# SELECTION PROCEDURE

For the recruitment of Soldier General Duty in the Indian Army, the application forms are no longer invited. Now on a fixed place and fixed time, an open recruitment rally is conducted, in which, Physical Test is held and the eligible candidates are called for the Written Examination.

**Minimum Educational Qualification:** 10th Class Pass.

**Age :** 17½ - 21 Years.

# SYLLABUS FOR THE TEST

There will be one written paper for all categories of 100 marks and of one hour duration.

**Mathematics (30 Marks):** In this portion, the questions will be from Arithmetic, Mensuration, Algebra, Set Theory, Geometry.

**General Science (40 Marks):** In this portion, the questions will be from Physics, Chemistry and Biology.

**General Knowledge (30 Marks):** In this portion the questions will be framed from History, Geography, Constitution of India, UNO, Abbreviation and from Current Events.

# CONTENTS



## MATHEMATICS

### ARITHMETIC



### ALGEBRA



## GENERAL SCIENCE

### Physics

**R. Gupta's**®

## POPULAR MASTER GUIDE

# Indian Army

# Soldier

## GENERAL DUTY

## Recruitment Exam

- According to the Latest Pattern of Examination
- Three Model Test Papers (Solved)

PREVIOUSLY KNOWN AS **NER – GENERAL DUTY**

## 2020 EDITION

**RAMESH PUBLISHING HOUSE,** New Delhi

***Published by***
O.P. Gupta *for* Ramesh Publishing House

***Admin. Office***
12-H, New Daryaganj Road, Opp. Officers' Mess,
New Delhi-110002 ① 23261567, 23275224, 23275124

E-mail: info@rameshpublishinghouse.com
Website: www.rameshpublishinghouse.com

***Showroom***
● Balaji Market, Nai Sarak, Delhi-6 ① 23253720, 23282525
● 4457, Nai Sarak, Delhi-6, ① 23918938



**Book Code: R-165**

**ISBN: 978-93-87918-26-9**

**HSN Code: 49011010**

## Chemistry



## Biology



# GENERAL KNOWLEDGE

## India

## World

# MODEL PAPERS

## MODEL PAPER I

*Time : 1 Hour*                     ***Maximum Marks : 100***

## GENERAL KNOWLEDGE

**Choose the correct answer**

1. Which is the deepest ocean in the world?
   - (*a*) Indian Ocean
   - (*b*) Atlantic Ocean
   - (*c*) Pacific Ocean
   - (*d*) Arabian Sea

2. What is the term for a member of the Rajya Sabha?
   - (*a*) 5 Years
   - (*b*) 4 Years
   - (*c*) 2 Years
   - (*d*) 6 Years

3. Who was the first Indian to be appointed President of the International Court of Justice?
   - (*a*) Nagendra Singh
   - (*b*) Bhagat Singh
   - (*c*) Dr. Hardayal
   - (*d*) None of these

4. Which day is observed as Human Right Day?
   - (*a*) 24$^{th}$ October
   - (*b*) 4$^{th}$ July
   - (*c*) 10$^{th}$ December
   - (*d*) None of these

5. India's biggest multipurpose river valley project is ............... .
   - (*a*) Hirakund
   - (*b*) Bhakra Nangal
   - (*c*) Damodar Valley
   - (*d*) None of these

6. In which state is 'Sanchi Stupa' situated?
   - (*a*) Madhya Pradesh
   - (*b*) Uttar Pradesh
   - (*c*) Bihar
   - (*d*) Maharashtra

7. 'Each one Teach one' programme relates to .................. .
   - (*a*) Adult education
   - (*b*) Regular education
   - (*c*) Non-formal education
   - (*d*) Awakened citizen

8. When was 'Shimla Pact' between India and Pakistan inked?
   - (*a*) 1955
   - (*b*) 1971
   - (*c*) 1962
   - (*d*) 1972

9. The River Mahanadi originates from ...................... .
   - (*a*) Raipur
   - (*b*) Patna
   - (*c*) Ujjain
   - (*d*) Dehradun

10. Who has written the book 'Anand Math'?
    - (*a*) Bankim Chandra Chatterjee
    - (*b*) Abdul Fazal

(*c*) Kalidas

(*d*) Sarat Chandra Chatterjee

**11.** ..................... is the author of 'Meghdoot'

(*a*) Kalidas     (*b*) Tulsidas

(*c*) Kautilya     (*d*) Vedvyas

**12.** ..................... is the largest planet of the solar system.

(*a*) Jupiter     (*b*) Mercury

(*c*) Venus     (*d*) None of these

**13.** Which of these is not part of our Parliament?

(*a*) President

(*b*) Lok Sabha

(*c*) Chief Justice

(*d*) None of these

**14.** Where did Ashoka fight his last battle?

(*a*) Malaya     (*b*) Kalinga

(*c*) Kochin     (*d*) None of these

**15.** Gautam Bhuddha was born in ........................

(*a*) Gaya     (*b*) Sarnath

(*c*) Patna     (*d*) Lumbini

## GENERAL SCIENCE

**16.** What is the heart beat rate of a young and healthy man?

(*a*) 50 times per min.

(*b*) 72 times per min.

(*c*) 108 times per min.

(*d*) None of these

**17.** Brain is responsible for ............

(*a*) Thinking

(*b*) Balancing the body

(*c*) Both (*a*) and (*b*)

(*d*) Only (*a*)

**18.** Blood is purified by ....................

(*a*) Lungs     (*b*) Intestine

(*c*) Kidney     (*d*) None of these

**19.** ................ is used in thermometer to show the temperature.

(*a*) Lead     (*b*) Mercury

(*c*) Silver     (*d*) None of these

**20.** ............. are a set of cold blooded animals.

(*a*) Crow, Earthworm, Frog

(*b*) Frog, Crow, Whale

(*c*) Penguin, Salamander, Monkey

(*d*) Rohu, Frog, Cobra

**21.** Solar Eclipse occur when ...........

(*a*) Earth comes between sun and moon.

(*b*) Moon comes between sun and earth.

(*c*) During crisis

(*d*) Sun comes between moon and earth

**22.** Good conductor of electricity is ........................

(*a*) Glass     (*b*) Paper

(*c*) Copper     (*d*) None of these

**23.** Beri Beri is caused due to deficiency of vitamin ..................

(*a*) A     (*b*) B

(*c*) C     (*d*) D

**24.** ATP is ..........................

   (*a*) Adenosine tetraphosphate

   (*b*) Adenine triphosphate

   (*c*) Adenosine triphosphate

   (*d*) None of these

**25.** ........................ law was put forth by Ernst Haeckel.

   (*a*) Law of inheritance

   (*b*) The biogenic law

   (*c*) Law of dominance

   (*d*) Law of segregation

**26.** Melting point of ice is ............... .

   (*a*) $100°C$    (*b*) $4°C$

   (*c*) $0°C$    (*d*) $5°C$

**27.** Hemoglobin is found in ............. .

   (*a*) Vein    (*b*) Urine

   (*c*) Blood    (*d*) AIDS

**28.** The nucleus of an atom consists of .................... .

   (*a*) Electrons and Neutrons

   (*b*) Electrons and Protons

   (*c*) Protons and Neutrons

   (*d*) Neutrons only

**29.** A mixture of metal dissolved in mercury is known as ................... .

   (*a*) Amalgam

   (*b*) Alloy

   (*c*) Mercury salt

   (*d*) Solution

**30.** The formula of Ammonium Chloride is ................... .

   (*a*) $NH_4Cl$    (*b*) $NH_4Cl_2$

   (*c*) $NHCl_2$    (*d*) $NH_4Cl_4$

**31.** Rusting of Iron is a ................... .

   (*a*) Physical change

   (*b*) Chemical change

   (*c*) Biochemical change

   (*d*) Electrochemical change

**32.** Penicillin is a/an ...................... .

   (*a*) Antibiotic    (*b*) Fats

   (*c*) Enzymes    (*d*) Proteins

**33.** The male and female gamates in the flower are called pollen and ................... .

   (*a*) Zygote    (*b*) Ova

   (*c*) Pupa    (*d*) Sperms

**34.** ............ is the fundamental particle that constitutes an atom other than the proton and electron.

   (*a*) Neuron    (*b*) Photon

   (*c*) Meson    (*d*) Anon

**35.** ...................... is not a compound.

   (*a*) Air    (*b*) Steel

   (*c*) Water    (*d*) Brass

## ( MATHEMATICS )

**Choose the correct answer:**

**36.** The value of 2-(2) is ................ .

   (*a*) 0    (*b*) 4

   (*c*) 8    (*d*) 16

**37.** If two angles of a triangle are 30 and 105, then the third angle will be ............ .

   (*a*) 75    (*b*) 45

   (*c*) 65    (*d*) 60

**38.** What is the value of 7/9 of 45 ?

    (*a*) 33            (*b*) 35

    (*c*) 38            (*d*) 28

**39.** If $\dfrac{(0.4z - 3)}{(1.5z + 9)} = -7/5$. Find the value of $z$.

    (*a*) 98/25          (*b*) 26/35

    (*c*) –96/25        (*d*) None of these

**40.** Find the area of a playground of 300m length and 200m breadth.

    (*a*) 60,000 m$^2$    (*b*) 500 m

    (*c*) 10,000 m$^2$    (*d*) 60,000 m$^3$

**41.** If 8 men can do a piece of work in 15 days, then in how many days could 20 men do the same work ?

    (*a*) 7 days         (*b*) 8 days

    (*c*) 10 days       (*d*) None of these

**42.** What is the fractional value of 4.21?

    (*a*) 421/100       (*b*) 121/10

    (*c*) 121/1000     (*d*) 21/100

**43.** Find the value of $\dfrac{1}{2} + \dfrac{1}{4}$ ?

    (*a*) 3/4            (*b*) 3/2

    (*c*) 5/4            (*d*) 1/8

**44.** What is the square root of 0.0036?

    (*a*) 0.06          (*b*) 0.6

    (*c*) 00.6         (*d*) 6

**45.** Perimeter of a square is 1000 cm. Find one side of that square ?

    (*a*) 10 cm       (*b*) 100 cm

    (*c*) 20 cm       (*d*) 250 cm

**46.** 3 hrs = .............. minutes ?

    (*a*) 1080        (*b*) 180

    (*c*) 108         (*d*) 1800

**47.** $(x + 4)(x + 5) = $ ?

    (*a*) $x^2 + x - 20$    (*b*) $x^3 + 9x - 20$

    (*c*) $x^2 + 5x + 1$    (*d*) $x^2 + 9x + 20$

**48.** If the average of 40, 10, 25, 20, 35 and $x$ is 25, then the value of $x$ is:

    (*a*) 20           (*b*) 30

    (*c*) 35           (*d*) None of these

**49.** Simplify : $81 \times 81 + 68 \times 68 - 2 \times 81 \times 68$

    (*a*) 169         (*b*) 196

    (*c*) 201         (*d*) None of these

**50.** Area of square ?

    (*a*) side × side

    (*b*) length × breadth

    (*c*) length × length

    (*d*) 4 × side

## EXPLANATORY ANSWERS

| | | | | |
|---|---|---|---|---|
| **1.** (*c*) | **2.** (*d*) | **3.** (*a*) | **4.** (*c*) | **5.** (*b*) |
| **6.** (*a*) | **7.** (*c*) | **8.** (*d*) | **9.** (*a*) | **10.** (*a*) |
| **11.** (*a*) | **12.** (*a*) | **13.** (*c*) | **14.** (*b*) | **15.** (*d*) |
| **16.** (*b*) | **17.** (*c*) | **18.** (*c*) | **19.** (*b*) | **20.** (*d*) |
| **21.** (*b*) | **22.** (*c*) | **23.** (*b*) | **24.** (*b*) | **25.** (*b*) |
| **26.** (*b*) | **27.** (*c*) | **28.** (*c*) | **29.** (*a*) | **30.** (*a*) |
| **31.** (*b*) | **32.** (*a*) | **33.** (*b*) | **34.** (*a*) | **35.** (*a*) |

**36.** (*a*) The value of 2–(2) = 0.

**37.** (*b*) $\angle A + \angle B + \angle C = 180°$

$\Rightarrow 30° + 105° + \angle C = 180°$

$\angle C = 180° - 135° = 45°$

Hence, third angle = 45°.

**38.** (*b*) $\dfrac{7}{9}$ of $45° = \dfrac{7}{9} \times 45 = 35$

**39.** (*c*) $\therefore \dfrac{0.4z - 3}{1.5z + 9} = -\dfrac{7}{5}$

$\Rightarrow 2z - 15 = -10.5z - 63$

$\Rightarrow 12.5z = -48$

$\Rightarrow \dfrac{125}{10}z = -48$

$\Rightarrow z = -\dfrac{10 \times 48}{125} = -\dfrac{96}{25}$

**40.** (*a*) Area of the playground $= l \times b$

$= 300 \times 200 = 60{,}000 \ \text{m}^2$

**41.** (*d*) $\because$ 8 men can do a work in 15 days

$\therefore$ 1 man can do this work in

$15 \times 8$ days

$\therefore$ 20 men can do this work in

$\dfrac{15 \times 8}{20}$ days

$= 6$ days.

**42.** (*a*) $4.21 = \dfrac{421}{100}$

**43.** (*a*) $\dfrac{1}{2} + \dfrac{1}{4} = \dfrac{2+1}{4} = \dfrac{3}{4}$

**44.** (*a*) $\sqrt{0.0036} = \sqrt{\dfrac{36}{10000}} = \sqrt{\dfrac{6 \times 6}{100 \times 100}}$

$= \dfrac{6}{100} = 0.06$

**45.** (*d*) Side of Square $= \dfrac{\text{Perimeter}}{4}$

$= \dfrac{1000}{4} = 250 \ \text{cm}.$

**46.** (*b*) 3 hrs = 3 × 60 min. = 180 minutes.

**47.** (*d*) $(x+4)(x+5)$

$= x(x+5) + 4(x+5)$

$= x^2 + 5x + 4x + 20$

$= x^2 + 9x + 20$

**48.** (*a*) Average

$= \dfrac{40 + 10 + 25 + 20 + 35 + x}{6}$

$\Rightarrow x + 130 = 6 \times 25 = 150$

$\Rightarrow x = 150 - 130 = 20$

**49.** (*a*) $81 \times 81 + 68 \times 68 - 2 \times 81 \times 68$

Let $81 = a$ and $68 = b$

$\therefore$ The given expression is

$a \times a + b \times b - 2a \times b$

$= a^2 + b^2 - 2ab = (a-b)^2$

$= (81 - 68)^2$

$= (13)^2 = 13 \times 13 = 169$

**50.** (*a*) Area of square $= (\text{side})^2 = \text{side} \times \text{side}.$

# MODEL PAPER II

*Time : 1 Hour*                                    *Max. Marks : 100*

## GENERAL KNOWLEDGE

1. Which one of the following is the most densely Populated Country in the world?
   (*a*) Bangladesh  (*b*) India
   (*c*) China       (*d*) Britain

2. The boundary between China and India is called
   (*a*) Durand Line
   (*b*) McMohan Line
   (*c*) 24th Parallel
   (*d*) 17th Parallel

3. The Battle of Plassey was fought in the year:
   (*a*) 1757  (*b*) 1747
   (*c*) 1737  (*d*) 1761

4. The maximum strength of Rajya Sabha is
   (*a*) 250  (*b*) 232
   (*c*) 234  (*d*) 225

5. The Rajya Sabha can delay a money bill passed by the Lok Sabha at the most for :
   (*a*) One month
   (*b*) Three months
   (*c*) Six months
   (*d*) 14 days

6. The places Tarapur, Narora and Kalpakkam have
   (*a*) Thermal Stations
   (*b*) Oil refineries
   (*c*) Hydro Stations
   (*d*) Nuclear Power plants

7. The Mausoleum of Sher Shah Suri is in :
   (*a*) Rohtas   (*b*) Agra
   (*c*) Sasaram  (*d*) Lahore

8. What is the retirement age of a Supreme Court Judge in India?
   (*a*) 58 years  (*b*) 60 years
   (*c*) 62 years  (*d*) 65 years

9. With which sport is the term "grand slam" associated?
   (*a*) Shooting  (*b*) Archery
   (*c*) Tennis    (*d*) Golf

10. NATO has its headquarters in
    (*a*) Brussels  (*b*) London
    (*c*) Paris     (*d*) Madras

11. Who among the following was known as the "Grand Old Man" of India?
    (*a*) Dadabhai Naoroji
    (*b*) W.C. Banerjee
    (*c*) Pherozeshah Mehta
    (*d*) Surendranath Banerjee

12. In which year did the Congress adopt "Poorna Swaraj" or Complete Independence as its goal?
    (*a*) 1930  (*b*) 1929
    (*c*) 1928  (*d*) 1942

13. Which country is the largest producer of Coffee in the world?
    (*a*) India  (*b*) Brazil
    (*c*) China  (*d*) Sri Lanka

**14.** The Rangaswamy cup is associated with
(*a*) Football
(*b*) Hockey
(*c*) Table Tennis
(*d*) Badminton

**15.** Parliament of which country is named Diet?
(*a*) Sweden
(*b*) Japan
(*c*) Israel
(*d*) Spain

## GENERAL SCIENCE

**16.** Which of the following is the most stable element found in nature?
(*a*) Oxygen    (*b*) Hydrogen
(*c*) Lead    (*d*) Uranium

**17.** A transformer
(*a*) stores energy
(*b*) regulates voltage
(*c*) speeds up transmission of energy
(*d*) changes electrical energy into mechanical energy

**18.** Leprosy is caused by
(*a*) Bacterium    (*b*) Virus
(*c*) Protozoa    (*d*) Helminthes

**19.** How is energy in the sun generated?
(*a*) Nuclear fusion
(*b*) Fission
(*c*) Magnetic force
(*d*) Gravitational force

**20.** Isobars are the places joining lines having equal
(*a*) temperature (*b*) height
(*c*) rainfall    (*d*) pressure

**21.** First atomic power plant in India was established at
(*a*) Tarapur    (*b*) Kota
(*c*) Narora    (*d*) Kalpakkam

**22.** Penicillin is obtained from
(*a*) Latex    (*b*) Penicillium
(*c*) Vaucheria    (*d*) Aspergillus

**23.** Water has highest density at
(*a*) 0°C    (*b*) 4°C
(*c*) 100°C    (*d*) 10°C

**24.** There is no reaction when steam is passed over heated
(*a*) Iron    (*b*) Copper
(*c*) Carbon    (*d*) Aluminium

**25.** The cells used in transistors are
(*a*) Voltaic cell
(*b*) Leclanche cell
(*c*) Dry cell
(*d*) Lead acid cell

**26.** Comets revolve around
(*a*) Sun    (*b*) Earth
(*c*) Venus    (*d*) Mars

**27.** The property of an object causes it to resist being set in motion is called
(*a*) equilibrium (*b*) momentum
(*c*) intertia    (*d*) impulse

**28.** The chemical formula of caustic soda is
(*a*) NaOH    (*b*) $Na(OH)_2$
(*c*) $Na_2O$    (*d*) None of these

**29.** Study of insects is called
(*a*) Entomology
(*b*) Anthropology
(*c*) Ontology
(*d*) Antonology

**30.** 1 Calorie =
   (*a*) 4.2 joules   (*b*) 3.2 joules
   (*c*) 9.2 joules   (*d*) 5.2 joules

**31.** Light year is the unit of:
   (*a*) time      (*b*) velocity
   (*c*) distance   (*d*) work

**32.** Temperature of the star is determined by:
   (*a*) colour     (*b*) size
   (*c*) distance   (*d*) None of these

**33.** The energy produced in the sun is due to:
   (*a*) chemical reaction
   (*b*) fission reaction
   (*c*) fussion reaction
   (*d*) None of these

**34.** Which of the following is chemical change?
   (*a*) Evaporation
   (*b*) Dissolution
   (*c*) Sublimation
   (*d*) Precipitation

**35.** Which of the following substance does not have melting point?
   (*a*) Bromine     (*b*) Mercury
   (*c*) Glass       (*d*) Soft

## ( MATHEMATICS )

Complete the following series :

**36.** 7, 14, 42, 168, .......
   (*a*) 480        (*b*) 560
   (*c*) 840        (*d*) 960

**37.** 3, 10, 29, 66, ........
   (*a*) 90         (*b*) 127
   (*c*) 140        (*d*) 176

**38.** $\left(2+\sqrt{2}\right)+\dfrac{1}{2+\sqrt{2}}-\dfrac{1}{\sqrt{2}-2}$ equals:
   (*a*) 2          (*b*) $2\sqrt{2}$
   (*c*) $2-\sqrt{2}$   (*d*) $2+\sqrt{2}$

**39.** The smallest number which when diminished by 3 is divisible by 21, 28, 36 and 45 is
   (*a*) 423        (*b*) 1257
   (*c*) 1263       (*d*) 1260

**40.** A retailer buys a radio for Rs. 225. His overhead expenses are Rs. 15. He sells the radio for Rs. 300. The profit per cent of the retailer is :
   (*a*) 10         (*b*) 25
   (*c*) 50         (*d*) 52

**41.** $(64)^{\frac{-2}{3}} \times \left(\dfrac{1}{4}\right)^{-2}$ is equal to :
   (*a*) 1          (*b*) $\dfrac{1}{4}$
   (*c*) 4          (*d*) 16

**42.** The value of $\dfrac{2^n + 2^{n-1}}{2^{n+1} - 2^n}$ is :
   (*a*) $\dfrac{1}{2}$        (*b*) $\dfrac{3}{2}$
   (*c*) $\dfrac{n-1}{2^{n+1}}$   (*d*) $\dfrac{1}{3}$

**43.** The expression
$$\left[\dfrac{1}{1.2}+\dfrac{1}{2.3}+\dfrac{1}{3.4}+...+\dfrac{1}{n(n+1)}\right]$$
for any natural number $n$, is:
   (*a*) always greater than 1
   (*b*) always less than 1
   (*c*) always equal to 1
   (*d*) None of these

**44.** If $\sqrt{4096} = 64$, then the value of

$\sqrt{40.96} + \sqrt{0.4096} + \sqrt{0.004096}$

$+ \sqrt{0.00004096} = ?$

   (*a*) 7.09        (*b*) 7.1014
   (*c*) 7.1104      (*d*) 7.12

**45.** From a group of boys and girls, 15 girls leave. There are then left 2 boys for each girl. After this, 45 boys leave. There are then 5 girls for each boy. The number of girls in the beginning was

   (*a*) 40          (*b*) 43
   (*c*) 29          (*d*) 50

**46.** Some money is divided among three persons A, B, C in such a way that 5 times A's share, 3 times B's share and 2 times C's share are all equal. The ratio between A, B and C's shares is:

   (*a*) 5 : 3 : 2     (*b*) 2 : 2 : 5
   (*c*) 15 : 10 : 6   (*d*) 6 : 10 : 15

**47.** Two pipes A and B can fill a cistern in 12 minutes and 16 minutes respectively. If both the pipes are opened together, then after how much time B should be closed so that the tank is full in 9 minutes ?

   (*a*) $3\dfrac{1}{2}$ min.     (*b*) 4 min.

   (*c*) $4\dfrac{1}{2}$ min.     (*d*) $4\dfrac{3}{4}$ min.

**48.** A person walks at 5 kmph for 6 hours and at 4 kmph for 12 hours. The average speed of the man is :

   (*a*) 4 kmph     (*b*) $4\dfrac{1}{3}$ kmph

   (*c*) $4\dfrac{1}{2}$ kmph   (*d*) $4\dfrac{2}{3}$ kmph

**49.** If $x = 2.3\dot{5}\dot{2}$, then $x$ is equal to :

   (*a*) $\dfrac{2352}{999}$       (*b*) $\dfrac{2329}{999}$

   (*c*) $\dfrac{2352}{990}$       (*d*) $\dfrac{2329}{990}$

**50.** If $x$ is positive real number, then the least value of $x + \dfrac{1}{x}$ is :

   (*a*) 2         (*b*) 4
   (*c*) 11        (*d*) 1

## EXPLANATORY ANSWERS

| | | | | |
|---|---|---|---|---|
| **1.** (*a*) | **2.** (*b*) | **3.** (*a*) | **4.** (*a*) | **5.** (*d*) |
| **6.** (*d*) | **7.** (*c*) | **8.** (*d*) | **9.** (*c*) | **10.** (*a*) |
| **11.** (*a*) | **12.** (*b*) | **13.** (*b*) | **14.** (*b*) | **15.** (*b*) |
| **16.** (*c*) | **17.** (*b*) | **18.** (*a*) | **19.** (*a*) | **20.** (*d*) |
| **21.** (*a*) | **22.** (*b*) | **23.** (*b*) | **24.** (*b*) | **25.** (*c*) |
| **26.** (*a*) | **27.** (*c*) | **28.** (*a*) | **29.** (*a*) | **30.** (*a*) |
| **31.** (*c*) | **32.** (*a*) | **33.** (*c*) | **34.** (*d*) | **35.** (*b*) |

**36.** (*c*) 840. To get the next number previous number is multiplied in the order 2, 3, 4, ......

**37.** (*b*) 127. Two are added in the cube of serial numbers.

**38.** (*a*) $\left(2+\sqrt{2}\right)+\dfrac{1}{2+\sqrt{2}}\times\dfrac{2-\sqrt{2}}{2-\sqrt{2}}$

$$-\dfrac{1}{2-\sqrt{2}}\times\dfrac{2+\sqrt{2}}{2+\sqrt{2}}$$

$$=\left(2+\sqrt{2}\right)+\dfrac{2-\sqrt{2}}{2}-\dfrac{2+\sqrt{2}}{2}$$

$$=2$$

**39.** (*c*) Required number = (LCM of 21, 28, 36, 45) + 3

$$= 1263$$

**40.** (*b*) C.P. = ₹ (225 + 15) = ₹ 240, S.P. = ₹ 300

$$\therefore \text{Gain \%} = \left(\dfrac{60}{240}\times 100\right)\%$$

$$= 25\%$$

**41.** (*a*) $(64)^{-\frac{2}{3}}\times\left(\dfrac{1}{4}\right)^{-2}$

$$= (4^3)^{-\frac{2}{3}}\times\left(\dfrac{1}{4}\right)^{-2}$$

$$= 4^{3\times\left(\frac{-2}{3}\right)}\times\left(\dfrac{1}{4}\right)^{-2}$$

$$= \left(4^{-2}\times\dfrac{1}{4^{-2}}\right)=1$$

**42.** (*b*) Given expression

$$= \dfrac{2^{n-1}(2+1)}{2^n(2-1)}=\dfrac{3}{2}$$

**43.** (*b*) Given expression

$$= 1-\dfrac{1}{2}+\dfrac{1}{2}-\dfrac{1}{3}+\dfrac{1}{3}-\dfrac{1}{4}+\dots$$

$$+\dfrac{1}{n}-\dfrac{1}{n+1}$$

$$= 1-\dfrac{1}{n+1}=\dfrac{1}{n+1}<1$$

**44.** (*c*) Expression = 6.4 + 0.64 + 0.064 + 0.0064 = 7.1104

**45.** (*a*) Let at present there be $x$ boys.

$\therefore$ Number of girls = $5x$

Before the boys have left,

Number of boys = $x + 45$

and number of girls = $5x$

$\therefore \qquad x + 45 = x \times 5x$

$\Rightarrow \qquad\qquad x = 5$

$\therefore$ Number of girls in the beginning = $5x + 15 = 40$

**46.** (*d*) 5A = 3B = 2C = K (let.)

Then, $A = \dfrac{K}{5}$, $B = \dfrac{K}{3}$

and $C = \dfrac{K}{2}$

$$\therefore A:B:C = \dfrac{K}{5}:\dfrac{K}{3}:\dfrac{K}{2}$$

$$= \dfrac{1}{5}:\dfrac{1}{3}:\dfrac{1}{2} = 6:10:15$$

**47.** (*d*) Let B be closed after $x$ minutes. Then part filled by (A + B) in $x$ minutes + part filled by A in $(9-x)$ min. = 1.

$$\Rightarrow x\left(\dfrac{1}{12}+\dfrac{1}{16}\right)+(9-x)\cdot\dfrac{1}{12}=1$$

$$\Rightarrow \frac{7x}{48} + \frac{9-x}{12} = 1$$

$$\Rightarrow 7x + 36 - 4x = 48$$

$$\Rightarrow x = 4 \text{ minutes}$$

**48.** (*b*) Total distance covered $= (5 \times 6 + 4 \times 12)$ km $= 78$ km

Total time taken $= 18$ hours

$$\therefore \text{Average speed} = \frac{78}{18} \text{ kmph}$$

$$= 4\frac{1}{3} \text{ kmph}$$

**49.** (*d*) $2.3\dot{5}\dot{2} = 2 + \frac{352-3}{990}$

$$= 2 + \frac{349}{990}$$

$$= \frac{1980 + 349}{990} = \frac{2329}{990}$$

**50.** (*a*) $x + \dfrac{1}{x}$

$$= \left(\sqrt{x}\right)^2 + \left(\frac{1}{\sqrt{x}}\right)^2 - 2\sqrt{x} \times \frac{1}{\sqrt{x}} + 2$$

$$= \left(\sqrt{x} - \frac{1}{\sqrt{x}}\right)^2 + 2 \geq 2$$

$$\therefore \text{Least value} = 2.$$

# MODEL PAPER III

*Time : 1 Hour*                    *Max. Marks : 100*

## GENERAL KNOWLEDGE

1. Which of the following is not a member of SAARC?
   (*a*) India   (*b*) Myanmar
   (*c*) Maldives   (*d*) Bhutan

2. The Constitution of India was adopted on :
   (*a*) 26 January, 1950
   (*b*) 26 January, 1949
   (*c*) 26 November, 1949
   (*d*) 31 December, 1949

3. 'Geet Govinda' the famous poem was written by :
   (*a*) Jayachandra (*b*) Jayadeva
   (*c*) Jayasimha   (*d*) Jayant

4. Thomas Cup is related to :
   (*a*) Badminton (*b*) Basketball
   (*c*) Cricket   (*d*) Tennis

5. One of the pairs not matched correctly is :
   (*a*) Dehradun—U.P.
   (*b*) Shimla—Himachal Pradesh
   (*c*) Darjeeling—West Bengal
   (*d*) Panchamarhi—M.P.

6. Where do you find the temple of Angkor Wat ?
   (*a*) In Thailand
   (*b*) In Malaysia
   (*c*) In Cambodia
   (*d*) In Myanmar

7. M.R.I. stands for :
   (*a*) Metered Resonance Imaging
   (*b*) Magnetic Resonance Imaging
   (*c*) Magnetic Reaction Imaging
   (*d*) Metered Reaction Imaging

8. Wular lake is situated in:
   (*a*) Kerala   (*b*) J & K
   (*c*) Punjab   (*d*) Tripura

9. Who replaced Planning Commission in 2015?
   (*a*) NIYAM Aayog
   (*b*) VIDHAN Aayog
   (*c*) NITI Aayog
   (*d*) None of these

10. Which is the hottest planet in the Solar System?
    (*a*) Jupiter   (*b*) Saturn
    (*c*) Venus   (*d*) Uranus

11. In India, one-rupee coins and notes and subsidiary coins are issued by :
    (*a*) The Reserve Bank of India
    (*b*) The Central Government
    (*c*) The State Bank of India
    (*d*) The Unit Trust of India

12. 'India Wins Freedom' is the autobiography of :
    (*a*) Abul Kalam Azad
    (*b*) Muhammad Ali
    (*c*) Zakir Hussain
    (*d*) Syed Ahmad Khan

13. Which is the India's largest lake ?
    (*a*) Naini   (*b*) Sambhar
    (*c*) Sishram   (*d*) Chilka

**14.** Which of the following States has rich forest of sandalwood?
(*a*) Andhra Pradesh
(*b*) Karnataka
(*c*) Kerala
(*d*) Madhya Pradesh

**15.** Which of the following is the smallest ocean of the world?
(*a*) Pacific    (*b*) Indian
(*c*) Atlantic    (*d*) Arctic

## ( GENERAL SCIENCE )

**16.** Cooking gas is a mixture of :
(*a*) carbon monoxide and carbondioxide
(*b*) butane and propane
(*c*) methane and ethylene
(*d*) carbon dioxide and oxygen

**17.** Marsh gas, formed from decaying organic matter and in coal mines, is :
(*a*) carbon dioxide
(*b*) methane
(*c*) ethane
(*d*) carbon monoxide

**18.** Water for civil supplies is commonly purified by :
(*a*) chlorination (*b*) distillation
(*c*) filtration (*d*) decantation

**19.** The raw material not found in nature is :
(*a*) water
(*b*) petrol
(*c*) vinyl chloride
(*d*) carbon dioxide

**20.** While sowing seeds, the fertiliser commonly used contains :
(*a*) nitrates (*b*) potash
(*c*) phosphorus (*d*) calcium

**21.** While cooking food, the compounds lost to the maximum extent are :
(*a*) fats
(*b*) carbohydrates
(*c*) proteins
(*d*) vitamins

**22.** A mixture of two or more metals is called a/an :
(*a*) amalgam
(*b*) alkali metal
(*c*) noble element
(*d*) alloy

**23.** An antipyretic is a drug that :
(*a*) lowers body temperature
(*b*) raises body temperature
(*c*) kills infection
(*d*) is used in viral attacks

**24.** Chemotherapy deals with :
(*a*) Industrial engineering
(*b*) the use of chemicals in warfare
(*c*) the study and uses of chemicals in the cure of diseases
(*d*) the use of chemicals in the food industry

**25.** Cholesterol is a :
(*a*) type of chlorophyll
(*b*) derivative of chloroform
(*c*) fatty alcohol found in animal fats
(*d*) chromium salt

**26.** The antibiotic 'mitomyein' is used to treat certain types of :
(*a*) cancer    (*b*) AIDS
(*c*) polio    (*d*) syphilis

27. The word meaning 'copper demon' was meant to denote the metallic element :
 (*a*) tin  (*b*) nickel
 (*c*) zinc  (*d*) iron

28. The process of extracting aluminium is called :
 (*a*) Dow Process
 (*b*) Haber Process
 (*c*) Hall Process
 (*d*) Electroplating

29. The dis-colorizer used in sugar refining is :
 (*a*) bone black
 (*b*) chlorine water
 (*c*) hydrogen peroxide
 (*d*) sulphur dioxide

30. The number of atoms represented in the formula $Ca_3(PO_4)_2$ are :
 (*a*) 5  (*b*) 3
 (*c*) 12  (*d*) 13

31. Which substance is used in making matchsticks?
 (*a*) red phosphorus
 (*b*) yellow phosphorus
 (*c*) sulphur
 (*d*) sodium

32. Which one of the following is not a fossil fuel?
 (*a*) petrol  (*b*) coke
 (*c*) charcoal  (*d*) coal

33. The neutron was discovered by:
 (*a*) Rutherford
 (*b*) Marie Curie
 (*c*) James Chadwick
 (*d*) Pierre Curie

34. The best material for the core of a transformer is:
 (*a*) stainless steel
 (*b*) soft iron
 (*c*) pure gold
 (*d*) mild steel

35. SONAR emits which of the following waves?
 (*a*) ultrasound  (*b*) radio
 (*c*) light  (*d*) visible

## ( MATHEMATICS )

Complete the following series :

36. $2, 3, 4, 9, 8, 27, \ldots\ldots$
 (*a*) 16  (*b*) 18
 (*c*) 30  (*d*) 32

37. $3, 5, 10, 12, 24, \ldots\ldots$
 (*a*) 14  (*b*) 26
 (*c*) 28  (*d*) 30

38. Find the area of the lateral surface of a right circular cylinder, the perimeter of whose base is 11 cm and its height is twice the diameter?
 (*a*) 77cm²  (*b*) 55cm²
 (*c*) 44cm²  (*d*) 40cm²

39. If $\left(x-\dfrac{1}{x}\right) = 6$, then $x^2 + \dfrac{1}{x^2} = ?$
 (*a*) 32  (*b*) 34
 (*c*) 36  (*d*) 38

40. The total area of right circular cone of radius R and height H is:
 (*a*) $\pi R(R+H)$
 (*b*) $\pi R(2R+H)$
 (*c*) $\pi R(R+\sqrt{H^2+R^2})$
 (*d*) $\pi R\left[2R+\dfrac{1}{3}\sqrt{H^2+R^2}\right]$

**41.** A restaurant hall is 20 metre long, 15 metre wide and 5 metre high. Its interior has to be covered with mat. What will be the total expenditure if it costs ₹ 60 per square metre ?

(a) ₹ 64000     (b) ₹ 57000

(c) ₹ 52000     (d) ₹ 45000

**42.** Find the smallest number which when divided by 6, 10 and 15 respectively leaves 5 as remainder in each case ?

(a) 35     (b) 40

(c) 45     (d) 50

**43.** Which of the following series is in ascending order?

(a) $\dfrac{7}{12}, \dfrac{9}{14}, \dfrac{11}{15}, \dfrac{17}{25}$

(b) $\dfrac{9}{14}, \dfrac{7}{12}, \dfrac{11}{15}, \dfrac{17}{25}$

(c) $\dfrac{17}{25}, \dfrac{11}{15}, \dfrac{9}{14}, \dfrac{7}{12}$

(d) $\dfrac{7}{12}, \dfrac{9}{14}, \dfrac{17}{25}, \dfrac{11}{15}$

**44.** The sides of the two triangles are 5 cm, 6 cm and 9 cm respectively. What is the ratio of their areas?

(a) $\sqrt{\dfrac{5}{18}}$     (b) $\sqrt{\dfrac{4}{15}}$

(c) $\sqrt{\dfrac{5}{12}}$     (d) $\sqrt{\dfrac{3}{8}}$

**45.** A company representative gives 4 pens free to a shopkeeper when he buys 20 pens and also 20% discount on the marked price. What per cent profit the shopkeeper earns if he sells the pens on the marked price?

(a) 30%     (b) 35%

(c) 40%     (d) 50%

**46.** C takes twice the time taken by A and B together to do a given work. To do the same work A and C together take $\dfrac{1}{3}$rd the time taken by B alone. A, B and C together complete the work in 10 days. How many days would A take to do the work alone?

(a) 30 days     (b) 24 days

(c) 20 days     (d) 16 days

**47.** Ram and Shyam go to a garden for morning walk. It has a circular path of radius 42 metres. Ram and Shyam walk on the circular path in the garden but in opposite directions at 17 m/minute and 16 m/minute respectively. At what intervals would they meet?

(a) 8 minutes     (b) 9 minutes

(c) 10 minutes     (d) 12 minutes

**48.** A person earns ₹ 416 as compound interest in 2 years on his investment of ₹ 2500. If the interest is compounded annually, what is the rate of interest?

(a) 4%     (b) 5%

(c) 8%     (d) 10%

**49.** A bag contains coins of ₹ 1, 50 paise and 25 paise in the ratio 9 : 5 : 4. If the sum of all the coins contained in the bag is ₹ 50, how many 25 paise coins does it have ?

(a) 40     (b) 36

(c) 20     (d) 16

**50.** Find the next number in the series—2, 6, 12, 20

(a) 25     (b) 30

(c) 35     (d) 40

# EXPLANATORY ANSWERS

| | | | | |
|---|---|---|---|---|
| **1.** (*b*) | **2.** (*c*) | **3.** (*b*) | **4.** (*a*) | **5.** (*a*) |
| **6.** (*c*) | **7.** (*b*) | **8.** (*b*) | **9.** (*c*) | **10.** (*c*) |
| **11.** (*b*) | **12.** (*a*) | **13.** (*d*) | **14.** (*b*) | **15.** (*d*) |
| **16.** (*b*) | **17.** (*b*) | **18.** (*a*) | **19.** (*c*) | **20.** (*a*) |
| **21.** (*d*) | **22.** (*d*) | **23.** (*a*) | **24.** (*c*) | **25.** (*a*) |
| **26.** (*a*) | **27.** (*b*) | **28.** (*c*) | **29.** (*a*) | **30.** (*d*) |
| **31.** (*a*) | **32.** (*c*) | **33.** (*a*) | **34.** (*b*) | **35.** (*a*) |

**36.** (*a*) 16. Two series one is becoming double and second is becoming triple.

**37.** (*b*) 26. Increasing in the form of $+2, \times 2, +2, \times 2$ etc.

**38.** (*a*) Perimeter $= \pi d = 11$ cm

$$d = \frac{11}{\pi} = 11 \times \frac{7}{22} = \frac{7}{2} \text{cm}$$

$$h = 2D = 2 \times \frac{7}{2} = 7\text{cm}$$

Area of lateral surface $= \pi dh$
$$= 11 \times 7 = 77 \text{ cm}^2.$$

**39.** (*d*) $\left(x - \dfrac{1}{x}\right)^2 = (6)^2$

$$x^2 + \frac{1}{x^2} - 2\, x\frac{1}{x} = 36$$

$$x^2 + \frac{1}{x^2} - 2 = 36$$

$$x^2 + \frac{1}{x^2} = 38$$

**40.** (*c*)

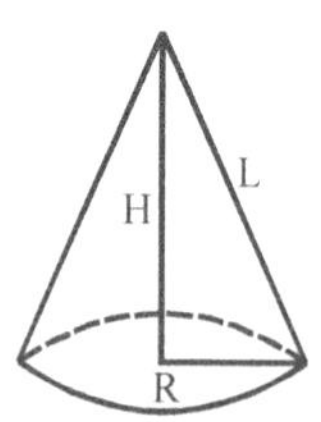


Area of the base $= \pi R^2$

Slant height, $L = \sqrt{H^2 + R^2}$

Area of the lateral surface $=$
$$\pi RL = \pi R\sqrt{H^2 + R^2}$$

$\therefore$ Total area $= \pi R^2 + \pi R\sqrt{H^2 + R^2}$
$$= \pi R\left[R + \sqrt{H^2 + R^2}\right]$$

**41.** (*b*) Total area of the hall to be covered with mat $= 2[lb + bh + lh]$
$= 2[20 \times 15 + 15 \times 5 + 20 \times 5]$ m$^2$
$= 2[300 + 75 + 100]$ m$^2$
$= 2 \times 475$ m$^2$ = 950 m$^2$
Total expenditure $= 60 \times 960$
$= ₹ 57000$

**42.** (*a*) LCM of 6, 10 and 15

| 2 | 6, | 10, | 15 |
|---|---|---|---|
| 3 | 3, | 5, | 15 |
| 5 | 1, | 5, | 5 |
| | 1, | 1, | 1 |

$\therefore$ LCM $= 2 \times 3 \times 5 = 30$
Required no. $= 30 + 5 = 35$

**43.** (*a*) LCM of 12, 14, 15 and 25.

| 2 | 12, | 14, | 15, | 25 |
|---|---|---|---|---|
| 3 | 6, | 7, | 15, | 25 |
| 5 | 2, | 7, | 5, | 25 |
| | 2, | 7, | 1, | 5 |

LCM $= 2 \times 3 \times 5 \times 2 \times 7 \times 5 = 2100$

$\therefore \dfrac{7}{12}, \dfrac{9}{14}, \dfrac{11}{15}, \dfrac{17}{25}$ can be written in an alternative equivalent form after rationalisation with common denominator as

$$\dfrac{7 \times 175,\ 9 \times 150,\ 11 \times 140, 17 \times 84}{2100}$$

$$= \dfrac{1225,\ 1350,\ 1540,\ 1428}{2100}$$

Comparing the numerators, the given fraction can be rearranged in ascending order as

$$\dfrac{7}{12}, \dfrac{9}{14}, \dfrac{17}{25}, \dfrac{11}{15}$$

**44.** (a) Areas of a triangle

$$= \sqrt{S\,(S-a)\,(S-b)\,(S-c)}$$

where S is semi-perimeter of the triangle and $a$, $b$, $c$ are sides of the triangle.

$$S = \dfrac{a+b+c}{2}$$

$$S_1 = \dfrac{5+6+9}{2} = 10 \text{ cm}$$

$$S_2 = \dfrac{7+9+14}{2} = 15 \text{ cm}$$

$$A_1 = \sqrt{10(10-5)\,(10-6)\,(10-9)}$$

$$A_1 = \sqrt{10 \times 5 \times 4 \times 1} = \sqrt{200}$$

$$A_2 = \sqrt{15(15-7)\,(15-9)\,(15-14)}$$

$$A_2 = \sqrt{15 \times 8 \times 6 \times 1} = \sqrt{720}$$

$$\therefore \dfrac{A_1}{A_2} = \dfrac{\sqrt{200}}{\sqrt{700}} = \sqrt{\dfrac{200}{720}} = \sqrt{\dfrac{5}{18}}$$

**45.** (d) Let the marked price of a pen be $x$.

$\therefore$ Marked price of 20 pens $= 20x$

Price after 20% discount

$$= (1 - 0.20)\,20x = 0.80 \times 20x = 16x$$

But the shopkeeper also gets 4 pens free. So, $16x$ is the cost price for 24 pens.

If the shopkeeper sells the pens at the marked price, the total selling price would be $24x$.

$$\therefore \% \text{ Profit} = \dfrac{24x - 16x}{16x} \times 100$$

$$= \dfrac{8x}{16x} \times 100 = 50\%.$$

**46.** (b) $(A + B + C)$ together can do the work in 10 days.

$$\therefore (A + B + C)\text{'s daily work} = \dfrac{1}{10}$$

2 times C's daily work

$= (A + B)$'s daily work.

On adding C's daily work on both sides we get,

3 times C's daily work

$$= (A + B + C)\text{'s daily work } \dfrac{1}{10}$$

$$\therefore C\text{'s daily work} = \dfrac{1}{30}$$

B's daily work $= \dfrac{1}{3}(A + C)$'s daily work.

or, 3 times B's daily work $= (A + C)$'s daily work

On adding B's daily work on both sides we get,

4 times B's daily work $= (A + B + C)$'s daily work $= \dfrac{1}{10}$

$$\therefore B\text{'s daily work} = \dfrac{1}{40}$$

A's daily work = (A + B + C)'s daily work – B's daily work – C's daily work

$$= \frac{1}{10} - \frac{1}{40} - \frac{1}{30}$$

$$= \frac{12 - 3 - 4}{120} = \frac{5}{120} = \frac{1}{24}$$

∴ A alone can do the work in 24 days.

**47.** (a) Radius of the circular path = 42 cm

Circumference of the path = $2\pi r$

$$= 2 \times \frac{22}{7} \times 42 = 264 \text{ m}$$

Relative speed
= 17 + 16 = 33m/minutes
Time interval between two successive encounters

$$= \frac{264}{33} = 8 \text{ minutes.}$$

**48.** (c) When the interest is compounded annually,
Amount = Principal Sum

$$\times \left[1 + \frac{\text{rate}}{100}\right]^n$$

$$\Rightarrow 2500 + 416 = 2500 \left(1 + \frac{r}{100}\right)^2$$

$$\Rightarrow \left(\frac{54}{50}\right)^2 = \left(1 + \frac{r}{100}\right)^2$$

$$\Rightarrow 1 + \frac{r}{100} = \frac{54}{50}$$

$$\Rightarrow \frac{r}{100} = \frac{54}{50} - 1$$

$$\therefore \quad r = \frac{4}{50} \times 100 = 8\%$$

**49.** (d) Let the no. of 25 p, 50 p and ₹ 1 coins be 4x, 5x and 9x respectively.

$$25p = ₹ \frac{1}{4}$$

$$50p = ₹ \frac{1}{2}$$

∴ Total value of all coins

$$= ₹ \left(\frac{4x}{4} + \frac{5x}{2} + 9x\right)$$

$$= ₹ \left(\frac{4x + 10x + 36x}{4}\right)$$

$$= ₹ \frac{50x}{4}$$

$$= ₹ \frac{25x}{2}$$

$$\Rightarrow \frac{25x}{2} = ₹ 50$$

$$\therefore \quad x = 50 \times \frac{2}{25} = 4$$

∴ No. of the 25 paise coins
$$= 4x = 4 \times 4 = 16.$$

**50.** (b)

| 2 | 6 | 12 | 20 | Next |
|---|---|----|----|------|
| ↓ | ↓ | ↓  | ↓  | ↓    |

$$1^2 + 1, \ 2^2 + 2, \ 3^2 + 3, \ 4^2 + 4, \ 5^2 + 5 = 30$$

or

2,   6,   12,   20,

+4   +6   +8   +10   = 30

# MATHEMATICS

# ARITHMETIC

# 1



## Number System

The development of the number system started with natural numbers. These are generally known as counting numbers.

### Natural Numbers

Numbers which start from 1 are known as natural numbers. It is denoted by N. The smallest natural number is 1. It is written as, $N = \{1, 2, 3, ..., \infty\}$

### Whole Numbers

A number which starts from zero (0) is known as whole number. It is denoted by W. It is written as, $W = \{0, 1, 2, 3, ..., \infty\}$

### Integers

Natural numbers along with 0 and their negatives are known as integers. It is denoted by I. It is written as, $I = \{..., -4, -3, -2, -1, 0, 1, 2, 3, 4, ...\}$

### Even Numbers

A number which is divisible by 2 is known as even numbers. Such as, 2, 4, 6, 10, 12, 128, 432 etc.

### Odd Numbers

A number which is not divisible by 2 is known as odd numbers: Such as, 1, 3, 5, 7, 9, 11, 13, 21, 29, 123 etc.

### Prime Numbers

A number which is divided by itself is known as prime numbers. The smallest prime number is 2. Such as, 2, 3, 5, 7, 11, 13, 17, 19, 23, ... etc.

*The formulae given below are quite useful for quick multiplication:*

$$(i)\ (a + b)^2 = a^2 + 2ab + b^2$$
$$(ii)\ (a - b)^2 = a^2 - 2ab + b^2$$
$$(iii)\ a^2 - b^2 = (a + b)(a - b)$$
$$(iv)\ a^2 + b^2 = (a + b)^2 - 2ab$$
$$(v)\ (a + b)^3 = a^3 + b^3 + 3ab(a + b)$$

(vi) $(a - b)^3 = a^3 - b^3 - 3ab\,(a - b)$
(vii) $a^3 + b^3 = (a + b)\,(a^2 - ab + b^2)$
(viii) $a^3 - b^3 = (a - b)\,(a^2 + ab + b^2)$

**Example :**  Simplify the following : $\dfrac{261 \times 261 \times 261 - 77 \times 77 \times 77}{261 \times 261 + 261 \times 77 + 77 \times 77}$

**Solution :**  $\dfrac{261 \times 261 \times 261 - 77 \times 77 \times 77}{261 \times 261 + 261 \times 77 + 77 \times 77}$

Let $\quad 261 = a$
and $\quad 77 = b$

$$\therefore \quad \frac{a^3 - b^3}{a^2 + ab + b^2} = \frac{(a-b)(a^2 + ab + b^2)}{(a^2 + ab + b^2)} = a - b$$

$$\therefore \quad 261 - 77 = 184.$$

## MULTIPLE CHOICE QUESTIONS

**1.** The face value of 8 in the numeral 458926 is:
   A. 8000            B. 8            C. 1000            D. 458000

**2.** $106 \times 106 + 94 \times 94 = x$, the value of $x$ is:
   A. 21032            B. 20032            C. 23032            D. 20072

**3.** If $m \times 48 = 173 \times 240$ then the value of $m$ is:
   A. 545            B. 685            C. 865            D. 495

**4.** $\left(1 - \dfrac{1}{3}\right)\left(1 - \dfrac{1}{4}\right)\left(1 - \dfrac{1}{5}\right)...\left(1 - \dfrac{1}{n}\right) = x$, then the value of $x$ is:

   A. $\dfrac{1}{n}$            B. $\dfrac{2}{n}$            C. $\dfrac{2(n-1)}{n}$            D. $\dfrac{2}{n(n+1)}$

**5.** When simplified the product $\left(2 - \dfrac{1}{3}\right)\left(2 - \dfrac{3}{5}\right)\left(2 - \dfrac{5}{7}\right)...\left(2 - \dfrac{997}{999}\right)$ is equal to:

   A. $\dfrac{5}{999}$            B. $\dfrac{1001}{999}$            C. $\dfrac{1001}{3}$            D. None of these

**6.** Which number should replace both the asterisks in $\left(\dfrac{*}{21}\right) \times \left(\dfrac{*}{189}\right) = 1$?

   A. 21            B. 63            C. 3969            D. 147

**7.** In a division sum, the divisor is 12 times the quotient and 5 times the remainder. If the remainder be 48, then the dividend is:

A. 240      B. 576      C. 4800      D. 4848

**8.** What least number must be subtracted from 1294 so that the remainder when divided by 9, 11, 13 will leave in each case the same remainder 6?

A. 0      B. 1      C. 2      D. 3

**9.** If $\sqrt{\left(1+\dfrac{27}{169}\right)} = \left(1+\dfrac{x}{13}\right)$, then the value of $x$ is:

A. 1      B. 3      C. 5      D. 7

**10.** If $\dfrac{x}{y} = \dfrac{3}{4}$, then the value of $\left(\dfrac{6}{7} + \dfrac{y-x}{y+x}\right)$ equals:

A. $\dfrac{5}{7}$      B. $1\dfrac{1}{7}$      C. 1      D. 2

**11.** The largest natural number by which the product of three consecutive even natural numbers is always divisible, is:

A. 16      B. 24      C. 48      D. 96

**12.** The least number of five digits which is exactly divisible by 12, 15 and 18 is:

A. 10080      B. 10800      C. 18000      D. 81000

**13.** The least number which when divided by 8, 9, 12, 16 and 20 leaves the same remainder 1 in each case is:

A. 712      B. 271      C. 721      D. 720

**14.** The value of 0.8693 + 0.092 + 0.87 + 0.4 equals:

A. 2.3213      B. 2.2331      C. 3.2313      D. 2.2313

**15.** The prime numbers between 1 to 50 are:

A. 8      B. 12      C. 15      D. 10

**16.** If $\dfrac{a}{b} = \dfrac{4}{3}$, then $\dfrac{3a+2b}{3a-2b}$ equals:

A. 6      B. 3      C. 5      D. −1

**17.** If $\sqrt{3^n} = 81$, then $n$ equals:

A. 2      B. 4      C. 6      D. 8

**18.** If $\sqrt{\dfrac{x}{196}} = \dfrac{72}{56}$, then $x$ equals:

A. 18      B. 14      C. 324      D. 212

**19.** If $a \times 48 = 173 \times 240$, then the value of $a$ is:

    A. 545      B. 685      C. 865      D. 495

**20.** If $\dfrac{80}{x} = \dfrac{x}{20}$, then the value of $x$ is:

    A. 40      B. 400      C. 800      D. 1600

**21.** If '$x$' and '$y$' are both odd numbers, which of the following numbers must be an even number?

    A. $x + y$      B. $x \times y$      C. $xy + 2$      D. $2x + y$

**22.** '$a$' is less than '$b$' then, which of the following numbers is greater than '$a$' and less than '$b$'?

    A. $\dfrac{a+b}{2}$      B. $\dfrac{ab}{2}$      C. $b^2 - a^2$      D. $ab$

**23.** $a + b + c + d$ is a positive number, a minimum of '$x$' of the number $a$, $b$, $c$ and $d$ must be positive, where '$x$' is equal to—

    A. $-1$      B. 2      C. 3      D. 4

**24.** There are four numbers A, B, C and D. Average of the first three i.e., A, B and C is 15 and that of B, C and D is 16. If the last number, i.e., D is 19, then the first number is—

    A. 15      B. 16      C. 17      D. 18

**25.** Think of a number, divide it by 9 and add 9 to it, if the result is 27, the number is—

    A. 18      B. 21      C. 100      D. 162

**26.** Of the three numbers, the first is twice the second and thrice the third. If the average of three is 22, the three numbers are—

    A. 12, 18, 36      B. 18, 12, 36      C. 36, 12, 18      D. 36, 18, 12

**27.** The number which when added to itself 10 times gives 264. The number is—

    A. 20      B. 22      C. 24      D. 26

**28.** If a person is standing on the sixth number in the queue from both the ends, the total persons in the queue are—

    A. 9      B. 11      C. 12      D. 13

**29.** A number '$x$' when multiplied by 5 and added to three times its own gives 64, the number is—

    A. 8      B. 12      C. 14      D. 18

**30.** If the sum of two numbers '$x$' and '$y$' is equal to twice the first number, the second number '$y$' is—

    A. $> x$                  B. $< x$

    C. $= x$                 D. negative number

## ANSWERS

| 1 | 2 | 3 | 4 | 5 | 6 | 7 | 8 | 9 | 10 |
|---|---|---|---|---|---|---|---|---|---|
| B | D | C | B | C | B | D | B | A | C |

| 11 | 12 | 13 | 14 | 15 | 16 | 17 | 18 | 19 | 20 |
|----|----|----|----|----|----|----|----|----|----|
| C | A | C | D | C | B | D | C | C | A |

| 21 | 22 | 23 | 24 | 25 | 26 | 27 | 28 | 29 | 30 |
|----|----|----|----|----|----|----|----|----|----|
| A | A | A | B | D | D | C | B | A | C |

## EXPLANATORY ANSWERS

**1.** The face value of 8 in the numeral 458926 is 8.

**3.** $\because m = \dfrac{173 \times 240}{48} = 865.$

**7.** Let quotient = Q and remainder = R
Then, divisor = 12Q = 5R        Now, R = 48
$\Rightarrow$ 12Q = 5 × 48 $\Rightarrow$ Q = 20 $\therefore$ Dividend = (20 × 240 + 48) = 4848

**11.** It is 2 × 4 × 6 = 48

**15.** The prime numbers between 1 to 50 are 2, 3, 5, 7, 11, 13, 17, 19, 23, 29, 31, 37, 41, 43, 47.
Hence, there are 15 prime numbers between 1 to 50.

**17.** $\because \sqrt{3^n} = 81 \Rightarrow 3^{\frac{n}{2}} = 3^4 \Rightarrow \dfrac{n}{2} = 4 \Rightarrow n = 8.$

**20.** $\because \dfrac{80}{x} = \dfrac{x}{20} \Rightarrow x^2 = 80 \times 20 \Rightarrow x^2 = 1600 \Rightarrow x = 40$

**21.** Since the sum of two odd numbers is always even number, therefore, $x + y$ is even number.

**22.** Average of two different numbers is always between the two numbers.

**23.** If all numbers were not positive, then the sum could not be positive. If $a, b, c$ were all $-1$ and $d$ were 5, then $a + b + c + d$ would be positive, so *(b), (c), (d)* are incorrect.

**25.** Let the number is $x$.

$\therefore \dfrac{x}{9} + 9 = 27$    or,    $\dfrac{x}{9} = 27 - 9 = 18$    $\therefore x = 18 \times 9 = 162.$

**29.** $5 \times x + 3x = 64 \Rightarrow 8x = 64$      $\therefore x = \dfrac{64}{8} = 8$

**30.** $x + y = 2x$      $\therefore y = 2x - x = x$

❖ ❖ ❖

**2**

# HCF and LCM

## Highest Common Factor

The HCF of two or more than two numbers is the greatest number that divides each of them exactly. The highest common factor is also known as Greatest Common Divisor or Greatest Common Measure.

There are two methods of determining the HCF of two or more numbers.

(*i*) HCF by Factorization method

(*ii*) HCF by Division method.

## HCF by Factorization Method

Express each one of the given number as the product of prime factors. Now choose common factors and take the product of these factors to obtain the required HCF.

**EXAMPLE :** Find the HCF of 126, 396 and 5400.

**SOLUTION :**
$$126 = 2 \times 3 \times 3 \times 7$$
$$396 = 2 \times 2 \times 3 \times 3 \times 11$$
$$5400 = 2 \times 2 \times 2 \times 3 \times 3 \times 3 \times 5 \times 5$$

Common factors are 2, 3 and 3.

Hence, the HCF = $2 \times 3 \times 3 = 18$.

## HCF by Division Method

Divide the larger number by the smaller one. Now, divide the divisor by the remainder. Repeat the process of dividing the preceding divisor by the remainder last obtained till zero is obtained as remainder. The last divisor is the required HCF.

**EXAMPLE:** Find the HCF of 48, 168 and 324.

**SOLUTION:** Firstly, we find the HCF of 48 and 168.

```
        48) 1 6 8 (3
            -1 4 4
            24) 4 8 (2
               - 4 8
               ______
                  0
```

Thus, HCF of 48 and 168 = 24.

Now, HCF of 24 and 324

```
           24) 3 2 4 (13
               - 2 4
               ______
                 8 4
                 7 2
               ______
               1 2) 2 4 (2
                    2 4
                    ____
                     0
```

Hence, HCF of 48, 168 and 324 = 12

## Lowest Common Multiple

The LCM of two or more numbers is the lowest or least number which is exactly divisible by each of them.

## LCM by Factorization

Resolve each one of the given numbers into a product of prime factors. Then LCM is the product of highest powers of all the factors.

**EXAMPLE:** Find the LCM of 72, 189 and 1026.

**SOLUTION:**
$$72 = 2^3 \times 3^2$$
$$189 = 3^3 \times 7$$
and
$$1026 = 2 \times 3^3 \times 19$$
$$\therefore \quad \text{LCM} = 2^3 \times 3^3 \times 7 \times 19$$
$$= 8 \times 27 \times 7 \times 19 = 28728$$

## FORMULA

Product of two numbers = HCF × LCM.

$$\text{LCM} = \frac{\text{Product of numbers}}{\text{HCF}} \qquad \text{HCF} = \frac{\text{Product of numbers}}{\text{LCM}}$$

$$\text{First number} = \frac{\text{LCM} \times \text{HCF}}{\text{2nd number}} \qquad \text{2nd number} = \frac{\text{LCM} \times \text{HCF}}{\text{First number}}$$

## HCF and LCM of Fractions

$$(i) \ \text{HCF} = \frac{\text{HCF of numerators}}{\text{LCM of denominators}} \qquad (ii) \ \text{LCM} = \frac{\text{LCM of numerators}}{\text{HCF of denominators}}$$

## MULTIPLE CHOICE QUESTIONS

1. HCF of 1485 and 4356 is:
   A. 189     B. 89     C. 99     D. 83

2. LCM of 18, 24, 42, 63 is:
   A. 302     B. 604     C. 504     D. 404

3. Which of the following fractions is the greatest of all? $\dfrac{7}{8}, \dfrac{6}{7}, \dfrac{4}{5}, \dfrac{5}{6}$

   A. $\dfrac{6}{7}$     B. $\dfrac{4}{5}$     C. $\dfrac{5}{6}$     D. $\dfrac{7}{8}$

4. Which of the following is in ascending order?

   A. $\dfrac{5}{7}, \dfrac{7}{8}, \dfrac{9}{11}$     B. $\dfrac{5}{7}, \dfrac{9}{11}, \dfrac{7}{8}$     C. $\dfrac{7}{8}, \dfrac{5}{7}, \dfrac{9}{11}$     D. $\dfrac{9}{11}, \dfrac{7}{8}, \dfrac{5}{7}$

**5.** HCF of three numbers is 12. If they be in the ratio 1 : 2 : 3, the numbers are:
   A. 12, 24, 36      B. 10, 20, 30     C. 5, 10, 15     D. 4, 8, 12

**6.** The largest natural number which exactly divides the product of any four consecutive natural numbers is:
   A. 6             B. 12           C. 24          D. 120

**7.** The traffic lights at three different road crossings change after every 48 seconds, 72 seconds and 108 seconds respectively. If they all change simultaneously at 8 : 20 : 00 hrs; then they will again change simultaneously at:
   A. 8 : 27 : 12 hrs                B. 8 : 27 : 24 hrs
   C. 8 : 27 : 36 hrs                D. 8 : 27 : 48 hrs

**8.** The HCF of two numbers is 16 and their LCM is 160. If one of the number is 32, then the other number is:
   A. 48          B. 80          C. 96          D. 112

**9.** The HCF of two numbers is 12 and their difference is also 12. The numbers are:
   A. 66, 78      B. 70, 82      C. 94, 106     D. 84, 96

**10.** The largest number which exactly divides 210, 315, 147 and 161 is:
   A. 3           B. 7           C. 21         D. 4410

**11.** The least perfect square number which is divisible by 3, 4, 5, 6 and 8 is:
   A. 900       B. 1200      C. 2500     D. 3600

**12.** The smallest number which is divisible by 12, 15 and 20 is a perfect square, is:
   A. 400       B. 900       C. 1600     D. 3600

**13.** The sum of two numbers is 216 and their HCF is 27. The numbers are:
   A. 54, 162     B. 108, 108    C. 27, 189    D. None of these

**14.** The HCF and LCM of two numbers are 44 and 264 respectively. If the first number is divided by 2, the quotient is 44. The other number is:
   A. 33          B. 66          C. 132       D. 264

**15.** The number of prime factors in $2^{222} \times 3^{333} \times 5^{555}$ is:
   A. 3           B. 1107      C. 1110      D. 1272

**16.** The number of prime factors in the expression $(6)^{10} \times (7)^{17} \times (11)^{27}$ is:
   A. 54          B. 64          C. 71          D. 81

**17.** Three measuring rods are 64 cm, 80 cm and 96 cm in length. The least length of cloth that can be measured exact number of times using any one of the above rod is:
   A. 0.96 m      B. 19.20 m    C. 9.60 m     D. 96.00 m

**18.** The product of two numbers is 1600 and their HCF is 5. The LCM of the numbers is:
A. 320              B. 1605              C. 1595              D. 8000

**19.** About the number of pairs which have 16 as their HCF and 136 as their LCM, we can definitely say that:
A. Only one such pair exists              B. Only two such pairs exist
C. Many such pairs exist              D. No such pair exist

**20.** The total number of prime factors of the product $(8)^{20} \times (15)^{24} \times (7)^{15}$ is:
A. 59              B. 98              C. 123              D. 138

**21.** A number $n$ is said to be perfect, if the sum of all its divisors (excluding $n$ itself) is equal to $n$. A perfect number is
A. 21              B. 15              C. 9              D. 6

**22.** HCF of $4 \times 27 \times 3125$, $8 \times 9 \times 25 \times 7$ and $16 \times 81 \times 5 \times 11 \times 49$ is
A. 1260              B. 540              C. 360              D. 180

**23.** Which is of the following is a co-primes?
A. (23, 92)              B. (21, 35)              C. (18, 25)              D. (16, 62)

**24.** The LCM of $2^3 \times 3^2 \times 5 \times 11$, $2^4 \times 3^4 \times 5^2 \times 7$

and $2^5 \times 3^3 \times 5^3 \times 7^2 \times 11$ is :

A. $2^5 \times 3^4 \times 5^3$                               B. $2^3 \times 3^2 \times 5$

C. $2^5 \times 3^4 \times 5^3 \times 7^2 \times 11$              D. $2^3 \times 3^2 \times 5 \times 7 \times 11$

**25.** The G.C.D. of 1.08, 0.36 and 0.9 is
A. 0.108              B. 0.18              C. 0.9              D. 0.03

**26.** H.C.F. of 3240, 3600 and a third number is 36 and their L.C.M. is $2^4 \times 3^5 \times 5^2 \times 7^2$. The third number is
A. $2^3 \times 3^5 \times 7^2$       B. $2^5 \times 5^2 \times 7^2$       C. $2^2 \times 5^3 \times 7^2$  D. $2^2 \times 3^5 \times 7^2$

**27.** The ratio of two numbers is 3 : 4 and their H.C.F. is 4. Find their L.C.M.
A. 48              B. 24              C. 16              D. 12

**28.** Three numbers are in the ratio 1 : 2 : 3 and their HCF is 12. Find the numbers.
A. 12, 24, 36              B. 10, 20, 30              C. 5, 10, 15              D. 4, 8, 12

**29.** If the sum of two numbers is 55 and the H.C.F. and L.C.M. of these numbers are 5 and 120 respectively. Find the sum of their reciprocals.

A. $\dfrac{120}{11}$              B. $\dfrac{11}{120}$              C. $\dfrac{601}{55}$              D. $\dfrac{55}{601}$

**30.** The L.C.M. of two numbers is 495 and their HCF is 5. If the sum of the numbers is 100, then find their difference.
A. 90              B. 70              C. 46              D. 10

## ANSWERS

| 1 | 2 | 3 | 4 | 5 | 6 | 7 | 8 | 9 | 10 |
|---|---|---|---|---|---|---|---|---|---|
| C | C | D | B | A | C | A | B | D | B |

| 11 | 12 | 13 | 14 | 15 | 16 | 17 | 18 | 19 | 20 |
|---|---|---|---|---|---|---|---|---|---|
| D | D | C | C | C | B | C | A | D | C |

| 21 | 22 | 23 | 24 | 25 | 26 | 27 | 28 | 29 | 30 |
|---|---|---|---|---|---|---|---|---|---|
| D | D | C | C | B | D | A | A | B | D |

## EXPLANATORY ANSWERS

**2.**

$$
\begin{array}{r|rrrr}
2 & 18, & 24, & 42, & 63 \\
\hline
3 & 9, & 12, & 21, & 63 \\
\hline
3 & 3, & 4, & 7, & 21 \\
\hline
7 & 1, & 4, & 7, & 7 \\
\hline
& 1, & 4, & 1, & 1
\end{array}
$$

LCM of 18, 24, 42, 63 $= 2 \times 3^2 \times 7 \times 4 = 504$.

**5.** Let the numbers be $x$, $2x$ and $3x$.
Then, their HCF $= x$
According to the question, $x = 12$
$\therefore$ The numbers are 12, 24, 36.

**6.** $1 \times 2 \times 3 \times 4 = 24$
$\therefore$ Required number $= 24$.

**10.** HCF of 210, 315, 147 and 161 $= 7$ Hence, the required number $= 7$.

**12.** LCM of 12, 15 and 20 $= 60$
Hence, required number $= 60 \times 60 = 3600$.

**15.** The number of prime factors in the given product
$= (222 + 333 + 555) = 1110$

**19.** HCF is always a factor of LCM. So no two numbers exist with HCF $= 16$ and LCM $= 136$.

**24.** $2^3 \times 3^2 \times 5 \times 11$;  $2^4 \times 3^4 \times 5^2 \times 7$
and $2^5 \times 3^3 \times 5^3 \times 7^2 \times 11$
$\therefore$ LCM $= 2^5 \times 3^4 \times 5^3 \times 7^2 \times 11$

**25.** GCD of 108, 36 and 90 $= 18$
Hence, GCD of 1.08, 0.36 and 0.9 $= 0.18$.

**27.** Let the numbers be $3x$ and $4x$; HCF = 4; Hence, $x = 4$
Then, numbers will be 12 and 16;
$\therefore$ Their LCM = 48.

**28.** Let the numbers are $x$, $2x$ and $3x$;
Their HCF = 12
Then, $x = 12$,
so the numbers will be 12, 24, 36.

**29.** Let the number be $x$ and $y$.
Then, $x + y = 55$;
$xy = \text{HCF} \times \text{LCM} = 5 \times 120$

$$\therefore \text{ Sum of their reciprocals} = \frac{1}{x} + \frac{1}{y} = \frac{x+y}{xy} = \frac{55}{5 \times 120} = \frac{11}{120}$$

**30.** Let the number be $x$ and $(100 - x)$
Now, $x\,(100 - x) = 5 \times 495$
$\Rightarrow x^2 - 100x + 2475 = 0$
$\Rightarrow x^2 - 55x - 45x + 2475 = 0$
$\Rightarrow x\,(x - 55) - 45\,(x - 55) = 0$
$\Rightarrow (x - 45)\,(x - 55) = 0$
Either, $x = 45$ or, $x = 55$
Hence, the numbers are 45 and 55
So, their difference = $55 - 45 = 10$

❖ ❖ ❖

# 3

# Simplification

Simplification means expressing in a simpler form. In order to simplify an expression we use the operations in the following order which is easily remembered as "BODMAS".

(*i*) Bracket (*ii*) Of (*iii*) Division (*iv*) Multiplication (*v*) Addition (*vi*) Subtraction.

'Of' means multiplication but it is operated even before division.

While removing brackets, first of all bar bracket '—' and after that small bracket '( )' is removed. Thereafter curley bracket '{ }' and at last square bracket '[ ]' is removed.

**EXAMPLE:** Simplify: $10 - \left[ 6 - \left\{ 7 - \left( 6 - \overline{8 - 5} \right) \right\} \right]$

**SOLUTION:** $10 - \left[ 6 - \left\{ 7 - \left( 6 - 3 \right) \right\} \right]$

$$= 10 - [6 - \{7 - 3\}] \qquad = 10 - [6 - 4] = 10 - 2 = 8.$$

## MULTIPLE CHOICE QUESTIONS

1. $\dfrac{48 - 12 \times 3 + 9}{12 - 9 \div 3}$ equals:

   A. 3      B. 21      C. $\dfrac{7}{3}$      D. $\dfrac{1}{3}$

2. $\dfrac{69 - 14 \times 3 + 2}{9 \times 5 - (5)^2}$ equals:

   A. 1.45      B. 2.75      C. 26.5      D. 265

3. If $\dfrac{17.28 \div x}{3.6 \times 0.2} = 2$ then, the value of $x$ is:

   A. 120      B. 1.20      C. 12      D. 0.12

4. $171 \div 19 \times 9$ equals:

   A. 0      B. 1      C. 18      D. 81

5. $3120 \div 26 + 13 \times 30$ equals:

   A. 2400      B. 3900      C. 536      D. None of these

---

**6.** $\dfrac{31}{10} \times \dfrac{3}{10} + \dfrac{7}{5} \div 20$ equals:

   A. 0        B. 1        C. 100        D. $\dfrac{107}{200}$

**7.** The simplification of $1 + \dfrac{1}{2 + \dfrac{1}{1 - \dfrac{1}{3}}}$ yields the result:

   A. $\dfrac{2}{7}$        B. $\dfrac{7}{9}$        C. $\dfrac{9}{7}$        D. $\dfrac{13}{7}$

**8.** The value of $1 + \dfrac{1}{4 \times 3} + \dfrac{1}{4 \times 3^2} + \dfrac{1}{4 \times 3^3}$ up to four places of decimals is:

   A. 1.1202        B. 1.1203        C. 1.1204        D. None of these

**9.** $\dfrac{\dfrac{1}{2} \div 4 + 20}{\dfrac{1}{2} \times 4 + 20}$ equals:

   A. $\dfrac{81}{88}$        B. $2\dfrac{3}{11}$        C. $\dfrac{161}{176}$        D. 1

**10.** $3 \div \left[ (8 - 5) \div \left\{ (4 - 2) \div \left( 2 + \dfrac{8}{13} \right) \right\} \right]$ equals:

   A. $\dfrac{13}{17}$        B. $\dfrac{68}{13}$        C. $\dfrac{17}{13}$        D. $\dfrac{13}{68}$

**11.** $10 - [9 - \{8 - (7 - 6)\}] - 5$ is equal to:

   A. $-5$        B. 1        C. 3        D. 9

**12.** $\dfrac{\dfrac{1}{5} \div \dfrac{1}{5} \text{ of } \dfrac{1}{5}}{\dfrac{1}{5} \text{ of } \dfrac{1}{5} \div \dfrac{1}{5}}$ is equal to:

   A. 1        B. 5        C. $\dfrac{1}{5}$        D. 25

**13.** The value of $1 + \dfrac{1}{1 + \dfrac{1}{1 + \dfrac{1}{9}}}$ is:

   A. $\dfrac{29}{19}$        B. $\dfrac{10}{19}$        C. $\dfrac{29}{10}$        D. $\dfrac{10}{9}$

**14.** $\dfrac{3}{48}$ is what part of $\dfrac{1}{12}$?

A. $\dfrac{3}{7}$          B. $\dfrac{1}{12}$          C. $\dfrac{4}{3}$          D. None of these

**15.** How many $\dfrac{1}{8}$ s are there in $37\dfrac{1}{2}$?

A. 300          B. 400
C. 500          D. Cannot be determined

**16.** $\dfrac{885 \times 885 \times 885 + 115 \times 115 \times 115}{885 \times 885 + 115 \times 115 - 885 \times 115}$ is equal to:

A. 115          B. 770          C. 885          D. 1000

**17.** The value of $\dfrac{9^2 \times 18^4}{3^{16}}$ is:

A. $\dfrac{2}{3}$          B. $\dfrac{4}{9}$          C. $\dfrac{16}{81}$          D. $\dfrac{32}{243}$

**18.** $\left(1\dfrac{3}{5} - \dfrac{2}{3} \div \dfrac{12}{13} + \dfrac{7}{5} \times \dfrac{1}{3}\right)$ is equal to:

A. $1\dfrac{31}{90}$          B. $\dfrac{19}{30}$          C. $\dfrac{11}{30}$          D. 30

**19.** The value of $48 \div 12 \times \left(\dfrac{9}{8} \text{ of } \dfrac{4}{3} \div \dfrac{3}{4} \text{ of } \dfrac{2}{3}\right)$ is:

A. $1\dfrac{1}{3}$          B. $5\dfrac{1}{3}$          C. 3          D. 12

**20.** $(20 \div 5) \div 2 + (16 \div 8) \times 2 + (10 \div 5) \times (3 \div 2)$ is equal to
A. 9          B. 12          C. 15          D. 18

**21.** The sum of 1/9, 1/3, 1/6 and 7/18 of a number is 150. The number is
A. 120          B. 130          C. 140          D. 150

**22.** Which is the greatest?  .999, .1011, .1995, .9985
A. .999          B. .1011          C. .1995          D. .9985

**23.** In decimal system, $9\dfrac{1}{8}$ may be represented as
A. 9.18          B. 9.125          C. 9.025          D. 9.225

**24.** $2.205 \div 0.15 = ?$
A. 1.47          B. 14.7          C. 147          D. 0.147

**25.** G.C.M. of .24, 3.2 and 16.0 is
   A. 80             B. 8             C. .8             D. .08

**26.** L.C.M. of .24, 3.2 and 16.0 is
   A. .48           B. 4.8           C. 48           D. 480

**27.** A pole has 0.5 of its length in mud, 0.25 of its length in water and 2 metres above water. The total length of the pole is
   A. 8 metres       B. 5 metres       C. 4 metres       D. 2 metres

**28.** $\sqrt{1/3}$ is equal to
   A. 0.57         B. 0.35         C. 0.30         D. 3.00

**29.** How many times does 2/3 of 1/2 go into half of third?
   A. 2            B. 1/2           C. 1/3           D. 2/3

**30.** The eleventh part of $990\dfrac{990}{990}$ is
   A. 99.0         B. 99.99         C. 90         D. 90.9

## ANSWERS

| 1 | 2 | 3 | 4 | 5 | 6 | 7 | 8 | 9 | 10 |
|---|---|---|---|---|---|---|---|---|----|
| C | A | C | D | D | B | C | B | C | A |

| 11 | 12 | 13 | 14 | 15 | 16 | 17 | 18 | 19 | 20 |
|----|----|----|----|----|----|----|----|----|----|
| C | D | A | D | A | D | C | A | D | A |

| 21 | 22 | 23 | 24 | 25 | 26 | 27 | 28 | 29 | 30 |
|----|----|----|----|----|----|----|----|----|----|
| D | A | B | B | D | C | A | A | B | C |

## EXPLANATORY ANSWERS

**4.** $171 \div 19 \times 9 = 9 \times 9 = 81.$

**5.** $3120 \div 26 + 13 \times 30 = 120 + 390 = 510.$

**6.** $\dfrac{31}{10} \times \dfrac{3}{10} + \dfrac{7}{5} \div 20 = \dfrac{31}{10} \times \dfrac{3}{10} + \dfrac{7}{5} \times \dfrac{1}{20}$

$= \dfrac{93}{100} + \dfrac{7}{100} = \dfrac{93+7}{100} = \dfrac{100}{100} = 1$

**11.** $10 - [9 - \{8 - (7 - 6)\}] - 5$
$= 10 - [9 - \{8 - 1\}] - 5$
$= 10 - [9 - 7] - 5$
$= 10 - 2 - 5 = 10 - 7 = 3$

**22.** .999 is the greatest.

**23.** $9\dfrac{1}{8} = 9 + \dfrac{1}{8} = 9 + .125 = 9.125$

**26.** L.C.M. of .24, 3.2 and 16.0 = L.C.M. of $\dfrac{24,\ 320\ \text{and}\ 1600}{100}$

$= \dfrac{4800}{100} = 48.$

**27.** Let total length of the pole $= x$
Pole above water $= x - [0.5x + 0.25x]$
$= 0.25x$; But, $0.25x = 2$ metres
$\therefore x = \dfrac{2 \times 100}{25} = 8$ metres

**28.** $\qquad \sqrt{\dfrac{1}{3}} = \dfrac{1}{\sqrt{3}} \times \dfrac{\sqrt{3}}{\sqrt{3}} = \dfrac{\sqrt{3}}{3} = \dfrac{1.732}{3} = .57$

**29.** $\qquad \dfrac{2}{3}$ of $\dfrac{1}{2} = \dfrac{2}{3} \times \dfrac{1}{2} = \dfrac{1}{3}$

$\qquad\qquad \dfrac{1}{2}$ of $\dfrac{1}{3} = \dfrac{1}{6}$

$\therefore \qquad \dfrac{1}{6} \div \dfrac{1}{3} = \dfrac{1}{6} \times \dfrac{3}{1} = \dfrac{1}{2}$

**30.** $\qquad$ Eleventh part of $990\dfrac{990}{990} = 990\dfrac{990}{990} \div 11 = \dfrac{990}{11} = 90$

❖ ❖ ❖

4

# Surds and Indices

## Surds

If '$a$' is a rational number and $n$ is a positive integer such that $n$th root of '$a$', i.e., $a^{1/n}$ or $\sqrt[n]{a}$ is an irrational number, then $a^{1/n}$ is called a surd or radical.

**For example,** $\sqrt{2} = 2^{1/2}$ = Square root of 2

$$\sqrt[3]{5} = 5^{1/3} = \text{Cube root of } 5$$

### *Important Formulae Based on Surds*

$\sqrt[n]{a} = a^{1/n}$ and it is called a surd of order $n$.

(i) $\sqrt[n]{a^n} = a$        (ii) $\sqrt[n]{ab} = \sqrt[n]{a}\,\sqrt[n]{b}$

(iii) $\sqrt{a} \times \sqrt{b} = \sqrt{ab}$        (iv) $\left(\sqrt{a} + \sqrt{b}\right)^2 = a + b + 2\sqrt{ab}$

(v) $\left(\sqrt{a} - \sqrt{b}\right)^2 = a + b - 2\sqrt{ab}$

(vi) $\left(\sqrt{a} + \sqrt{b}\right)\left(\sqrt{a} - \sqrt{b}\right) = a - b$ where $a$ and $b$ are positive rational numbers.

## Indices

The expression $a^n$ is termed as power function or simply power, $a$ is called the base and $n$ is called index or exponent of the power $a^n$.

For example, $2^2$ = square of 2, $2^3$ = cube of 2, etc.

## Laws of Indices

(i) $a^m \times a^n = a^{m+n}$        (ii) $a^m \times a^n \times a^p \times ... = a^{m+n+p+...}$

(iii) $\dfrac{a^m}{a^n} = a^{m-n}$, if $m > n$        (iv) $(a^m)^n = a^{mn}$

(v) $(ab)^n = a^n b^n$        (vi) $a^0 = 1$

(vii) If $a^m = a^n$ then $m = n$        (viii) If $a^m = b^m$ then $a = b$

## MULTIPLE CHOICE QUESTIONS

**1.** If the infinite series is $x = \sqrt{6 + \sqrt{6 + \sqrt{6 + ...}}}$ then the value of $x$ is:

   A. 2.5        B. 3        C. 6        D. 8

**2.** If $\dfrac{9^n \cdot 3^2 \cdot 3^n - (27)^n}{3^{3m} \cdot 2^3} = \dfrac{1}{27}$, then the value of $(m - n)$ is:

    A. 1                B. 2                C. $\sqrt{3}$           D. $\sqrt{\dfrac{2}{3}}$

**3.** If $x = \dfrac{\sqrt{5} + \sqrt{3}}{\sqrt{5} - \sqrt{3}}$ and $y = \dfrac{\sqrt{5} - \sqrt{3}}{\sqrt{5} + \sqrt{3}}$, then $(x + y)$ is equal to:

    A. 8                B. 6                C. $2\sqrt{15}$         D. $2\left(\sqrt{5} + \sqrt{3}\right)$

**4.** $2^{x+1} + 2^{x+3} = 2560$, then $x$ is equal to:
    A. 12             B. 11            C. 8              D. 6

**5.** If $\dfrac{5 + 2\sqrt{3}}{7 + 4\sqrt{3}} = a + b\sqrt{3}$, then $b$ is equal to:

    A. –6           B. 6              C. –11         D. 11

**6.** If $\dfrac{(21)^{5.36}}{(21)^{3.47}} = (21)^x$, then the value of $x$ is:

    A. 8.88         B. 1.54         C. 9.32        D. 1.89

**7.** $\sqrt{24} + \sqrt{12}$ equal to:
    A. $\sqrt{36}$         B. $2\sqrt{6} + 2\sqrt{3}$    C. $6\sqrt{2}$        D. $\sqrt{288}$

**8.** If $a^b = 64$, where $a$ and $b$ are positive integers then $(a - b)^{a+b-4}$ is:

    A. 0             B. 1              C. 2           D. $\dfrac{1}{2}$

**9.** The value of $\dfrac{5^{10+n} \cdot 25^{3n-4}}{5^{7n}}$ is:

    A. 5             B. 8             C. 25          D. 16

**10.** $3^x - 3^{x-1} = 18$, then the value of $x^x$ is:
    A. 3             B. 8             C. 27          D. 216

**11.** If $x = \sqrt{10 + \sqrt{25 + \sqrt{121}}}$, then $x$ is equal to:
    A. –2 only       B. 2 only       C. ± 4         D. 4 only

**12.** If $a^x = b^y = c^z$ and $b^2 = ac$, then $y$ is equal to:

    A. $\dfrac{xz}{x + z}$        B. $\dfrac{xz}{2(x - z)}$     C. $\dfrac{xz}{2(z - x)}$    D. $\dfrac{2xz}{x + z}$

**13.** $\dfrac{5^{n+3} - 6 \times 5^{n+1}}{9 \times 5^n - 5^n \times 2^2}$ is equal to:

   A. 5        B. 19        C. 25        D. 95

**14.** The value of $\left(\dfrac{x^a}{x^b}\right)^{(a+b)} \times \left(\dfrac{x^b}{x^c}\right)^{(b+c)} \times \left(\dfrac{x^c}{x^a}\right)^{(c+a)}$ is equal to:

   A. 0        B. 2        C. 1        D. 3

**15.** If $\sqrt{3^n} = 729$, then the value of $n$ is:

   A. 12        B. 8        C. 10        D. 6

**16.** The value of $4\sqrt{3} - 3\sqrt{12} + 2\sqrt{75}$ is:

   A. $2\sqrt{3}$        B. $4\sqrt{3}$        C. $6\sqrt{3}$        D. $8\sqrt{3}$

**17.** The value of $\sqrt{50} - \sqrt{98} + \sqrt{162}$ is:

   A. $5\sqrt{2}$        B. $7\sqrt{2}$        C. $3\sqrt{2}$        D. $4\sqrt{2}$

**18.** If $x = 1 - \sqrt{2}$, the value of $\left(x - \dfrac{1}{x}\right)^3$ is:

   A. 1        B. 4        C. 8        D. 2

**19.** If $a = 7 - 4\sqrt{3}$, then the value of $\sqrt{a} + \dfrac{1}{\sqrt{a}}$ is equal to:

   A. 1        B. 4        C. 2        D. 3

**20.** The value of $\dfrac{4\sqrt{18}}{\sqrt{12}} - \dfrac{8\sqrt{75}}{\sqrt{32}} + \dfrac{9\sqrt{2}}{\sqrt{3}}$ is:

   A. 0        B. 2        C. 1        D. 3

**21.** If $(625)^2 = 390625$, then the value of $\sqrt{.00390625}$ will be:

   A. .0625        B. 0.625        C. .00625        D. .000625

**22.** $x \otimes y = \sqrt{(x+1)(y+1)^2}$, then the value of $3 \otimes 7$ will be:

   A. 21        B. 16        C. 18        D. 28

**23.** The cube root of $8^4$ is:

   A. 16        B. 8        C. 4        D. 64

**24.** By what smallest number 270 be multiplied so that the resulting number becomes a perfect cube?

    A.  121        B.  109        C.  100        D.  99

**25.** By what smallest number 675 be multiplied so that the product becomes a perfect square number?

    A.  2        B.  $\dfrac{3}{5}$        C.  4        D.  3

**26.** If the approximate square root of 80 is 8.94. What will be the value of $\sqrt{20}$ ?

    A.  3.37        B.  4.47        C.  4.87        D.  4.40

**27.** What will be the value of $\sqrt[3]{32+\sqrt{1012+\sqrt{144}}}$ ?

    A.  4        B.  6        C.  5        D. 8

**28.** What will be the square root of $\left(\sqrt[3]{0.00000064}\right) \times \sqrt{2.56}$ ?

    A.  .06        B.  .08        C.  .05        D.  .04

**29.** If $\dfrac{\sqrt{?}}{4}=\dfrac{1}{3}$ , what will be in place of (?)?

    A.  $\dfrac{16}{3}$        B.  $\dfrac{16}{9}$        C.  $\dfrac{21}{16}$        D.  $\dfrac{4}{3}$

**30.** If 30% of $\sqrt{?}$ + 15% of 40 = 11, what should replace the sign of interrogation (?)?

    A.  $\dfrac{2500}{9}$        B.  $\dfrac{2400}{7}$        C.  $\dfrac{2300}{11}$        D.  $\dfrac{2200}{7}$

## ANSWERS

| 1 | 2 | 3 | 4 | 5 | 6 | 7 | 8 | 9 | 10 |
|---|---|---|---|---|---|---|---|---|---|
| B | A | A | C | A | D | B | B | C | C |

| 11 | 12 | 13 | 14 | 15 | 16 | 17 | 18 | 19 | 20 |
|----|----|----|----|----|----|----|----|----|----|
| D | D | B | C | A | D | B | C | B | A |

| 21 | 22 | 23 | 24 | 25 | 26 | 27 | 28 | 29 | 30 |
|----|----|----|----|----|----|----|----|----|----|
| A | B | A | C | D | B | A | B | B | A |

## EXPLANATORY ANSWERS

**6.** $$\frac{(21)^{5.36}}{(21)^{3.47}} = (21)^x$$

$\Rightarrow \quad (21)^{5.36\,-\,3.47} = (21)^x$

$\Rightarrow \qquad\qquad x = 1.89$

**7.** $\sqrt{24} + \sqrt{12} = 2\sqrt{6} + 2\sqrt{3}$

**8.** $a^b = 64 = (4)^3 \Rightarrow a = 4,\ b = 3$

$\therefore (a-b)^{a+b-4} = (4-3)^{4+3-4} = (1)^3 = 1$

**13.** $$\frac{5^{n+3} - 6 \times 5^{n+1}}{9 \times 5^n - 5^n \times 2^2} = \frac{5^n \times 5^3 - 6 \times 5^n \times 5}{9 \times 5^n - 4 \times 5^n}$$

$$= \frac{5^n(125 - 30)}{5^n(9 - 4)} = 5^0 \times \frac{95}{5}$$

$$= 1 \times 19 = 19.$$

**15.** $\sqrt{3^n} = 729 \Rightarrow 3^{n/2} = 3^6$

$\Rightarrow \qquad\qquad \dfrac{n}{2} = 6$

$\Rightarrow \qquad\qquad n = 12.$

**25.** $675 = 3 \times 3 \times 3 \times 5 \times 5 = 3 \times 3^2 \times 5^2$

From the above, we find that only a factor 3 is left unpaired

$\therefore$ If we multiply 675 by 3 the product would be $\underline{3 \times 3} \times 3^2 \times 5^2$ which is a perfect square.

$\therefore$ The required smallest number is 3.

**27.** $\because \sqrt[3]{32 + \sqrt{1012 + \sqrt{144}}} = \sqrt[3]{32 + \sqrt{1012 + 12}}$

$= \sqrt[3]{32 + \sqrt{1024}} = \sqrt[3]{32 + 32} = \sqrt[3]{64} = \sqrt[3]{4 \times 4 \times 4} = 4$

**29.** $\dfrac{\sqrt{?}}{4} = \dfrac{1}{3} \Rightarrow \sqrt{?} = \dfrac{4}{3} \qquad \Rightarrow ? = \dfrac{4}{3} \times \dfrac{4}{3} = \dfrac{16}{9}$

$\therefore$ Sign of interrogation (?) should be replaced by $\dfrac{16}{9}$.

**5**

# Ratio, Proportion & Partnership

## Ratio

When comparison is made by dividing one quantity by another of the same kind, the result is called ratio. If $a$ and $b$ are two numbers, ratio of $a$ to $b$ is denoted by $a : b$ or $\dfrac{a}{b}$. The first term $a$ is called antecedent and the second term $b$ is called consequent.

## Proportion

Equality of two ratios is called proportion. If $a : b = c : d$, then $a$, $b$, $c$, $d$ are called in proportion. In a proportion $a : b :: c : d$, then $a$ and $d$ are called extremes and $b$ and $c$ are called means.

Product of extremes = Product of means

**Comparison of Ratio:** Suppose $\dfrac{a}{b} > \dfrac{c}{d}$ then we say that $a : b > c : d$.

**Compounded Ratio:** The compound ratio of the ratios $a : b$, $c : d$ and $e : f$ is $ace : bdf$.

**Duplicate Ratio:** The duplicate ratio of $a : b$ is $a^2 : b^2$.

**Triplicate Ratio:** The triplicate ratio of $a : b$ is $a^3 : b^3$.

**EXAMPLE:** If $A : B = 3 : 4$ and $B : C = 8 : 9$ then find $A : C$.

**SOLUTION:** $A : B = 3 : 4 \Rightarrow \dfrac{A}{B} = \dfrac{3}{4}$

$B : C = 8 : 9 \Rightarrow \dfrac{B}{C} = \dfrac{8}{9}$ $\qquad$ $\dfrac{A}{C} = \dfrac{A}{B} \times \dfrac{B}{C} = \dfrac{3}{4} \times \dfrac{8}{9} = \dfrac{2}{3}$

$\Rightarrow A : C = 2 : 3$

## Partnership

**Partnership** is a form of association of two or more persons who contribute resources like money together in order to carry on a business. It may be of simple or compound type.

**Simple partnership** is one in which the capitals of the partners are invested for the same time. The profits or losses are divided among the partners in the ratio of their investments.

**Compound partnership** is one in which the capitals of the partners are invested for different periods. In such cases, equivalent capitals are calculated for each partner by multiplying their capital contributions with time. The profits or losses are then divided in the ratio of these equivalent capitals.

The partner who invests the money in the business as well as takes part in its management, is known as **Working partner**.

The partner who only invests the money in the business and does not work, is known as **Sleeping partner**.

## MULTIPLE CHOICE QUESTIONS

1. If $A : B = 2 : 3$ and $B : C = 4 : 5$, then $C : A$ is equal to:
   A. $15 : 8$      B. $12 : 10$      C. $8 : 5$      D. $8 : 15$

2. If 10% of $x$ is the same as 20% of $y$, then $x : y$ is equal to:
   A. $1 : 2$      B. $2 : 1$      C. $5 : 1$      D. $10 : 1$

3. The mean proportional to $6 + \sqrt{27}$ and $6 - \sqrt{27}$ is:
   A. 3      B. 9      C. 10      D. $\sqrt{10}$

4. If $x : y = 9 : 11$, the value of $\dfrac{5x + 3y}{3x + 5y}$ is:
   A. $45 : 55$      B. $18 : 22$      C. $37 : 41$      D. $39 : 41$

5. If $a + b : b + c : c + a = 6 : 7 : 8$ and $a + b + c = 14$, then the value of $c$ is:
   A. 14      B. 7      C. 8      D. 6

6. Two numbers are in the ratio $2 : 3$. If 5 is added to each number, the ratio becomes $5 : 7$. The bigger number is:
   A. 30      B. 40      C. 60      D. 20

7. What should be added to each of the numbers 12, 30, 40 and 86, so that they are in proportion?
   A. 6      B. 4      C. –6      D. –4

8. The ratio of males and females of a village is $5 : 3$. If there are 800 males in the village, females are:
   A. 240      B. 480      C. 840      D. 488

9. In a mixture of 60 litres, the ratio of ethanol to ether is $4 : 1$. How much ether must be added to the mixture to make this ratio $2 : 1$?
   A. 10 litres      B. 12 litres      C. 18 litres      D. 24 litres

**10.** The proportion of zinc and copper in a brass piece is 4 : 5. How much zinc will be there in 180 kg of such a piece?
A. 40 kg  B. 80 kg  C. 100 kg  D. 120 kg

**11.** The prices of a scooter and a television set are in the ratio 3 : 2. If a scooter costs ₹ 6000 more than the television set, the price of the television set is:
A. ₹ 18000  B. ₹ 12000  C. ₹ 10000  D. ₹ 6000

**12.** The weight of a 13 metres long iron rod be 23.4 kg. The weight of 6 metres long of such rod will be:
A. 7.2 kg  B. 12.4 kg  C. 10.8 kg  D. 18 kg

**13.** The ratio between the ages of Gayatri and Savitri is 6 : 5 and the sum of their ages is 44 years. The ratio of their ages after 8 years will be:
A. 5 : 6  B. 7 : 8  C. 8 : 7  D. 14 : 13

**14.** Two numbers are such that the ratio between them is 3 : 5 but if each is increased by 10, the ratio between them becomes 5 : 7. The numbers are:
A. 3, 5  B. 7, 9  C. 13, 22  D. 15, 25

**15.** A, B and C share the profit in the ratio of 3 : 5 : 7. If the gain is ₹ 2040, then C's share is:
A. ₹ 360  B. ₹ 600  C. ₹ 952  D. ₹ 120

**16.** A, B and C started a business with ₹ 47000. A puts in ₹ 5000 more than B and B ₹ 3000 more than C. The share of A out of the profit of ₹ 14100 will be:
A. ₹ 3600  B. ₹ 4500  C. ₹ 6000  D. ₹ 6300

**17.** A starts a business with ₹ 5000. After 4 months B joins him with a sum of ₹ 4000. In the end of the year there is a profit of ₹ 8970. The share of A in the profit will be:
A. ₹ 3120  B. ₹ 4020  C. ₹ 5850  D. ₹ 6360

**18.** A, B, C are three partners in a business. The profit share of A is $\frac{3}{16}$ of the profit and B's share is $\frac{1}{4}$ of the profit. If C receives ₹ 243, then the amount received by B will be:
A. ₹ 90  B. ₹ 96  C. ₹ 108  D. ₹ 120

**19.** A, B and C share the profit in the ratio 2 : 3 : 7. If the average gain is ₹ 8000, then B's share is:
A. ₹ 2000  B. ₹ 1000  C. ₹ 1500  D. ₹ 3000

**20.** Ashok started a business investing ₹ 90,000. After 3 months Shabir joined him with a capital of ₹ 1,20,000. If at the end of one year the total profit made by them was ₹ 96,000, what will be the difference between their shares?

A. ₹ 24000      B. ₹ 8000      C. ₹ 20000      D. None of these

**21.** If $a : b = 2 : 3$, $b : c = 4 : 5$ and $c : d = 6 : 7$, then $a : d$ is equal to:

A. $2 : 7$      B. $7 : 8$      C. $4 : 13$      D. $16 : 35$

**22.** The mean proportional between 0.32 and 0.02 is:

A. 0.34      B. 0.3      C. 0.16      D. 0.08

**23.** The sum of three numbers is 98. If the ratio between the first and second be $2 : 3$ and that between the second and third be $5 : 8$, then what is the second number?

A. 20      B. 30      C. 10      D. 40

**24.** One man adds 3 litres of water to 12 litres of milk and another 4 litres of water to 10 litres of milk. What is the ratio of the strenghts of the milk in the two mixtures?

A. $15 : 25$      B. $25 : 28$      C. $28 : 25$      D. None of these

**25.** ₹ 425 is divided among 4 men, 5 women and 6 boys such that the share of a man, a woman and a boy may be in the ratio of $9 : 8 : 4$. What is the share of a woman?

A. ₹ 34      B. ₹ 24      C. ₹ 44      D. None

**26.** A vessel contains liquids P and Q in the ratio $5 : 3$. If 6 litres of the mixture are removed and the same quantity of liquid $q$ is added, the ratio becomes $3 : 5$. What quantity does the vessel hold?

A. 40 litres      B. 50 litres      C. 30 litres      D. None of these

**27.** A bucket contains a mixture of two liquids P and Q in the proportion $7 : 5$. If 9 litres of the mixture is replaced by 9 litres of liquid Q, then the ratio of the two liquid becomes $7 : 9$. How much of the liquid P was there in the bucket?

A. 11 litres      B. 21 litres      C. 31 litres      D. None of these

**28.** Three glasses P, Q and R with their capacities in the ratio $2 : 3 : 4$ are filled with a mixture of spirit and water. The ratio of spirit to water in P, Q and R is $1 : 5$, $3 : 5$ and $5 : 7$ respectively. If the contents of these glasses are mixed together, what is the ratio of spirit to water in the mixture?

A. $14 : 27$      B. $23 : 47$      C. $25 : 47$      D. None of these

**29.** A and B are two alloys of gold and copper prepared by mixing metals in proportions 7 : 2 and 7 : 11 respectively. If equal quantities of the alloys are melted to form a third alloy C, the proportion of gold and copper in C will be

A. 5 : 9      B. 5 : 7      C. 7 : 5      D. 9 : 5

**30.** Gold is 19 times as heavy as water and copper 9 times as heavy as water. The ratio in which these two metals be mixed so that the mixtures is 15 times as heavy as water is:

A. 1 : 2      B. 2 : 3      C. 3 : 2      D. 19 : 135

## ANSWERS

| 1 | 2 | 3 | 4 | 5 | 6 | 7 | 8 | 9 | 10 |
|---|---|---|---|---|---|---|---|---|----|
| A | B | A | D | D | A | A | B | B | B |

| 11 | 12 | 13 | 14 | 15 | 16 | 17 | 18 | 19 | 20 |
|----|----|----|----|----|----|----|----|----|----|
| B | C | C | D | C | C | C | C | A | D |

| 21 | 22 | 23 | 24 | 25 | 26 | 27 | 28 | 29 | 30 |
|----|----|----|----|----|----|----|----|----|----|
| D | D | B | C | A | A | B | C | C | C |

## EXPLANATORY ANSWERS

**3.** Mean proportional $= \sqrt{\left(6+\sqrt{27}\right)\left(6-\sqrt{27}\right)}$

$$= \sqrt{36-27} = \sqrt{9} = 3$$

**8.** Ratio of Males : Females = 5 : 3

$$\Rightarrow \frac{800}{x} = \frac{5}{3} \Rightarrow 5x = 3 \times 800$$

$$\Rightarrow x = \frac{3 \times 800}{5} = 3 \times 160 = 480$$

Hence, number of females = 480.

**10.** In 9 kg of brass, zinc = 4 kg

$$\therefore \text{ In 180 kg of brass, zinc} = \frac{4}{9} \times 180 = 80 \text{ kg.}$$

**12.** Weight of 13 m long iron rod = 23.4 kg

Weight of 6 m long iron rod

$$= \frac{23.4}{13} \times 6 \text{ kg} = 1.8 \times 6 = 10.8 \text{ kg.}$$

**15.** C's share $= \dfrac{7}{15} \times 2040 = ₹\ 952.$

**19.**  B's share $= \dfrac{3}{2+3+7} \times 8000 = \dfrac{3 \times 8000}{12} = ₹\ 2000$

**22.** Mean proportional $= \sqrt{0.32 \times 0.02} = \sqrt{0.0064} = 0.08$

**23.** The ratio among the three numbers is

$$2 \quad : \quad 3$$
$$5 \quad : \quad 8$$
$$\text{and} \quad 10 \quad : \quad 15 \quad : \quad 24$$

$\therefore$ The second number $= \dfrac{98}{10+15+24} \times 15 = 30$

**25.** The ratio of shares of group of men, women and boys
$$= 9 \times 4 : 8 \times 5 : 4 \times 6 = 9 : 10 : 6$$

$\therefore$ Share of 5 women $= \dfrac{425}{9+10+6} \times 10 = ₹\ 170$

$\therefore$ Share of 1 woman $= \dfrac{170}{5} = ₹\ 34$

**29.** Gold in C $= \left(\dfrac{7}{9} + \dfrac{7}{18}\right) = \dfrac{21}{18} = \dfrac{7}{6}$

Copper in C $= \left(\dfrac{2}{9} + \dfrac{11}{18}\right) = \dfrac{15}{18} = \dfrac{5}{6}$

$\therefore$ Gold : Copper $= \dfrac{7}{6} : \dfrac{5}{6} = 7 : 5$

# 6   *Average*

The sum of all the quantities of same kind divided by their number is called average (or mean) of those quantities.

## FORMULAE

1. Average $= \left( \dfrac{\text{Sum of observations}}{\text{Number of observations}} \right)$

2. Sum of the first $n$ natural numbers $= 1 + 2 + 3 + \ldots + n = \dfrac{n(n+1)}{2}$

3. Sum of the squares of the first $n$ natural numbers

$$= 1^2 + 2^2 + \ldots + n^2 = \frac{n(n+1)(2n+1)}{6}$$

4. Sum of the cubes of the first $n$ natural numbers

$$= 1^3 + 2^3 + \ldots + n^3 = \left\{ \frac{n(n+1)}{2} \right\}^2$$

5. Sum of the first $n$ odd numbers $= 1 + 3 + 5 + \ldots + (2n - 1) = n^2$

Different kinds of mean or average:

(*a*) Arithmetic mean, (*b*) Geometric mean, (*c*) Harmonic mean

$$\text{A.M.} = \frac{x_1 + x_2 + x_3 + \ldots + x_n}{n}$$

$$\text{G.M.} = (x_1 \cdot x_2 \cdot x_3 \ldots x_n)^{1/n}$$

$$\text{H.M.} = \frac{n}{\dfrac{1}{x_1} + \dfrac{1}{x_2} + \ldots + \dfrac{1}{x_n}}.$$

**EXAMPLE 1. :** Find the average of first ten prime numbers.

**SOLUTION:** First ten prime numbers are 2, 3, 5, 7, 11, 13, 17, 19, 23 and 29.

$$\therefore \text{ Average} = \frac{2+3+5+7+11+13+17+19+23+29}{10}$$

$$= \frac{129}{10} = 12.9$$

**EXAMPLE 2. :** The average of 11 results is 50. If the average of first six results is 49 and that of last six is 52, find the sixth result.

**SOLUTION:** Sum of 11 results $= 11 \times 50 = 550$

Sum of first 6 results $6 \times 49 = 294$

Sum of last 6 results $= 6 \times 52 = 312$

$\therefore$ 6th result $= 294 + 312 - 550 = 56$

**EXAMPLE 3. :** The average age of three boys is 15 years. If their ages are in the ratio 3 : 5 : 7. What is the age of the youngest boy?

**SOLUTION:** Let the ages of the three boys be $3x$, $5x$ and $7x$.

$$\text{Average age} = \frac{3x + 5x + 7x}{3} = 5x \text{ and } 5x = 15 \Rightarrow x = 3$$

The age of the youngest boy $= 3x = 3 \times 3 = 9$ years.

## MULTIPLE CHOICE QUESTIONS

1.  The average of first five multiples of 3 is:
    A. 3      B. 9      C. 12      D. 15

2.  The average of 25 results is 18, that of first 12 is 14 and of the last 12 is 17. Thirteenth result is:
    A. 78      B. 85      C. 28      D. 72

3.  Out of three numbers, the first is twice the second and is half of the third. If the average of the three numbers is 56, the three numbers in order are:
    A. 48, 96, 24      B. 48, 24, 96      C. 96, 24, 48      D. 96, 48, 24

4.  The sum of three numbers is 98. If the ratio between first and second be 2 : 3 and that between second and third be 5 : 8, then the second number is:
    A. 30      B. 20      C. 58      D. 48

5.  The average age of a committee of seven trustees is the same as it was 5 years ago; a young man having been substituted for one of them. The new man compared to the replaced old man, is younger in age by:
    A. 5 years      B. 7 years      C. 12 years      D. 35 years

6.  The average expenditure of a man for the first five months is ₹ 120 and for the next seven months is ₹ 130. His monthly average income if he saves ₹ 290 in that year, is:
    A. ₹ 160      B. ₹ 170      C. ₹ 150      D. ₹ 140

7.  The average salary of 20 workers in an office is ₹ 1900 per month. If the manager's salary is added, the average becomes ₹ 2000 per month. The manager's salary is:
    A. ₹ 24000      B. ₹ 25200      C. ₹ 45600      D. None of these

**8.** The average temperature of first 3 days is 27°C and of the next 3 days is 29°C. If the average of the whole week is 28.5°C, the temperature of the last day is:

    A. 31.5°C      B. 10.5°C      C. 21°C      D. 42°C

**9.** A cricketer scored 180 runs in the first test and 258 runs in the second. How many runs should he score in the third test so that his average score in the three tests would be 230 runs?

    A. 219      B. 242      C. 334      D. None of these

**10.** The average of first five prime numbers is:

    A. 5.0      B. 5.2      C. 5.6      D. 6.0

**11.** The average weight of 3 men A, B and C is 84 kg. Another man D joins the group and the average now becomes 80 kg. If another man E, whose weight is 3 kg more than that of D, replaces A, then average weight of B, C, D and E becomes 79 kg. The weight of A is:

    A. 70 kg      B. 72 kg      C. 75 kg      D. 80 kg

**12.** The average age of A, B, C, D and E is 45 years. By including $x$, the present average of all the six is 49 years. The present age of $x$ is:

    A. 64 years      B. 69 years      C. 45 years      D. 40 years

**13.** The average height of 30 boys, out of a class of 50, is 160 cm. If the average height of the remaining boys is 165 cm, the average height of the whole class (in cm) is:

    A. 161      B. 162      C. 163      D. 164

**14.** The average age of an adult class is 40 years. 12 new students with an average age of 30 years join the class, thereby decreasing the average of the class by 4 years. The original strength of the class was:

    A. 10      B. 18      C. 12      D. 15

**15.** If $a$, $b$, $c$, $d$, $e$ are five consecutive even numbers, their average is:

    A. $5(a + 4)$                              B. $\dfrac{abcde}{5}$

    C. $5(a + b + c + d + e)$      D. None of these

**16.** Of the three numbers, second is twice the first and is also thrice the third. If the average of the three numbers is 44, the largest number is:

    A. 24      B. 36      C. 72      D. 108

**17.** The average of 50 numbers is 38. If two numbers namely, 45 and 55 are discarded, the average of remaining number is:

    A. 36.50      B. 37.00      C. 37.50      D. 37.52

18. The average height of 30 girls out of a class of 40 is 160 cm and that of the remaining girls is 156 cm. The average height of the whole class is:
    A. 158 cm      B. 158.5 cm      C. 159 cm      D. 159.5 cm

19. The average of $n$ numbers is $x$. If 36 is subtracted from any two numbers each, then new average is $(x - 8)$. The value of $n$ is:
    A. 6      B. 8      C. 9      D. 72

20. The average salary of male employees in a firm is ₹ 520 and that of female employees is ₹ 420. The mean salary of all the employees is ₹ 500. The percentage of female employees is:
    A. 40%      B. 30%      C. 25%      D. 20%

21. Out of three numbers, the first is twice the second and is half of the third. If the average of the three numbers is 56, the three numbers in order are
    A. 48, 96, 24      B. 48, 24, 96      C. 96, 24, 48      D. 96, 48, 24

22. The average age of 30 students in a class is 12 years. The average age of a group of 5 of the students is 10 years and that of another group of 5 of them is 14 years. The average age of the remaining students is
    A. 8 years      B. 10 years      C. 12 years      D. 14 years

23. Out of four numbers, the average of first three is 15 and that of the last three is 16. If the last number is 19, the first is
    A. 15      B. 16      C. 18      D. 19

24. The average age of an adult class is 40 years. 12 new students with an average age of 32 years join the class, thereby decreasing the average by 4 years. The original strength of the class was
    A. 10      B. 11      C. 12      D. 15

25. The average age of 24 students in a class is 10. If the teacher's age is included, the average increases by one. The age of the teacher is
    A. 25      B. 30      C. 35      D. 40

26. The average age of A, B, C and D five years ago was 45 years. By including X, the present age of all the five is 49 years. The present age of X is
    A. 64 years      B. 48 years      C. 45 years      D. 40 years

27. The average expenditure of a man for the first five months is ₹ 120 and for the next seven months it is ₹ 130. If he saves ₹ 290 in that year, his monthly average income is
    A. ₹ 1000      B. ₹ 1800      C. ₹ 2000      D. ₹ 2500

**28.** The average weight of a class of 40 students is 40 kg. If the weight of the teacher be included, the average weight increases by 500 gms. The weight of the teacher is

A. 40.5 kg    B. 60 kg    C. 60.5 kg    D. 62 kg

**29.** The average weight of 8 persons is increased by 2.5 kg when one of them whose weight is 56 kg is replaced by a new man. The weight of the new man is

A. 66 kg    B. 75 kg    C. 76 kg    D. 86 kg

**30.** If $a$, $b$, $c$, $d$, $e$ are five consecutive odd numbers, their average is

A. $5(a + 4)$

B. $\dfrac{abcde}{5}$

C. $5(a + b + c + d + e)$

D. None of these

## ANSWERS

| 1 | 2 | 3 | 4 | 5 | 6 | 7 | 8 | 9 | 10 |
|---|---|---|---|---|---|---|---|---|----|
| B | A | B | A | D | C | D | A | D | C |

| 11 | 12 | 13 | 14 | 15 | 16 | 17 | 18 | 19 | 20 |
|----|----|----|----|----|----|----|----|----|----|
| C | B | B | B | D | C | C | C | C | D |

| 21 | 22 | 23 | 24 | 25 | 26 | 27 | 28 | 29 | 30 |
|----|----|----|----|----|----|----|----|----|----|
| B | C | B | C | C | C | B | C | C | D |

## EXPLANATORY ANSWERS

**1.** Average $= \dfrac{3(1+2+3+4+5)}{5} = \dfrac{(3 \times 15)}{5} = 9$

**6.** Total income for 12 months $= ₹\ (120 \times 5 + 130 \times 7 + 290) = ₹\ 1800$

Average monthly income $= ₹\dfrac{1800}{12} = ₹150$

**10.** Average $= \dfrac{2+3+5+7+11}{5} = \dfrac{28}{5} = 5.6.$

**13.** Total height of 30 boys $= 30 \times 160 = 4800$
Total height of 20 boys $= 20 \times 165 = 3300$
Total height of 50 boys $= 8100$

Average height of 50 boys $= \dfrac{8100}{50} = 162.$

**19.** $\dfrac{nx - 36 - 36}{n} = x - 8$

$\Rightarrow nx - 72 = nx - 8n$

$\Rightarrow 8n = 72 \Rightarrow \quad n = 9$

**23.** Sum of four numbers $= (15 \times 3 + 19) = 64$
Sum of last three numbers $= (16 \times 3) = 48$
$\therefore$ First number $= (64 - 48) = 16$

**24.**    Let the original strength$= x$
     Then, $40x + 12 \times 32 = (x + 12) \times 36$
$\Rightarrow \qquad\qquad 40x + 384 = 36x + 432$
$\Rightarrow \qquad\qquad\qquad\quad 4x = 48$
$\Rightarrow \qquad\qquad\qquad\quad x = 12$

**25.**       Age of the teacher $= (25 \times 11 - 24 \times 10)$ years $= 35$ years

**26.**      Present age of $x = [(49 \times 5) - (4 \times 45 + 4 \times 5)]$ years
$= 45$ years

**27.**         Total income $= (120 \times 5 + 130 \times 7 + 290) = ₹\ 1800$

**28.**    Weight of the teacher $= (41 \times 40.5 - 40 \times 40)$ kg $= 60.5$ kg

**29.**       Total increase $= (8 \times 2.5)$ kg $= 20$ kg
Weight of new man $= (56 + 20)$kg $= 76$ kg

**30.**  Average $= \dfrac{a + (a + 2) + (a + 4) + (a + 6) + (a + 8)}{5}$

$= (a + 4)$

❖ ❖ ❖

7

Percentage

The word 'per cent' or 'percentage' means 'for every one hundred'. In other words, it gives an indication of rate per hundred. It is denoted by the symbol %.

For example, 5% means 5 out of one hundred or $\dfrac{5}{100}$.

## Important Facts:

For quickly solving the problems related to percentage, remember following rules:

   (*a*) Of the given two numbers if the first is $x\%$ more than the second, then the second will be $\left(\dfrac{100 \times x}{100 + x}\right)\%$ less than the first.

   (*b*) Of the given two numbers if the first is $x\%$ less than the second, then the second will be $\left(\dfrac{100 \times x}{100 - x}\right)\%$ more than the first.

   (*c*) If two numbers are respectively $x\%$ and $y\%$ more than a third number, then the first number will be $\left(\dfrac{100 + x}{100 + y} \times 100\right)\%$ of the second.

   (*d*) If two numbers are respectively $x\%$ and $y\%$ less than a third number, then the first number will be $\left(\dfrac{100 - x}{100 - y} \times 100\right)\%$ of the second.

**Example 1. :** A's income is 150% more than B's income. By how much per cent is B's income less than A's income?

**Solution :** Here, A's income is 150% more than B's income, *i.e.*, $x = 150$

$\therefore$ B's income will be $\left(\dfrac{100 \times 150}{100 + 150}\right)\%$ less than A's income,

$$\left(\dfrac{100 \times 150}{100 + 150}\right)\% = \dfrac{100 \times 150}{250}\% = 60\%$$

**Example 2. :** If a number is increased by 10% and thereafter decreased by 10%, then by how much per cent the number has been increased or decreased?

36

**Solution :** ∵ The number is first increased by 10% and later the new number is decreased by 10%

∴ Percentage decrease in the number $= \left(\dfrac{(10)^2}{100}\right)\% = 1\%$

**Example 3. :** The population of a town is 40,000. If the population increases 20% every year, find the population after 3 years.

**Solution:** Population after 3 years $= 40000\left(1+\dfrac{20}{100}\right)^3$

$= 40000 \times \dfrac{6}{5} \times \dfrac{6}{5} \times \dfrac{6}{5} = 69120$

## MULTIPLE CHOICE QUESTIONS

1. If $x$ is 90% of $y$, then what per cent of $x$ is $y$?
   A. 90      B. 190      C. 101.1      D. 111.1

2. A number exceeds 20% of itself by 40. The number is :
   A. 50      B. 60      C. 80      D. 320

3. The price of an article is cut by 10%. To restore it to the former value, the new price must be increased by :

   A. 10%      B. $9\dfrac{1}{11}\%$      C. $11\dfrac{1}{9}\%$      D. 11%

4. The income of a broker remains unchanged though the rate of commission is increased from 4% to 5%. The percentage of slump business is :
   A. 8%      B. 1%      C. 20%      D. 80%

5. 5% income of A is equal to 15% income of B and 10% income of B is equal to 20% income of C. If income of C is ₹ 2000, then total income of A, B and C is :
   A. ₹ 6000      B. ₹ 18000      C. ₹ 20000      D. ₹ 14000

6. A student who secures 20% marks in an examination fails by 30 marks. Another student who secures 32% gets 42 marks more than those required to pass. The percentage of marks required to pass is:
   A. 20      B. 25      C. 28      D. 30

7. In a college election, a candidate secured 62% of the votes and is elected by a majority of 144 votes. The total number of votes polled is :
   A. 600      B. 800      C. 925      D. 1200

**8.** What will be 80% of a number whose 200% is 90?

   A. 144           B. 72           C. 36           D. None of these

**9.** $p$ is six times as large as $q$. The per cent that $q$ is less than $p$, is :

   A. $83\dfrac{1}{3}$           B. $16\dfrac{2}{3}$           C. 90           D. 60

**10.** The price of an article has been reduced by 25%. In order to restore the original price, the new price must be increased by :

   A. $33\dfrac{1}{3}\%$           B. $11\dfrac{1}{9}\%$           C. $9\dfrac{1}{11}\%$           D. $66\dfrac{2}{3}\%$

**11.** The price of cooking oil has increased by 25%. The percentage of reduction that a family should effect in the use of cooking oil so as not to increase the expenditure on this account is :

   A. 25%           B. 30%           C. 20%           D. 15%

**12.** In an organisation, 40% of the employees are matriculates, 50% of the remaining are graduates and the remaining 180 are postgraduates. How many employees are graduates?

   A. 360           B. 240           C. 300           D. 180

**13.** In 40% of the people read newspaper X, 50% read newspaper Y, and 10% read both the papers. What percentage of the people read neither newspaper?

   A. 10%           B. 15%           C. 20%           D. 25%

**14.** The population of a town increases by 5% annually. If its population in 2008 was 138915, what it was in 2005?

   A. 110000           B. 100000           C. 120000           D. 90000

**15.** The population of a village is 4500. $\dfrac{5}{9}$th of them are males and rest females. If 40% of the males are married, then the percentage of married female is :

   A. 35           B. 40           C. 50           D. 60

**16.** A's income is 10% more than B's. How much per cent is B's income is less than A's?

   A. 10%           B. 7%           C. $9\dfrac{1}{11}\%$           D. $6\dfrac{1}{2}\%$

**17.** A mixture of 40 litres of milk and water contains 10% water. How much water must be added to make water 20% in the new mixture?

   A. 10 litres           B. 7 litres           C. 5 litres           D. 3 litres

**18.** If $z = \dfrac{x^2}{y}$ and $x$, $y$ both are increased in value by 10%, then the value of $z$ is :
A. unchanged
B. increased by 10%
C. increased by 11%
D. increased by 20%

**19.** In an examination, 35% of the examinees failed in G.K. and 25% in English. If 10% of the examinees failed in both, then the percentage of examinees passed will be:
A. 40%
B. 45%
C. 48%
D. 50%

**20.** If the price of a television set is increased by 25%, then by what percentage should the new price be reduced to bring the price back to original level?
A. 15%
B. 20%
C. 25%
D. 30%

**21.** A candidate needs 35% marks to pass. If he gets 96 marks and fails by 16 marks, then the maximum marks are :
A. 250
B. 320
C. 300
D. 425

**22.** In an election one of the two candidates gets 40% votes and loses by 100 votes. Total number of votes is :
A. 500
B. 400
C. 600
D. 1000

**23.** If the income tax is decreased by 26%, a man's net income increases by $\dfrac{2}{3}$%. The rate of income tax is:
A. $3\dfrac{1}{2}$%
B. $2\dfrac{1}{2}$%
C. $1\dfrac{1}{2}$%
D. 3%

**24.** The gross income of a person is ₹ 20000. 10% of his income is exempted from income tax and his net income is ₹ 19100. The rate of income tax is :
A. 3%
B. 2%
C. 4%
D. 5%

**25.** If the rate of income tax is 5%, the net income of a person is ₹ 17100. If the rate of income tax is 6%, how much will be the net income?
A. 15820
B. 16920
C. 17820
D. 18920

**26.** The gross income of a person is ₹ 15000, 20% of his income is exempted from income tax and the rate of income tax is ₹ 4%. The net income is :
A. 14520
B. 14620
C. 15520
D. 15620

**27.** The gross income of a person is ₹ 16000. A part of his income is exempted from income tax and his net income is ₹ 14480. If the rate of income tax is 8%, the income exempted from income tax is :
A. 1600
B. 1700
C. 1800
D. 1500

**28.** One-eight of a number is 17.25. What will 73% of number be?

  A. 82.66      B. 96.42      C. 100.74    D. 138.00

**29.** If 58% of 960 − $x$% of 635 = 277.4, find the value of $x$.

  A. 24       B. 36       C. 44       D. 58

**30.** There are 1225 employees in an organisation, out of which 40% got transferred to different places. How many such employees got transferred?

  A. 490      B. 540      C. 630      D. 710

## ANSWERS

| 1 | 2 | 3 | 4 | 5 | 6 | 7 | 8 | 9 | 10 |
|---|---|---|---|---|---|---|---|---|---|
| D | A | C | C | B | B | A | C | A | A |

| 11 | 12 | 13 | 14 | 15 | 16 | 17 | 18 | 19 | 20 |
|---|---|---|---|---|---|---|---|---|---|
| C | D | C | C | C | C | C | B | D | B |

| 21 | 22 | 23 | 24 | 25 | 26 | 27 | 28 | 29 | 30 |
|---|---|---|---|---|---|---|---|---|---|
| B | A | B | D | B | A | D | C | C | A |

## EXPLANATORY ANSWERS

**2.** $x - 20\%$ of $x = 40$

$$\Rightarrow x - \frac{x}{5} = 40 \Rightarrow \frac{4x}{5} = 40$$

$$\Rightarrow x = \frac{40 \times 5}{4} = 50$$

**3.** Required percentage $= \dfrac{10}{100-10} \times 100$

$$= \frac{10}{90} \times 100 = 11\frac{1}{9}\%$$

**7.** $(62\%$ of $x - 38\%$ of $x) = 144$

$$\Rightarrow 24\% \text{ of } x = 144$$

$$\Rightarrow x = \frac{144 \times 100}{24}$$

$$= 600$$

**10.** Required percentage $= \dfrac{25}{100-25} \times 100 = \dfrac{25}{75} \times 100 = 33\dfrac{1}{3}\%$

**13.** Number of people read either one or both = 40 + 50 − 10 = 80%
Hence, number of people read neither newspaper = 100 − 80 = 20%

**16.** Required percentage $= \left[\dfrac{10}{(100+10)} \times 100\right]\% = 9\dfrac{1}{11}\%$

**21.** 35% of $x = 96 + 16 = 112$

$$\Rightarrow \frac{35}{100} \times x = 112 \Rightarrow x = \frac{112 \times 100}{35} = 320$$

**22.** Out of 100, difference in votes = (60 − 40) = 20
20% of $x = 100$

$$\therefore \quad x = \frac{100 \times 100}{20} = 500$$

**25.** Gross income $= \dfrac{100}{95} \times 17100 = ₹\,18000$

New net income $= \dfrac{94}{100} \times 18000 = ₹\,16920$

**28.** The number = 8 × 17.25 = 138.00

73% of the number $= \dfrac{73}{100} \times 138 = \dfrac{10074}{100} = 100.75$

**30.** The number of employess got transferred $= \dfrac{40}{100} \times 1225 = 490$

# Profit & Loss

## Cost Price (CP)

The price at which an article is purchased is called the cost price of the article.

## Selling Price (SP)

The price at which an article is sold is called the selling price of the article.

## Profit or Gain

If SP is greater than the CP, the seller is said to have a profit or gain.

Clearly,      Gain = SP – CP

## Loss

If SP is less than CP, the seller is said to have a loss.

Clearly,      Loss = CP – SP

Profit or loss per cent is calculated on cost price.

$$\text{Profit \%} = \frac{\text{Profit}}{\text{CP}} \times 100$$

$$\text{Loss \%} = \frac{\text{Loss}}{\text{CP}} \times 100$$

If an article is sold at a gain of 20%,

then,      SP = (120% of CP)

If an article is sold at a loss of 20%,

then,      SP = (80% of CP)

**EXAMPLE 1. :** Ravi buys an article for ₹ 5000 and sells it at 20% gain. Find it selling price.

**SOLUTION:**      $\text{Profit} = 20\% \text{ of CP} = \dfrac{20}{100} \times 5000$

$\Rightarrow$      Profit = ₹ 1000

SP = CP + Profit

= 5000 + 1000

= ₹ 6000

**EXAMPLE 2. :** A man sells an article at 20% gain for ₹ 3600. Find its cost price.

**SOLUTION:**    Let CP = ₹ 100

then      SP = 100 + 20 = ₹ 120

When SP ₹ 120 then CP = ₹ 100

When SP ₹ 3600 then CP = $\dfrac{100}{120} \times 3600$

Hence             CP = ₹ 3000

## MULTIPLE CHOICE QUESTIONS

1. A loss of 5% was suffered by selling a plot for ₹ 4085. The cost price of the plot was:
   A. ₹ 4350          B. ₹ 4259.25     C. ₹ 4200        D. ₹ 4300

2. On selling an article for ₹ 240, a trader loses 4%. In order to gain 10%, he must sell that article for:
   A. ₹ 264.00        B. ₹ 273.20      C. ₹ 275.00      D. ₹ 280.00

3. A man purchased a watch for ₹ 400 and sold it at a gain of 20% of the selling price. The selling price of the watch is:
   A. ₹ 300           B. ₹ 320         C. ₹ 440         D. ₹ 500

4. If 5% more is gained by selling an article for ₹ 350 than by selling it for ₹ 340, the cost of the article is:
   A. ₹ 50            B. ₹ 160         C. ₹ 200         D. ₹ 225

5. Profit after selling a commodity for ₹ 425 is same as loss after selling it for ₹ 355. The cost of the commodity is:
   A. ₹ 385           B. ₹ 390         C. ₹ 395         D. ₹ 400

6. The cost price of an article, which on being sold at a gain of 12% yields ₹ 6 more than when it is sold at a loss of 12%, is:
   A. ₹ 30            B. ₹ 25          C. ₹ 20          D. ₹ 24

7. The CP of an article which is sold at a loss of 25% for ₹150, is:
   A. ₹ 125           B. ₹ 175         C. ₹ 200         D. ₹ 225

8. When the price of pressure cooker was increased by 15%, its sale fell down by 15%. The effect on the money receipt was:
   A. no effect                        B. 15% decrease
   C. 7.5% increase                    D. 2.25% decrease

9. A man sells 320 mangoes at the cost price of 400 mangoes. His gain per cent is:
   A. 10%             B. 25%           C. 15%           D. 20%

10. By selling 12 oranges for one rupee a man loses 20%. How many for a rupee should he sell to get a gain of 20%?
    A. 5              B. 8             C. 10            D. 15

11. A man sells a car to his friend at 10% loss. If the friend sells it for ₹ 54000 and gains 20%, the original CP of the car was:
    A. ₹ 25000       B. ₹ 37500       C. ₹ 50000       D. ₹ 60000

12. The loss incurred on selling an article for ₹ 270 is as much as the profit made after selling it at 10% profit. The CP of the article is:
    A. ₹ 90       B. ₹ 110       C. ₹ 363       D. ₹ 300

13. An item costing ₹ 200 is being sold at 10% loss. If the price is further reduced by 5%, the selling price will be:
    A. ₹ 179       B. ₹ 175       C. ₹ 171       D. ₹ 170

14. A trader lists his articles 20% above CP and allows a discount of 10% on cash payment. His gain per cent is:
    A. 10%       B. 6%       C. 8%       D. 5%

15. A discount series of 10%, 20% and 40% is equal to a single discount of:
    A. 50%       B. 56.80%       C. 70%       D. 70.28%

16. An umbrella marked at ₹ 80 is sold for ₹ 68, the rate of discount is:
    A. 12%       B. 15%       C. $17\frac{11}{17}\%$       D. 20%

17. A reduction of 20% in the price of mangoes enables a person to purchase 12 more for ₹ 15. The price of 16 mangoes before reduction was:
    A. ₹ 5       B. ₹ 6       C. ₹ 7       D. ₹ 9

18. Tarun bought a TV with 20% discount on the labelled price. Had he bought it with 25% discount, he would have saved ₹ 500. At what price did he buy the TV?
    A. ₹ 5,000       B. ₹ 10,000       C. ₹ 12,000       D. None of these

19. If a commission of 10% is given on the marked price of a book, the publisher gains 20%. If the commission is increased to 15%, the gain is:
    A. $16\frac{2}{3}\%$       B. $13\frac{1}{3}\%$       C. $15\frac{1}{6}\%$       D. None of these

20. There would be 10% loss if rice is sold at ₹ 5.40 per kg. At what price per kg should it be sold to earn a profit of 20%?
    A. ₹ 7.20       B. ₹ 7.02       C. ₹ 6.48       D. ₹ 6

21. At what price must Kantilal sell a mixture of 80 kg sugar at ₹ 6.75 per kg with 120 kg at ₹ 8 per kg to gain 20%?
    A. ₹ 7.50 per kg                 B. ₹ 8.20 per kg
    C. ₹ 8.35 per kg                 D. ₹ 9 per kg

**22.** Subhash purchased a taperecorder at $\dfrac{9}{10}$ of its selling price and sold it at 8% more than its S.P. His gain is :
   A. 8%  B. 10%  C. 18%  D. 20%

**23.** A dealer marks his goods 20% above cost price. He then allows some discount on it and makes a profit of 8%. The rate of discount is :
   A. 12%  B. 10%  C. 6%  D. 4%

**24.** A trader lists his articles 20% above C.P. and allows a discount of 10% on cash payment. His gain per cent is :
   A. 10%  B. 8%  C. 6%  D. 4%

**25.** Tarun bought a T.V. with 20% discount on the labelled price. Had he bought it with 25% discount, he would have saved Rs. 500. At what price did he buy the T.V.?
   A. ₹ 5000  B. ₹ 8000  C. ₹ 10000  D. ₹ 12000

**26.** While selling a watch, a shopkeeper gives a discount of 5%. If he gives a discount of 7%, he earns ₹ 15 less as profit. The marked price of the watch is :
   A. ₹ 697.50  B. ₹ 712.50  C. ₹ 787.50  D. None of these

**27.** Kabir buys an article with 25% discount on its marked price. He makes a profit of 10% by selling it at ₹ 660. The marked price is :
   A. ₹ 600  B. ₹ 700  C. ₹ 800  D. ₹ 885

**28.** A person bought an article and sold it at a loss of 10%. If he had bought it for 20% less and sold it for ₹ 55 more, he would have had a profit of 40%. The C.P. of the article is :
   A. ₹ 200  B. ₹ 225  C. ₹ 250  D. None of these

**29.** The purchase tax on an article is levied at the rate of $66\dfrac{2}{3}\%$ of its wholesale price, while the retailer's profit amounts to 20% of the retail price of the article. What is the wholesale price of an article which is retailed at ₹ 12.50?
   A. ₹ 4  B. ₹ 6  C. ₹ 8  D. ₹ 2

**30.** The catalogue price of a radio is ₹ 720. If it is sold at a discount of $16\dfrac{2}{3}\%$ of the catalogue price, the gain is 25%. Find the gain or loss per cent, if it is sold for ₹ 160 below the catalogue price.
   A. $16\dfrac{2}{3}\%$  B. 16%  C. 18%  D. 20%

## ANSWERS

| 1 | 2 | 3 | 4 | 5 | 6 | 7 | 8 | 9 | 10 |
|---|---|---|---|---|---|---|---|---|----|
| D | C | D | C | B | B | C | D | B | B |

| 11 | 12 | 13 | 14 | 15 | 16 | 17 | 18 | 19 | 20 |
|----|----|----|----|----|----|----|----|----|----|
| C | D | C | C | B | B | A | D | B | A |

| 21 | 22 | 23 | 24 | 25 | 26 | 27 | 28 | 29 | 30 |
|----|----|----|----|----|----|----|----|----|----|
| D | D | B | B | B | D | C | C | B | A |

## EXPLANATORY ANSWERS

**1.** Loss = 5%, SP = ₹ 4085

$\qquad$ Let CP = ₹ 100

$\therefore \qquad$ SP = ₹ 100 – 5 = ₹ 95

When SP ₹ 95 then CP = ₹ 100

When SP ₹ 4085 then CP = $\dfrac{100}{95} \times 4085$ = 4300

Hence, the cost price of the plot was ₹ 4300.

**5.** Let CP = ₹ $x$, $\qquad$ then, $425 - x = x - 355 \Rightarrow 2x = 780 \Rightarrow x = 390$

Hence, the cost of commodity is ₹ 390.

**7.** $100 - 25 = 75$

When SP 75 then CP = ₹ 100

When SP 150 then CP = ₹ $\dfrac{100}{75} \times 150 = ₹\ 200$

**9.** Let CP of each mango be ₹ 1.

Then, $\qquad$ CP of 400 mangoes = ₹ 400

$\therefore \qquad$ CP of 320 mangoes = ₹ 320

$\qquad$ SP of 320 mangoes = ₹ 400

$\qquad$ Profit = 400 – 320 = ₹ 80

$$\text{Profit\%} = \dfrac{80}{320} \times 100 = 25\%$$

**11.** SP = ₹ 54000 and gain earned = 20%

$$CP = ₹\left(\dfrac{100}{120} \times 54000\right) = ₹\ 45000$$

Now, SP = ₹ 45000 and Loss = 10%

$$\therefore CP = ₹\left(\dfrac{100}{90} \times 45000\right) = ₹\ 50000$$

**13.** SP = 90% of ₹ 200 = ₹ 180

Further, SP = (95% of ₹180) = ₹ 171

**16.** Marked price = ₹ 80, SP = ₹ 68

Discount = MP − SP = 80 − 68 = ₹ 12

Discount % = $\dfrac{\text{discount}}{\text{MP}} \times 100 = \dfrac{12}{80} \times 100 = 15\%$

**22.** Let S.P. = ₹ 100; C.P. for Subhash = $\dfrac{9}{10} \times 100$ = ₹ 90 and S.P. = ₹ 108

Hence, gain % for Subhash = $\dfrac{108 - 90}{90} \times 100 = 20\%$

**23.** Let C.P. be ₹ 100; then Marked price = ₹ 120 and S.P. = ₹ 108

∴ Discount = $\left(\dfrac{12}{120} \times 100\right)\% = 10\%$

**24.** Let C.P. be ₹ 100

Then, marked price = ₹ 120

S.P. = ₹ $\left(\dfrac{90}{100} \times 120\right)$ = ₹ 108 ∴ Gain % = $\left(\dfrac{8}{100} \times 100\right)\% = 8\%$

**26.** Let the marked price = ₹ $x$

Then, $\dfrac{7x}{100} - \dfrac{5x}{100} = 15$

$\Rightarrow \dfrac{x}{50} = 15 \qquad \therefore x = ₹\ 750$

**27.** C.P. = $\dfrac{100}{110} \times 660$ = ₹ 600

Hence, M.P. = $\dfrac{100}{75} \times 600$ = ₹ 800

# 9

# Simple & Compound Interest

In any money transaction there is a **lender** who gives money, and a **borrower** who receives money. The amount of loan borrowed, is called the principal (P). The borrower pays a certain amount for the use of this money. This is called **Interest (I)**. Interest is always calculated on the principal borrowed. The borrowing is for a specified **Time (t)** and on specified terms. The specified term is expressed as per cent of the principal and is called rate of interest. The sum of the principal and the interest is called the **Amount (A)**.

Interest is of two kinds—**Simple Interest and compound Interest**. If the interest is calculated only, on a certain sum borrowed it is called Simple Interest. The simple interest (SI) on a principal P at R% per annum for T years is given by: $SI = \dfrac{P \times R \times T}{100}$

Compound Interest differs from Simple Interest that in CI the interest for the future period is calculated not only on the principal but also on the interest earned until the previous period. The difference between the final amount (A) obtained at the last unit of time and the original principal is called the **Compound Interest**.

## Important Relations

| Principal | = | ₹ P (in rupees) |
| Rate | = | R % (in per cent per annum) |
| Time period | = | T years (in years) |
| Amount | = | ₹ A (in rupees) |

When interest is compounded annually, $A = P\left[1 + \dfrac{R}{100}\right]^{T}$

When interest is compounded half-yearly,

$$A = P\left[1 + \dfrac{R/2}{100}\right]^{2T} = P\left[1 + \dfrac{R}{200}\right]^{2T}$$

[R is divided by 2 and T is multiplied by 2.]

$CI = A - P$

**EXAMPLE 1. :** Find the simple interest on ₹ 1000 for 3 years at 10% p.a.

**SOLUTION:** $SI = \dfrac{P \times R \times T}{100} = \dfrac{1000 \times 10 \times 3}{100} = ₹\ 300$

**EXAMPLE 2. :** Find the amount of ₹ 600 in 4 years at 3% p.a.

**SOLUTION:** $SI = \dfrac{P \times R \times T}{100} = \dfrac{600 \times 3 \times 4}{100} = ₹\ 72$

∴ Amount = P + SI = 600 + 72 = ₹ 672

**EXAMPLE 3. :** In what time will ₹ 7000 give ₹ 3675 as interest at the rate of 7% p.a. simple interest?

**SOLUTION:** $T = \dfrac{SI \times 100}{P \times R} = \dfrac{3675 \times 100}{7000 \times 7} = \dfrac{15}{2} = 7\dfrac{1}{2}$ years.

## MULTIPLE CHOICE QUESTIONS

1. The simple interest on ₹ 500 for 6 years at 5% p.a. is:
   A. ₹ 250    B. ₹ 150    C. ₹ 140    D. ₹ 120

2. A certain sum of money at SI amounts to ₹ 1012 in $2\dfrac{1}{2}$ years and to ₹ 1067.20 in 4 years. The rate of interest per annum is:
   A. 2.5%    B. 3%    C. 4%    D. 5%

3. ₹ 1200 amounts to ₹ 1632 in 4 years at a certain rate of simple interest. If the rate of interest is increased by 1%, it would amount to how much?
   A. ₹ 1635    B. ₹ 1644    C. ₹ 1670    D. ₹ 1680

4. A man will get ₹ 87 as simple interest on ₹ 725 at 4% per annum in:
   A. 3 years    B. 3½ years    C. 4 years    D. 5 years

5. At simple interest, a sum doubles after 20 years. The rate of interest per annum is:
   A. 5%    B. 10%
   C. 20%    D. Data inadequate

6. A lent ₹ 600 to B for 2 years and ₹ 150 to C for 4 years and received altogether from both ₹ 90 as simple interest. The rate of interest is:
   A. 12%    B. 10%    C. 5%    D. 4%

7. Interest on a certain sum of money for $2\dfrac{1}{3}$ years at $3\dfrac{3}{4}$% per annum is ₹ 210. The sum is:
   A. ₹ 2800    B. ₹ 1580    C. ₹ 2400    D. None of these

8. A certain sum of money at simple interest amounts to ₹ 1260 in 2 years and to ₹ 1350 in 5 years. The rate per cent per annum is:
   A. 2.5%    B. 3.75%    C. 5%    D. 7.5%

**9.** A sum of money doubles itself in 5 years. It will become 4 times itself in:
A. 10 years      B. 12 years      C. 15 years      D. 20 years

**10.** The simple interest on a sum of money will be ₹ 600 after 10 years. If the principal is trebled after 5 years, the total interest at the end of 10 years will be:
A. ₹ 600                      B. ₹ 900
C. ₹ 1200                   D. Data inadequate

**11.** ₹ 800 amounts to ₹ 920 in 3 years at simple interest. If the interest rate is increased by 3%, it would amount to how much?
A. ₹ 1056      B. ₹ 1112      C. ₹ 1182      D. ₹ 992

**12.** A sum of money at simple interest amounts to ₹ 2240 in 2 years and ₹ 2600 in 5 years. The sum is:
A. ₹ 1880                   B. ₹ 2000
C. ₹ 2120                   D. Data inadequate

**13.** If ₹ 7500 are borrowed at CI at the rate of 4% per annum, then after 2 years the amount to be paid is:
A. ₹ 8082      B. ₹ 7800      C. ₹ 8100      D. ₹ 8112

**14.** Simple interest on a sum at 4% per annum is ₹ 80 in 2 years. The compound interest on the same sum for the same period is:
A. ₹ 81.60      B. ₹ 160      C. ₹ 1081.60    D. None of these

**15.** ₹ 800 at 5% per annum compound interest will amount to ₹ 882 in:
A. 1 year      B. 2 years      C. 3 years      D. 4 years

**16.** What is the principal amount which earns ₹ 132 as compound interest for the second year at 10% per annum?
A. ₹ 1000      B. ₹ 1200      C. ₹ 1320      D. None of these

**17.** The difference between the compound interest and the simple interest on a certain sum at 5% per annum for 2 years is ₹ 1.50. The sum is:
A. ₹ 600      B. ₹ 500      C. ₹ 400      D. ₹ 300

**18.** The compound interest on a certain sum of money for 2 years at 10% per annum is ₹ 420. The simple interest on the same sum at the same rate and for the same time will be:
A. ₹ 350      B. ₹ 375      C. ₹ 380      D. ₹ 400

**19.** A sum amounts to ₹ 2916 in 2 years and to ₹ 3149.28 in 3 years at compound interest. The sum is :
A. ₹ 1500      B. ₹ 2000      C. ₹ 2500      D. ₹ 3000

**20.** A sum of money amounts to ₹ 10648 in 3 years and ₹ 9680 in 2 years. The rate of interest is:
A. 5%      B. 10%      C. 15%      D. 20%

**21.** If the simple interest on a certain sum of money at 6% per annum for 3 years is ₹ 90, the sum will be:
A. ₹ 500        B. ₹ 450        C. ₹ 525        D. ₹ 560

**22.** If the simple interest on Re. 1 for 1 month is 1 paise, the rate per cent p.a. will be :
A. 10%        B. 8%        C. 12%        D. 6%

**23.** A sum of money doubles itself in 20 years. In how many years will it triple itself at the same rate of simple interest?
A. 30 years        B. 50 years        C. 40 years        D. 45 years

**24.** If the simple interest on Rs. 500 for 4 years is Rs. 40, find the rate per cent p.a.
A. 3½%        B. 2%        C. 2½%        D. 3%

**25.** After what time will the sum of ₹ 2000 become ₹ 2240 at 4% per annum simple interest?
A. 3 years        B. 2 years        C. 5 years        D. 4 years

**26.** What will be the compound interest on ₹ 8000 for 3 years at 5% p.a.?
A. ₹ 1361        B. ₹ 1261        C. ₹ 1260        D. ₹ 1250

**27.** What will be the amount if a sum of ₹ 2500 is invested for 1 year at 4% per annum compound interest, interest being compounded half-yearly?
A. ₹ 2625        B. ₹ 2601        C. ₹ 2830        D. ₹ 2901

**28.** Find the compound interest on ₹ 2560 for ½ year at 12½% per annum, interest payable quarterly.
A. ₹ 3720.50        B. ₹ 2722.50        C. ₹ 2752.50        D. ₹ 2250.50

**29.** After how many years will ₹ 3375 become ₹ 4096 at $6\frac{2}{3}\%$ per annum compound interest?
A. 4 years        B. 2 years        C. 2½ years        D. 3 years

**30.** A certain sum of money placed at compound interest amounts to Rs. 110 in 1 year and to Rs. 121 in 2 years. The rate of interest per annum is :
A. 5%        B. 10%        C. 8%        D. 4%

## ANSWERS

| 1 | 2 | 3 | 4 | 5 | 6 | 7 | 8 | 9 | 10 |
|---|---|---|---|---|---|---|---|---|---|
| B | C | D | A | A | C | C | A | C | C |
| 11 | 12 | 13 | 14 | 15 | 16 | 17 | 18 | 19 | 20 |
| D | B | D | A | B | B | A | D | C | B |
| 21 | 22 | 23 | 24 | 25 | 26 | 27 | 28 | 29 | 30 |
| A | C | C | B | A | B | B | B | D | B |

## EXPLANATORY ANSWERS

**1.** $\text{SI} = \dfrac{P \times R \times T}{100} = \dfrac{500 \times 5 \times 6}{100} = ₹\ 150$

**3.** $R = \dfrac{\text{SI} \times 100}{P \times T} = \dfrac{432 \times 100}{1200 \times 4} = 9\%$

New rate $= (9 + 1)\% = 10\%$

$$\text{SI} = \dfrac{P \times R \times T}{100} = \dfrac{1200 \times 10 \times 4}{100} = ₹\ 480$$

Amount $= P + \text{SI} = 1200 + 480 = ₹\ 1680$

**4.** $T = \dfrac{\text{SI} \times 100}{P \times R} = \dfrac{87 \times 100}{725 \times 4} = 3$ years

**5.** Let P be $₹\ x$ then $A = ₹\ 2x$

$\text{SI} = A - P = 2x - x = ₹\ x$

$$R = \dfrac{\text{SI} \times 100}{P \times T} = \dfrac{x \times 100}{x \times 20} = 5\%$$

**12.** SI for 3 years $= 2600 - 2240 = ₹\ 360$

SI for 2 years $= \dfrac{360}{3} \times 2 = ₹\ 240$

$\therefore$ Sum $= 2240 - 240 = ₹\ 2000$

**13.** $A = P\left(1 + \dfrac{R}{100}\right)^{T} = 7500\left(1 + \dfrac{4}{100}\right)^{2}$

$$= 7500 \times \dfrac{26}{25} \times \dfrac{26}{25} = ₹\ 8112$$

**21.** $P = \dfrac{90 \times 100}{6 \times 3} = ₹\ 500$

**22.** Rate $= \dfrac{1 \times 100}{100 \times \dfrac{1}{12}} = 12\%.$

**23.** Let principal $= ₹\ x$; Amount $= ₹\ 2x$; then $I = 2x - x = ₹\ x$

$\therefore\ R = \dfrac{x \times 100}{x \times 20} = 5\%$

Again, if principal $= ₹\ x$; Amount $= ₹\ 3x$; then $I = 3x - x = ₹\ 2x$

Hence, $T = \dfrac{2x \times 100}{x \times 5} = 40$ years

24. Rate $= \dfrac{40 \times 100}{500 \times 4} = 2\%$

25. Here, $I = 2240 - 2000 = ₹\ 240$

$\therefore\ T = \dfrac{240 \times 100}{2000 \times 4} = 3$ years

26. $\therefore\ \text{C.I.} = 8000\left[\left(1 + \dfrac{5}{100}\right)^3 - 1\right] = 8000\left[\left(\dfrac{21}{20}\right)^3 - 1\right]$

$= \dfrac{8000 \times 1261}{8000} = ₹\ 1261$

27. $A = 2500\left(1 + \dfrac{2}{100}\right)^2 = 2500\left(\dfrac{51}{50}\right)^2 = \dfrac{2500 \times 51 \times 51}{50 \times 50} = ₹\ 2601$

28. Amount $= 2560\left(1 + \dfrac{25}{8 \times 100}\right)^2 = \dfrac{2560 \times 33 \times 33}{32 \times 32} = ₹\ 2722.50$

29. Here, $4096 = 3375\left(1 + \dfrac{20}{3 \times 100}\right)^n \Rightarrow \dfrac{4096}{3375} = \left(1 + \dfrac{1}{15}\right)^n$

$\Rightarrow \left(\dfrac{16}{15}\right)^3 = \left(\dfrac{16}{15}\right)^n \quad \therefore\ n = 3$ years

# Time & Work

The problems on Time and Work can be solved by following two methods:

(*i*) **Ratio and Proportion Method:** Since problems concerning to Time and Work have proportional relation, these can be solved by this method.

(*ii*) **Unitary Method:** In this method, we first proceed to reduce the problem to either work done by one person or work done in 1 day and so on as per the requirement of the problem.

If $M_1$ persons can do $W_1$ works in $D_1$ days and $M_2$ persons can do $W_2$ works in $D_2$ days then we have a very general formula in the relationship of

$$M_1 \, D_1 \, W_2 = M_2 \, D_2 \, W_1$$

The above relationship can be taken as a very basic and all-in-one formula we also derive:

(*i*) More men less days and conversely more days less men.

(*ii*) More men more work and conversely more work more men.

(*iii*) More days more work and conversely more work more days.

$$M_1 \, D_1 \, T_1 \, W_2 = M_2 \, D_2 \, T_2 \, W_1$$

**EXAMPLE:** 5 men can prepare 10 toys in 6 days working 6 hrs a day. How many days can 12 men prepare 16 toys working 8 hrs a day?

**SOLUTION:** $M_1 \, D_1 \, T_1 \, W_2 = M_2 \, D_2 \, T_2 \, W_1$

$$5 \times 6 \times 6 \times 16 = 12 \times D_2 \times 8 \times 10$$

$$D_2 = \frac{5 \times 6 \times 6 \times 16}{12 \times 8 \times 10} = 3 \text{ days.}$$

**EXAMPLE:** A and B together can do a piece of work in 12 days, B alone can finish it in 30 days. In how many days can A alone finish the work?

**SOLUTION:** (A + B)'s 1 day's work $= \dfrac{1}{12}$

B's 1 day's work $= \dfrac{1}{30}$

$\therefore$ A's 1 day's work $= \dfrac{1}{12} - \dfrac{1}{30} = \dfrac{5-2}{60} = \dfrac{3}{60} = \dfrac{1}{20}$

Hence, A alone can finish the work in 20 days.

# MULTIPLE CHOICE QUESTIONS

1. A and B can together do a piece of work in 15 days. B alone can do it in 20 days. In how many days can A alone do it?
   A. 30 days      B. 40 days      C. 45 days      D. 60 days

2. A can do a piece of work in 30 days while B can do it in 40 days. A and B working together can do it in:
   A. 70 days      B. $42\dfrac{3}{4}$ days      C. $27\dfrac{1}{7}$ days      D. $17\dfrac{1}{7}$ days

3. A can do $\dfrac{1}{3}$ of the work in 5 days and B can do $\dfrac{2}{5}$ of the work in 10 days. In how many days both A and B together can do the work?
   A. $7\dfrac{3}{4}$ days      B. $8\dfrac{4}{5}$ days      C. $9\dfrac{3}{8}$ days      D. 10 days

4. A, B and C can do a piece of work in 6, 12 and 24 days respectively. They altogether will complete the work in:
   A. $3\dfrac{3}{7}$ days      B. $\dfrac{7}{24}$ days      C. $4\dfrac{4}{5}$ days      D. $\dfrac{5}{24}$ days

5. A, B and C contract a work for ₹ 550. Together A and B are to do $\dfrac{7}{11}$ of the work. The share of C should be:
   A. ₹ $183\dfrac{1}{3}$      B. ₹ 200      C. ₹ 300      D. ₹ 400

6. A and B finish a job in 12 days while A, B and C can finish it in 8 days. C alone will finish the job in:
   A. 20 days      B. 14 days      C. 24 days      D. 16 days

7. 12 men can complete a work in 8 days. Three days after they started the work, 3 more men joined them. In how many days will all of them together complete the remaining work?
   A. 2      B. 4      C. 5      D. 6

8. Mahesh and Umesh can complete a work in 10 and 15 days respectively. Umesh starts the work and after 5 days Mahesh joins him. In all, the work would be completed in:
   A. 9 days      B. 7 days      C. 11 days      D. None of these

**9.** Sunil completes a work in 4 days whereas Dinesh completes the work in 6 days. Ramesh works $1\frac{1}{2}$ times as fast as Sunil. How many days it will take for the three together to complete the work?

   A. $\frac{7}{12}$        B. $1\frac{5}{12}$        C. $1\frac{5}{7}$        D. None of these

**10.** A can complete a work in 6 days and B in 5 days. They work together, finish the job and receive ₹ 220 as wages. B's share should be:
   A. ₹ 120        B. ₹ 110        C. ₹ 100        D. ₹ 90

**11.** 12 men and 8 children can finish a piece of work in 9 days. If each child takes twice the time taken by a man to finish the work, in how many days will 12 men finish the same work?
   A. 8 days        B. 15 days        C. 9 days        D. 12 days

**12.** A, B and C together earn ₹ 150 per day while A and C together earn ₹ 94 and B and C together earn ₹ 76. The daily earning of C is:
   A. ₹ 75        B. ₹ 56        C. ₹ 34        D. ₹ 20

**13.** If 5 men or 9 women can finish a piece of work in 19 days, 3 men and 6 women will do the same work in:
   A. 10 days        B. 12 days        C. 13 days        D. 15 days

**14.** A can do a piece of work in 12 days. B is 60% more efficient than A. The number of days, it takes B to do the same piece of work, is:

   A. $7\frac{1}{2}$ days        B. $6\frac{1}{4}$ days        C. 8 days        D. 6 days

**15.** A and B can do a piece of work in 45 and 40 days respectively. They began the work together, but A leaves after some days and B finished the remaining work in 23 days. After how many days did A leave?
   A. 6 days        B. 8 days        C. 9 days        D. 12 days

**16.** 12 men can complete a work within 9 days. After 3 days they started the work, 6 men joined them to replace 2 men. How many days will they take to complete the remaining work?

   A. 2 days        B. 3 days        C. 4 days        D. $4\frac{1}{2}$ days

**17.** 10 men can finish a piece of work in 10 days whereas it takes 12 women to finish it in 10 days. If 15 men and 6 women undertake to complete the work, how many days will they take to complete it?
   A. 2 days        B. 4 days        C. 5 days        D. 11 days

**18.** A can do a piece of work in 80 days. He works at it for 10 days and then B alone finishes the work in 42 days. The two together could complete the work in:

A. 24 days       B. 25 days       C. 30 days       D. 35 days

**19.** A and B can together finish a work in 30 days. They worked for it for 20 days and then B left. The remaining work was done by A alone in 20 more days. A alone can finish the work in:

A. 48 days       B. 50 days       C. 54 days       D. 60 days

**20.** A can complete a job in 9 days, B in 10 days and C in 15 days. B and C start the work and are forced to leave after 2 days. The time taken by A alone to complete the remaining work is:

A. 13 days       B. 10 days       C. 9 days       D. 6 days

**21.** 12 boys can do a piece of work in 16 days. In how many days can 6 boys do the same work?

A. 16 days       B. 32 days       C. 23 days       D. 24 days

**22.** A can do a piece of work in 8 days while B can do the same work in 16 days. If they start working together, how long would they take to complete half portion of this work?

A. $2\dfrac{2}{3}$ days       B. $3\dfrac{5}{7}$ days       C. $4\dfrac{1}{2}$ days       D. $3\dfrac{1}{2}$ days

**23.** A can do a piece of work in 4 days. B is 50% more efficient than A. How long would B alone take to finish this work?

A. $3\dfrac{1}{3}$ days       B. $5\dfrac{1}{4}$ days       C. $2\dfrac{2}{3}$ days       D. $1\dfrac{2}{3}$ days

**24.** A and B working together complete a work in 35 days. If A takes 60 days to complete it, how long would B alone take to complete it?

A. 64 days       B. 72 days       C. 81 days       D. 84 days

**25.** A few children working together can do a piece of work in 18 days. If the number of children employed on the work is made double, how long would they take to complete half of the work?

A. $4\dfrac{1}{2}$ days       B. $2\dfrac{1}{3}$ days       C. $8\dfrac{3}{4}$ days       D. $6\dfrac{1}{2}$ days

**26.** 10 men or 18 boys can do a piece of work in 15 days. In how many days would 25 men and 15 boys complete the same work working together?

A. $5\dfrac{1}{2}$ days       B. $4\dfrac{1}{2}$ days       C. $6\dfrac{2}{3}$ days       D. $2\dfrac{1}{3}$ days

**27.** A can do a piece of work in 40 days. He starts working, but having some other engagements he drops out after 5 days. Thereafter B completes this work in 21 days. How many days would A and B take to complete this work working together?

A. 15 days    B. 16 days    C. 17 days    D. 11 days

**28.** Two persons A and B can complete a piece of work in 8 hours and 16 hours respectively. If they work at it alternately for an hour, A starting first, in how many hours will the work be finished?

A. $9\frac{1}{3}$ hours    B. $10\frac{1}{2}$ hours    C. $11\frac{1}{2}$ hours    D. $8\frac{1}{2}$ hours

**29.** 15 men can complete a work in 210 days. They started the work but at the end of 10 days 15 additional men, with double efficiency, were inducted. How many days, in whole, did they take to finish the work?

A. $76\frac{2}{3}$ days    B. $84\frac{3}{4}$ days    C. $72\frac{1}{2}$ days    D. 70 days

**30.** A and B working together can complete a piece of work in 12 days and B and C working together can complete the same work in 16 days. A worked at it for 5 days and B worked at it for 7 days. C finished the remaining work in 13 days. How many days would C alone take to complete it?

A. 10 days    B. 24 days    C. 32 days    D. 40 days

## ANSWERS

| 1 | 2 | 3 | 4 | 5 | 6 | 7 | 8 | 9 | 10 |
|---|---|---|---|---|---|---|---|---|---|
| D | D | C | A | B | C | B | A | D | A |

| 11 | 12 | 13 | 14 | 15 | 16 | 17 | 18 | 19 | 20 |
|----|----|----|----|----|----|----|----|----|----|
| D | D | D | A | C | D | C | C | D | D |

| 21 | 22 | 23 | 24 | 25 | 26 | 27 | 28 | 29 | 30 |
|----|----|----|----|----|----|----|----|----|----|
| B | A | C | D | A | B | A | B | A | B |

## EXPLANATORY ANSWERS

**1.** (A + B)'s 1 day's work = $\dfrac{1}{15}$

B's 1 day's work = $\dfrac{1}{20}$

A's 1 day's work = $\dfrac{1}{15} - \dfrac{1}{20} = \dfrac{4-3}{60} = \dfrac{1}{60}$

∴ A can do this work alone in 60 days.

**5.** Work to be done by C $= \left(1 - \dfrac{7}{11}\right) = \dfrac{4}{11}$

$\therefore$ (A + B) : C $= \dfrac{7}{11} : \dfrac{4}{11} = 7 : 4$

$\therefore$ C's share $= ₹\dfrac{4}{11} \times 550 = ₹\ 200$

**10.** Ratio of time taken by A and B = 6 : 5

Ratio of work done in same time = 5 : 6

So, the money is to be divided among A and B in the ratio 5 : 6.

$\therefore$ B's share $= ₹\dfrac{6}{11} \times 220 = ₹\ 120$

**11.** 2 children = 1 man

$\therefore$ 8 children + 12 men = 4 + 12 = 16 men

Now, less men, more days

$12 : 16 :: 9 : x \Rightarrow \dfrac{12}{16} = \dfrac{9}{x} \Rightarrow x = 12$ days

**12.** B's daily earning $= ₹\ (150 - 94) = ₹\ 56$

A's daily earning $= ₹\ (150 - 76) = ₹\ 74$

C's daily earning $= ₹\ [150 - (56 + 74)] = ₹\ 20$

**17.** 10 men = 12 women $\Rightarrow$ 1 man $= \dfrac{6}{5}$ women

$\therefore$ 15 men + 6 women $= 15 \times \dfrac{6}{5} + 6$

$\qquad\qquad\qquad\qquad = 18 + 6 = 24$ women

12 women can do the work in 10 days

24 women can do the same work in $\dfrac{10 \times 12}{24} = 5$ days

**20.** (B + C)'s 2 day's work $= 2\left(\dfrac{1}{10} + \dfrac{1}{15}\right) = \dfrac{1}{3}$

Remaining work $= 1 - \dfrac{1}{3} = \dfrac{2}{3}$

Now, $\dfrac{1}{9}$ work is done by A in 1 day

$\therefore \dfrac{2}{3}$ work will be done by A in $9 \times \dfrac{2}{3} = 6$ days

**21.** $\because$    12 boys can do a piece of work in 16 days.

    $\therefore$    1 boy will do the same piece of work in 16 × 12 days.

    $\therefore$    6 boys will do the same piece of work in $\dfrac{16 \times 12}{6}$ days = 32 days.

**23.** A's 1 day's work $= \dfrac{1}{4}$ ;         Hence, B's 1 day's work $= \dfrac{150}{100} \times \dfrac{1}{4} = \dfrac{3}{8}$

    So, B will do the whole work in $\dfrac{8}{3} = 2\dfrac{2}{3}$ days.

**25.** Let number of children be $x$;

    Now $x$ children can do the work in 18 days.

    Hence, $2x$ children will do $\dfrac{1}{2}$ of the work in $\dfrac{18 \times x}{2x \times 2} = \dfrac{9}{2}$ days $= 4\dfrac{1}{2}$ days.

**27.** A's 5 days' work $= 5 \times \dfrac{1}{40} = \dfrac{1}{8}$

    Remaining work $= 1 - \dfrac{1}{8} = \dfrac{7}{8}$, which is done by B in 21 days.

    Hence, B's 1 day's work $= \dfrac{7}{8 \times 21} = \dfrac{1}{24}$

    Now, (A + B)'s 1 day's work $= \dfrac{1}{40} + \dfrac{1}{24} = \dfrac{8}{120} = \dfrac{1}{15}$

    Hence, (A + B) will complete the work in 15 days.

**28.** In 2 hours the part of work $= \dfrac{1}{8} + \dfrac{1}{16} = \dfrac{3}{16}$ will be completed.

    Hence, in 5 pairs of hours the part of work

    $= 5 \times \dfrac{3}{16} = \dfrac{15}{16}$ will be completed

    Remaining work $= 1 - \dfrac{15}{16} = \dfrac{1}{16}$ which will be done by A.

    Time taken by A to complete the $\dfrac{1}{16}$ work $= \dfrac{1/16}{1/8} = \dfrac{1}{2}$ hour.

    Hence, required number of hours $= 10 + \dfrac{1}{2} = 10\dfrac{1}{2}$ hours.

❖ ❖ ❖

$$\boxed{11}$$

# Time & Distance

## Important Formulae:

1. Speed = Distance ÷ Time
2. Distance = Time × Speed
3. Time = Distance ÷ Speed
4. $x$ km/hr $= \left( x \times \dfrac{5}{18} \right)$ m/sec
5. $x$ metres/sec $= \left( x \times \dfrac{18}{5} \right)$ km/hr.
6. If the speed of a body is changed in the ratio $m : n$, then the ratio of the time taken changes in the ratio $n : m$.
7. When a man covers a certain distance with a speed of $x$ km/h and another equal distance at the rate of $y$ km/h, then for the whole journey, the average speed is given by Average speed $= \dfrac{2xy}{x+y}$ km/h.

**Example :** A boy goes to school at a speed of 4 km/h and returns to the house at a speed of 3 km/h. If he takes 5 hrs. in all, what is the distance between the house and the school?

**Solution:** Let the distance between house and the school be $x$ km.

$$\frac{x}{4} + \frac{x}{3} = 5 \qquad \Rightarrow \qquad \frac{7x}{12} = 5 \qquad \therefore \quad x = \frac{60}{7} \text{ km}$$

## MULTIPLE CHOICE QUESTIONS

1. A car moving at 48 km/hr completes a journey in 10 hours. By how much the speed of this car should be increased so as to do this journey in 8 hours?
   A. 8 km/hr.     B. 12 km/hr     C. 10 km/hr     D. 15 km/hr

2. Starting from a point at a speed of 4 km/hr a man reaches at a cerain place and returns back to the point from where he had started journey on bicycle at the speed of 16 km/hr. His average speed during the entire journey will be :
   A. 6.4 km/h     B. 8.4 km/h     C. 5.4 km/h     D. 10 km/h

3. A motorist covers a certain distance at a average speed of 48 km/h in 45 minutes. What speed in km/h he must maintain to cover the same distance in 30 minutes?
   A. 66 km/h     B. 79 km/h     C. 80 km/h     D. 72 km/h

**4.** Two points A and B are 150 km apart. A man completes his onward journey from A to B in 3 hours 20 minutes and return journey from B to A in 4 hours 10 minutes. His average speed during the entire journey will be less than his average speed during the journey from A to B by :
A. 5 km/h          B. 7.5 km/h          C. 9 km/h          D. 3 km/h

**5.** A policeman saw a thief at a distance of 200 m. The policeman and the thief started running at the same time. If the policeman runs at a speed of $4\frac{1}{6}$ m per second and the thief at a speed of $3\frac{1}{3}$ m per second, after what time the policeman will catch the thief?
A. 12 min          B. 10 min          C. 9 min          D. 4 min

**6.** Kanchan walks from her home at 4 kms per hour and reaches her school 5 minutes late. If she walks at 5 kms per hour, she reaches the school 2½ minutes earlier. How far is the school from her home?
A. 3.5 kms          B. 2.5 kms          C. 2.75 kms          D. 3.2 kms

**7.** A monkey wants to climb up a glazed pole. He climbs 12 metres in 1 minute and then he slips back 3 metres in the next minute. If the pole is 63 metre high, how long does he take to climb at the top of the pole?
A. $11\frac{1}{4}$ min          B. $12\frac{1}{2}$ min          C. $12\frac{3}{4}$ min          D. $14\frac{3}{4}$ min

**8.** A and B start walking at the same time on a circular path with circumference 35 metre. If they walk in the same direction at 4 km/hr and 5 km/hr respectively, after what time will they meet together?
A. 35 hours          B. 27 hours          C. 24 hours          D. 40 hours

**9.** While walking at $\frac{3}{5}$ of his usual speed Kamalkant reaches at his destination late by 30 minutes. His usual time consumed in reaching to his destination is:
A. 32 min          B. 40 min          C. 45 min          D. 42 min

**10.** The distance between two stations A and B is 300 km. A train leaves the station A with a speed of 40 km/hr. At the same time another train departs from the station B with a speed of 50 km/hr. How much time will these two trains take to cross each other?
A. 3 hrs 40 min     B. 3 hrs 20 min   C. 2 hrs 20 min   D. 3 hrs 45 min

**11.** Gulshan starts from a place P at 2 p.m. and walks to Q at 5 km per hour. Tarun starts from P at 3 p.m. and follows Gulshan on bicycle at 10 km per hour. By when Tarun will catch Gulshan?
A. At 5.30 p.m.     B. At 4.00 p.m.   C. At 4.30 p.m.   D. At 6.00 p.m.

12. Nilesh goes to school from his village at the speed of 4 km/hr and returns from school to village at the speed of 2 km/hr. If he takes 6 hours in all, then what is the distance between the village and the school?
    A. 8 km            B. 6 km            C. 5 km           D. 4 km

13. A school bus covers a distance from a village to school at the speed of 12 km/hr and reaches the school 8 minute late. The next day the bus covers the same distance at the speed of 20 km/hr and reaches the school 10 minutes early. What is the distance between village and the school?
    A. 6 km            B. 9 km            C. 12 km        D. 15 km

14. By increasing the speed of the bus by 10 km/hr the time of journey for 72 km is reduced by 36 minutes. What was the original speed of the bus?
    A. 30 km/hr      B. 35 km/hr      C. 40 km/hr    D. 45 km/hr

15. A car completes a fixed journey in 8 hours. It covers half distance at the speed of 40 km/hr and rest at the 60 km/hr, the distance of the journeyTis:
    A. 400 km      B. 420 km      C. 384 km    D. 350 km

16. A car covers four consecutive extensions of 3 km each at the speeds of 10 km/hr, 20 km/hr, 30 km/hr and 60 km/hr. Its average speed of journey is:
    A. 30 km/hr      B. 25 km/hr      C. 20 km/hr    D. 10 km/hr

17. A girl rides her bicycle 10 km at an average speed of 12 km/hr and another 12 km at an average speed of 10 km/hr. Her average speed for the entire journey is approximately:
    A. 12.2 km/hr    B. 11.2 km/hr    C. 10.8 km/hr  D. 10.4 km/hr

18. Raman drove from home to a neighbouring town at the speed of 50 km/hr and on his returning journey, he drove at the speed of 45 km/hr and also took an hour longer to reach home. What distance did he cover each way?
    A. 900 km      B. 500 km      C. 450 km    D. 225 km

19. A man takes 6 hours 35 minutes in walking to a certain place and riding back. He would have taken 2 hours less by riding both ways. What would be the time he would take to walk both ways?
    A. 10 hours                  B. 8 hours 35 minutes
    C. 8 hours 25 minutes        D. 8 hrs

20. A man covers a distance of 6 km at the rate of 4 km/hr and other 4 km at 3 km/hr this average speed is

    A. $3\dfrac{5}{9}$ km/hr    B. $3\dfrac{9}{17}$ km/hr    C. $5\dfrac{9}{17}$ km/hr  D. $9\dfrac{3}{17}$ km/hr

**21.** A cyclist rides 24 km at 16 km/h and further 36 km at 15 km/hr. Find his average speed for the journey.

    A. 15.38 km/hr    B. 15.5 km/hr    C. 16 km/hr    D. 16.5 km/hr

**22.** A car is running at a speed of 108 km/hr. Find the distance covered by it in 15 seconds.

    A. 450 m    B. 475 m    C. 500 m    D. 550 m

**23.** How long will a boy take to run round a square field of side 35 meters, If he runs at the rate of 9 km/hr?

    A. 56 sec.    B. 54 sec.    C. 52 sec.    D. 50 sec.

**24.** A person crosses a 600 m long street in 5 minutes. Find his speed in km/hr.

    A. 10    B. 8.4    C. 7.2    D. 3.6

**25.** A man walking at the rate of 5 km/hr crosses a bridge in 15 minutes. What is the length of the bridge in meters?

    A. 1250    B. 1000    C. 750    D. 600

**26.** A truck covers a distance of 550 m in 1 minute whereas a bus covers a distance of 33 km in 45 minutes. The ratio of their speeds is:

    A. 50 : 3    B. 3 : 5    C. 4 : 3    D. 3 : 4

**27.** A train travels at an average of 50 miles/hr for $2\frac{1}{2}$ hrs and then travels at a speed of 70 miles/hr for $1\frac{1}{2}$ hrs. Find the distance travelled by the train in entire 4 hrs.

    A. 230 miles    B. 200 miles    C. 150 miles    D. 120 miles

**28.** Sound is said to travel in air at about 1100 feet/sec. A man hears the axe striking the tree $\frac{11}{5}$ seconds after he sees it strike the tree. Find the distance between the man and the wood chopper.

    A. 2629 ft.    B. 2500 ft.    C. 2420 ft.    D. 2197 ft.

**29.** A motor car starts with the speed of 70 km/hr with its speed increasing every two hours by 10 km/hr. What is the time taken (in hours) in covering 345 km by it?

    A. 5 hrs.    B. $4\frac{1}{2}$ hrs.    C. 4 hrs 5 min.    D. 4 hrs

**30.** A person has to cover a distance of 6 km in 45 minutes. If he covers one-half of the distance in two-thirds of the total time. Find his speed (in km/hr) to cover the remaining distance in remaining time.

    A. 15    B. 12    C. 8    D. 6

## ANSWERS

| 1 | 2 | 3 | 4 | 5 | 6 | 7 | 8 | 9 | 10 |
|---|---|---|---|---|---|---|---|---|---|
| B | A | D | A | D | B | C | A | C | B |

| 11 | 12 | 13 | 14 | 15 | 16 | 17 | 18 | 19 | 20 |
|----|----|----|----|----|----|----|----|----|----|
| B | A | B | A | C | C | C | C | B | B |

| 21 | 22 | 23 | 24 | 25 | 26 | 27 | 28 | 29 | 30 |
|----|----|----|----|----|----|----|----|----|----|
| A | A | A | C | A | D | A | C | B | B |

## EXPLANATORY ANSWERS

**2.** Average speed during the entire journey

$$= \frac{2xy}{x+y} = \frac{2 \times 4 \times 16}{4+16} = \frac{8 \times 16}{20} = 6.4 \text{ km/hr.}$$

**3.** Let required speed be $x$ km/hr; then

$$x \times \frac{1}{2} = 48 \times \frac{3}{4} \qquad \therefore \ x = 48 \times \frac{3}{4} \times 2 = 72 \text{ km/hr}$$

**5.** Suppose the policeman will catch the thief after $t$ seconds

then, $\left(\dfrac{25}{6} - \dfrac{10}{3}\right) t = 200 \Rightarrow \dfrac{5}{6} t = 200 \ \therefore t = \dfrac{200 \times 6}{5} = 240$ sec = 4 min.

**11.** Let Tarun will catch Gulshan after $t$ hours the starting of Tarun; then,
$10t = 5(t + 1) \Rightarrow 5t = 5 \ \therefore \ t = 1$ hr
Hence, required time = 3 p.m. + 1 hr. = 4 p.m.

**21.** Required average speed $= \dfrac{24+36}{\dfrac{24}{16}+\dfrac{36}{15}} = \dfrac{60}{\dfrac{3}{2}+\dfrac{12}{5}} = \dfrac{60 \times 10}{39} = 15.38$ km/hr

**22.** Required distance $= 108 \times \dfrac{15}{60 \times 60}$ km $= \dfrac{9}{20}$ km $= \dfrac{9}{20} \times 1000 = 450$ m

**23.** $9$ km/hr $= 9 \times \dfrac{5}{18} = \dfrac{5}{2}$ m/s

Time taken $= \dfrac{4 \times 35}{5/2} = 4 \times 7 \times 2 = 56$ sec.

**24.** Speed $= \dfrac{600 \text{m}}{5 \times 60 \text{ s}} = 2 \text{m}/s = 2 \times \dfrac{18}{5}$ km/hr $= \dfrac{36}{5} = 7.2$ km/hr.

❖ ❖ ❖

**12**

# *Mensuration*

## Perimeter

Perimeter of a geometrical figure is the total length of the sides enclosing the figure.

## Triangle

A triangle is a plane figure bounded by three sides. It includes three angles. It is denoted by the symbol $\Delta$. The sum of angles of a triangle is $180°$.

(*i*) **Equilateral Triangle:** A triangle in which all sides are equal is called an equilateral triangle.

(*ii*) **Isosceles Triangle:** A triangle in which two sides are equal is called an isosceles triangle.

(*iii*) **Scalene Triangle:** A triangle in which all sides are different or unequal is called scalene triangle.

(*iv*) **Right Angled Triangle:** A triangle having one of the angles equal to $90°$ is called a right angled triangle. The side opposite to the right angle of a triangle is called its hypotenuse.

## Quadrilateral

A plane figure bounded by four straight lines is called a quadrilateral.

## Various Types of Quadrilaterals:

(*i*) **Rectangle:** A quadrilateral whose opposite sides are equal and all angles are at right angles. The diagonals of a rectangle are equal.

(*ii*) **Square:** A rectangle having all sides are equal is called a square.

(*iii*) **Parallelogram:** A quadrilateral whose opposite sides are equal and parallel is called parallelogram.

(*iv*) **Rhombus:** A parallelogram having all the sides equal is called a rhombus. Diagonals of a rhombus are not equal and they bisect each other at right angles.

(*v*) **Trapezium:** A quadrilateral having one pair of opposite sides parallel, is called a trapezium.

## Circle

The path traced by a point which moves in such a way that its distance from a fixed point is always same, is called a circle. The fixed point is called its centre and fixed distance is called its radius.



R-165 (Math)-5-II

(*i*) **Arc:** Any part of the circumference of a circle is called an arc.

(*ii*) **Chord:** The straight line joining the ends of an arc of a circle is called a chord.

(*iii*) **Diameter:** The chord passing through the centre of a circle is called its diameter.

(*iv*) **Segment:** The area enclosed by an arc and a chord is called a segment.

(*v*) **Sector:** The area bounded by an arc and two radii is called a sector.

## Formulae for Area of Various Figures:

(*i*) **Rectangle:**

Area of rectangle $= l \times b$    Perimeter of rectangle $= 2(l + b)$.

(*ii*) **Square:**

Area of square $= (\text{side})^2$    Perimeter of square $= 4 \times \text{side}$

Area of room $= l \times b$

Area of 4 walls of a room $= 2(l + b) \times h$

(*iii*) **Parallelogram:**

Area of Parallelogram $= b \times h$    Area of rhombus $= \dfrac{1}{2} \times d_1 \times d_2$.

(*iv*) **Trapezium:**

Area of trapezium $= \dfrac{1}{2}(\text{sum of parallel sides}) \times (\text{distance between them})$

(*v*) **Triangle:**

(*a*) Area of right triangle $= \dfrac{1}{2} \times b \times h$

(*b*) Area of equilateral triangle $= \dfrac{\sqrt{3}}{4} \times (\text{side})^2$

(*c*) Area of scalene triangle $= \sqrt{s(s-a)(s-b)(s-c)}$ where, $s = \dfrac{a+b+c}{2}$

(*vi*) **Circle:**

(*a*) Area of circle $= \pi r^2$    (*b*) Circumference of a circle $= 2\pi r$

(*c*) Length of arc $= \dfrac{\theta}{360} \times 2\pi r$    (*d*) Area of sector $= \dfrac{\theta}{360} \times \pi r^2$

## Polygon

A polygon is plane figure bounded by multiple number of sides. Normally, it is used for figures enclosed by more than four sides: *e.g.,* pentagon, hexagon, octagon etc.

## Regular Polygon

It is a polygon whose all sides are equal. For a regular polygon of $n$ equal sides,

its vertex angle $\theta$ is given by $\theta = \left(\dfrac{n-2}{n}\right) \times 180°$

**EXAMPLE:** Find the area and perimeter of a rectangle whose length is 25 m and breadth is 15 m.

**SOLUTION:** Area of rectangle $= l \times b = 25 \times 15 = 375$ m²

Perimeter of rectangle $= 2(l + b) = 2(25 + 15) = 80$ m

**EXAMPLE:** Find the area of a parallelogram whose base is 35 m and altitude 18 m.

**SOLUTION:** Area of parallelogram $= b \times h = 35 \times 18 = 630$ m²

**EXAMPLE:** Find the circumference and the area of a circle of radius 3.5 cm.

**SOLUTION:** Circumference $= 2\pi r = 2 \times \dfrac{22}{7} \times 3.5 = 22$ cm

Area of circle $= \pi r^2 = \dfrac{22}{7} \times 3.5 \times 3.5 = 38.5$ cm²

## Volume and Surface Area

**Cuboid:**

| | |
|---|---|
| Volume of cuboid | $= l \times b \times h$ cubic units |
| Whole surface area | $= 2(lb + bh + hl)$ square units |
| Diagonal of cuboid | $= \sqrt{l^2 + b^2 + h^2}$ units |
| Area of 4 walls of a room | $= 2(l + b) \times h$ square units |

**Cube:**

| | |
|---|---|
| Volume of cube | $= a^3$ cubic units |
| Side of cube | $= \sqrt[3]{\text{Volume}}$ |
| Lateral surface area | $= 4a^2$ square units |
| Total surface area | $= 6a^2$ square units |
| Diagonal of the cube | $= \left(\sqrt{3}\,a\right)$ units |

**Cylinder:**

| | |
|---|---|
| Volume of cylinder | $= \pi r^2 h$ cubic units |
| Lateral surface area | $= 2\pi rh$ square units |
| Total surface area | $= 2\pi r(h + r)$ square units |

**Cone:**

| | |
|---|---|
| Volume of cone | $= \dfrac{1}{3}\pi r^2 h$ cubic units |
| Lateral surface area | $= \pi rl$ square units |

Total surface area $\qquad = \pi r(l + r)$ square units

Slant height $(l)$ $\qquad = \sqrt{r^2 + h^2}$

**Sphere:**

Volume of sphere $\qquad = \dfrac{4}{3}\pi r^3$ cubic units

Surface area $\qquad = 4\pi r^2$ square units

**Hemisphere:**

Volume $\qquad = \dfrac{2}{3}\pi r^3$ cubic units

Lateral surface area $\qquad = 2\pi r^2$ square units

Total surface area $\qquad = 3\pi r^2$ square units

**Frustum:**

Volume $\qquad = \dfrac{1}{3}\pi h(r_1^2 + r_1 r_2 + r_2^2)$ cubic units

Curved surface area $\qquad = \pi(r_1 + r_2) \times l$ square units

Total surface area $\qquad = \pi\left[r_1^2 + r_2^2 + (r_1 + r_2)l\right]$ square units

**Pyramid:** Volume $= \dfrac{1}{2} \times$ (area of base) $\times$ height cubic units

**EXAMPLE:** Three cubes whose edges measure 3 cm, 4 cm and 5 cm respectively form a single cube. Find the total surface area of the new cube.

**SOLUTION:** Let the edge of new cube $= x$ cm

$$
\begin{aligned}
x^3 &= 3^3 + 4^3 + 5^3 \\
&= 27 + 64 + 125 = 216 \text{ cm}^3 \\
\Rightarrow x^3 &= 6 \times 6 \times 6 \Rightarrow x = 6 \text{ cm}
\end{aligned}
$$

Total surface area of cube $= 6(x)^2 = 6 \times 6 \times 6 = 216$ cm$^2$

Hence, total surface area of new cube $= 216$ cm$^2$.

## MULTIPLE CHOICE QUESTIONS

1. The length of a plot is four times its breadth. A playground measuring 1200 square metres occupies a third of the total area of the plot. What is the length of the plot, in metres?

   A. 20 $\qquad$ B. 30 $\qquad$ C. 60 $\qquad$ D. None of these

2. The width of a rectangular hall is $\dfrac{3}{4}$ of its length. If the area of the hall is 300 m$^2$, then the difference between its length and width is:

   A. 3 m $\qquad$ B. 4 m $\qquad$ C. 5 m $\qquad$ D. 15 m

**3.** The length and breadth of a rectangular piece of land are in ratio of 5 : 3. The owner spent ₹ 3000 for surrounding it from all the sides at ₹ 7.50 per metre. The difference between its length and breadth is:
A. 50 m     B. 100 m     C. 150 m     D. 200 m

**4.** A room 8 m × 6 m is to be carpeted by a carpet 2 m wide. The length of carpet required is:
A. 12 m     B. 36 m     C. 24 m     D. 48 m

**5.** The length of a rectangle is increased by 60%. By what per cent would the width have to be decreased to maintain the same area?

A. $37\dfrac{1}{2}\%$     B. 60%     C. 75%     D. 120%

**6.** A man walked 20 m to cross a rectangular field diagonally. If the length of the field is 16 m, the breadth of the rectangle is:
A. 4 m
B. 16 m
C. 12 m
D. Cannot be determined

**7.** If the ratio of the areas of two squares is 9 : 1, the ratio of their perimeters is:
A. 9 : 1     B. 3 : 1     C. 3 : 4     D. 1 : 3

**8.** The perimeter of both, a square and a rectangle are each equal to 48 m and the difference between their areas is 4 m$^2$. The breadth of the rectangle is:
A. 10 m     B. 12 m     C. 14 m     D. None of these

**9.** Area of a square with side $x$ is equal to the area of a triangle with base $x$. The altitude of the triangle is:

A. $\dfrac{x}{2}$     B. $x$     C. $2x$     D. $4x$

**10.** If only the length of the rectangular plot is reduced to $\dfrac{2}{3}$rd of its original length, the ratio of original area to reduced area is:
A. 2 : 3     B. 3 : 2     C. 1 : 2     D. None of these

**11.** If the radius of a circle be reduced by 50%, its area is reduced by:
A. 25%     B. 50%     C. 75%     D. 100%

**12.** The perimeter of a rhombus is 52 m while its longer diagonal is 24 m. Its other diagonal is:
A. 5 m     B. 10 m     C. 20 m     D. 28 m

**13.** The circumference of a circle is 352 m, then its area in m$^2$ is:
A. 9856     B. 8956     C. 6589     D. 5986

**14.** A wheel makes 100 revolutions in covering a distance of 88 km. The diameter of the wheel is:

A. 240 m  B. 400 m  C. 280 m  D. 140 m

**15.** If the diameter of a circle is increased by 100%, its area is increased by:

A. 100%  B. 200%  C. 300%  D. 400%

**16.** The area of a sector of a circle of radius 5 cm formed by an arc of length 3.5 cm, is:

A. 35 cm$^2$  B. 17.5 cm$^2$  C. 8.75 cm$^2$  D. 55 cm$^2$

**17.** A circular wire of radius 42 cm is cut and bent in the form of a rectangle whose sides are in the ratio 6 : 5. The smaller side of the rectangle is:

A. 30 cm  B. 60 cm  C. 72 cm  D. 132 cm

**18.** The length of a minute hand on a wall clock is 7 cm. The area swept by the minute hand in 30 minutes is:

A. 147 cm$^2$  B. 210 cm$^2$  C. 154 cm$^2$  D. 77 cm$^2$

**19.** A circle and a square have same area. The ratio of the side of the square and the radius of the circle is:

A. $\sqrt{\pi} : 1$  B. $1 : \sqrt{\pi}$  C. $1 : \pi$  D. $\pi : 1$

**20.** The dimensions of the floor of a rectangular hall are 4 m $\times$ 3 m. The floor of the hall is to be tiled fully with 8 cm $\times$ 6 cm rectangular tiles without breaking tiles to smaller sizes. The number of tiles required is:

A. 4800  B. 2600  C. 2500  D. 2400

**21.** The surface area of a cube is 726 m$^2$. The volume of cube is:

A. 1300 m$^3$  B. 1331 m$^3$  C. 1452 m$^3$  D. 1542 m$^3$

**22.** Sum of the length, width and depth of a cuboid is $s$ and its diagonal is $d$. Its surface area is:

A. $s^2$  B. $d^2$  C. $s^2 - d^2$  D. $s^2 + d^2$

**23.** A wooden box of dimensions 8 m $\times$ 7 m $\times$ 6 m is to carry rectangular boxes of dimensions 8 cm $\times$ 7 cm $\times$ 6 cm. The maximum number of boxes that can be carried in 1 wooden box is:

A. 1200000  B. 1000000  C. 9800000  D. 7500000

**24.** The length of the longest rod that can be placed in a room 30 m long, 24 m broad and 18 m high is:

A. 30 m  B. $15\sqrt{2}$ m  C. 60 m  D. $30\sqrt{2}$ m

**25.** If the volume of two cubes are in the ratio 8 : 1, the ratio of their edges is:

A. 8 : 1  B. $2\sqrt{2} : 1$  C. 2 : 1  D. None of these

**26.** A metal sheet 27 cm long 8 cm broad and 1 cm thick is melted into a cube. The difference between the surface areas of two solids will be:
    A. 284 cm$^2$        B. 296 cm$^2$        C. 286 cm$^2$    D. 300 cm$^2$

**27.** If each edge of a cube is increased by 50%, the percentage increase in surface area is:
    A. 50%        B. 75%        C. 100%    D. 125%

**28.** If a right circular cone of vertical height 24 cm has a volume of 1232 cm$^3$, then the area of its curved surface in cm$^2$ is:
    A. 1254        B. 704        C. 550    D. 154

**29.** Two cubes have volumes in the ratio 1 : 27. The ratio of their surface areas is:
    A. 1 : 3        B. 1 : 8        C. 1 : 9    D. 1 : 18

**30.** If the volumes of two cones are in the ratio 1 : 4 and their diameters are in the ratio 4 : 5, then the ratio of their heights is:
    A. 1 : 5        B. 5 : 4        C. 5 : 16    D. 25 : 64

**31.** The radius of a wire is decreased to one-third. If volumes remains the same, length will increase:
    A. 1 time        B. 3 times        C. 6 times    D. 9 times

**32.** A cylindrical piece of metal of radius 2 cm and height 6 cm is shaped into a cone of same radius. The height of cone is:
    A. 18 cm        B. 14 cm        C. 12 cm    D. 8 cm

**33.** If 1 cubic cm of cast iron weight 21 g then the weight of a cast iron pipe of length 1 m with a bore of 3 cm and in which the thickness of the metal is 1 cm, is:
    A. 21 kg        B. 24.2 kg        C. 26.4 kg    D. 18.6 kg

**34.** The number of solid spheres, each of diameter 6 cm, that could be moulded to form a solid metal cylinder of height 45 cm and diameter 4 cms, is:
    A. 3        B. 4        C. 5    D. 6

**35.** A right cylinder and a right circular cone have the same radius and the same volume. The ratio of the height of the cylinder to that of the cone is:
    A. 3 : 5        B. 2 : 5        C. 3 : 1    D. 1 : 3

**36.** If a solid sphere of radius 10 cm is moulded into 8 spherical solid balls of equal radius, then surface area of each ball (in cm$^2$) is:
    A. 100$\pi$        B. 75$\pi$        C. 60$\pi$    D. 50$\pi$

**37.** The radii of two spheres are in the ratio 1 : 2. The ratio of their surface areas, is:
    A. 1 : 2        B. 1 : 4        C. 1 : $\sqrt{2}$    D. 3 : 8

**38.** The radii of two cylinders are in the ratio 2 : 3 and their heights are in the ratio 5 : 3, then their volumes will be in ratio:
A. 4 : 9          B. 27 : 20          C. 20 : 27          D. 9 : 4

**39.** The volume of a hemisphere is 19404 cm$^3$. The total surface area is:
A. 2772 cm$^2$          B. 4158 cm$^2$          C. 5544 cm$^2$          D. 1386 cm$^2$

**40.** If the volume and surface area of a sphere are numerically the same, then its radius is:
A. 1 unit          B. 2 units          C. 3 units          D. 4 units

**41.** A rectangle measures 50 cm × 25 cm. Its area is
A. 1150 sq. cm.          B. 1250 sq. cm.          C. 1275 sq. cm. D. 1280 sq. cm.

**42.** A field is in the form of a square whose perimeter is 580 m. Area of this field is
A. 21025 sq. m.                              B. 20225 sq. m.
C. 30025 sq. m.                              D. 19975 sq. m.

**43.** Find the area of the square whose each side measures 20 cm.
A. 300 sq. cm.                              B. 380 sq. cm.
C. 360 sq. cm.                              D. 400 sq. m.

**44.** Area of a circle is 154 sq. cm. Its circumference will be
A. 44 cm          B. 48 cm          C. 54 cm          D. 68 cm

**45.** The base and the height of a triangle is 8 cm and 10 cm respectively. Its area will be
A. 40 sq. cm.          B. 20 sq. cm.          C. 49 sq. cm.          D. 64 sq. cm.

**46.** A solid in the form of a cuboid is 4 cm × 3 cm × 2 cm. Its volume will be
A. 20 cu cm          B. 22 cu cm          C. 28 cu cm          D. 24 cu cm

**47.** A reservoir is 3 m long, 2 m wide and 1 m deep. Its capacity in litres is
A. 8000 litres                              B. 10000 litres
C. 6500 litres                              D. 6000 litres

**48.** Surface area of a cube is 1014 sq. cm. Its volume will be
A. 2197 cu cm                              B. 2297 cu cm
C. 2179 cu cm                              D. 2117 cu cm

**49.** If the volumes of two cubical blocks are in the ratio of 8 : 1, what will be the ratio of their edges?
A. 1 : 2          B. 2 : 1          C. 4 : 1          D. 2 : 3

**50.** Two spheres have their surface areas in the ratio 9 : 16. Their volumes are in the ratio of
A. 64 : 27          B. 27 : 64          C. 16 : 27          D. 11 : 27

## ANSWERS

| 1 | 2 | 3 | 4 | 5 | 6 | 7 | 8 | 9 | 10 |
|---|---|---|---|---|---|---|---|---|---|
| D | C | A | C | A | C | B | A | C | B |

| 11 | 12 | 13 | 14 | 15 | 16 | 17 | 18 | 19 | 20 |
|----|----|----|----|----|----|----|----|----|----|
| C | B | A | C | C | C | B | D | A | C |

| 21 | 22 | 23 | 24 | 25 | 26 | 27 | 28 | 29 | 30 |
|----|----|----|----|----|----|----|----|----|----|
| B | C | B | D | C | C | D | C | C | D |

| 31 | 32 | 33 | 34 | 35 | 36 | 37 | 38 | 39 | 40 |
|----|----|----|----|----|----|----|----|----|----|
| D | A | C | C | D | A | B | C | B | C |

| 41 | 42 | 43 | 44 | 45 | 46 | 47 | 48 | 49 | 50 |
|----|----|----|----|----|----|----|----|----|----|
| B | A | D | A | A | D | D | A | B | B |

## EXPLANATORY ANSWERS

**1.** Area of the plot = $3 \times 1200 = 3600$ m$^2$
Let breadth be $x$ m. Then length = $4x$ m
According to the question,
$4x \times x = 3600 \Rightarrow x^2 = 900 \Rightarrow x = 30$
Hence, length of the plot = $4 \times 30 = 120$ m.

**4.** Length of the carpet = $\dfrac{8 \times 6}{2} = 24$ m.

**6.** Breadth $= \sqrt{(20)^2 - (16)^2}$
$= \sqrt{400 - 256} = \sqrt{144} = 12$ m.

**12.** Side of rhombus = $\dfrac{52}{4} = 13$ m

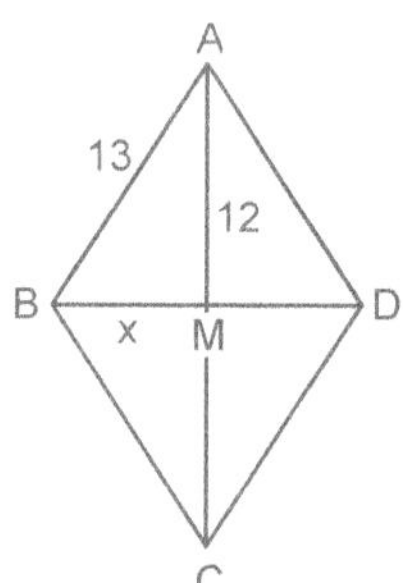


In $\triangle ABM$,
$$x^2 = (13)^2 - (12)^2$$
$$x^2 = 169 - 144$$
$$x^2 = 25$$
$\Rightarrow \qquad x = 5$ m
$\therefore$ Another diagonal = $2 \times 5 = 10$ m

**16.** Area of sector $= \left( \dfrac{1}{2} \times r^2 \times \dfrac{\text{arc}}{r} \right)$

$= \dfrac{1}{2} \times 5 \times 3.5 = 8.75$ cm$^2$

**21.** Surface area of cube = $6a^2$

$$6a^2 = 726 \Rightarrow a^2 = \frac{726}{6} = 121 \Rightarrow a = 11 \text{ m}$$

Volume of cube = $a^3 = 11 \times 11 \times 11 = 1331 \text{ m}^3$

**23.** Number of boxes = $\dfrac{800 \times 700 \times 600}{8 \times 7 \times 6} = 1000000$

**25.** Let their volumes be $8x^3$ and $x^3$.
Then, their sides are $2x$ and $x$
$\therefore$ Ratio of their edges = $2 : 1$

**38.** Let the radii of cylinders are $2r$ and $3r$ and heights are $5x$ and $3x$

$$\text{Ratio of their volumes} = \frac{\pi(2r)^2 \times 5x}{\pi(3r)^2 \times 3x} = \frac{4r^2 \times 5}{9r^2 \times 3} = \frac{20}{27}$$

**39.** Volume of hemisphere = 19404

$$\Rightarrow \qquad \frac{2}{3}\pi r^3 = 19404 \Rightarrow \frac{2}{3} \times \frac{22}{7} r^3 = 19404$$

$$\Rightarrow \qquad r^3 = \frac{3 \times 19404 \times 7}{2 \times 22} = 9261$$

$$\Rightarrow \qquad r = 21 \text{ cm}$$

$$\text{Surface area} = 3\pi r^2 = 3 \times \frac{22}{7} \times 21 \times 21 = 4158 \text{ cm}^2$$

**40.** $\dfrac{4}{3}\pi r^3 = 4\pi r^2$

$$\Rightarrow \frac{r}{3} = 1 \Rightarrow r = 3 \text{ units}$$

**41.** Area of the rectangle = $l \times b = 50 \times 25 = 1250$ sq. cm

**42.** Here, $4 \times$ side = $580 \Rightarrow$ side = $\dfrac{580}{4} = 145$ m

$\therefore$ Area $=$ (side)$^2 = (145)^2 = 21025$ sq. m.

**43.** Area of the square = (side)$^2 = (20)^2 = 400$ sq. cm.

**44.** Area of the circle = $\pi r^2 \Rightarrow \pi r^2 = 154 \Rightarrow r^2 = \dfrac{154 \times 7}{22} \Rightarrow r = 7 \text{ cm}$

$\therefore$ Circumference of the circle = $2\pi r = 2 \times \dfrac{22}{7} \times 7 = 44$ cm.

**45.** Area of the triangle $= \dfrac{1}{2} \times 8 \times 10 = 40$ sq. cm.

**46.** Volume of the cuboid $= l \times b \times h = 4 \times 3 \times 2 = 24$ cu. cm.

**47.** Volume of the reservoir $= l \times b \times h = 3 \times 2 \times 1 = 6$ cu. m

($\because$ 1 cu m = 1000 litre)

$\therefore$ Capacity of the reservoir $= 6 \times 1000 = 6000$ litre.

**48.** Here, $6 \times (\text{side})^2 = 1014 \Rightarrow (\text{side})^2 = \dfrac{1014}{6} = 169$

$\therefore$ side $= \sqrt{169} = 13$ cm

Hence, Volume of the cube $= (\text{side})^3 = (13)^3 = 2197$ cu cm.

**49.** Here, $a_1^3 : a_2^3 = 8 : 1$

$\therefore \left(\dfrac{a_1}{a_2}\right)^3 = \left(\dfrac{2}{1}\right)^3 \Rightarrow a_1 : a_2 = 2 : 1$

Therefore, ratio of their edges $= 2 : 1$.

**50.** Here, $4\pi r_1^2 : 4\pi r_2^2 = 9 : 16 \Rightarrow r_1^2 : r_2^2 = 9 : 16$

$\Rightarrow \left(\dfrac{r_1}{r_2}\right)^2 = \left(\dfrac{3}{4}\right)^2 \Rightarrow r_1 : r_2 = 3 : 4$

$\Rightarrow \dfrac{r_1^3}{r_2^3} = \dfrac{27}{64}$

$\Rightarrow r_1^3 : r_2^3 = 27 : 64.$

Therefore, ratio of their volumes $= \dfrac{4}{3}\pi r_1^3 : \dfrac{4}{3}\pi r_2^3 = r_1^3 : r_2^3$

$= 27 : 64$

# ALGEBRA

## 13 — Set Theory

**Set :** It is a well defined collection of objects. The objects which belong to a set are called its member or elements.

**Method of Representing a Set**

(a) Tabular Form or the Roster Form

(b) Set Builder Form or Rule Method

**Tabular Form :** In this form all the elements of the set are separated by commas and enclosed between brackets { }, *e.g.,* : N = {1, 2, 3, 4, ............}.

**Rule Method :** In this form, the elements of the set are represented in terms of one or several characteristic properties, *e.g.,* N = $\{x \mid x \in N\}$

**Empty or Null Set :** The set which contains no element is called the empty set. The symbols for the empty set is $\phi$, *e.g.,* $\phi$ = { }.

The set of odd numbers is divisible by 2.

**Singleton :** A set containing only one element is called a singleton, *e.g.,* {1}, {$a$} etc.

**Equal Sets :** Two sets A ana B are said to be equal if both have the same elements. e.g., A = {$a, b, c, d$} and B = {$b, c, a, d$}, Then A = B.

**Equivalent Sets :** Two sets A and B are said to be equivalent if we can find a one-to-one correspondence between the element of the two sets.

*e.g.,* A = {1, 2, 3, 4} and {$b, c, a, d$}, Then A ~ B but A ≠ B.

**Note :** Equal sets are always equivalent but vice-versa is not true.

**Finite and Infinite Set :** The set which contains a definite number of element is called a finite set. *e.g.,* The set of days in a week. The set which contains an infinite number of element is called an infinite set. *e.g.,* The set of natural numbers.

**Disjoint Sets :** Two sets A and B are said to be disjoint if they do not have any elements in common. *e.g.,* A = {1, 2, 3}, B = {4, 5, 6} are disjoint set.

**Subsets :** If every member of set A is also in set B then A is said to be a subset of B and B is called a super set A. e.g., : A = {1, 2, 3}, B = {1, 2, 3, 4, 5, 6} ∴ A ⊂ B.

**Power Set :** The set of all the subset of a set is called the power set. If *n* is the number of element of a set A then the number of subset of A, *i.e.,* the no. of elements of $P(A) = 2^n$. A = {1, 2, 3} ∴ $P(A) = 2^3 = 8$.

**Universal Set :** The largest set containing every set is called universal set. It is denoted by U.

**Union of Sets :** The union of two sets A and B is the set of all elements of A with all the elements of B. It is denoted by A ∪ B.

*e.g.,* A = {1, 2, 3}, B = {1, 3, 4}, ∴ A ∪ B = {1, 2, 3, 4}

**Intersection of Sets :** The intersection of two sets is the set of all elements which are in A and also in B. It is written as A ∩ B.

e.g., A = {1, 2, 3}, B = {2, 3, 4}, ∴ A ∩ B = {2, 3}.

**Complement of a Set :** The set of three elements of universal set (U) which are not the element of A is called the complement of A and is denoted by $A^1$ of $A^c$. e.g., If U = {1, 2, 3, 4, 5, 6} and A = {1, 3, 5}, $A^1$ = {2, 4, 6}.

**Complement of a Union and Intersection of Two Sets :**

(a) $(A \cup B)^1 = A^1 \cap B^1$      (b) $(A \cap B)^1 = A^1 \cup B^1$.

**Important Result**

(a) $n(A \cup B) = n(A) + n(B)$, If A and B are disjoint set.

(b) $n(A \cup B) = n(A) + n(B) - n(A \cap B)$.

## MULTIPLE CHOICE QUESTIONS

1. Let $a$ = {$x : x$ is a multiple of 3} and B = {$x : x$ is a multiple of 5}. Then A ∩ B is given by
   A. {3, 6, 9, ...}            B. {5, 10, 15, 20, ...}
   C. {15, 30, 45, ...}         D. None of these

2. If X and Y are two sets, then X ∪ (Y ∩ X)' equals
   A. X           B. Y           C. φ           D. None of these

3. Let A = {1, 2, 3, 4, 5}, B = 2, 3, 6, 7}. Then the number of elements in (A × B) ∩ (B × A) is
   A. 18          B. 6          C. 4          D. 0

4. In a group of 52 persons, 16 drink tea but not coffee and 33 drink tea. It is assumed that every person takes tea or coffee. Then the number of persons who take coffee but not tea is given by
   A. 19                  B. 36
   C. Cannot be found by the given data   D. None of these

5. A survey of 100 Indians shows that 60 like cheese whereas 70 like apples. let $n$ be the number of persons who like both cheese and apple. Then
   A. $n = 30$      B. $n = 60$      C. $n = 10$      D. None of these

6. Let $n(U) = 700, n(A) = 200, n(B) = 300, n(A \cap B) = 100$. Then $n(A' \cap B') =$
   A. 400          B. 600          C. 300          D. None of these

**7.** Two finite sets have $m$ and $n$ elements. The total number of subsets of the first set is 56 more than the total number of subsets of the second set. The values of $m$ and $n$ are
   A. 7, 6  B. 6, 3  C. 5, 1  D. 8, 7

**8.** Let $A = \{1, 2, 3\}$, $B = \{1, 3, 5\}$. A relation $R : A \to B$ is defined by $R = \{(1, 3), (1, 5), (2, 1)\}$. Then $R^{-1}$ is  defined by
   A. $\{(1, 2), (3, 1), (1, 3), (1, 5)\}$  B. $\{(1, 2), (3, 1), (2, 1)\}$
   C. $\{(1, 2), (5, 1), (3, 1)\}$  D. None of these

**9.** The relation R is defined on the set of natural numbers as $\{(a, b): a = 2b\}$. Then $R^{-1}$ is given by
   A. $\{(2, 1), (4, 2), (6, 3)...\}$  B. $\{(1, 2), (2, 4), (3, 6)...\}$
   C. $R^{-1}$ is not defined  D. None of these

**10.** The relation R defined on the set of natural numbers as $\{(a, b) : a$ differs from $b$ by $3\}$, is given by
   A. $\{(1, 4), (2, 5), (3, 6), ...\}$  B. $\{(4, 1), (5, 2), (6, 3), ...\}$
   C. $\{(1, 3), (2, 6), (3, 9), ...\}$  D. None of these

**11.** A relation R defined on the set of integers by $R = \{(a, b): a$ divides $b\}$. Then R is
   A. reflexive  B. symmetric  C. transitive  D. equivalence

**12.** Given two finite sets A and B such that $n(A) = 2$, $n(B) = 3$. Then total number of relations from A to B is
   A. 4  B. 8  C. 64  D. None of these

**13.** The solution set of $8x \equiv 6 \pmod{14}$, $x \in Z$, are
   A. $[8] \cup [6]$  B. $[8] \cup [14]$
   C. $[6] \cup [13]$  D. $[8] \cup [6] \cup [13]$

**14.** Let $n(A) = n$. Then the number of all relations on A is
   A. $2^n$  B. $2^{(n)!}$  C. $2^{n^2}$  D. None of these

**15.** If A and B be two subsets of a set U, then which of the following is false?
   A. $A \cap B = A$  B. $A \cap U = A$  C. $A \cap B \in A$  D. $B \cup A \cap B$

**16.** It is given that $n(P(S)) = 64$, where $P(S)$ is power set of S, then $n(S)$ is:
   A. 2  B. 4  C. 8  D. 6

**17.** If A and B are two sets, then $A \cup (A \cap B)$ is:
   A. $A \cap B$  B. A  C. B  D. none of these

**18.** If A and B are two subsets of universal set U, then $A - B$ is equal to:
   A. $A \cap B$  B. $A \cap B'$  C. $A' \cap B$  D. $A' \cap B'$

**19.** If $P, Q \subset U$, then $P \cap (P \cup Q)$; is equal to:
   A. P  B. Q  C. f  D. none of these

**20.** In a town of 840 persons, 450 persons read Hindi, 300 read English and 200 read both. The number of persons who read neither, is:
A. 210      B. 290      C. 180      D. 260

**21.** Let A and B have 2 and 5 elements respectively. What can be the maximum and minimum number of elements in $A \cap B$?
A. 5 and 2      B. 5 and 0      C. 25 and 4      D. 2 and 0

**22.** If $A = \{a, c, d, g\}$ and $B = \{b, d, j, k\}$, then which of the following is true?
A. $A \cap B$ is a null set      B. A and B are disjoint sets
C. $A \cap B$ is a singleton set      D. All of the above are true

**23.** If A and B are subsets of a set X, then $[A \cap (X - B)] \cup B$ is equal to:
A. $A \cup B$      B. $A \cap B$      C. A      D. B

**24.** If $A = \{1, 2\}$, $B = \{2, 5\}$, $C = \{5, 7\}$ then
$(A \times B) \cap (A \times C)$ is equal to:
A. $\{(2, 5), (1, 5)\}$      B. $\{(2, 2), (5, 5)\}$
C. $\{(2, 7), (1, 5)\}$      D. none of these

**25.** Let $A = \{a, b, c, d, \}$, which one of the following subsets of $A \times A$ is not a function on A?
A. $\{(a, d), (d, a), (a, b), (d, c)\}$      B. $\{(d, a), (a, b), (b, c), (c, d)\}$
C. $\{(a, d), (b, a), (c, b), (d, c)\}$      D. $\{(d, a), (a, d), (b, a), (c, c)\}$

## ANSWERS

| 1 | 2 | 3 | 4 | 5 | 6 | 7 | 8 | 9 | 10 |
|---|---|---|---|---|---|---|---|---|----|
| C | C | C | A | A | C | B | C | B | D |

| 11 | 12 | 13 | 14 | 15 | 16 | 17 | 18 | 19 | 20 |
|----|----|----|----|----|----|----|----|----|----|
| C | C | C | C | A | D | B | B | C | B |

| 21 | 22 | 23 | 24 | 25 |
|----|----|----|----|----|
| D | C | A | A | A |

## EXPLANATORY ANSWERS

**2.** $X \cap (Y \cup X)'$
$\qquad = X \cap (Y' \cap X')$
$\qquad = (X \cap X') \cap Y'$
$\qquad = \phi \cap X' = \phi$

**5.** Let A = Apples, C ≡ Cheese
Then $n(A \cap C) \leq n(A)$
$n(A \cap C) \leq n(C)$
$\Rightarrow n(A \cap C) \leq 60$
Also $n(A \cap C) = n(A) + n(C) - n(A \cup C)$

$\geq 70 + 60 - 100 = 30$

$\therefore 30 \leq n(A \cap C) \leq 60$

**6.** $n(A' \cap B') = n(A \cup B)'$

$= 700 - n(A \cup B)$

$= 700 - [200 + 300 - 100]$

$= 300$

**7.** $2^m = 2^n + 56$

which is satisfied when $m = 6$, $n = 3$.

**8.** $(x, y) \in R \Leftrightarrow (y, x) \in R^{-1}$,

$\therefore R^{-1} = \{(3, 1), (5, 1), (1, 2)\}$

**9.** $R = \{(2, 1), (4, 2), (6, 3), ...\}$

so $R^{-1} = \{(1, 2), (2, 4), (3, 6), ...\}$

**10.** $R = \{(a, b): a, b \in N, A \sim b = 3\}$

$= \{(n, n + 3), (n + 3, n) : n \in N\}$

$= \{(1, 4), (4, 1), (2, 5), (5, 2), ...\}$

**23.** See the figures

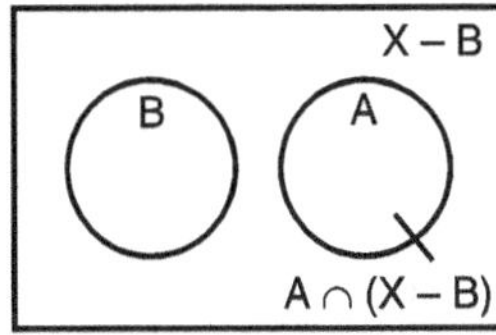

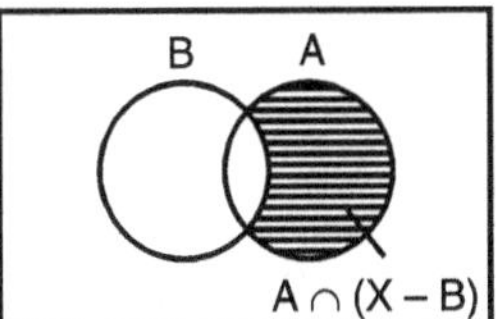


In both cases

**24.** $A \times B = \{(1, 2) (1, 5), (2, 2), (2, 5)\}$

$A \times C = \{(1, 5), (1, 7), (2, 5), (2, 7)\}$

$\therefore (A \times B) \cap (A \times C) = \{(1, 5), (2, 5)\}$

**14**

# Simplification & Factorization

A function $p(x)$ defined by $p(x) = a_0 + a_1 x + a_2 x^2 + \ldots + a_n x^n$ is called a polynomial function in $x$.

Where, $a_0, a_1 \ldots a_n$ are real numbers and called co-efficient of the polynomial.

**Factor Theorem:** If $f(x)$ is completely divisible by $(x - a)$, then $f(a) = 0$ Thus, $(x - a)$ is a factor of $f(x)$.

## Some Important Formulae

1. $(a + b)^2 = a^2 + 2ab + b^2$

2. $(a - b)^2 = a^2 - 2ab + b^2$

3. $a^2 - b^2 = (a + b)(a - b)$

4. $a^2 + b^2 = (a + b)^2 - 2ab$

5. $(a + b + c)^2 = a^2 + b^2 + c^2 + 2ab + 2bc + 2ca$

6. $(a + b)^3 = a^3 + 3a^2 b + 3ab^2 + b^3$
$$= a^3 + b^3 + 3ab(a + b)$$

7. $(a - b)^3 = a^3 - 3a^2 b + 3ab^2 - b^3$
$$= a^3 - b^3 - 3ab(a - b)$$

8. $a^3 + b^3 = (a + b)(a^2 - ab + b^2)$ [for factorisation]

    $a^3 + b^3 = (a + b)^3 - 3ab(a + b)$ [for evaluation when $a+b$ and $ab$ are given]

9. $a^3 - b^3 = (a - b)(a^2 + ab + b^2)$ [for factorisation]

    $a^3 - b^3 = (a - b)^3 + 3ab(a - b)$ [for evaluation]

10. If $a + b + c = 0$, then $a^3 + b^3 + c^3 = 3abc$

## MULTIPLE CHOICE QUESTIONS

1. If $\left( x + \dfrac{1}{x} \right) = 5,$ then $\left( x^2 + \dfrac{1}{x^2} \right)$ is equal to:

    A. 20      B. 24      C. 27      D. 23

2. If $\left( x + \dfrac{1}{x} \right) = 4,$ then $\left( x^4 + \dfrac{1}{x^4} \right)$ is equal to:

    A. 190      B. 180      C. 193      D. 194

**3.** If $\left(x^2 + \dfrac{1}{x^2}\right) = 66,$ then $\left(x - \dfrac{1}{x}\right)$ is equal to:

    A. 6            B. 12            C. 8            D. 9

**4.** If $a + b = 8,$ $a - b = 4,$ then $a^2 + b^2$ is equal to:
    A. 20            B. 40            C. 10            D. 30

**5.** If $x^2 + 5x - 2k,$ is exactly divisible by $(x - 1),$ then the value of $k$ is:
    A. 1            B. 2            C. 3            D. 4

**6.** If $(x - 2),$ is a factor of $x^2 + 4x - 2k,$ then the value of $k$ is:
    A. 1            B. 3            C. 4            D. 6

**7.** If $x^{100} + 2x^{99} + k,$ is divisible by $(x + 1),$ then the value of $k$ is:
    A. 1            B. 4            C. 3            D. 0

**8.** Value of $k$ for which $(x - 2)$ is a factor of $(x^2 - kx + 2)$ is:
    A. 2            B. 3            C. 4            D. 5

**9.** If $x - \dfrac{1}{x} = 3.$ The value of $x^2 + \dfrac{1}{x^2}$ is :

    A. 2            B. 12            C. 10            D. 11

**10.** If $x - \dfrac{1}{x} = 2,$ then $x^3 - \dfrac{1}{x^3}$ is :

    A. 14            B. 16            C. 15            D. 12

**11.** If $x - 2$ is a factor of $x^2 + 3ax - 2a,$ then $a$ is equal to
    A. 2            B. –2            C. 1            D. –1

**12.** The value of $k$ for which $x - 1$ is a factor of $4x^3 + 3x^2 - 4x + k,$ is :
    A. 3            B. 1            C. –2            D. –3

**13.** If $x - a$ is a factor of $x^3 - 3x^2a + 2a^2x + b,$ then the value of $b$ is :
    A. 0            B. 2            C. 1            D. 3

**14.** If $x^{140} + 2x^{151} + k$ is divisible by $x + 1,$ then the value of $k$ is :
    A. 1            B. –3            C. 2            D. –2

**15.** If $x + 2$ and $x - 1$ are the factors of $x^3 + 10x^2 + mx + n,$ then the values of $m$ and $n$ are respectively :
    A. 5 and –3       B. 17 and –8     C. 7 and –18    D. 23 and –19

**16.** Let $f(x)$ be a polynomial such that $f\left(-\dfrac{1}{2}\right) = 0,$ then a factor of $f(x)$ is :

    A. $2x - 1$         B. $2x + 1$         C. $x - 1$         D. $x + 1$

**17.** When $x^3 - 2x^2 + ax - b$ is divided by $x^2 - 2x - 3$, the remainder is $x - 6$. The values of $a$ and $b$ are respectively :
A. –2, –6      B. 2 and –6      C. –2 and 6      D. 2 and 6

**18.** One factor of $x^4 + x^2 - 20$ is $x^2 + 5$. The other factor is :
A. $x^2 - 4$      B. $x - 4$      C. $x^2 - 5$      D. $x + 2$

**19.** If $(x - 1)$ is a factor of polynomial $f(x)$ but not of $g(x)$, then it must be a factor of :
A. $f(x)\, g(x)$      B. $-f(x) + g(x)$
C. $f(x) - g(x)$      D. $\{f(x) + g(x)\}\, g(x)$

**20.** $(x + 1)$ is a factor of $x^n + 1$ only if :
A. $n$ is an odd integer      B. $n$ is an even integer
C. $n$ is a negative integer      D. $n$ is a positive integer

**21.** If $x^2 + \dfrac{1}{x^2} = 7$, then the values of $x + \dfrac{1}{x}$ is :
A. 2      B. 3      C. 5      D. 6

**22.** If $x + \dfrac{1}{x} = 4$, then the value of $x^3 + \dfrac{1}{x^3}$ is :
A. 52      B. 64      C. 68      D. 76

**23.** The factors of $x^8 + x^4 + 1$ are :
A. $\left(x^4 + 1 - x^2\right), \left(x^2 + 1 + x\right), \left(x^2 + 1 - x\right)$
B. $\left(x^4 + 1 - x^2\right), \left(x^2 - 1 + x\right), \left(x^2 + 1 + x\right)$
C. $\left(x^4 - 1 + x^2\right), \left(x^2 - 1 + x\right), \left(x^2 + 1 + x\right)$
D. $\left(x^4 - 1 + x^2\right), \left(x^2 + 1 - x\right), \left(x^2 + 1 + x\right)$

**24.** The expression $10xy^4 - 10x^4 y$ can be expressed in factors as :
A. $10xy\left(x - y\right)\left(x^2 + xy + y^2\right)$      B. $10xy\left(y - x\right)\left(x^2 - xy + y^2\right)$
C. $10xy\left(y - x\right)\left(x^2 + xy + y^2\right)$      D. None of these

**25.** The algebraic expression $4x^2 + 9y^2 + 25z^2 + 12xy - 30yz - 20zx$ can be factorised as :
A. $\left(2x + 3y + 5z\right)^2$      B. $\left(2x + 3y - 5z\right)^2$
C. $\left(2x - 3y + 5z\right)^2$      D. None of these

**26.** One of the factors of the expressions $x^2 + 5x + 25$ is :

A. $x+5$ 

B. $x-5$

C. $x+\sqrt{5}$ 

D. Cannot be factorised

**27.** If $x+y=8$ and $xy=7$ then the value of $x^3+y^3$ is :

A. 344 

B. 342 

C. 345 

D. 340

**28.** The expression $49x^2 + 64$ when expressed as factors is :

A. $(7x+8)^2$ 

B. $(7x+8)(7x-8)$

C. $(7x-8)^2$ 

D. Cannot be factorised

**29.** $(4x+3y)^2 + (4x-3y)^2$ is equal to :

A. $16x^2 - 9y^2$ 

B. $32x^2 + 18y^2$ 

C. $16x^2 + 9y^2$ 

D. $32x^2 + 9y^2$

**30.** The expression $32x^3 + 108y^3$ can be expressed in factors as :

A. $(4x+3y)(4x^2 - 6xy + 9y^2)$ 

B. $(4x-3y)(4x^2 + 6xy + 9y^2)$

C. $(4x+3y)(4x^2 + 6xy + 9y^2)$ 

D. None of these

## ANSWERS

| 1 | 2 | 3 | 4 | 5 | 6 | 7 | 8 | 9 | 10 |
|---|---|---|---|---|---|---|---|---|----|
| D | D | C | B | C | D | A | B | D | A |

| 11 | 12 | 13 | 14 | 15 | 16 | 17 | 18 | 19 | 20 |
|----|----|----|----|----|----|----|----|----|----|
| D | D | A | A | C | B | C | A | A | A |

| 21 | 22 | 23 | 24 | 25 | 26 | 27 | 28 | 29 | 30 |
|----|----|----|----|----|----|----|----|----|----|
| B | A | A | C | B | D | A | D | B | D |

## EXPLANATORY ANSWERS

**1.** $\because \left(x+\dfrac{1}{x}\right) = 5$

$\therefore x^2 + \dfrac{1}{x^2} = \left(x+\dfrac{1}{x}\right)^2 - 2 = 25 - 2 = 23$

**4.** $\because$ $(a + b)^2 + (a - b)^2 = 2a^2 + 2b^2 = 2(a^2 + b^2)$

$\Rightarrow \qquad (8)^2 + (4)^2 = 2(a^2 + b^2)$

$\qquad\qquad 64 + 16 = 2\,(a^2 + b^2)$

$\Rightarrow \qquad\qquad 80 = 2(a^2 + b^2)$

$\therefore \qquad\qquad a^2 + b^2 = 40$

**8.** $\because$ $x - 2 = 0 \Rightarrow x = 2$

$x^2 - kx + 2 = 0 \Rightarrow 4 - k(2) + 2 = 0$

$6 - 2k = 0 \Rightarrow 2k = 6$

$k = 3.$

**10.** $\because \quad x - \dfrac{1}{x} = 2$

$\therefore \quad x^3 - \dfrac{1}{x^3} = \left(x - \dfrac{1}{x}\right)^3 + 3x \cdot \dfrac{1}{x}\left(x - \dfrac{1}{x}\right)$

$\qquad\qquad = (2)^3 + 3(2) = 8 + 6 = 14.$

**18.** $\because$ One factor of $x^4 + x^2 - 20$ is $x^2 + 5$

$\qquad (x^2 + 5)\,(x^2 - 4) = x^4 + x^2 - 20$

$\therefore$ Other factor $= x^2 - 4.$

**22.** $\because \quad x + \dfrac{1}{x} = 4$

$\therefore \quad x^3 + \dfrac{1}{x^3} = \left(x + \dfrac{1}{x}\right)^3 - 3 \cdot x \cdot \dfrac{1}{x}\left(x + \dfrac{1}{x}\right)$

$\qquad\qquad = (4)^3 - 3(4)$

$\qquad\qquad = 64 - 12 = 52$

**27.** $\because$ $x + y = 8$ and $xy = 7$

$\therefore \quad x^3 + y^3 = (x + y)^3 - 3xy(x + y)$

$\qquad\qquad = (8)^3 - 3(7)(8)$

$\qquad\qquad = 512 - 168 = 344.$

**29.** $(4x + 3y)^2 + (4x - 3y)^2 = 2(4x)^2 + 2(3y)^2$

$\qquad = 32x^2 + 18y^2$

$$[\because\ (a + b)^2 + (a - b)^2 = 2a^2 + 2b^2].$$

# 15

# Linear equation & Quadratic Equation

## The System of Equations

$a_1x + b_1y + c_1 = 0$ and $a_2x + b_2y + c_2 = 0$ may be either unique solution or no solution or infinitely many solutions.

Unique solution is known as consistent or not parallel. No solution is known as inconsistent or parallel, while many solutions are known as coincident or dependent.

(*a*) **For unique solution:** $\dfrac{a_1}{a_2} \neq \dfrac{b_1}{b_2}$

(*b*) **For no solution:** $\dfrac{a_1}{a_2} = \dfrac{b_1}{b_2} \neq \dfrac{c_1}{c_2}$

(*c*) **For many solutions:** $\dfrac{a_1}{a_2} = \dfrac{b_1}{b_2} = \dfrac{c_1}{c_2}$

## Algebraic Methods of Solving Simultaneous Linear Equations in Two Variables

(*a*) Substitution Method
(*b*) Elimination Method
(*c*) Cross Multiplication Method

## Quadratic Equation

**Definition :** A polynomial equation in which the highest power of the unknown variable is two. The general form of a quadratic equation in the variable $x$ is

$$ax^2 + bx + c = 0$$

where, $a$, $b$ and $c$ are constant.

## Solution of a Quadratic Equation

$$x = \frac{-b \pm \sqrt{b^2 - 4ac}}{2a}$$

$b^2 - 4ac = D$ is called discriminant.

(*a*) If $D > 0$ then there are real and distinct roots given by

$$\alpha = \frac{-b+\sqrt{b^2-4ac}}{2a}, \quad \beta = \frac{-b-\sqrt{b^2-4ac}}{2a}$$

(*b*) If $D = 0$, there are real and equal roots

$$\alpha = \beta = \frac{-b}{2a}$$

(*c*) If $D < 0$, there are no real roots.

Sum of the roots

$$\alpha + \beta = \frac{-b}{a}$$

Product of the roots

$$\alpha\beta = \frac{c}{a}$$

**Ex. 1 :** The roots of the equation $6x^2 - 5x - 21 = 0$ are

**Sol.** $\qquad 6x^2 - 14x + 9x - 21 = 0$

$\Rightarrow \qquad 2x(3x - 7) + 3(3x - 7) = 0$

$\Rightarrow \qquad (3x - 7)(2x + 3) = 0$

$\Rightarrow \qquad x = \dfrac{7}{3}, \ x = -\dfrac{3}{2}$

**Ex. 2 :** If $\alpha$ and $\beta$ are the roots of the quadratic equation $3x^2 + 3x + 2 = 0$ then $\alpha^3 + \beta^3 = $ ......

**Sol.** $\qquad a = 3, \ b = 3, \ c = 2$

$\Rightarrow \qquad \alpha + \beta = -1, \ \alpha\beta = \dfrac{2}{3}$

$$\alpha^3 + \beta^3 = (-1)^3 - 3 \times \frac{2}{3} \times (-1)$$

$$= -1 + 2 = 1$$

## MULTIPLE CHOICE QUESTIONS

1. The system of linear equations $2x + 3y = 7$ and $4x + 6y = 10$ has :
   A. no solution
   B. unique solution
   C. infinite solution
   D. no conclusion can be drawn

2. The value of $k$ for which the system of equations $x + 2y + 7 = 0$ and $2x + ky + 14 = 0$ will have infinitely many solutions is :
   A. 2            B. 4            C. 6            D. 8

3. For what value of $\alpha$, the system of equations $\alpha x + 3y = \alpha - 3$ and $12x + \alpha y = \alpha$ will have a unique solution?
   A. $\alpha \neq \pm 6$      B. $\alpha \neq \pm 3$      C. $\alpha \neq \mp 6$      D. None of these

4. For what value of $k$, the system of equations will represent the coincident lines $x + 5y - 7 = 0$ and $4x + 20y + k = 0$?
   A. 28      B. $-28$      C. $-26$      D. None of these

5. A lady has 50 paise and ₹ 1 coins in her purse. If in all, she has 40 coins totally ₹ 25.50 how many of each type of coins does she have?
   A. 26, 11      B. 11, 29      C. 29, 11      D. None of these

6. A father is three times as old as his son. After twelve years his age will be twice as the age of his son. Find their present ages in years.
   A. 12, 26      B. 24, 36      C. 36, 12      D. None of these

7. Ten years ago, father was twelve times as old as his son. Ten years after, he will be twice as old as his son will be. Find their present ages in years.
   A. 12, 36      B. 12, 24      C. 12, 34      D. None of these

8. The present age of a father is 3 years more than three times the age of son. Three years hence father's age will be 10 years more than twice the age of son. Determine their present ages in years.
   A. 10, 33      B. 33, 10      C. 10, 30      D. None of these

9. In a triangle $ABC$, $\angle C = 3\angle B = 2(\angle A + \angle B)$.
   Find three angles in degrees.
   A. $20°, 50°, 120°$             B. $30°, 40°, 120°$
   C. $20°, 40°, 120°$             D. None of these

10. The fraction becomes 2 when 1 is added to both the numerator and the denominator, and it becomes 3 when 1 is subtracted from both the numerator and denominator. The given fraction is :
    A. $\dfrac{7}{3}$      B. $\dfrac{4}{7}$      C. $\dfrac{3}{7}$      D. $\dfrac{7}{4}$

11. In the system of equations $x + y = 13$ and $2x + 3y = 32$, the values of $x$ and $y$ are:
    A. 5 and 6      B. 7 and 8      C. 7 and 6      D. 6 and 7

12. If $y = 4$, find the value of $x$ in the equation $3x + 4y = 25$.
    A. 3      B. 8      C. 5      D. 4

13. The equation whose roots are 5, 9 is :
    A. $x^2 - 5x + 14 = 0$             B. $x^2 - 14x + 14 = 0$
    C. $x^2 - 45x + 14 = 0$            D. $x^2 - 14x + 45 = 0$

**14.** If $\alpha$, $\beta$ be the values of $x$ satisfying the equation $x^2 - px + q = 0$, the value of $\dfrac{1}{\alpha} + \dfrac{1}{\beta}$ is :

   A. $\dfrac{q}{p}$        B. $-\dfrac{p}{q}$        C. $\dfrac{p}{q}$        D. $\dfrac{1}{q}$

**15.** If one of the roots of the equation is $2 + \sqrt{3}$, the other has to be :

   A. $\sqrt{3} - 2$        B. $2$        C. $2 - \sqrt{3}$        D. $\sqrt{3}$

**16.** If $\alpha$, $\beta$ are the roots of $2x^2 - x + 1 = 0$, the value of $\alpha^2 + \beta^2$ is :

   A. $1$        B. $0$        C. $5/4$        D. $-3/4$

**17.** Find the values of '$p$' for which the quadratic equation $px^2 + 4x + 1 = 0$ has real roots.

   A. $p \le 4$        B. $p \ge 6$        C. $p \ge 4$        D. None of these

**18.** Determine '$k$' such that the quadratic equation $x^2 + 7(3 + 2k) - 2x(1 + 3k) = 0$ has equal roots.

   A. $2, -10/9$        B. $3, -10/9$        C. $2, 10/9$        D. None of these

**19.** For what value of '$k$' the equation $(k + 3) x^2 - (5 - k)x + 1 = 0$ has coincident roots?

   A. $1, 13$        B. $1, 12$        C. $3, 13$        D. None of these

**20.** Find the value of '$k$' so that the sum of the roots of equation $3x^2 + (2x + 1) x - k + 5 = 0$ is equal to the product of roots.

   A. $4$        B. $2$        C. $3$        D. $-6$

**21.** Find the value of '$p$' so that equation $4x^2 - 8px + 9 = 0$ has roots whose difference is 4.

   A. $\pm 3$        B. $\pm 2/5$        C. $\pm 5/2$        D. None of these

**22.** Find the value of '$m$' so that the equation $9x^2 - 8mx - 9 = 0$ has one root as the negative of the other.

   A. $0$        B. $1$        C. $2$        D. None of these

**23.** If $\alpha$ and $\beta$ are the roots of $x^2 - 2x - 1 = 0$, find the value of $\alpha^2\beta + \beta^2\alpha$.

   A. $-3$        B. $-2$        C. $2$        D. None of these

**24.** If $a$ and $b$ are the roots of the equation $x^2 - 5x + 6 = 0$, find the value of $(a^2 - b^2)$.

   A. $\pm 3$        B. $\pm 5$        C. $\pm 4$        D. None of these

**25.** For what values of '$p$' for which the quadratic equation $px^2 - 4x + p$ has real linear factors?

   A. $-2 \le p < 3$        B. $-2 \le p \le 2$        C. $-2 \ge p \le 2$        D. None of these

**26.** The numerical difference of the roots of $x^2 - 6x + 6 = 0$ is

    A. 0               B. $\sqrt{6}$           C. $\sqrt{12}$        D. $\sqrt{18}$

**27.** If one root of $5x^2 + 13x + k = 0$ is reciprocal of the other, then $k$ is equal to

    A. 0               B. 5            C. 1/6        D. 6

**28.** If one root of the equation
$x^2 + px + 12 = 0$ is 4, while the equation
$x^2 + px + q = 0$ has equal roots, the value of $q$ is

    A. 49/4         B. 4/49        C. 4        D. None of these

**29.** If $\alpha$ and $\beta$ are the roots of the equation
$ax^2 + bx + c = 0$, then $(1 + \alpha + \alpha^2)(1 + \beta + \beta^2) =$

    A. 0          B. positive      C. negative    D. None of these

**30.** If the roots of $ax^2 + bx + c = 0$ are $\alpha$, $\beta$ and the roots of $Ax^2 + bx + C = 0$ are
$\alpha - k$, $\beta - k$ then $(B^2 - 4AC)/(b^2 - 4ac)$ is equal to

    A. 0          B. 1         C. $(A/a)^2$    D. $(a/A)^2$

## ANSWERS

| 1 | 2 | 3 | 4 | 5 | 6 | 7 | 8 | 9 | 10 |
|---|---|---|---|---|---|---|---|---|---|
| A | B | A | B | C | A | C | A | C | A |

| 11 | 12 | 13 | 14 | 15 | 16 | 17 | 18 | 19 | 20 |
|----|----|----|----|----|----|----|----|----|----|
| C | A | D | C | C | D | A | A | A | D |

| 21 | 22 | 23 | 24 | 25 | 26 | 27 | 28 | 29 | 30 |
|----|----|----|----|----|----|----|----|----|----|
| C | A | B | B | B | C | B | A | B | C |

## EXPLANATORY ANSWERS

**3.** Since, the given equations have unique solution.

$$\therefore \quad \frac{a_1}{a_2} \neq \frac{b_1}{b_2}$$

$$\frac{\alpha}{12} \neq \frac{3}{\alpha} \Rightarrow \alpha^2 \neq 36 \Rightarrow \alpha \neq \pm 6$$

**4.** Since, the given set of equations represent coincident lines.

$$\text{then, } \frac{1}{4} = \frac{5}{20} = \frac{-7}{K} \Rightarrow K = -28$$

**12.** $3x + 4y = 25$

$\Rightarrow \quad 3x + 4 \times 4 = 25 \quad (\because y = 4)$

or $\qquad 3x + 16 = 25 \Rightarrow 3x = 25 - 16$

$\Rightarrow \qquad 3x = 9 \Rightarrow x = 9/3 = 3$

**13.** Roots are 5 and 9

Sum of the roots $= 5 + 9 = 14$

Product of roots $= 5 \times 9 = 45$

$\therefore x^2 -$ Sum of roots $(x) +$ Product of roots $= 0$

$\Rightarrow x^2 - 14x + 45 = 0$

**14.** $\alpha + \beta = p, \quad \alpha\beta = q$

$$\therefore \frac{1}{\alpha} + \frac{1}{\beta} = \frac{\alpha+\beta}{\alpha\beta} = \frac{p}{q}$$

**17.** For real roots $D \geq 0$

$$\Rightarrow (4)^2 - 4.p.1 \geq 0 \qquad\qquad \Rightarrow 16 \geq 4p$$

$$\Rightarrow 4p \leq 16 \qquad\qquad \Rightarrow p \leq 4$$

**20.** $\alpha + \beta = \alpha\beta$

$$\frac{-(2k+1)}{3} = \frac{-k+5}{3}$$

$-2k-1 = -k+5 \qquad k = -6$

**23.** Here, $\qquad \alpha + \beta = 2, \alpha\beta = -1$

Now, $\quad \alpha^2\beta + \alpha\beta^2 = \alpha\beta(\alpha + \beta)$

$$= -1(2) = -2$$

**26.** $\alpha + \beta = 6, \alpha\beta = 6$

$\therefore \alpha - \beta = \sqrt{[(\alpha + \beta)^2 - 4\alpha\beta]} = \sqrt{(12)}$

**27.** Let $\alpha$ and $1/\alpha$ be the roots.

$\therefore$ Product of roots $= \alpha(1/\alpha) = 1$

$\qquad = k/5 \Rightarrow k = 5$

**28.** $\because$ One root of equation

$x^2 + px + 12 = 0$ is 4

$\therefore 16 + 4p + 12 = 0 \Rightarrow p = -7$

If equation $x^2 + px + q = 0$ has equal roots,

then $p^2 - 4q = 0 \Rightarrow q = p^2/4 = 49/4$

## Definition

The logarithm of any number to a given base is the index of the power to which the base must be raised in order to equal the given number.

If $b$ be any number and $p$ and N two other numbers such that $b^p = $ N, then $p$ is called the logarithm of N to the base $b$ and is written as $\log_b$ N. Thus the exponential identity $b^p = $ N is equivalent to logarithmic identity $\log_b$ N $= p$.

| *Exponential* | *Logarithmic* |
|---|---|
| $b^p = n$ | $\log_b N = p$ |
| $3^2 = 9$ | $\log_3 9 = 2$ |
| $4^{-2} = \dfrac{1}{16}$ | $\log_4\left(\dfrac{1}{16}\right) = -2$ |
| $4^{-2} = 0.0625$ | $\log_4 (0.0625) = -2$ |
| $64^{1/3} = 4$ | $\log_{64}(4) = \dfrac{1}{3}$ |

## Properties of Logarithms:

(i) $a^{\log_a^x} = x;\ a \neq 0, \pm 1, x > 0.$

(ii) $a^{\log_b^x} = x^{\log_b^a};\ a > 0, b > 0, \neq 1, x > 0.$

(iii) $\log_a a = 1,\ \log_a 1 = 0;\ a > 0, \neq 1.$

(iv) $\log_a x = \dfrac{1}{\log_x a};\ x, a > 0, \neq 1.$

(v) $\log_a x = \log_b x.\log_a b = \dfrac{\log_b x}{\log_b a};\ a, b > 0, \neq 1, x > 0.$

(vi) For $x, y > 0, a > 0, \neq 1$

    (a) $\log_a (x.y) = \log_a x + \log_a y$

    (b) $\log_a (x/y) = \log_a x - \log_a y$

    (c) $\log_a (x^n) = n \log_a x.$

**Example :** Compute $\log_{30} 8$ if $\log_{30} 3 = a$ and $\log_{30} 5 = b.$

**Solution :** $\log_{30} 8 = 3 \log_{30} 2 = 3\log_{30} \dfrac{30}{15} = 3[1 - \log_{30} 3 - \log_{30} 5]$

$= 3 (1 - a - b)$

## MULTIPLE CHOICE QUESTIONS

**1.** $\log_5 5 \, \log_4 9 \, \log_3 2$ simplifies to:
   A. 2        B. 1        C. 5        D. None of these

**2.** $\log_3 11 . \log_{11} 13 . \log_{13} 15 . \log_{15} 27 = ?$
   A. 1        B. 2        C. 3        D. None of these

**3.** $\log_{2\sqrt{2}} 512 = ?$
   A. 4        B. 5        C. 6        D. 7

**4.** If $A = \log_2 \log_2 \log_4 256 + 2\log_{\sqrt{2}} 2$, then A equals:
   A. 2        B. 3        C. 5        D. 7

**5.** $25^{\left(1/2 + \log_{1/5} 27 + \log_{125} 81\right)} = ?$
   A. 0        B. 1        C. 10/81        D. $5\sqrt[3]{9/81}$

**6.** The domain of the function $\sqrt{(\log_{0.5} x)}$ is:
   A. $(1, \infty)$        B. $(0, \infty)$        C. $(0, 1)$        D. $(0.5, 1)$

**7.** If $\log_{10} 3 = 0.477$, the no. of digits in $3^{40}$ is:
   A. 18        B. 19        C. 20        D. 21

**8.** If $a^x = b$, $b^y = c$, $c^z = a$, then value of $xyz$ is:
   A. 0        B. 1        C. 2        D. 3

**9.** $7 \log (16/15) + 5 \log (25/24) + 3 \log (81/80) = ?$
   A. 0        B. 1        C. $\log 2$        D. $\log 3$

**10.** If $\log_{16} x + \log_4 x + \log_2 x = 14$, then $x = ?$
   A. 16        B. 32        C. 64        D. None of these

**11.** If $N = m!$ ($m$ is a fixed positive integer $> 2$), then

$$\frac{1}{\log_2 N} + \frac{1}{\log_3 N} + \cdots\cdots + \frac{1}{\log_m N} \text{ is equal to:}$$

   A. $-1$        B. 0        C. 1        D. 2

**12.** $\log (\log_{ab} a + 1/\log_b ab) = ?$
   A. 0        B. 1        C. $\log ab$        D. None of these

**13.** The value of $\sqrt{(\log^2_{0.5} 4)}$ is:
   A. $-2$        B. $\sqrt{(-4)}$        C. 2        D. None of these

**14.** If $\dfrac{\log_8 17}{\log_9 23} - \dfrac{\log_{2\sqrt{2}} 17}{\log_3 23} = ?$
   A. 0        B. 1        C. 17/8        D. 23/17

**15.** $\dfrac{1}{\log_{xy} xyz} + \dfrac{1}{\log_{yz} xyz} + \dfrac{1}{\log_{zx} xyz} = ?$

    A. 0      B. 1      C. 2      D. $\log_x xyz$

**16.** The equation $\log_e x + \log_e (1 + x) = 0$ can be written as:

    A. $x^2 + x - 1 = 0$          B. $x^2 + x + 1 = 0$

    C. $x^2 + x - e = 0$          D. $x^2 + x + e = 0$

**17.** If $2 \log_{16} (x^2 + x) - \log_4 (x + 1) = 2$, then $x = ?$

    A. $-1$      B. 16      C. 2      D. None of these

**18.** If $\dfrac{1}{\log_a x} + \dfrac{1}{\log_c x} = \dfrac{2}{\log_b x}$ , then $a, b, c$ are in:

    A. A.P.      B. G.P.      C. H.P.      D. None of these

**19.** $\log_{10} \tan 1° + \log_{10} \tan 2° + ... + \log_{10} \tan 89° = ?$

    A. 0      B. 1      C. 2      D. 3

**20.** The number $\log_2 7$ is:

    A. an integer          B. a rational number

    C. an irrational number          D. a prime number

**21.** If $\log_{10} 3 = 0.477$, the number of digits in $3^{50}$ is:

    A. 23      B. 24      C. 50      D. 150

**22.** If $\log_8 m + \log_8 {}^{1/6} = \dfrac{2}{3}$; then $m$ is equal to:

    A. 4      B. 12      C. 18      D. 24

**23.** If the logarithm of a number of the base $\sqrt{8}$ is 6, then the number is:

    A. $\sqrt{48}$      B. $\dfrac{\sqrt{8}}{6}$      C. $6\sqrt{8}$      D. 512

**24.** If $\log 2 = 0.3010$ and $\log 3 = 0.4771$, then the value of $\log 48$ is

    A. 1.6731      B. 1.6811      C. 1.6911      D. 1.8611

**25.** If $\log_4 7 = x$, then $\log_7 16$ is equal to:

    A. $2/x$      B. $x$      C. $2x$      D. $x^2$

**26.** The value of the real number $x$ satisfying $\log_9 x - \log_9\left(\dfrac{x}{10} + \dfrac{1}{9}\right) = 1$ is:

    A. 2      B. 4      C. 9      D. 10

**27.** The value of $\log_2 \log_2 \log_3 \log_3 27^3$ is

    A. 0      B. 1      C. 2      D. 3

**28.** $\log_{10}{}^{10} + \log_{10}{}^{100} + \ldots + \log_{10} 1\underbrace{0000\ldots0}_{n}$ is equal to:

 A. $n$      B. $(n+1)$     C. $(n^2 + n + 1)$   D. $\dfrac{n(n+1)}{2}$

**29.** If $\log_{10}(x + 5) + \log_{10}{}^{10} = 4$, then the value of $x$ is:

 A. 795      B. 890      C. 995      D. 1000

**30.** If $\log_4{}^{x^2(x-1)^2} - \log_2{}^{(x-1)} = 1$, then the value of $x$ will be:

 A. 1       B. 2       C. 3       D. 4

## ANSWERS

| 1 | 2 | 3 | 4 | 5 | 6 | 7 | 8 | 9 | 10 |
|---|---|---|---|---|---|---|---|---|----|
| B | C | C | C | D | C | C | B | C | D |

| 11 | 12 | 13 | 14 | 15 | 16 | 17 | 18 | 19 | 20 |
|----|----|----|----|----|----|----|----|----|----|
| C | A | C | A | C | A | B | B | A | C |

| 21 | 22 | 23 | 24 | 25 | 26 | 27 | 28 | 29 | 30 |
|----|----|----|----|----|----|----|----|----|----|
| B | D | D | B | A | D | A | D | C | B |

## EXPLANATORY ANSWERS

**1.** Given expression $= 1. \log_{2^2} 3^2 . \log_3 2$

$$= \frac{2}{2} \log_2 3.1/(\log_2 3) = 1.$$

**2.** Given expression $= \log_3 27 = \log_3 3^3 = 3 \log_3 3 = 3.$

**3.** $\log_{2\sqrt{2}} 512 = \log_{2^{3/2}} 2^9 = \{9/(3/2)\} \log_2 2 = 6.$

**8.** $a = c^z = (b^y)^z = b^{yz} = (a^x)^{yz}$

$$= a^{xyz} \Rightarrow xyz = 1.$$

**21.** Let $x = 3^{50}$

$\Rightarrow \log x = 50 \log 3 = 50 \times 0.477 = 23.850$

Hence, requried number of digits $= 23 + 1 = 24$

**22.** $\log_8{}^m + \log_8{}^{1/6} = \dfrac{2}{3} \Rightarrow \log_8{}^{\left(m \times \frac{1}{6}\right)} = \dfrac{2}{3}$

$$\Rightarrow m \times \frac{1}{6} = 8^{2/3} \qquad \Rightarrow \frac{m}{6} = \left(2^3\right)^{2/3}$$

$$\Rightarrow \frac{m}{6} = 4 \quad \therefore m = 24$$

**23.** $\log_{\sqrt{8}} x = 6 \qquad \Rightarrow x = \left(\sqrt{8}\right)^6 = \left(2^{3/2}\right)^6$

$\therefore x = 2^9 = 512$

**24.** $\log 48 = \log\left(2^4 \times 3\right) = 4\log 2 + \log 3$

$= 4 \times 0.3010 + 0.4771 = 1.6811$

**25.** $\log_4 7 = x \qquad \Rightarrow \log_7 4 = \dfrac{1}{x} \qquad \Rightarrow 2\log_7 4 = \dfrac{2}{x}$

$\Rightarrow \log_7 4^2 \qquad \Rightarrow \log_7 16 = \dfrac{2}{x}$

**26.** $\log_9 x - \log_9\left(\dfrac{x}{10}+\dfrac{1}{9}\right) = 1 \qquad \Rightarrow \log_9 x - \log_9\left(\dfrac{x}{10}+\dfrac{1}{9}\right) = \log_9 9$

$\Rightarrow \log_9 x / \left(\dfrac{x}{10}+\dfrac{1}{9}\right) = \log_9 9 \qquad \Rightarrow \log_9\left(\dfrac{90x}{9x+10}\right) = \log_9 9$

$\Rightarrow \dfrac{90x}{9x+10} = 9 \qquad \Rightarrow 90x = 81x + 90 \qquad \Rightarrow 9x = 90 \qquad \Rightarrow x = 10$

**27.** $\log_2 \log_2 \log_3 \log_3 27^3 = \log_2 \log_2 \log_3 \log_3 \left(3^3\right)^3 = \log_2 \log_2 \log_3 9\log_3 3$

$= \log_2 \log_2 \log_3 3^2 \times 1 = \log_2 \log_2 2 \log_3 3 = \log_2 \log_2 2 \times 1$

$= \log_2 \times 1 = \log_2 1 = 0$

**28.** $\log_{10} 10 + \log_{10} 100 + \ldots + \log_{10} 1\underbrace{00000\ldots0}_{n}$

$= \log_{10} 10 + \log_{10} 10^2 + \ldots + \log_{10} 10^n$

$= \log_{10} 10 + 2\log_{10} 10 + \ldots + n\log_{10} 10$

$= 1 + 2 + \ldots + n = \dfrac{n(n+1)}{2}$

**29.** $\log_{10}(x+5) + \log_{10} 10 = 4 \qquad \Rightarrow \log_{10}(x+5) + 1 = 4$

$\Rightarrow \log_{10}(x+5) = 3 \quad \Rightarrow x + 5 = 10^3 \qquad \therefore x = 1000 - 5 = 995$

**30.** $\log_4 x^2(x-1)^2 - \log_2(x-1) = 1 \qquad \Rightarrow \log_{2^2}[x(x-1)]^2 - \log_2(x-1) = 1$

$\Rightarrow \dfrac{2}{2}\log_2 x(x-1) - \log_2(x-1) = 1 \Rightarrow \log_2 \dfrac{x(x-1)}{x-1} = 1$

$\Rightarrow \log_2 x = 1 \qquad \therefore x = 2^1 = 2$

❖ ❖ ❖

# 17

# *Geometry*

## Important Definations and facts

**Line :** To connect two points on a plane is called a line. It may be straight line, a curved line (a line has only length, it has no breadth).

**Point :** On a given point there passes infinitely many lines.

**Parrallel straight lines :** Two lines on a plane which never intersect each other are called parrallel lines.

**Angle :** An angle is the union of two non-collinear rays with a common initial point.

1. **Right angle :** An angle whose measure is $90°$ is called a right angle.

2. **Actute angle :** An angle whose measure is less than $90°$ is called an actue angle.

3. **Obtuse angle :** An angle whose measure is more than $90°$ less than $180°$ is called an obtuse angle.

4. **Reflex angle :** An angle having measure more than $180°$ and less than $360°$ is called a reflex angle.

5. **Supplementary angle :** Two angles, the sum of whose measures is $180°$ are called supplementary angle.

6. **Complementary angle :** Two angles, the sum of whose measure is $90°$ are called complementary angles.

   For example : 70 and 110 are a pair of summple- mentary angles while 50 and 40 are a pair of complementary angles.

7. **Adjacent angle :** Two angles are called adjacent angle if they have the same vertex, they have a common arm and uncommon arms are on either side of the common arm.

## Triangle

**Triangle :** Figure on a plane formed by three lines.

## Types of Triangles

(*a*) Types of triangle on the basis of sides.

(*i*) Equilateral Triangle : All three sides are equal.

(*ii*) Isosceles Triangle : Two sides are equql.

(*iii*) Scalence Triangle : Non of side is equal (unequal)

(*b*) Types of triangle on the bases of angle :

(*i*) Right angle triangle : One angle is of a right angle ($90°$)

(*ii*) Obtuse angle triangle : Triangle with one angle an obtuse angle.

   **Note :** The sum of the three angles of a triangle is $180°$.

## Quadrilateral

**Quadrilateral :** Figure on a plane formed by four lines. The sum is interior angles is $360°$

## The Types of Triangles Quadrilateral

(*i*) **Square :** All the four sides are equal and each angle is of $90°$. The diagnonals are equal and intersect at $90°$.

(*ii*) **Rhombus :** All the four sides are equal and angles are not necessary to be right angle. In a rhombus. (a) Diagonals intersect at $90°$ to each other. (b) Diagonals bisect each other.

(*iii*) **Rectangle :** It is a parallelogram having all the angles of $90°$ but the length and breadth are unequal.

(*iv*) **Parallelogram :** A quadrilateral which has both pairs of opposite sides parallel.

**In a parallelogram :** (a) Each pair of opposite side are equal. (b) Each pair of opposite angles are equal.

(*v*) **Trapezium :** A qudrilateral which has one pair of opposite sides parallel.

## Interior Angles of a Polygon:

1. Sum of the exterior angles of any polygon is $360°$.

2. Sum of the interior angles of any polygon is $(2n - 4)$ 90, here $n$ stands for number of sides.

*For example :*

(*i*) Find the sum of the interior angles of a hexagon (figure with six angles).

**Sol.** $(2 \times 6 - 4)$ $90 = 8 \times 90 = 720°$.

(*ii*) Find the sum of the interior angles of a pentagon (figure with five angle).

**Sol.** $(2 \times 5 - 4)$ $90 = 6 \times 90 = 540°$.

(*iii*) Each angle of a regular polygon $= \dfrac{2(n - 4)90}{n}$

*For example :*

(*iv*) Find the value of each angle of a regular hexagon.

**Sol.** $\dfrac{(2 \times 6 - 4)90}{6}$ or $\dfrac{8 \times 90}{6} = 120°$

## MULTIPLE CHOICE QUESTIONS

1. A tangent to a circle is a line that intersect the circle in only:
   A. two points      B. three points    C. four points   D. one point

2. A line intersecting a circle in two points is called:
   A. tangent                          B. secant
   C. point of contact                 D. None of these

3. The longest chord of a circle is called its:
   A. radius           B. secant          C. diameter      D. tangent

4. A tangent PQ at a point P of a circle of radius 5 cm meets a line through the centre O at a point Q, so that OQ = 12 cm. Length PQ is:
   A. $\sqrt{119}$ cm      B. 13 cm           C. 10 cm          D. 12 cm

5. In a right angled triangle hypotenuse is:
   A. Any side of the triangle         B. Side opposite to right angle
   C. Side opposite to acute angle     D. None of these

6. If the perimeter and area of a circle are numerically equal, then the radius of the circle is :
   A. 6 units          B. $\pi$ units       C. 4 units       D. 2 units

7. The area of a circle is 301.84 cm$^2$. Then its radius is :
   A. 9.2 cm           B. 9.3 cm          C. 9.8 cm         D. 9.6 cm

8. If three altitudes of a triangle are equal then the triangle is :
   A. Right angled     B. Equilateral     C. Isosceles     D. Scalene

9. The height of an equilateral triangle is :
   A. $\dfrac{\sqrt{3}}{4} \times$ Side      B. $\dfrac{\sqrt{3}}{2} \times$ Side      C. $\dfrac{\sqrt{3}}{4} \times$ Side$^2$  D. None of these

10. ABC is an isosceles right triangle. If AB$^2$ = 2AC$^2$ then right angle is at:
    A. C                 B. A                C. B                 D. None of these

11. The length of an altitude of an equilateral triangle of side $2a$ is :
    A. $\sqrt{2}\,a$ cm      B. $\sqrt{3}\,a$ cm      C. 2 cm          D. 1 cm

12. If $\angle A = 100°$, AB = AC, CD bisects $\angle$ACB and BD bisects $\angle$ABC. The values of $x$ and $y$ are:
    A. 15° and 70°                      B. 20° and 140°
    C. 10° and 160°                     D. 20° and 125°

13. A perpendicular at the end of the radius of a circle is :
    A. diameter         B. tangent         C. chord          D. anyline

14. ABC and BDF are two equilateral triangles such that D is the mid-point of BC. The ratio of the areas of triangles ABC and BDF is :
    A. 2 : 1       B. 1 : 2       C. 4 : 1       D. 1 : 4

15. The exterior angle of a quadrilateral are $x°$, $(x + 5)°$, $(x + 10)°$ and $(x + 25)°$, then value of $x$ is :
    A. 50°       B. 80°       C. 60°       D. 70°

16. The point equidistant from the three sides of a triangle is :
    A. circumference       B. centroid       C. incentre       D. orthocentre

17. In $\triangle ABC$, AB = $6\sqrt{3}$ cm AC = 12 cm and BC = 6 cm. The $\angle CAB$ and $\angle ABC$ are:
    A. 90° and 60°       B. 30° and 90°
    C. 60° and 90°       D. 90° and 30°

18. Chords AC and BD of a circle intersect each other, than the figure ABCD formed will be :
    A. square       B. rectangle
    C. parallelogram       D. quadrilateral

19. Sides of two similar triangles are in the ratio of 4 : 9 then area of these triangles are in the ratio :
    A. 2 : 3       B. 4 : 9       C. 81 : 16       D. 16 : 81

20. In the given figure $\angle AOB = 80°$. The value of $x$ is :

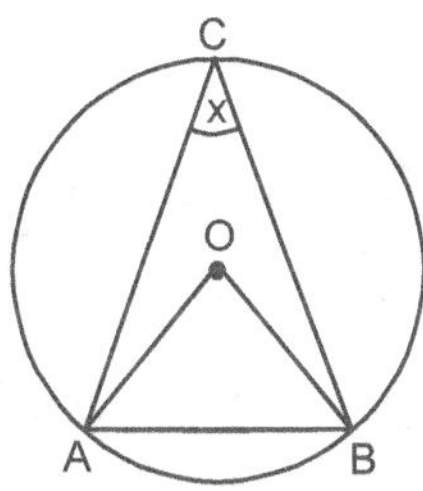


    A. 10°       B. 25°       C. 40°       D. 160°

## ANSWERS

| 1 | 2 | 3 | 4 | 5 | 6 | 7 | 8 | 9 | 10 |
|---|---|---|---|---|---|---|---|---|---|
| D | B | C | A | B | D | C | B | B | A |

| 11 | 12 | 13 | 14 | 15 | 16 | 17 | 18 | 19 | 20 |
|---|---|---|---|---|---|---|---|---|---|
| B | B | D | C | B | C | B | B | D | C |

## EXPLANATORY ANSWERS

1. A line meeting a circle in one point is called a tangent to the circle.
2. A line, which intersects a cirlce in two distinct points is called secant of the circle.

5.

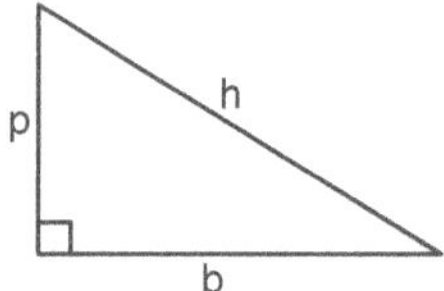


In any right-angled triangle hypotenuse is opposite to right angle.

6. From question,
   circumference of circle = Area of circle
   $$2\pi r = \pi r^2$$
   $$\Rightarrow \quad r = 2$$
   $$\therefore \quad \text{Radius} = 2 \text{ units.}$$

7. Area of the circle $= \pi r^2$
   According to the question,
   $$\pi r^2 = 301.84$$
   $$\Rightarrow \quad \frac{22}{7} r^2 = 301.84$$
   $$r^2 = \frac{7 \times 301.84}{22} = 96.04$$
   $$\therefore \quad r = \sqrt{96.04} = 9.8 \text{ cm.}$$

8. If the altitudes of a triangle are equal then it is equilateral.

10. Let $\angle C = 90°$
    In $\triangle ACB$,
    $$(AB)^2 = (AC)^2 + (BC)^2$$
    $$(AB)^2 = (AC)^2 + (AC)^2$$
    $$AB^2 = 2AC^2$$
    $$\therefore \quad \angle C = 90°.$$

13. A tangent to a circle is at right angle to the radius.

15. We have,
    $$x° + (x + 5)° + (x + 10)° + (x + 25)° = 360°$$
    $$4x + 40° = 360°$$

$$4x = 320°$$
$$x = 80°.$$

**16.** Point of concurrence of the bisector of the angles of a triangle is called incentre.

**17.** In $\triangle ABC$

$$(12)^2 = (6)^2 + \left(6\sqrt{3}\right)^2$$
$$144 = 36 + 108 = 144$$

$\therefore$ $\triangle ABC$ is right-angled triangle

$\therefore$ $\qquad \angle B = 90°$

$$\sin A = \frac{BC}{AC} = \frac{6}{12} = \frac{1}{2}$$

$\Rightarrow \qquad \sin A = \sin 30°$

$$A = 30°$$

$\therefore$ The angles $\angle CAB$ and $\angle ABC$ are 30° and 90° respectively.

**18.** Chords AC and BD must pass through the centre of the circle and will intersect at the centre,

$\therefore$ $\square ABCD$ is a rectangle.

**19.** $\because$ $\triangle ABC \sim \triangle DEF$

$$\therefore \quad \frac{ar\triangle ABC}{ar\triangle DEF} = \frac{(4)^2}{(9)^2} = \frac{16}{81} = 16 : 81.$$

**20.** We have,

$$\angle AOB = 2\angle ACB$$

[Angle of the centre is twice at the angle of circumference]

$$80° = 2x$$

$\therefore \qquad x = \frac{80}{2} = 40°.$

# 18

# *Trigonometry*

The word 'trigonometry' literally means the science which deals with the measurement of triangles.

## Angle

An angle is a figure formed by two rays (called the arms) with the common initial point (called the vertex).

It is determined by rotating a ray about its end point.

## Positive and Negative Angles

Angles determined by a **counter clockwise** rotation are said to be **positive** and angles determined by **clockwise** rotation are said to be **negative**.

The six trigonometric ratios of the acute angle $\theta$ are defined as follows :

$$\sin\theta = \frac{p}{h} = \frac{AB}{AC} \qquad\qquad \cos\theta = \frac{b}{h} = \frac{BC}{AC}$$

$$\tan\theta = \frac{p}{b} = \frac{AB}{BC} \qquad\qquad \cot\theta = \frac{b}{p} = \frac{BC}{AB}$$

$$\sec\theta = \frac{h}{b} = \frac{AC}{BC} \qquad\qquad \csc\theta = \frac{h}{p} = \frac{AC}{AB}$$

$$\begin{bmatrix} p = \text{perpendicular} \\ \qquad\text{or opposite} \\ b = \text{base or adjacent} \\ h = \text{hypotenuse} \end{bmatrix}$$

## *IMPORTANT FORMULAE*

**A.**   (*i*) $\tan\theta = \dfrac{\sin\theta}{\cos\theta} = \dfrac{1}{\cot\theta}$           (*ii*) $\cot\theta = \dfrac{\cos\theta}{\sin\theta} = \dfrac{1}{\tan\theta}$

    (*iii*) $\sec\theta = \dfrac{1}{\cos\theta}$                (*iv*) $\csc\theta = \dfrac{1}{\sin\theta}$

**B.**   (*i*) $\sin^2\theta + \cos^2\theta = 1$

       $\sin^2\theta = 1 - \cos^2\theta \Rightarrow \sin\theta = \sqrt{1-\cos^2\theta}$

       $\cos^2\theta = 1 - \sin^2\theta \Rightarrow \cos\theta = \sqrt{1-\sin^2\theta}$

(*ii*) $1 + \tan^2\theta = \sec^2\theta$

$\sec^2\theta - \tan^2\theta = 1$

$\sec^2\theta - 1 = \tan^2\theta$

(*iii*) $1 + \cot^2\theta = \csc^2\theta$

$\csc^2\theta - \cot^2\theta = 1$

$\csc^2\theta - 1 = \cot^2\theta$

(*iv*) $\tan^2\theta = \dfrac{\sin^2\theta}{\cos^2\theta}$

(*v*) $\cot^2\theta = \dfrac{\cos^2\theta}{\sin^2\theta}$

(*vi*) $\sec^2\theta = \dfrac{1}{\cos^2\theta}$

(*vii*) $\csc^2\theta = \dfrac{1}{\sin^2\theta}$

**C.** (*i*) $\sin(90 - \theta) = \cos\theta$

(*ii*) $\cos(90 - \theta) = \sin\theta$

(*iii*) $\tan(90 - \theta) = \cot\theta$

(*iv*) $\cot(90 - \theta) = \tan\theta$

(*v*) $\sec(90 - \theta) = \csc\theta$

(*vi*) $\csc(90 - \theta) = \sec\theta$

**D.** (*i*) $\sin(A \pm B) = \sin A \times \cos B \pm \cos A \times \sin B$

(*ii*) $\cos(A \pm B) = \cos A \times \cos B \mp \sin A \times \sin B$

**E.** (*i*) $\sin 2\theta = 2\sin\theta \cdot \cos\theta$

(*ii*) $\cos 2\theta = \cos^2\theta - \sin^2\theta = 1 - 2\sin^2\theta = 2\cos^2\theta - 1$

(*iii*) $\tan 2\theta = \dfrac{2\tan\theta}{1 - \tan^2\theta}$

**F.** (*i*) $\sin 3\theta = 3\sin\theta - 4\sin^3\theta$

(*ii*) $\cos 3\theta = 4\cos^3\theta - 3\cos\theta$

## T-Ratios of Standard Angles

| $\theta$ | $0°$ | $30°$ | $45°$ | $60°$ | $90°$ |
|---|---|---|---|---|---|
| $\sin\theta$ | $0$ | $\dfrac{1}{2}$ | $\dfrac{1}{\sqrt{2}}$ | $\dfrac{\sqrt{3}}{2}$ | $1$ |
| $\cos\theta$ | $1$ | $\dfrac{\sqrt{3}}{2}$ | $\dfrac{1}{\sqrt{2}}$ | $\dfrac{1}{2}$ | $0$ |
| $\tan\theta$ | $0$ | $\dfrac{1}{\sqrt{3}}$ | $1$ | $\sqrt{3}$ | $\infty$ |
| $\cot\theta$ | $\infty$ | $\sqrt{3}$ | $1$ | $\dfrac{1}{\sqrt{3}}$ | $0$ |
| $\sec\theta$ | $1$ | $\dfrac{2}{\sqrt{3}}$ | $\sqrt{2}$ | $2$ | $\infty$ |
| $\csc\theta$ | $\infty$ | $2$ | $\sqrt{2}$ | $\dfrac{2}{\sqrt{3}}$ | $1$ |

# MULTIPLE CHOICE QUESTIONS

**1.** If $\cos\theta = \dfrac{1}{2}$, find the value of $\dfrac{2\sec\theta}{1+\tan^2\theta}$

   A. 1                 B. 2                 C. 3                 D. 4

**2.** If $\sin\theta = \dfrac{5}{13}$ and $0 < \theta < 90°$, find out the value of $\cos\theta$.

   A. $\dfrac{5}{12}$         B. $\dfrac{12}{13}$         C. $\dfrac{13}{12}$         D. $\dfrac{12}{5}$

**3.** If $5\tan\theta = 4$, find the value of $\dfrac{5\sin\theta - 3\cos\theta}{5\sin\theta + 2\cos\theta}$

   A. 2         B. $\dfrac{3}{2}$         C. $\dfrac{1}{6}$         D. $\dfrac{2}{3}$

**4.** If $3\cot\theta = 2$, find the value of $\dfrac{4\sin\theta - 3\cos\theta}{2\sin\theta + 6\cos\theta}$

   A. $\dfrac{2}{3}$         B. $\dfrac{3}{2}$         C. $\dfrac{1}{3}$         D. 3

**5.** If $3\tan\theta = 2$, find the value of $\dfrac{4\sin\theta - \cos\theta}{2\sin\theta + \cos\theta}$

   A. $\dfrac{3}{2}$         B. $\dfrac{5}{7}$         C. $\dfrac{3}{7}$         D. 1

**6.** If $3\cot\theta = 4$, find the value of $\dfrac{5\sin\theta - 3\cos\theta}{5\sin\theta + 3\cos\theta}$

   A. $\dfrac{1}{9}$         B. $\dfrac{2}{7}$         C. 3         D. 4

**7.** If $\tan\theta = \dfrac{3}{4}$, find the value of $\dfrac{4\sin\theta - 2\cos\theta}{4\sin\theta + 3\cos\theta}$

   A. $\dfrac{2}{3}$         B. $\dfrac{4}{3}$         C. $\dfrac{1}{6}$         D. $\dfrac{5}{6}$

**8.** If $\tan A = \dfrac{5}{12}$, find the value of $\sin A + \cos A$, where A is an acute angle.

   A. $\dfrac{13}{17}$         B. $\dfrac{17}{13}$         C. $\dfrac{12}{5}$         D. $\dfrac{5}{17}$

**9.** If $\tan \theta = \dfrac{2}{3} \ (0° < \theta < 90°),$ then find the value of $\sin \theta$

  A. $\dfrac{2}{\sqrt{13}}$      B. $\dfrac{3}{\sqrt{12}}$      C. 1      D. 0

**10.** If $2 \tan \theta = 1,$ find the value of $\dfrac{3\cos\theta + 2\sin\theta}{2\cos\theta - \sin\theta}$

  A. $\dfrac{8}{3}$      B. $\dfrac{5}{3}$      C. $\dfrac{2}{3}$      D. 2

**11.** Evaluate : $(\operatorname{cosec} \theta - \sin \theta)(\sec \theta - \cos \theta)(\tan \theta + \cot \theta)$
  A. 1      B. 2      C. 3      D. 0

**12.** Evaluate : $(\sin A + \cos A)(\tan A + \cot A)$
  A. $\sin A + \cos A$             B. $\sec A + \operatorname{cosec} A$
  C. $\sin A$                   D. $\cos A$

**13.** Evaluate $\dfrac{\sin \theta}{1 + \cos\theta} + \dfrac{1 + \cos\theta}{\sin \theta}$
  A. 2 sin A      B. 2 cosec A      C. 2 tan A      D. 2 cos A

**14.** Evaluate $\dfrac{\tan A + \sec A - 1}{\tan A - \sec A + 1}$
  A. $\sec A + \tan A$      B. $\sin A$      C. 1      D. 0

**15.** If $\sin x + \sin^2 x = 1,$ then $\cos^2 x + \cos^4 x$ is :
  A. 1      B. 2      C. 3      D. 4

**16.** If $\cos \theta - \sin \theta = \sqrt{2} \sin \theta,$ then $\cos \theta + \sin \theta$ is:

  A. $\sqrt{2} \sin \theta$      B. $\sqrt{2} \cos \theta$      C. $\sin \theta$      D. $\cos \theta$

**17.** Find the value of
$4(\sin^4 30° + \cos^4 60°) - 3(\sin^2 45° - 2 \cos^2 45°).$
  A. 1      B. 2      C. 0      D. 3

**18.** Express $\cos 79° + \sec 79°$ in terms of angles between 0° and 45°
  A. 1                       B. 2
  C. $\sin 11° + \operatorname{cosec} 11°$         D. $\cos 11° + \sec 11°$

**19.** Using the formula
$\cos (A - B) = \cos A \cos B + \sin A \sin B,$ find the value of $\cos 15°.$

  A. $\dfrac{\sqrt{3} - 1}{2\sqrt{2}}$      B. $\sqrt{3} - 1$      C. $\dfrac{\sqrt{3} + 1}{2\sqrt{2}}$      D. $\sqrt{3} + 1$

**20.** Using the formula

sin $(A - B) = \sin A \cos B - \cos A \sin B$, find the value of sin $15°$

   A. $\sqrt{3}$      B. $\sqrt{3}+1$      C. $\dfrac{\sqrt{3}-1}{2\sqrt{2}}$      D. $\dfrac{\sqrt{3}+1}{2\sqrt{2}}$

**21.** sin $\theta$ cos $(90° - \theta)$ + cos $\theta$ sin $(90° - \theta)$ equal to :
   A. 0      B. 1      C. $-1$      D. 2

**22.** $\cos^2 72° + \cos^2 18° = ?$
   A. 0      B. 1      C. $-1$      D. 2

**23.** $3 \tan^2 30° + \sec^4 45° - \tan^2 60°$ is equal to :
   A. 0      B. 1      C. 2      D. 3

**24.** The value of sin $79°$ cos $11°$ + cos $79°$ sin $11°$.
   A. 1      B. 0      C. 2      D. $-2$

**25.** (sin $\theta$ + cos $\theta$) $(1 - \sin\theta \cos \theta)$ can be written as :
   A. sin $\theta$ + cos $\theta$            B. $\sin^3 \theta - \cos^3 \theta$
   C. $\sin^3 \theta + \cos^3 \theta$         D. sin $\theta$ $-$ cos $\theta$

**26.** If $\cot^2 \theta = \dfrac{7}{8}$ and $0 < \theta < 90°$, then the value of $\dfrac{(1+\sin\theta)(1-\sin\theta)}{(1+\cos\theta)(1-\cos\theta)}$ is

equal to :

   A. $\dfrac{7}{8}$      B. $\dfrac{7}{6}$      C. $\dfrac{7}{5}$      D. $\dfrac{7}{4}$

**27.** $\sin 40°.\sec 50° - \dfrac{\tan 40°}{\cot 50°} + 1 =$
   A. 0      B. 1      C. $-1$      D. 2

**28.** The value of sin $20°$ $-$ cos $70°$ is :
   A. 1      B. 2      C. 3      D. 0

**29.** The value of $\operatorname{cosec}^2 (90° - \theta) - \tan^2 \theta$ is
   A. 2      B. 3      C. 0      D. 1

**30.** If $\theta = 45$ then $\dfrac{2\tan\theta}{1+\tan^2\theta}$ is :
   A. 1      B. 0      C. 2      D. 3

**31.** The value of cos $1°$ cos $2°$ ... cos $100°$ is
   A. 1      B. $-1$      C. 0      D. None of these

**32.** cos $24°$ + cos $5°$ + cos $175°$ + cos $204°$ + cos $300°$ =
   A. 1/2      B. $-1/2$      C. $\sqrt{(3/2)}$      D. None of these

**33.** $\tan 5° \tan 25° \tan 45° \tan 65° \tan 85° =$
   A. 1        B. 1/2        C. 3/4        D. None of these

**34.** $\tan\dfrac{\pi}{20}\tan\dfrac{3\pi}{20}\tan\dfrac{5\pi}{20}\tan\dfrac{7\pi}{20}\tan\dfrac{9\pi}{20} =$
   A. 1        B. $-1$        C. 1/2        D. None of these

**35.** $\sin^2(\pi/18) + \sin^2(\pi/9) + \sin^2(7\pi/18) + \sin^2(4\pi/9)$
   A. 1        B. 2        C. 4        D. None of these

**36.** $\tan\theta \sin(\pi/2 + \theta)\cos(\pi/2 - \theta) =$
   A. 1        B. $-1$        C. $1/2 \sin 2\theta$        D. None of these

**37.** $\log\sin 1° \, \log\sin 2° \, ... \, \log\sin 179° =$
   A. 1        B. 0        C. $1/\sqrt{2}$        D. None of these

**38.** $\log\tan 1° + \log\tan 2° + ... + \log\tan 89° =$
   A. 1        B. 0        C. $\pi/4$        D. None of these

**39.** The value of $\sin 12° \sin 48° \sin 54°$ is
   A. 1/2        B. 1/3        C. 1/6        D. 1/8

**40.** If $f(x) = \cos^2 x + \sec^2 x$, its value always is
   A. $f(x) < 1$        B. $f(x) = 1$        C. $2 > f(x) > 1$        D. $f(x) \geq 2$

**41.** If $A = \cos^2\theta + \sin^4\theta$, then for all values of $\theta$
   A. $1 \leq A \leq 2$        B. $13/16 \leq A \leq 1$
   C. $3/4 \leq A \leq 13/16$        D. $3/4 \leq A \leq 1$

**42.** If $x = r\cos\theta\cos\phi$, $y = r\cos\theta\sin\phi$, $z = r\sin\theta$, then $x^2 + y^2 + z^2 =$
   A. 0        B. 1        C. $r$        D. $r^2$

**43.** If $x = a\cos^3\theta$, $y = b\sin^3\theta$, then
   A. $(x/a)^{2/3} + (y/b)^{2/3} = 1$        B. $(x/b)^{2/3} + (y/a)^{2/3} = 1$
   C. $(a/x)^{2/3} + (b/y)^{2/3} = 1$        D. $(b/x)^{2/3} + (a/y)^{2/3} = 1$

**44.** The equation $x = \dfrac{2a\theta}{1+\theta^2}, \ y = \dfrac{a(1-\theta^2)}{1+\theta^2}$, where $a$ is a constant, is the parametric equation of the curve:
   A. $x - y^2 = a^2$        B. $x^2 + y^2 = a^2$        C. $x^2 + 4y^2 = 4a^2$        D. $x = 2y$

**45.** The expression
$$3\left[\sin^4\left\{\frac{3}{2}\pi - \alpha\right\} + \sin^4(3\pi + \alpha)\right] - 2\left[\sin^6\left(\frac{1}{2}\pi + \alpha\right) + \sin^6(5\pi - \alpha)\right] \text{ is}$$
equal to
   A. 0        B. 1        C. 3        D. $\sin 4\alpha + \cos 6\alpha$

**46.** $\dfrac{1}{\sin 10°} - \dfrac{\sqrt{3}}{\cos 10°}$ is equal to

    A. 2          B. 4          C. 3          D. None of these

**47.** $\sqrt{3}$ cosec 20° − sec 20° is equal to

    A. 2          B. 2 sin 20°/sin 40°

    C. 4          D. 4 sin 20°/sin 40°

**48.** If $\tan A = \dfrac{a}{a+1}$ and $\tan B = \dfrac{1}{2a+1}$, then the value of A + B is

    A. 0          B. $\pi/2$          C. $\pi/3$          D. $\pi/4$

**49.** In a triangle PQR, $\angle$ R = $\pi/2$. If tan (P/2) and tan (Q/2) are the roots of the equation $ax^2 + bx + c = 0$, then

    A. $a + b = c$          B. $b + c = a$          C. $a + c = b$          D. $b = c$

**50.** $\sqrt{(\log_3 \tan x)}$ is real for

    A. $n\pi + \pi/4 \leq x < n\pi + \pi/2$          B. $n\pi < x < n\pi + \pi/2$

    C. $n\pi \pm \pi/4 \leq x < n\pi \pm \pi/2$          D. None of these

## ANSWERS

| 1 | 2 | 3 | 4 | 5 | 6 | 7 | 8 | 9 | 10 |
|---|---|---|---|---|---|---|---|---|----|
| A | B | C | C | B | A | C | B | A | A |
| **11** | **12** | **13** | **14** | **15** | **16** | **17** | **18** | **19** | **20** |
| A | B | B | A | A | B | B | C | C | C |
| **21** | **22** | **23** | **24** | **25** | **26** | **27** | **28** | **29** | **30** |
| B | B | C | A | C | A | B | D | D | A |
| **31** | **32** | **33** | **34** | **35** | **36** | **37** | **38** | **39** | **40** |
| C | A | A | A | B | D | B | B | D | D |
| **41** | **42** | **43** | **44** | **45** | **46** | **47** | **48** | **49** | **50** |
| D | D | A | B | B | B | C | D | A | A |

## EXPLANATORY ANSWERS

**18.** cos 79° + sec 79°

    = cos (90° − 11°) + sec (90° − 11°)

    = sin 11° + cosec 11°.

**28.** sin 20° − cos(90° − 20°) = sin 20° − sin 20° = 0.

**29.** $\sec^2\theta - \tan^2\theta = \dfrac{1}{\cos^2\theta} - \dfrac{\sin^2\theta}{\cos^2\theta} = \dfrac{1-\sin^2\theta}{\cos^2\theta} = \dfrac{\cos^2\theta}{\cos^2\theta} = 1.$

**30.** $\dfrac{2\tan 45°}{1+\tan^2 45°} = \dfrac{2\times 1}{1+1} = \dfrac{2}{2} = 1.$

**31.** $\because \cos 90° = 0$

$\therefore$ Given expression

$= \cos 1° \cos 2° \,...\, \cos 89°.0 \cos 91°$           $...\cos 100° = 0.$

**32.** Given expression

$= \cos 24° + \cos 5° + \cos (180° - 5°) + \cos (180° + 24°) + \cos (360° - 60°)$

$= \cos 24° + \cos 5° - \cos 5° - \cos 24° + \cos 60° = 1/2.$

**33.** Given expression

$= \tan 5° \tan 25°.1 \tan (90° - 25°) \times \tan(90° - 5°)$

$= \tan 5° \tan 25° \cot 25° \cot 5° = 1.$

**37.** $\because \log \sin 90° = \log 1 = 0$

$\therefore$ Given expression $= 0.$

**38.** Given expression

$= \log (\tan 1°.\tan 2° \,...\, \tan 44°. \tan 45°.\cot 44°.\cot 43° \,...\, \cot 1°)$

$= \log 1 = 0.$

**39.** $\sin 12° \sin 48°. \sin 54°$

$= \dfrac{1}{2} (\cos 36° - \cos 60°) \cos 36°$

$= \dfrac{1}{4} (2 \cos^2 36° - \cos 36°)$

$= \dfrac{1}{4} (1 + \cos 72° - \cos 36°)$

$= \dfrac{1}{4} (1 + \sin 18° - \cos 36°) = \dfrac{1}{4}\cdot\left(\dfrac{1}{2}\right) = \dfrac{1}{8}.$

**40.** $f(x) = (\cos x - \sec x)^2 + 2 \Rightarrow f(x) \geq 2$

**47.** Given expression

$= \dfrac{\sqrt{3}\cos 20° - \sin 20°}{\cos 20° \sin 20°}$

$$= \frac{2\left[\left(\frac{1}{2}\sqrt{3}\right)\cos 20° - \frac{1}{2}\sin 20°\right]}{\frac{1}{2}\sin 40°}$$

$$= \frac{4\sin(60° - 20°)}{\sin 40°} = 4.$$

**48.** $\tan(\theta + \phi) = (\tan\theta + \tan\phi)/(1 - \tan\theta\tan\phi)$
$= 1 \Rightarrow \theta + \phi = \pi/4.$

**49.** $\tan(P/2) + \tan(Q/2) = -b/a,$
$\tan(P/2).\tan(Q/2) = c/a$
$\angle P + \angle Q = \pi/2$

$$\tan\left(\frac{1}{2}P + \frac{1}{2}Q\right) = 1$$

$$= \frac{\tan(P/2) + \tan(Q/2)}{1 - \tan(P/2)\tan(Q/2)}$$

$$= \frac{-b/a}{1 - c/a} = \frac{-b}{a - c}$$

$\Rightarrow a + b = c.$

**50.** $\sqrt{(\log_3 \tan x)}$ is real if $\log_3 \tan x \geq 0$
*i.e.*, $\tan x \geq 1$ (as base $= 3 > 1$)
$\therefore \ \pi/4 \leq x < \pi/2.$ General values are given by
$n\pi + \pi/4 \leq x < n\pi + \pi/2.$

# GENERAL SCIENCE

# PHYSICS

## UNITS AND MEASUREMENT

Unit is that physical quantity which expresses the length, mass and time.

*Types of Units:* There are three systems of the fundamental units which are commonly used and internationally recognized these are:

*(i)* **Metric System Unit (M.K.S.):** In this system of unit 'M' stands for metre, 'K' for kilogram and S for second (time). Metre as unit of length, Kilogram as unit of mass and Second as unit of time.

*(ii)* **C.G.S. System of unit:** In this system 'C' stands for centimetre 'G' stands for gram and 'S' for Second. Centimetre is the unit of length, Gram is the unit of mass and Second is the unit of time.

*(iii)* **F.P.S. System of Unit:** In this system of unit 'F' stands for foot, 'P' stands for pound and 'S' for second. Foot is the unit of length, Pound is unit of mass, second is unit of time.

## Scientific Instruments

1. **Altimeter**—It is used for measuring altitudes specially used in aircraft.
2. **Ammeter**—It is used for measuring the strength of the current in amperes.
3. **Barometer**—It is used for measuring the atmospheric pressure.
4. **Dynamo**—It is used to convert mechanical energy into electrical energy.
5. **Galvanometer**—It is used for detecting the presence of current.
6. **Hygrometer**—It is used for measuring humidity in air.
7. **Periscope**—A device to see the objects which are above the eye level of the observer.
8. **Potentiometer**—It is used for measuring or adusting electrical potential.
9. **Sextant**—It is used for measuring angular elevation.
10. **Transformer**—It is used to decrease or increase the voltage of an alternating current.
11. **Thermocouple**—It is based on thermoelectricity used for measuring temperature.
12. **Thermometer**—It is used measuring temperature.
13. **Viscometer**—It is used for measuring viscosity of liquids.
14. **Voltmeter**—It measures the potential difference.

## MECHANICS

Branch of science dealing with the study of motion of object in called mechanics.

*Distance:* The length of path traversed by a particle in a given time is known as distance.

*Displacement:* The distance covered by a particle in a particular direction with respect to the point of reference is known as displacement.

*Speed:* The distance travelled by a particle in unit time is defined as its speed.



(165) Sci.-(E)-1

***Average or Mean Speed:*** The ratio of the total distance travelled by a particle to the time taken to cover that distance is defined as its average speed.

***Velocity:*** The ratio of the total displacement of a particle to the time taken to cover that displacement is defined as average velocity.

***Acceleration:*** The change in velocity of a particle in unit time is defined as its average acceleration.

***Retardation:*** The rate of decrease of velocity of a particle is defined as retardation. It is a negative acceleration.

***Inertia:*** The property of a body by virtue of which it opposes any change in its state is defined as its inertia.

***Mass:*** The quantity of matter contained in a body is defined as its mass.

(*a*)   The mass of a body can never be zero.

(*b*)   The mass of a body remains constant at all places of earth.

(*c*)   It can be determined by a physical balance.

(*d*)   There are two types of mass, *i.e.*, (*i*) gravitational mass, and (*ii*) inertial mass.

***Gravitational Mass:*** The ratio of the weight of a body and acceleration due to gravity at that place is defined as gravitational mass. The mass determined by a chemical or physical balance is the gravitational mass.

***Inertial Mass:*** The ratio of the force applied and the acceleration produced in a body at a place with zero gravity is defined as the inertial mass.

***Force:*** The push or pull which one system exerts on another is defined as force.

***Momentum:*** The product of mass and velocity of a moving body is known as its linear momentum.

***Impulse:*** The product of applied force on a body and the time internal for which the force acts is defined as impulse.

***Energy:*** The capacity of doing work is known as energy. Energy can be converted from one form to another form.

***Mechanical Energy:*** The energy present in a body on account of its position or motion is defined as mechanical energy. This is of two type viz., (*i*) Potential energy and (*ii*) Kinetic energy.

***Newton's Laws of Motion***

(*i*)    *First Law or Law of Inertia:* A body to be in its state of rest or of uniform motion until and unless it is acted upon by some external forces. This law defines forces.

(*ii*)   *Second Law:* The force applied to a body is equal to the rate of change of its momentum.

(*iii*)  *Third Law or Law of Action and Reaction:* To every action force there is an equal and opposite reaction force.

***Gravitational Field:*** The region of space around a body in which gravitational force is experienced by other bodies is defined as the gravitational field of that body.

***Newton's Law of Gravitation:*** Every particle in the universe attracts energy other particle with a force which is directly proportional to the product of their masses and inversely proportional to the square of distance between them.

***Force of Gravity:*** The force with which earth attracts anybody towards its centre is defined as the force of gravity. The force exerted by earth on the body is known as the weight of the body.

*Acceleration due to Gravity:* The rate of change of velocity of a body falling freely due to earth's force of gravity is defined as acceleration due to gravity

*Satellites:* The bodies revolving around a planet in its gravitational field are defined as satellites.

*Natural Satellites:* The natural heavenly bodies which revolve around a planet are known as natural satellites, *e.g.*, moon is the natural satellite of earth.

*Artificial Satellites:* The man made bodies which are established in a particular orbit and are made to revolve around the earth are known as artificial satellites, *e.g.*, Aryarbhatta, Rohini, Bhaskar.

*Orbital Satellite:* The satellites which always revolve in different orbits around earth are known as orbital satellites.

*Communication Satellites:* The satellite which remain stationary with respect to earth are known as communication satellites, *e.g.*, INSAT, 1B, 2A, 2E etc.

*Power:* The rate of doing work by a machine or a person is defined as power.

*Law of Conservation of Momentum:* In the absence of an external force, the total momentum of a system remains constant.

*Deforming Force:* The external force acting on a body on account of which is size or shape or both change is defined as the deforming force.

*Elasticity:* The property of a body, by virtue of which it regains its original form (size and shape) after the removal of external deforming force, is defined as elasticity.

*Perfectly Elastic Body:* The body which perfectly regains its original form on removing the external deforming force, is defined as a perfectly elastic body, *e.g.*, quartz.

*Plastic Body:* The body which does not have the property of opposing the external deforming force is known as a plastic body.

*Elastic Limit:* The maximum deforming force after which a body loses its property of elasticity and it gets permanently deformed, is defined as the elastic limit.

*Stress:* The internal reactional force per unit area developed as a result of applied external force is defined as stress.

*Strain:* The change in dimensions per unit original dimensions due to applied deforming force is defined as strain.

*Hooke's Law:* Within elastic limit, stress is directly proportional to strain.

*Cohesive Force:* The force of attraction acting between the molecules of same material is defined as cohensive force, *e.g.*, the force acting between water molecule.

*Adhesive Force:* The force of attraction acting between the molecules of two different materials is defined as adhesive force, *e.g.*, the force acting between the molecules of paper and ink.

*Surface Tension:* The property of a liquid, on account of which it lends to keep surface area in its free surface, is defined as surface tension.

*Viscosity:* The property of fluids, by virtue of which they oppose the relative motion between their different layers, is known as viscosity.

# HEAT

*Temperature:* Temperature of a body is that property which tells us that how much hot or cold a particular body is.

*Scales of Temperature:*

(*i*)    Temperature in Kelvin = Temperature in Celsius + 273

(*ii*)   $1°C$ temperature difference = $1°$ K

(*iii*)  The temperature of $-40°C$ is same in $°C$ and $°F$

(*iv*)  The temperature of a normal person is $37°C$ or $98.6°F$.

*Heat:* Heat is a form of energy which is exchanged among various bodies or systems on account of temperature difference.

*Latent Heat:* The amount of heat used to change the state of matter, without changing its temperature is defined as latent heat.

*Specific Heat:* The amount of heat required to increase the temperature of 1 gm of material by $1°C$ is defined as its specific heat.

*Boyles Law:* At a constant temperature the volume of the given mass of gas is inversely proportional to its pressure.

*Charle's Law:* At constant pressure the volume of a given mass of gas is directly proportional to its absolute temperature. At constant pressure the volume of a given mass of gas increases by $\dfrac{1}{273}$ of its volume at $0°C$ for $1°C$ size in its temperature.

*Gay Lussac's Law:* At constant volume, the pressure of given mass of gas is directly proportional to its absolute temperature.

*Graham's Law of Diffusion:* At constant temperature and pressure, the rate of diffusion of a gas is inversely proportional to the square root of its density.

*Dalton's Law of Partial Pressure:* The total pressure exerted by the mixture of inactive gases in a vessel is equal to the sum of the partial pressures due to individual gas.

*Avogadro's Law:* If the temperature, pressure and volume of two gases are same then the number of molecules in them will also be equal.

# SOUND

*Wave:* A disturbance created in the medium which propagates in the forward direction with constant velocity without changing its shape, is defined as a wave.

*Wave Motion:* The mode of energy transfer in which a disturbance advances in the forward direction by affecting the medium without mass transfer, is defined as wave motion.

## Characteristics of Wave Motion:

(*i*)    The particle of the medium do not leave their mean positions rather they keep on vibrating about their mean positions.

(*ii*)   The medium itself does not move.

(*iii*)  The energy and momentum are transferred in the medium.

(*iv*)  The phase of various particle of the medium keep on changing constantly.

## Properties of Medium Necessary for Wave Propagation

(*i*)    The medium should have the property of inertia.

(*ii*)   The medium should posses the property of elasticity.

(*iii*)  The medium should have low resistance.

*Longitudinal Waves:* In these waves the particles of the medium vibrate in the direction of propagation of waves.

*Transverse Waves:* In these waves the particles of the medium vibrate at right angles to the direction.

*Ultrasonic Waves:* The waves with frequency greater than that of sound, *i.e.*, $20 \times 10^3$ Hz are defined as Ultrasonic waves.

*Shock Waves:* When a sound source move with a velocity greater than that of sound then it leave behind it waves whose wave front is conical. These waves are defined as shock wave.

## Terms Related to Wave Motion

(*i*) **Displacement:** The distance covered by a particle from mean position in a particular direction in SHM is known as displacement.

(*ii*) **Amplitude:** The maximum displacement of a particle executing SHM from its mean position, is defined as amplitude.

(*iii*) **Time Period:** The time taken by a particle in completing one vibration is defined as time period.

(*iv*) **Frequency:** The number of vibrations per second made by any particle of the medium is defined as its frequency.

(*v*) **Wavelength:** The distance between two nearest particles in one complete vibraton is defined as the wavelength.

(*vi*) **Wave Number:** The number of wave present in unit length is defined as the wave number.

(*vii*) **Wave Velocity:** The velocity with which the crests and troughs or compression and rarefactions travel in medium, is defined as wave velocity.

(*viii*) **Beats:** When two waves of nearly same frequency, travelling in the same direction of the medium, superimpose over each other then the intensity at any point of the medium changes periodically with time. This phenomenon is defined as beats.

(*ix*) **Beat Frequency:** The number of beats heard per second is defined as beat frequency.

(*x*) **Note:** Any musical sound which is produced by the SHM of sound source is known as note.

(*xi*) **Tone:** Every component of musical sound is known as a tone. Every musical sound consists of a number of components of different frequencies. Every component is known as a tone.

(*xii*) **Organ Pipe:** The pipe filled with air and which when vibrated produces sound waves is known as organ pipe.

(*xiii*) **Loudness:** It is that characteristic of sound, on account of which the sound appears to be intense or slow is defined as loudness of sound or the power crossing per unit area at any point of the medium is defined as loundness.

(*xiv*) **Pitch:** It is that characteristic of sound on account of which it appears to be shrill or grave, is known as pitch.

# LIGHT

*Light:* The light is an electromagnetic radiation with the help of which our eyes experience the sensation of vision is known as light.

*Ray of Light:* The path of light energy from one point to another is known as a ray of light.

*Properties of Light*

(*i*)  It propagates in straight line.

(*ii*)  It exhibits the phenomenon of reflection, refraction, interference, diffraction, polarisation and double refraction.

(*iii*)  The properties of the medium through which light passes remain unchanged.

(*iv*)  Its velocity is different in different media. In rarer medium it is more and in denser medium it is less.

(*v*)  Its velocity in vacuum is maximum whose value is $3 \times 10^8$ m/s.

*Reflection of Light:* The phenomenon of returning of incident light in the same medium is known as reflection.

*Laws of Reflection:*

(*i*)  The incident ray, the reflected ray and the normal all lie in the same plane.

(*ii*)  In regular reflection the angle of incidence is equal to the angle of reflection.

(*iii*)  When light is reflected by a rarer medium then its phase remains unchanged whereas phase difference of a path difference of $\lambda/2$ or time difference T/2 is created when it is reflected by a denser medium. This is also known as Stoke's Law.

*Refraction of Light:* When a ray of light enters from one medium to another then at the boundary of separation it deviates from its initial path. This phenomenon is known as refraction.

*Law of Refraction:*

(*i*)  The incident ray, the refracted ray and the normal all three lie in the same plane.

(*ii*)  For given two media and for a given wavelength, the ratio of the sine of angle of incidence to the sine of angle of refraction always remain constant.

(*iii*)  Light bends towards the normal if passes through rarer medium to denser medium.

(*iv*)  Light bends away from the normal if passes through denser medium to rarer medium.

*Critical Angle:* When a ray of light enters from denser to rarer medium, then the angle of incidence corresponding to which the angle of refraction is 90°, is defined as the critical angle.

*Total Internal Reflection:* When a ray of light passes from a denser to rarer medium at an angle greater than the critical angle, then it gets totally reflected. This phenomenon is known as total internal reflection.

*Refractive Index:* The ratio of velocities of light in two media is defined as refractive index.

*Dispersion of Light:* The phenomenon of spliting of a ray of light into difference colours by a prism is defined as dispersion.

*Spectrum:* The whole band of colours from violet to red colour is known as spectrum. There are seven colours in the spectrum in the following order Violet, Indigo, Blue, Green, Yellow, Orange and Red or VIBGYOR.

*Rainbow:* The seven coloured curved strip formed as a result of dispersion of light through water droplets which keep suspended in the atmosphere after rains, is known as rainbow.

**LASER** (Light Amplification by Stimulated Emission of Radiation)

(*i*) The light amplification by induced emission of radiation is known as laser.

(*ii*) It is highly coherent and highly monochromatic light.

(*iii*) It is perfectly unidirectional and highly intense and powerful.

*Polaroids:* Microcrystals of iodo-sulphate of quinine are deposited on thin sheet of nitro-cellulose and then squeezed them out through a fine slit. In this process only the crystals having axes parallel to the slit pass through it and form a sheet. These sheets are kept between ordinary glass plates and called polaroids.

*Uses of Polaroids:* In winds screen; Window panes of aeroplanes; Camera filters and sun glasses in 3-D movies.

*Luminous Flux:* The luminous flux through a given surface is the amount of luminous energy that passes through the surface in one second in a direction normal to surface.

*Lumen:* One lumen is the amount of luminous flux emitted per unit solid angle by a source of light of luminous intensity one candela.

*Luminous Intensity:* The luminous intensity of a source is defined as the luminous flux emitted per unit solid angle by the source. It is also known as illuminating power.

*Candela:* One candela is the luminous intensity in a given direction due to a source, which emits monochromatic radiation of frequency $5.4 \times 10^{14}$ Hz and whose radiant intensity in that direction is 1/683 watt per steradian.

*Mirror:* The highly polished reflecting surface is known as mirror. Mirror are of three tyes: Plane mirror;  Concave mirror and  Convex mirror.

## Properties of Image Formed by Plane Mirror

(*i*) The image formed by a plane mirror is erect, virtual laterally reversed.

(*ii*) The size of image formed by it is equal to that of the object.

(*iii*) The image is formed behind the mirror at a distance equal to the distance of the object in front of mirror.

(*iv*) When the mirror is rotated through an angle $\theta$, then the reflected ray rotates through an angle $2\theta$.

(*v*) When two mirrors are kept parallel to each other, then the number of images will be infinity as

*Spherical Mirror:* The smooth, polished spherical surface is known as spherical mirror, or the reflecting surface which is a part of a sphere is known as spherical mirror. It is of two types: (*i*) Concave mirror and (*ii*) Convex mirror

*Magnification (m):* The ratio of the size of image to size of object is defined as the magnification of spherical mirror,

$$\text{or } \textit{magnification} = \frac{\text{Size of image}}{\text{Size of object}}$$

$$\text{or } \textit{magnification} = \frac{\text{Length of image}}{\text{Length of object}}$$

*Use of Plane Mirrors:*
(*a*)  In dressing tables
(*b*)  In looking-glass
(*c*)  In scientific apparatus. Plane mirrors are used to bend the paths of rays of light in scientific apparatus.

*Uses of Concave Mirror:*
(*a*)  As shaving and hair dressing mirrors.
(*b*)  As reflectors—concave mirrors are used as reflectors in search lights and head light.
(*c*)  The ENT specialists use concave mirror for viewing the inner parts of ear, nose and throat.
(*d*)  In lighthouses in seas.
(*e*)  In a torch for hunting purpose.

*Use of Convex Mirror:*
(*a*)  To spread light on roads.
(*b*)  As side mirrors on cars in order to view the vehicle following the cars.
(*c*)  For decoration purpose as these form the very small images which look beautiful.

*Lens:* The part of an isotropic transparent medium by two spherical, cylindrical, parabolic or one plane and another spherical surfaces is defined as lens.

*Lenses are of Two types:*
(*i*)  Concave lens or diverging lens.
(*ii*)  Convex lens or converging lens.

*Concave lenses are of three types:*
(*i*)  *Concave-concave lens:* Both of its surfaces are concave. The radii of curvature of its two concave surfaces may be same or different.
(*ii*)  *Plano-concave lens:* Its one surface is plane and second surface is concave.
(*iii*)  *Convexo-concave:* One of its surfaces is convex and another surface is concave. The radii of curvature of convex and concave surfaces are different.

*Convex Lenses are of Three Types:*
(*i*)  *Convexo-convex:* Both of its surface are convex. The radii of curvature of its convex surfaces may be same or different.
(*ii*)  *Plano-convex:* One of its surfaces is convex and another one is plane.
(*iii*)  *Concavo-convex:* One of its surfaces is concave and another one is convex. The radii of its concave and convex surfaces are different.

*Power of Lens*
The power of a thin lens is equal to the reciprocal of its focal length measured in meter, *i.e.,* $P = \dfrac{1}{f}$. The unit of power of lens is dioptre.

(*ii*)  When two lenses are kept in contact then the power of compound lens is equal to the sum of power of two lenses, *i.e.,* $P = P_1 + P_2$.
(*iii*)  When a concave lens and a convex lens of equal focal lengths are kept in contact then the power of the compound lens becomes zero, *i.e.,* it behaves like a plane glass plate.
(*iv*)  Magnification: The ratio of the size of image formed by lens to the size of object is defined as its linear magnification.

## Images Formed by Concave and Convex Mirror

| Mirror | Position of Object | Position of Image | Nature of Image | Size of Image | Ray Diagram of Image Formation |
|---|---|---|---|---|---|
| Concave | at $\infty$ | at focus in front of the mirror | real and erect | smaller than object | 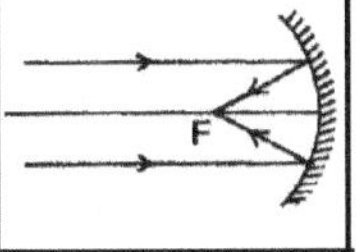 |
| Concave | farther from centre of curvature | between focus and centre of the mirror | real and inverted | smaller than object | 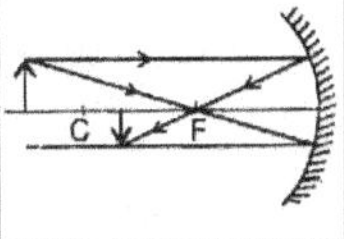 |
| Concave | at centre of curvature | at centre of curvature in front of the mirror | real and inverted | at the size of object | 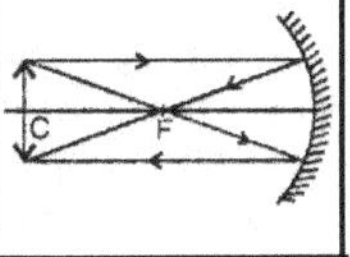 |
| Concave | between focus and centre of curvature | farther from centre of curvature | real and inverted | bigger than object | 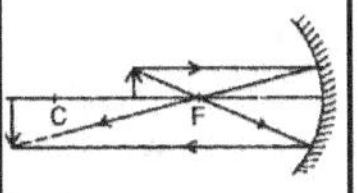 |
| Concave | at focus | at $\infty$ in front of mirror | real and inverted | bigger than object | 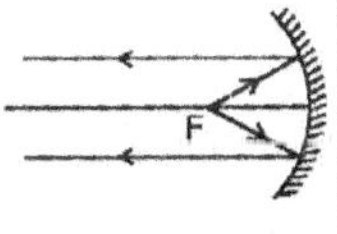 |
| Concave | between focus and pole | behind the mirror | virtual and erect | bigger than object | 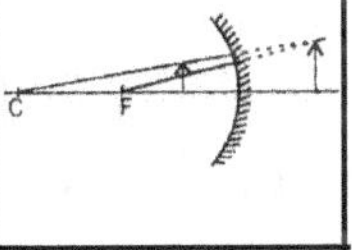 |
| Convex | at $\infty$ | at focus | erect and point image | | 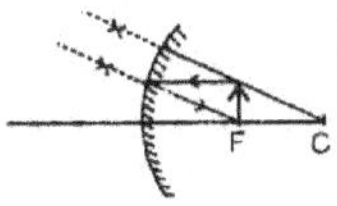 |
| Convex | between pole and $\infty$ | between pole and focus behind mirror | erect | smaller than object | 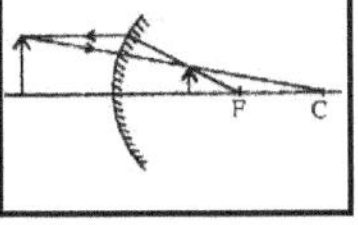 |

*Prism:* An isotropic transparent medium closed by surfaces inclined at an angle is define as a prism.

*Dispersion:* The phenomen of splitting of a white ray of light into seven colours is defined as dispersion.

*Visible Spectrum:* The spectrum which can be viewed with the help of eye is known as visible spectrum. The spectrum spreads from violet and (wavelength 3500Å).

# MAGNETISM

*Magnet:* A piece of matter, which when suspended freely rests in a particular direction (North-South) and which possesses a net magnetic moment and which attracts ferrous bodies towards it, is called a magnet.

*Natural Magnet:* The magnet which is found naturally in mines is called a natural magnet, e.g., magnetite. Its shape and size are indefinite, hence it cannot be used for scientific purpose. Its magnetism is quite weak.

*Artificial Magnet:* The magnet which are artificially prepared are known as artificial magnets. There are generally made of iron, steel and nickel. Its shape and size are definite.

*Bar Magnet:* A system composed of two poles, equal in magnitude but opposite in polarity, plane, at a small displacement apart is known as a bar magnet. It is also known as a magnetic dipole.

*Properties of a Magnet:* Like pole repel and unlike pole attract each other; it can be magnetically saturated; it can be demagnetized by beating, mechanical jerks, heating and with lapse of time; it produces magnetism in other materials by induction.

*Magnetism:* It is the property of a magnet, by virtue of which it attracts ferromagnetic materials towards it and rests itself in North-South direction, is known as magnetism. The magnetism of materials is mainly due to the spin motion of its electrons.

*Magnetic Poles:* The two points at the ends of a magnet at which magnetism is maximum are defined as magnetic poles. The magnetic poles are of two types—(*i*) North pole, (*ii*) South pole.

*Magnetic Axis:* The imaginary line joining the two poles of a magnet is defined as magnetic axis.

*Magnetic Meridian:* An imaginary plane passing through the axis of a freely suspended stationary magnet is defined as magnetic meridian. It is not a particular plane rather it is the direction of earth's magnetic field.

*Pole Strength:* The strength of a magnetic pole to attract magnetic materials towards it is known as pole strength.

*Magnetic Field:* The space around a magnet in which a torque acts on a magnetic needle is known as magnetic field.

*Magnetic Dipole:* The structure, which tend to align along the direction of magnetic field, are known as magnetic dipoles.

*Magnetic Flux:* The number of lines of forces passing through a given area is defined as magnetic flux.

*Magnetic Moment:* The product of the pole strength of a magnet and its length is defined as its magnetic moment.

*Electromagnetic Induction:* The phenomenon of production of electromotive force on account of change in magnetic flux linked with a circuit, is defined as electromagnetic induction.

*Induced emf:* The emf generated on account of change in magnetic flux linked with a plane or a circuit, is defined as induced emf.

*Induced Charge:* The electric charge flowing in a closed circuit on account of induced current is defined as induced charge.

*Transformer:* The device based on the principle of mutual induction used to change the value of alternating voltage is defined as transformer. There are two types of transformer: (*a*) Step-up transformer, (*b*) Step-down transformer

*Dynamo:* The device used to convert mechanical energy into electrical energy is known as dynamo.

# ☰ ELECTROSTATICS AND CURRENT ELECTRICITY ☰

*Electrostatics:* The branch of physics in which we study charges at rest, is known as electrostatics.

*Electric Charge:* It is a fundamental property of matter which can never be isolated from matter.

*Charges are of two types:* (*a*) Positive charges;   (*b*) Negative charges

*Positive Charges:* The deficiency of electron on a body or particle is known as positive charge.

*Negative Charge:* The excess of electrons on a body or a particle is known as negative charge. When a negative charge is given to a body then its mass some what increases.

*Properties of Charges:*
(*i*)   Like charges repel and unlike charges attract each other.
(*ii*)  A charged body attracts other uncharged light particles.
(*iii*) Total charge of an isolated physical system is always conserved.

*Law of Conservation of Charge:* Charges can neither be created nor be destroyed, rather these can be transferred from one body to another.

*Coulomb's Law:* The force of attraction or repulsion acting between two stationary point charges is directly proportional to the product of strengths of charges and inversely proportional to the square of distance between two charges. Its direction is along the line joining the two charges.

*Electric Field:* The region of space around a charge in which any other charge experiences coloumb forces is known as electric field.

*Electric Intensity:* The resultant coulomb force per unit test charge at any point in an electric field is defined as the intensity of electric field at that point.

*Electromotive Force:* The total work done in carrying a unit positive test charge around a closed path in an electric field, is defined as electromotive force.

*Electric Potential:* The work done against electric field in carrying a unit positive test charge from infinity to any point in electric field is defined as electric potential at that point.

*Potential Difference:* The negative of work done in carrying a unit positive test charge from one point to another point in an electric field is defined as electric potential difference between those two points.

*Capacitance:* It is numerically equal to that electric charge which raises its potential by unity. Unit of capacitance is farad.

*Condenser:* The pair of conductors of opposite charges, on which sufficient quantity of charge may be accommodated is defined as condenser.

*Current:* The rate of flow of charge in a circuit is defined as current. Electric current is equal to the charge that flow in one second.

*Conductor:* The materials, in which the number of free electron is very large are defined as conductors, *e.g.*, silver, copper, aluminium, etc.

*Insulator:* The materials, in which the number of free electrons at ordinary temperatures is negligible, are defined as insulators.

*Resistance:* The property of a conductor by virtue of which it opposes the flow of current in it is defined as resistance.

*Ohm's Law:* If the physical circumstances of the conductor (temperature, etc.) remains constant, then the applied potential difference is directly proportional to the current flowing in it.

*Resistivity:* The resistivity of a material is equal to the resistance of the wine of that material with unit cross-sectional area and unit length.

*Conductivity* : The reciprocal of specific resistance is defined as specific conductance.

# NUCLEAR PHYSICS

*Isotopes:* The elements which have same atomic number, same chemical properties, same electron number and same structure, but different mass is called isotopes.

*Isobars:* The elements which have same atomic mass, but different atomic number, physical and chemical properties is called isobars.

*Photo-electric Cell:* The device, by which light energy is directly converted into electrical energy, is known as the photo-electric cell.

*X-rays:* There are electromagnetic waves whose wavelength is more than that of $\gamma$-rays but less than that of ultraviolet rays, *i.e.*, these rays lie in between the ultraviolet region and $\gamma$-rays region of electromagnetic spectrum.

*Mass Defect:* When neutrons and protons combine to form a nucleus, then the mass of the nucleus is some what less then the sum of masses of its constituent particles.

Mass defect $(\Delta m)$ = total mass of all the neutrons present inside nucleus + total mass of protons − mass of the nucleus.

*Binding Energy:* The minimum energy required to keep the neutrons and protons bound inside the nucleus, is defined as binding energy.

*Nuclear Fission:* The phenomenon in which a heavy unstable nuclear breaks into two parts of nearly same mass, is defined as nuclear fission.

*Chain Reaction:* The process of nuclear fission, which when once started, continues spontaneously is defined as chain reaction.

*Nuclear Reactor:* The device in which energy is generated by chain reaction of nuclear fission is known as nuclear reactor.

*Nuclear Fusion:* The process in which two or more than two lighter nuclei combine to form a heavier nucleus, is known as nuclear fusion.

*Radioactivity:* The phenomenon of spontaneous disintegration of nuclei of unstable atoms is defined as radioactivity.

*Decay Constant:* It is equal to the reciprocal of that time in which the number of radioactive atoms remains its initial value.

*Half-life:* The time, in which the number of atoms (N) reduces to half of its initial value is defined as the half-life of the element.

*Mean-life:* The time, for which a radioactive remains active, is defined as mean life of that material.

# Multiple Choice Questions

1. In a simple harmonic motion, the energy of the particle in SHM is
   (*a*) directly proportional to half of its mass
   (*b*) inversly proportional to its amplitude
   (*c*) directly proportional to the square of its amplitude
   (*d*) directly proportional to its angular velocity

2. A body of mass 1kg was moving with a velocity of 5 ms$^{-1}$ when it was suddenly stopped by a force. The body came to a halt. What was the magnitude of the force?
   (*a*) 2.5 N          (*b*) 3.2 N
   (*c*) 1.0 N          (*d*) 1.9 N

3. Two identical bodies move on two concentric circular paths. The speed and radius of the path of the outer body is double than that of the inner body. The force experienced by them will be
   (*a*) more for outer body
   (*b*) more for inner body
   (*c*) same for both the bodies
   (*d*) insufficient information to predict

4. A bob of mass 150 g is replaced by a mass of 200 g in a simple pendulum. The time period of the simple pendulum will
   (*a*) decrease
   (*b*) increase
   (*c*) not be affected
   (*d*) depend upon the material at the new bob

5. What would happen if friction were missing?
   (*a*) Cars would stop with the help of hydraulic brakes
   (*b*) Machines with a belts would not work
   (*c*) Walking would be easier
   (*d*) Writing on the paper would be smoother

6. Two circular discs have masses in the ratio of 1:2 and diameters in the ratio of 2:1. The ratio of their moments of inertia is
   (*a*) 1 : 1          (*b*) 2 : 1
   (*c*) 4 : 3          (*d*) 3 : 4

7. The time period of a simple pendulum is 2s. If its length be increased from times, the new time period would become
   (*a*) 6 seconds      (*b*) 8 seconds
   (*c*) 4 seconds      (*d*) 4$\pi$ seconds

8. A ball P is dropped vertically from a point. Another ball Q is thrown horizontally from the same point when would they reach the ground?
   (*a*) At the same time
   (*b*) Ball A would reach first
   (*c*) Ball B would reach first
   (*d*) Cannot be predicted

9. A copper disc has a circular hole at its centre. When the copper disc is heated to raise its temperature, the diameter of the hole will
   (*a*) increase
   (*b*) decrease
   (*c*) first increase, then decrease
   (*d*) first decrease, then increase

10. Why does a table tennis ball keep on dancing on a water jet with pressure?
   (*a*) The ball has the tendency to do so
   (*b*) The ball remains at the top of the jet due to the thrust of water and is not able to change its state
   (*c*) The ball falls down occasionally
   (*d*) None of the above

11. The centripetal force
   (*a*) always works in the direction of motion
   (*b*) always acts at right angle to the direction of motion
   (*c*) always acts parallel to the path of motion
   (*d*) None of the above

**12.** A solid metallic ball collides with an identical ball which is at rest. The first one is observed to become stationery immediately upon collision. The second ball

    (*a*) will remain at rest

    (*b*) will go forward with one-third of the velocity of the first ball (in motion)

    (*c*) will go forward with the same velocity as that of the first ball (in motion)

    (*d*) None of the above

**13.** Under isothermal conditions, the elasticity of a gas is equal to its

    (*a*) pressure

    (*b*) volume

    (*c*) molar volume

    (*d*) None of the above

**14.** Two spheres of the same size are made of the same metal. But one is hollow and the other one is solid. They are heated to the same temperature,

    (*a*) the hollow sphere will expand more

    (*b*) the solid sphere will expand more

    (*c*) both spheres will expand almost equally

    (*d*) None of the above

**15.** Which one of the following changes in the parameters of an ideal gas will change its volume four times?

    (*a*) Both temperature and pressure are doubled

    (*b*) Temperature is reduced to one-half and pressure is doubled

    (*c*) Temperature is reduced to one-fourth and there is no change in pressure

    (*d*) Pressure is reduced to one-fourth and there is no change in temperature

**16.** The pressure of a gas in a metal cylinder is 4 atmosphere at 27°C. The pressure at 54°C is (in atmospheres)

    (*a*) 3.36 atm       (*b*) 4.36 atm

    (*c*) 6.23 atm       (*d*) 5.36 atm

**17.** The coefficient of linear expansion for a solid is 0.000231°C. The coefficient of volume expansion of the same solid will be

    (*a*) double the coefficient of linear expansion

    (*b*) thrice the coefficient of linear expansion

    (*c*) one-half of the coefficeint of linear expansion

    (*d*) equal to the coefficient of linear expansion

**18.** Specific heat of a gas at constant pressure is greater than specific heat of that gas at constant volume. It is so because

    (*a*) at constant volume, work is done against external pressure

    (*b*) at constant pressure, work is done while expanding the gas

    (*c*) at constant pressure, force of attraction of molecules of the gas is greater

    (*d*) none of the above

**19.** A perfect white body is a body, which

    (*a*) reflects all the energy falling on it

    (*b*) absorbs all the energy falling on it

    (*c*) acts as a black body at times

    (*d*) None of the above

**20.** How many calories of heat are required by 1 gram of water at 99°C to boil off?

    (*a*) 530          (*b*) 640

    (*c*) 540          (*d*) 500

**21.** What is the relative humidity of a place when it is raining?

    (*a*) 50%        (*b*) 80%

    (*c*) 0%          (*d*) 100%

**22.** Which one of the following is not an internal combustion engine?

    (*a*) Steam engine

    (*b*) Truck engine

    (*c*) Motorcycle engine

    (*d*) Diesel engine set's engine

23. The temperature, to which a gas must be cooled before it can be liquefied by pressure alone, is known as its
    (a) saturation point
    (b) freezing point
    (c) liquification temperature
    (d) critical temperature

24. A pressure cooker works on the basis of the following principle
    (a) boiling point is lowered by increasing the pressure on the surface of the liquid
    (b) boiling point is raised by increasing the pressure on the surface of the liquid
    (c) more heat energy is consumed when the pressure is lowered
    (d) more heat energy is consumed when the quantity of liquid is increased

25. The rate at which, a hot body loses heat, is proportional to the
    (a) temperature of the body
    (b) square of temperature of the body
    (c) difference between the temperature of the body and the temperature of the surroundings
    (d) square root of the temperature of the body

26. If the scale of temperature is in degrees F instead of in degrees C, the value of specific heat will be
    (a) greater
    (b) same in both the cases
    (c) lesser
    (d) cannot predict

27. The most important principle of kinetic theory of gases is that
    (a) lighter gas molecules have higher average energies than heavier gas molecules
    (b) lighter gas molecules have lower average energies than heavier gas molecules
    (c) all the molecules in a gas have the same average energy value
    (d) All of the above are true

28. In isothermal expansion of an ideal gas
    (a) heat content remains constant
    (b) temperature remains constant
    (c) both heat and temperature remain constant
    (d) pressure and temperature of the gas remain constant

29. Which one of the following statements is true?
    (a) Ventilation of rooms is essential for good health because fresh air can enter into the room
    (b) The direct formation of a vapour from a solid is known as vaporisation
    (c) Ice is a good refrigeration because it has a high specific heat
    (d) The temperature of boiling water in steam engine boiler may be as high as 300°C as there is high pressure inside the boiler

30. Mercury is used as a thermometric substance because
    (a) it is a metal available in liquid state
    (b) it has high density and so, the length of the mercury column will be small
    (c) its vapour pressure will be the same
    (d) it has a uniform coefficent of volume expansion

31. When a liquid boils, the vapour pressure of the vapour is
    (a) equal to the atmospheric pressure
    (b) less than the atmospheric pressure
    (c) more than the atmospheric pressure
    (d) None of the above

32. The door of a refrigerator, which is working when left open
    (a) the temperature of the room will fall
    (b) the temperature of the room will rise
    (c) the room will have the same temperature as has been maintained within the refrigerator
    (d) None of the above

**33.** What will be the state of a gas below to critical temperature?
(*a*) Vapour
(*b*) Solid
(*c*) Liquid
(*d*) Solid and vapours

**34.** Which one of the following does not have a melting point?
(*a*) Glass     (*b*) Oxygen
(*c*) Mercury     (*d*) Aluminium

**35.** Why cotton cloth (double layer) acts as a warm cloth in winter?
(*a*) Cotton has insulating property
(*b*) The layer of air trapped between the two layers acts as a bad conductor of heat
(*c*) The human body adjusts its temperature
(*d*) All of the above

**36.** How do the molecules of a gas behave?
(*a*) Flexible, inelastic spheres
(*b*) Flexible, elastic spheres
(*c*) Rigid, perfectly elastic spheres
(*d*) Depends upon the type of the gas

**37.** Two sound waves, passing through air, have their wavelength in the ratio of 4:5. Their frequencies are in the ratio of
(*a*) $4 : 5$     (*b*) $3 : 4$
(*c*) $5 : 4$     (*d*) $1 : 1$

**38.** The ratio of frequency of a fundamental note in an open pipe to that in a closed pipe of the same length is
(*a*) $2 : 1$     (*b*) $2 : 3$
(*c*) $3 : 2$     (*d*) $1 : 2$

**39.** Two coupled vibrating systems are said to be in resonance if their
(*a*) amplitudes are equal
(*b*) frequencies are equal
(*c*) damping factors are equal
(*d*) temperature are equal

**40.** In which medium, would you be able to hear the sound of a train (the train is at a great distance from you)?
(*a*) From the air
(*b*) From the steel rails
(*c*) From the wooden planks under the rails
(*d*) It is not possible to hear the sound

**41.** Why the auditoria walls are provided with cardboard panels and porons wall furnishings?
(*a*) So that the sound from the stage may be heard properly
(*b*) So that the echo effect may be minimised
(*c*) So that the sound may appear to be pleasing on the ears of the listeners
(*d*) All of the above

**42.** A musical sound is the one that is produced
(*a*) at regular intervals
(*b*) in quick succession
(*c*) Both (*a*) and (*b*)
(*d*) None of (*a*) and (*b*)

**43.** The loudness of sound depends upon
(*a*) its velocity     (*b*) its pitch
(*c*) its amplitude     (*d*) its frequency

**44.** Transverse waves cannot travel through
(*a*) lubricating oil
(*b*) a stretched nylon string
(*c*) hydrogen gas
(*d*) an iron rod

**45.** For an organ pipe, the wavelength of the fundamental note is
(*a*) equal to the length of the pipe
(*b*) half the length of the pipe
(*c*) one-fourth the length of the pipe
(*d*) twice the length of the pipe

**46.** The frequency of sound can remain unchanged even if we double the length of the wire, provided
(*a*) tension of the wire is doubled
(*b*) tension of the wire is decreased four-fold
(*c*) tension of the wire is halved
(*d*) tension of the wire is increased four-fold.

47. Which characteristic of sound enables us to distinguish two musical notes coming from different sources but having the same frequency and loudness?-
    (*a*) Timber
    (*b*) Pitch
    (*c*) Loudness
    (*d*) None of the above

48. As the length of a vibrating column increases, its frequency
    (*a*) decreases
    (*b*) increases
    (*c*) remains the same
    (*d*) increases if the vibrating column is not in air

49. The sound of frequency 512 Hz is higher than the sound of frequency 256 Hz by
    (*a*) one octave    (*b*) two octaves
    (*c*) half an octave (*d*) three octaves

50. Which one of the following rays has the greatest value of wavelength?
    (*a*) Red                (*b*) Yellow green
    (*c*) Ultra violet    (*d*) Infrared

51. When a train arriving at a railway platform approaches a person standing on the platform, the noise produced by the engine increases. This phenomenon is governed by
    (*a*) Kundt's Rule
    (*b*) Law of Tension
    (*c*) Law of Mass
    (*d*) Doppler's Effect

52. Plane waves are incident on a concave reflector. The reflected waves will be
    (*a*) plane
    (*b*) circular
    (*c*) parabolic
    (*d*) None of the above

53. Antinodes are the points of
    (*a*) minimum displacement
    (*b*) maximum displacement
    (*c*) nil displacement
    (*d*) None of the above

54. For a sound wave in air, the vibrations of the particles of a medium
    (*a*) are parallel to the direction of propagation
    (*b*) are perpendicular to the direction of propagation
    (*c*) may either be parallel or perpendicular to the direction of propagation
    (*d*) None of the above

55. For sound waves in air, the vibration are
    (*a*) electromagnetic
    (*b*) longitudinal
    (*c*) transverse
    (*d*) None of the above

56. If two vibrating systems are in resonance, then
    (*a*) their amplitudes are equal
    (*b*) their frequencies are equal
    (*c*) their temperatures are equal
    (*d*) their intensities are equal

57. How many nodes and antinodes are there in a tuning fork?
    (*a*) 6                (*b*) 5
    (*c*) 3                (*d*) 4

58. In which type of waves, there is no flow of energy?
    (*a*) Longitudinal  (*b*) Transverse
    (*c*) Progressive    (*d*) Stationary

59. The longer the length of the prong of a tunning fork is the frequency of vibration produced.
    (*a*) lower
    (*b*) higher
    (*c*) same
    (*d*) cannot be predicted

60. What is interference?
    (*a*) Two waves of different amplitudes travel in the same direction
    (*b*) Two waves of same amplitude travel in opposite directions
    (*c*) Two waves of different amplitudes travel in opposite directions
    (*d*) None of the above

**61.** The distance between two nearest troughs of a wave is called
(*a*) time period    (*b*) trough bar
(*c*) wavelength    (*d*) trough tide

**62.** The phenomenon of echo of sound waves is due to
(*a*) reflection    (*b*) interference
(*c*) diffraction    (*d*) all of the above

**63.** Velocity of sound in a medium is
(*a*) independent of its density
(*b*) inversely proportional to its density
(*c*) directly proportional to its density
(*d*) inversely proportional to the square root of its density

**64.** Which one of the following has the longest wavelength?
(*a*) Radio waves    (*b*) Sound waves
(*c*) X-rays    (*d*) Infrared ray

**65.** Which one of the following mirrors can form a virtual image?
(*a*) Concave Mirror
(*b*) Convex mirro
(*c*) Both (*a*) and (*b*)
(*d*) None of (*a*) and (*b*)

**66.** A person is suffering from myopia. What type of lens should be used by him to rectify his vision?
(*a*) A cylindrical lens
(*b*) A convex lens
(*c*) A concave lens
(*d*) None of the above

**67.** When a ray of light goes from a denser medium to a rarer medium, then the angle of refraction goes on
(*a*) increasing
(*b*) decreasing
(*c*) no change takes place
(*d*) insufficient information to predict

**68.** Which one of the following waves has the lowest wavelength?
(*a*) Heat radiations
(*b*) X-rays
(*c*) Light radiations
(*d*) Sound waves

**69.** Why does a diamond shine so brightly?
(*a*) Due to refraction
(*b*) Due to total internal reflection
(*c*) Due to reflection
(*d*) None of the above

**70.** Which one of the following colours suffers maximum deviation after dispersion through a prism?
(*a*) Green    (*b*) Red
(*c*) Yellow    (*d*) Violet

**71.** If in the case of a convex lens, the objective is at infinity, then the nature of the image is
(*a*) real, diminished and inverted
(*b*) real and highly diminished
(*c*) vertical and diminished
(*d*) None of the above

**72.** The power of a telescope to see the two objects distinctly is called its
(*a*) dispersive power
(*b*) magnifying power
(*c*) resolving power
(*d*) None of the above

**73.** What is the unit of power of lens?
(*a*) Candela    (*b*) Dioptre
(*c*) Metre    (*d*) Lux

**74.** Which one of the following mirrors is free from spherical abberration?
(*a*) Convex
(*b*) Concave
(*c*) Parabolic
(*d*) None of the above

**75.** Why the rainbow is formed after rains?
(*a*) The tiny water molecules act as slabs
(*b*) The tiny water molecules act as prisms
(*c*) The tiny water molecules act as convex lenses
(*d*) None of the above

**76.** Which type of mirror (reflector) is used in headlights of cars?
(*a*) Convex
(*b*) Concave
(*c*) Either of (*a*) or (*b*)
(*d*) None of (*a*) or (*b*)

**77.** When reflection takes place from a spherical mirror, positions of the object and its image are known as
(*a*) poles
(*b*) conjugate foci
(*c*) focal lengths
(*d*) None of the above

**78.** Cylindrical lenses are used to cure the following optic disease.
(*a*) Myopia      (*b*) Hypermetropia
(*c*) Astigmatism   (*d*) Presbyopia

**79.** Presbyopia is an eye defect in which, a person can see
(*a*) nearer objects clearly
(*b*) distant objects clearly
(*c*) both distant and nearer objects clearly
(*d*) None of the above

**80.** Light waves are similar in nature to
(*a*) Gamma Rays
(*b*) X-Rays
(*c*) Cathode Rays
(*d*) None of the above

**81.** Which one of the following is more monochromatic?
(*a*) Laser beam    (*b*) White light
(*c*) Sodium light   (*d*) Mercury light

**82.** Critical angle for the passage of light from glass to air is minimum in value for
(*a*) green rays     (*b*) yellow rays
(*c*) violet rays     (*d*) red rays

**83.** If there were no atmosphere on the earth, duration of daylight on the earth would
(*a*) increase
(*b*) decrease
(*c*) remain the same
(*d*) depends upon the weather

**84.** The dispersive power of a prism depends upon
(*a*) the material of prism
(*b*) the angle of the prism
(*c*) the size of the prism
(*d*) None of the above

**85.** A beam of monochromatic light is passing from one medium to another. Which one of the following qualities does not change?
(*a*) Amplitude     (*b*) Velocity
(*c*) Frequency     (*d*) Wavelength

**86.** The totally dark part of the shadow is known as
(*a*) umbra
(*b*) penumbra
(*c*) eclipse
(*d*) None of the above

**87.** A piece of cloth is red in colour. It is viewed in yellow light. What would be the colour of the cloth before our eyes?
(*a*) Red       (*b*) Orange
(*c*) Yellow     (*d*) Black

**88.** Total internal reflection cannot take place when a ray passes from
(*a*) glass to air   (*b*) air to glass
(*c*) glass to water (*d*) water to air

**89.** When a plane mirror is rotated through a certain angle, the reflected ray turns through double the angle. The size of the image
(*a*) is doubled
(*b*) becomes infinite
(*c*) is halved
(*d*) remains the same

**90.** In a compound microscope, the nature of final image is
(*a*) virtual, inverted, magnified
(*b*) real, inverted, diminshed
(*c*) virtual, inverted, diminished
(*d*) real, inverted, magnified

**91.** The angle of dip is the angle
(*a*) between the magnetic meridian and the geographical meridian
(*b*) between the direction of earth's magnetic field and the horizontal direction
(*c*) between the vertical component of earth's magnetic field and magnetic meridian
(*d*) None of the above

**92.** If the pole strength as well as the distance between the two magnetic poles is doubled, the force between them
(*a*) reduces by one-half
(*b*) remains unchanged
(*c*) increases two times
(*d*) increases four times

**93.** The magnetic field produced by electrons in atoms and molecules is
(*a*) due to their spin motions
(*b*) due to their orbital motions
(*c*) due to both of their spin and orbital motions
(*d*) neither due to their spin motions nor due to their orbital motions

**94.** What is angle between geographical and magnetic meridian known as?
(*a*) Angle of magnetic dip
(*b*) Angle of declination
(*c*) Angle of deflection
(*d*) None of the above

**95.** At the centre of a magnetic bar, the magnetism is
(*a*) maximum
(*b*) minimum
(*c*) zero
(*d*) cannot be predicted

**96.** If a metal is weakly repelled by a magnet, then the metal is expected to be
(*a*) non-magnetic    (*b*) paramagnetic
(*c*) diamagnetic    (*d*) ferromagnetic

**97.** The vertical plane, which passes through the magnetic axis of a freely suspended magnet, is known as
(*a*) magnetic moment
(*b*) magnetic length
(*c*) magnetic axis
(*d*) magnetic meridian

**98.** The magnet attracts both ends of a rod of magnetic substance (but not magnetised) due to the phenomenon of
(*a*) electric field
(*b*) magnetic induction
(*c*) polarisation
(*d*) None of the above

**99.** A magnet can be demagnetised by
(*a*) hammering a magnet
(*b*) putting it in water
(*c*) colling it
(*d*) putting it in contact with iron

**100.** The magnetic flux is expressed in
(*a*) Oersted      (*b*) Gauss
(*c*) Weber      (*d*) Lux

**101.** Magnetic storms are due to
(*a*) the rotation of the earth around its axis
(*b*) the revolution of the earth around the sun
(*c*) the sun spots
(*d*) None of the above

**102.** The line, which joins the North Pole and the South Pole of a magnet, is called its
(*a*) Magnetic Meridian
(*b*) Magnetic Axis
(*c*) Magnetic Flux
(*d*) None of the above

**103.** The effective length of a bar magnet is ............. its geometrical length
(*a*) one-sixth      (*b*) five-fourth
(*c*) two-third      (*d*) three-fourth

**104.** If the atom is to be electrically neutral, then
(*a*) proton = neutron
(*b*) neutron = electron
(*c*) proton = electron
(*d*) protons + electrons = neutrons

**105.** Which one of the following is a diamagnetic substance?
(*a*) Platinum      (*b*) Aluminium
(*c*) Copper      (*d*) Nickel

**106.** In which product, would you find the application of magnets?
(*a*) AC Motor
(*b*) Dynamo
(*c*) Steam locomotive
(*d*) Loud speaker

**107.** The permeability of a diamagnetic material is
(*a*) less than one
(*b*) greater than one

(*c*) equal to one
(*d*) difficult to determine

**108.** Which one of the following cannot be magnetised?
(*a*) Iron     (*b*) Cobalt
(*c*) Nickel     (*d*) Mica

**109.** Two parallel currents, flowing in the same direction
(*a*) repel one another
(*b*) attract one another
(*c*) do not exert any force on one another
(*d*) None of the above

**110.** Two parallel wires carry currents in opposite directions. They will
(*a*) attract each other
(*b*) repel each other
(*c*) neither attract nor repel
(*d*) Cannot be predicted

**111.** When the temperature of a metal is raised, its conductance
(*a*) increases
(*b*) decreases
(*c*) remains the same
(*d*) None of the above

**112.** Which device is used to step up or step down AC power?
(*a*) Convertor     (*b*) Rectifer
(*c*) Transformer     (*d*) DC generator

**113.** The safety fuse is able to protect the electrical devices because it has a low
(*a*) resistivity
(*b*) melting point
(*c*) conductivity
(*d*) None of the above

**114.** The transistor acts as a
(*a*) semiconductor (*b*) rectifier
(*c*) thermionic value (*d*) insulator

**115.** The commonly used material used in heating appliances is Nichrome, which is an alloy of
(*a*) Nickel and Lead
(*b*) Nickel and Chromium
(*c*) Lead and Chromium
(*d*) Nickel, Lead and Chromium

**116.** If the length and cross-section of a wire are doubled, then
(*a*) its resistance will increase four times
(*b*) its resistance will decrease four times
(*c*) its resistance will remain unchanged
(*d*) its resistance will remain unchanged

**117.** What is the unit of conductance?
(*a*) Ohm     (*b*) Henry
(*c*) Mho     (*d*) Oersted

**118.** What type of material is used for making the cores of transformers?
(*a*) CRGO     (*b*) Steel
(*c*) Chromium     (*d*) Copper

**119.** If silver is the best conductor of electricity, then why is it not used in transformers and motors?
(*a*) Difficult to obtain
(*b*) Difficult to draw in wires
(*c*) Costly
(*d*) All of the above

**120.** In which of the following materials, will there be a reduction in electrical resistance with the rise of its temperature?
(*a*) Nichrome     (*b*) Platinum
(*c*) Selenium     (*d*) Gold

**121.** When the cells are connected in parallel, the total emf will be equal to
(*a*) sum of emf values of all the cells
(*b*) the emf of a single cell
(*c*) half the sum of emf values of all the cells
(*d*) None of the above

**122.** An electric line of force is
(*a*) a curve, the tangent to which at any point gives the direction of the electric field at the point
(*b*) the path along which a unit positive charge would move, if free to do so, when placed in the electric field
(*c*) Both of the above
(*d*) None of the above

**123.** Lenz's law is a consequence of the law of conservation of
(*a*) momentum
(*b*) charge

(*c*) energy
(*d*) angular momentum

**124.** Which device uses a gate?
   (*a*) SCR       (*b*) Diode
   (*c*) Rectifier    (*d*) Convertor

**125.** The magnetic field produced in a solenoid coil and depend inversely upon
   (*a*) current
   (*b*) length
   (*c*) number of turns
   (*d*) constant K

**126.** In which device would you find the commutator?
   (*a*) AC generator  (*b*) DC generator
   (*c*) AC motor    (*d*) All of the above

**127.** The main source of energy of the sun is
   (*a*) fusion of heavy nuclei
   (*b*) fusion of light nuclei
   (*c*) fission of light nuclei
   (*d*) fission of heavy nuclei

**128.** A nuclear reactor is a device, which produces energy with the help of
   (*a*) nuclear fusion
   (*b*) nuclear fission
   (*c*) thermonuclear reaction
   (*d*) simple chemical reactions

**129.** If the chain reaction of the nuclear power plant were not controlled, the power plant would
   (*a*) become defunct
   (*b*) explode like a nuclear bomb
   (*c*) generate pollution due to leakage of chemicals
   (*d*) continue to work

**130.** Which material is used to produce nuclear power?
   (*a*) Platinum    (*b*) Radium
   (*c*) Uranium    (*d*) All of the above

**131.** The best method to find the life of an old wooden log is to
   (*a*) use carbon dating technique
   (*b*) count the number of rings in its stem
   (*c*) burn the piece of wood and find the amount of carbon in it
   (*d*) use either of the aforesaid methods

**132.** Which was the first nuclear research reactor of India?
   (*a*) Apsara    (*b*) Zerlina
   (*c*) Purnima    (*d*) Kaiga

**133.** Nucleii with the same atomic number are called
   (*a*) isomers    (*b*) isotopes
   (*c*) isotones    (*d*) isobars

**134.** When an electron and a positron combine, a new particle emerges. It is a/an
   (*a*) alpha particle
   (*b*) positron
   (*c*) neutron
   (*d*) None of the above

**135.** Why is heavy water used in nuclear power reactors?
   (*a*) To stop the flow of electrons
   (*b*) To regulate the speed of fast neutrons
   (*c*) To absorb the harmful radiations of the nuclear chain reaction
   (*d*) None of the above

**136.** What is the difference between the parts of a diode and those of a triode?
   (*a*) The anode missing in diode
   (*b*) The cathode missing in triode
   (*c*) The grid missing in triode
   (*d*) None of the above

**137.** Which particle initiates a chain reaction in uranium?
   (*a*) Neutron
   (*b*) $\alpha$-Particle
   (*c*) Electron
   (*d*) Any one of the above

**138.** Why fusion reaction is difficult to achieve?
   (*a*) Light nucleii are not a available
   (*b*) High values of temperature and pressure required to initiate the reaction
   (*c*) Heavey nucleii are not available
   (*d*) None of the above

**139.** In which place out of the following, heavy water is not being manufactured?

(*a*) Nangal     (*b*) Tuticorin
(*c*) Managura     (*d*) Vizag

**140.** Which element can be enriched to produce nuclear fission material?
(*a*) Thorium     (*b*) Iridium
(*c*) Silicon     (*d*) Lead

**141.** The junction of NPN transistor is rich in
(*a*) electrons
(*b*) holes
(*c*) neutrons
(*d*) None of the above

**142.** A transistor can be used effectively as a/an
(*a*) diode
(*b*) amplifier
(*c*) rectifier
(*d*) All of the above

**143.** Balmer series, in the emission spectrum of a hydrogen atom, lie in the
(*a*) ultra-violet region
(*b*) violet region
(*c*) infrared region
(*d*) visible region

**144.** Why a rocket is made to lose its fuel cylinders while it moves up in space?
(*a*) It must lose weight
(*b*) It must remove fuel cylinders else it could catch fire
(*c*) It must become streamlined
(*d*) All of the above

**145.** Atmosphere is present on earth due to
(*a*) gravitational attraction
(*b*) air
(*c*) cloud
(*d*) surface tension

**146.** The cause of weightlessness in space-ships revolving round the earth is
(*a*) zero gravity     (*b*) acceleration
(*c*) inertia     (*d*) surface tension

**147.** The escape velocity of a body projected from the surface of a planet does not depend upon
(*a*) the mass of the earth
(*b*) the direction of projection of the body
(*c*) the mass of the planet
(*d*) radius of the planet

**148.** The orbital velocity of Jupiter is
(*a*) zero
(*b*) equal to the orbital velocity of earth
(*c*) less than the orbital velocity
(*d*) more than the orbital velocity of earth

**149.** The weight of a body of mass $m$ when taken to the bottom of deep mine
(*a*) decrease
(*b*) increase
(*c*) its mass increases
(*d*) its mass decreases

**150.** Newton's law of gravitation is valid for
(*a*) all bodies
(*b*) only heavenly bodies
(*c*) only for small bodies
(*d*) only for changed bodies

═══════════════ ANSWERS ═══════════════

| 1 | 2 | 3 | 4 | 5 | 6 | 7 | 8 | 9 | 10 |
|---|---|---|---|---|---|---|---|---|---|
| (*a*) | (*c*) | (*a*) | (*c*) | (*b*) | (*b*) | (*c*) | (*a*) | (*a*) | (*b*) |
| **11** | **12** | **13** | **14** | **15** | **16** | **17** | **18** | **19** | **20** |
| (*b*) | (*c*) | (*a*) | (*c*) | (*d*) | (*b*) | (*b*) | (*c*) | (*a*) | (*c*) |
| **21** | **22** | **23** | **24** | **25** | **26** | **27** | **28** | **29** | **30** |
| (*d*) | (*a*) | (*d*) | (*b*) | (*d*) | (*c*) | (*c*) | (*b*) | (*d*) | (*d*) |

| 31 | 32 | 33 | 34 | 35 | 36 | 37 | 38 | 39 | 40 |
|---|---|---|---|---|---|---|---|---|---|
| (*a*) | (*c*) | (*a*) | (*a*) | (*a*) | (*c*) | (*c*) | (*a*) | (*b*) | (*b*) |
| 41 | 42 | 43 | 44 | 45 | 46 | 47 | 48 | 49 | 50 |
| (*b*) | (*d*) | (*c*) | (*c*) | (*d*) | (*c*) | (*a*) | (*a*) | (*a*) | (*d*) |
| 51 | 52 | 53 | 54 | 55 | 56 | 57 | 58 | 59 | 60 |
| (*d*) | (*b*) | (*b*) | (*a*) | (*b*) | (*b*) | (*d*) | (*a*) | (*d*) | (*c*) |
| 61 | 62 | 63 | 64 | 65 | 66 | 67 | 68 | 69 | 70 |
| (*c*) | (*a*) | (*d*) | (*b*) | (*a*) | (*d*) | (*a*) | (*b*) | (*b*) | (*c*) |
| 71 | 72 | 73 | 74 | 75 | 76 | 77 | 78 | 79 | 80 |
| (*b*) | (*b*) | (*b*) | (*b*) | (*b*) | (*b*) | (*b*) | (*c*) | (*a*) | (*a*) |
| 81 | 82 | 83 | 84 | 85 | 86 | 87 | 88 | 89 | 90 |
| (*b*) | (*c*) | (*b*) | (*a*) | (*c*) | (*a*) | (*b*) | (*b*) | (*d*) | (*a*) |
| 91 | 92 | 93 | 94 | 95 | 96 | 97 | 98 | 99 | 100 |
| (*b*) | (*b*) | (*c*) | (*b*) | (*c*) | (*c*) | (*d*) | (*b*) | (*a*) | (*c*) |
| 101 | 102 | 103 | 104 | 105 | 106 | 107 | 108 | 109 | 110 |
| (*c*) | (*b*) | (*b*) | (*c*) | (*c*) | (*c*) | (*a*) | (*d*) | (*c*) | (*b*) |
| 111 | 112 | 113 | 114 | 115 | 116 | 117 | 118 | 119 | 120 |
| (*b*) | (*c*) | (*b*) | (*b*) | (*b*) | (*d*) | (*c*) | (*a*) | (*c*) | (*c*) |
| 121 | 122 | 123 | 124 | 125 | 126 | 127 | 128 | 129 | 130 |
| (*b*) | (*d*) | (*c*) | (*a*) | (*a*) | (*b*) | (*b*) | (*b*) | (*b*) | (*c*) |
| 131 | 132 | 133 | 134 | 135 | 136 | 137 | 138 | 139 | 140 |
| (*a*) | (*a*) | (*b*) | (*a*) | (*b*) | (*c*) | (*a*) | (*b*) | (*d*) | (*a*) |
| 141 | 142 | 143 | 144 | 145 | 146 | 147 | 148 | 149 | 150 |
| (*a*) | (*b*) | (*d*) | (*a*) | (*a*) | (*b*) | (*b*) | (*c*) | (*a*) | (*a*) |

★ ★ ★ ★ ★

# CHEMISTRY



## ATOMS AND ITS STRUCTURE

*Nucleus:* The nucleus (atomic nucleus) is the center of an atom. It is composed of one or more protons and usually some neutrons as well. The simplest atom of all, hydrogen, has one protone in its nucleus.

*Proton* is a subatomic particle with a positive electric charge of $1.6 \times 10^{-19}$ coulomb and a mass of 938 MeV ($1.6726231 - 10^{-27}$ kg, or about 1800 times the mass of an electron).

*Neutron* is a subatomic particle with no net electric charge and a mass of 940 MeV (very slightly more than a proton). The nucleus of most atoms consists of protons and neutrons.

*Electron* is a subatomic particle with a negative charge. In an atom the electrons surround the nucleus of protons and neutrons. The electron has a negative electric charge of $-1.6 \times 10^{-19}$ coulombs, and a mass of about $9.10 \times 10^{-31}$ kg, which is 1/1800 of the proton mass.

## FAMOUS INVENTIONS

| | |
|---|---|
| Atomic Theory | **John Dalton** |
| Electron | **J.J.Thomson** |
| Proton | **Rutherford** |
| Neutron | **Masley** |
| Dynamite | **Alfred Nobel** |
| Atomic Number | **Chadwick** |
| Periodic Table | **Dmitry Mendeleyev** |
| Radioactivity | **Henri Becquerel** |
| Oxygen | **J.Priestly** |
| Hydrogen | **Cavendish** |

*Atomic Number:* The number of protons in an atoms nucleus is called the atomic number (Z), and determines the element (for example hydrogen, carbon, oxygen, etc.).

*Atomic Weight (A):* The atomic weight is the sum of neutrons and protons in the nucleus of the atom also called Mass Number.

*Molecular Weight:* The molecular weight of a molecule is the sum of the atomic weights of the atoms making up that molecule.

*Isotopes:* Isotopes are atoms of a chemical element whose nuclei have the same atomic number, Z, but different atomic weights, A.

*Isobars:* Isobars have the same isotopic mass but different atomic number. e.g. Argon, Potassium and calcium $^{18}Ar_{40}$, $^{19}K_{40}$, $^{20}Ca_{40}$.

*Isotone :* Isotone contains the same number of neutrons but different numbers of protons.

## ELEMENTS

Elements are substances compose of same type of atom. Hydrogen, oxygen, chlorine, sodium, and iron are examples of elements. Ninety two elements are known to occur in nature, and 22 more have been made artificially.

## Some common elements and their applications

*Nitrogen:* Nitrogen is the most abundant constituent in the atmosphere composes about four-fifths (78.03 per cent) by volume of the atmosphere. Nitrous oxide is known as laughing gas. Nitrous oxide is used as an anesthesia. Liquid nitrogen is used as coolant in cryogenics.

*Oxygen:* It was discovered by Joseph priestly. Oxygen composes 21 percent by volume of atmosphere. It is used in high-temperature welding torches, administered to patients whose breathing is impaired and oxygen-enriched air is used in open-hearth furnaces for steel manufacture. High-purity oxygen is used also in the metal-fabrication industries; in liquid form it is used in a propellant for guided missiles and rockets.

*Argon:* Argon is the third most prevalent gas in the earth atmosphere. Argon is also used in one type of neon lamp giving blue light whereas pure neon gives a red light. It is preferred because it requires a lower voltage than neon.

*Hydrogen:* Hydrogen exits as a gas at room temperature and is highly flammable. In stars, hydrogen nuclei combine with each other in nuclear reactions to form helium atoms. The isotopes of Hydrogen are Deuterium and tritium. Spacecrafts use hydrogen as fuel that reacts with fluorine or oxygen. Nuclear plants use D2O as a moderator.

*Carbon dioxide:* Carbon dioxide does not burn and support ordinary combustion; it is used in fire extinguishers. Solid carbon dioxide is known as Dry ice widely used as refrigerant. The presence of carbon dioxide in the blood stimulates breathing. For this reason, $CO_2$ is added to the oxygen in artificial respiration.

*Methane:* Methane also know as marsh gas, gas composed of carbon and hydrogen with formula $CH_4$, the first member of the paraffin or alkane series of hydrocarbons. It is lighter than air, colorless, odorless, and flammable. It occurs in natural gas, in coal mines, as a by-product of petroleum refining, and as a product of decomposition of matter in swamps.

*Iron:* Iron is a metal extracted from iron ore, and is hardly ever found in the free (elemental) state. Depending upon the carbon content Iron can be classified into: Pig Iron (4%–5%), Cast iron(2–3.5%), carbon steel(0.5–1.5%) and Wrought Iron( < 0.5%).

*Sodium:* Sodium is a constituent of table salt and baking soda. Sulfur, however, is a common impurity in fossil fuels used for home heating and the production of electricity. Large amounts of $SO^2$ are causing both local air pollution as well as acid rain.

*The halogens:* The halogens are: fluorine, chlorine, bromine, iodine, and astatine.

- Chlorine gas is greenish yellow. It is a powerful bleaching, and disinfecting agent. Chlorine is an important chemical in water purification.
- Bromine is a red volatile liquid at room temperature.
- Astatine is radioactive and heaviest of Halogens.
- Iodine is a bluish-black, lustrous solid. Potassium Iodide is used in Photography. Iodine 131 is used as a tracer in medicine.

# COMPOUND

Compound is a substance formed from two or more elements. eg. Water. **Mixture** is the product of a mechanical blending or mixing of chemical substances without other chemical change, so that each ingredient substance retains its own chemical properties. While there are no chemical changes in a mixture, physical properties of a mixture, such as its melting point, may differ from those of its components. Mixtures can usually be separated by mechanical means. There are different types of Compounds are Acids, Bases, Salts, Oxides and organic compounds.

*Acids:* An acid is a water-soluble, sour-tasting chemical compound. An acid always has a pH of less than 7 and turns litmus red. An acid reacts with a base in a neutralization reaction to form a salt.

| Acid | Used as |
|---|---|
| Ascetic Acid | Vinegar |
| Amino Acid | Basis of protein |
| Ascorbic Acid | Vitamin C |
| Carbolic Acid/Phenol | Disinfectant |
| Citric Acid | Citrus fruits |
| Nitrohydrochloric Acid(Aqua Regia) | Dissolving gold and platinum |
| Tartaric Acid | Used in baking powder |
| Carbonic Acid | Carbonated beverages |
| Formic Acid | Ants |
| Lactic Acid | Sour milk |
| Malic Acid | Unripe apples |
| Nitric Acid/Aqua Fortis | Used in explosives and rocket fuels |
| Prussic Acid/ Hydrocynic Acid | Poison |
| Salicylic Acid | Basis of aspirin |
| Tannic Acid/Tannin | Found in tea |
| Uric Acid | In the urine of birds and reptiles |
| Oxalic Acid | Spinach |

*Bases :* A base is a chemical compound that will neutralize an acid and form a salt and water. Bases are typically water-soluble, bitter tasting, turns litmus blue and always have a pH greater than 7 in solution. e.g. baking soda , sodium carbonate etc.

*Litmus:* A mixture of pigments extracted from certain lichens that turns blue in basic solution and red in acidic solution.

*Salt:* A salt is a neutral compound composed of cations bound to anions. A cation is a positively charged ion. Metals typically form cations where as anions are negatively charged ion.

*Organic compound:* These contain carbon chemically bound to hydrogen. They often contain other elements (particularly O, N, halogens, or S).

# METALS & NON METALS

*Metals:* Metals are shiny (lustre), high density, ductile and malleable, high melting point, hard, and conduct electricity and heat.

*Ores:* An ore is a mineral containing a metal as a proportion of its content. which is economical to extract its metallic component.

| Substance | Important Ores |
|---|---|
| Aluminium | Bauxite |
| Antimony | Stibnite |
| Beryllium | Beryl , Crysoberyl |
| Calcium | Lime stone, Marble, Chalk, Gypsum, Flurosper |

| Substance | Important Ores |
|---|---|
| Chromium | Chromite |
| Cobalt | Smaltite |
| Copper | Cuprite, Bornite |
| Iron | Hematite,        Magnatite |
| Lead | Galena,        Masicot, Serusite |
| Magnicium | Magnesite, Dolomite, Carnallite |
| Manganese | Pyrolusite, Hausmannite |
| Mercury | Cinnabar |
| Molybdenum | Molybdenite & wulfenite |
| Nickel | Pantilandite and Gargnierite |
| Phosphorous | Phosphorite Apatite, Chlorapatite |
| Potassium | Carnelite , Saltpetre |
| Silver | Argentite |
| Sodium | Rock Salt, Chile Saltpetre |
| Sulphur | Galena, Copper Pyrites & Iron Pyrites |
| Tin | Cassiterite,     Tin stone |
| Titanium | Rutile, Ilmenite |
| Uranium | Pitchblende |
| Zinc | Zinc Blends,   Calamine |

# SOME IMPORTANT PROCESSES

(*a*)  ***Gravity separation:*** The heavier metal or metallic mineral particles seperated from the lighter gangue. Gold and magnetite are separated in this way.

(*b*)  ***Flotation:*** In this method, finely ground ore is mixed with a liquid. The metal or metallic mineral floats while the gangue sinks.

(*c*)  ***Magnetic separation:*** Metals that have magnetic properties are seperated from the gangue e.g. magnetite.

(*d*)  ***Smelting:*** the ore is heated with a reducing agent and a flux to a high temperature. The reducing agent combines with the oxygen in a metallic oxide, leaving pure metal; and the flux combines with the gangue to form a slag that is liquid poured away from the metal. The production of pig iron extract copper, lead, nickel use this process.

(*e*)  ***Amalgamation*** is a metallurgical process that utilizes mercury to dissolve silver or gold to form an amalgam.

(*f*)  ***Electrolysis:*** In this process, the metal is deposited at the cathode from aqueous solutions or in an electrolytic furnace. Copper, nickel, zinc, silver, and gold are several examples of metals that are refined by deposition from aqueous solutions. Aluminium, barium, calcium, magnesium, beryllium, potassium, and sodium are metals that are processed in electrolytic furnaces.

# SOME INTERESTING POINTS

Osmium and iridium are the most dense metals, and lithium is the least dense. Bismuth has the lowest electrical conductivity of the metallic elements, and silver the highest at ordinary temperatures. Gallium, mercury, cesium, and rubidium are the only metal elements that melt near room temperature

*Metalloids* have intermediate in properties between the metals and the nonmetals. Most common is that metalloids are usually semiconductors rather than conductors. They are boron, silicon, germanium, arsenic, antimony, tellurium, Polonium.

*Non metal:* A non metal is a substance that conducts heat and electricity poorly, is brittle or waxy or gaseous, and cannot be hammered into sheets or drawn into wire. The nonmetals are: nitrogen, oxygen, fluorine, phosphorus, sulfur, chlorine, selenium.

*Alkali metals:* They are soft compared to other metals, have low melting points, and are so reactive that they are never found freely in nature. eg. lithium, sodium, potassium, rubidium, cesium, and francium. Francium exists only in a radioactive form.

*Alkaline Earth Metals:* They are brittle, the alkaline earth metals are malleable, conduct electricity and when heated, burn readily in air. eg. beryllium, magnesium, calcium, strontium, barium, and radium.

# ALLOYS

An alloy is a compound, of two or more elements, at least one of which is a metal.

| Alloy | Composition |
| --- | --- |
| Duraluminium | Aluminium, copper, magnesium, and manganese |
| Gun Metal | Copper, Tin |
| Steel | Iron, Carbon |
| Stainless Steel | Iron, carbon, chromium, tunsten |
| Petwar | Tin, Antimony & Copper |
| Bronze | Copper, Tin and Zinc |
| German Silver | Copper, Zinc and Nickel |
| Electrum | Gold & Silver |
| 18 carat Gold | Gold, Silver & copper |
| Dentist Amalgam | Mercury  Copper |
| Yellow Brass | Copper Zinc |
| Brass | Copper & Zinc |
| Nichrome | Nickel & Chromium |
| Plumbers Solder | Lead and tin |

# COMMON CHEMICALS AND THEIR CHEMICAL NAMES

| Common Name | Chemical Name |
| --- | --- |
| Grain alcohol | ethyl alcohol |
| Wood Alcohol | methyl alcohol |
| alum | aluminum potassium sulfate |
| alumina | aluminum oxide |
| baking soda | sodium bicarbonate |
| bleaching powder | chlorinated lime |
| blue vitriol | copper sulfate |
| brimstone | sulfur |

| Common Name | Chemical Name |
| --- | --- |
| carbolic acid | phenol |
| carbonic acid gas | carbon dioxide |
| epsom salts | gypsum |
| hypo (photography) | sodium thiosulfate solution |
| gypsum | natural calcium sulfate |
| lime | calcium oxide |
| lime, slaked | calcium hydroxide |
| limewater | calcium hydroxide |
| lunar caustic | silver nitrate |
| magnesia | magnesium oxide |
| mercury oxide, black | mercurous oxide |
| methanol | methyl alcohol |
| methylated spirits | methyl alcohol |
| pearl ash | potassium carbonate |

# IMPORTANT POINTS TO REMEMBER

- Temporary hardness of water is due to the presence of bicarbonates of calcium and magnesium in water. Whereas the permanent hardness is due to the presence of Calcium Sulphate, which can be eliminated by the use of Zeolites.
- The gas used in balloons is helium.
- gobar gas is obtained by decomposition of vegitable matter and animal dung.
- L.P.G (liquefied petroleum gas) consists of mainly propane and butane.
- Natural gas is composed primarily of methane and other light hydrocarbons.
- Ethylene gas is used for artificial fruit ripening
- Sodium and potassium react vigorously with cold water so it is preserved under kerosene while phosphorus is spontaneously inflammable in air so preserved under water.
- Nitrous oxide is called laughing gas, in mild doses it is used as anesthetic
- Nitric acid is used as fertilizers and explosives
- Tri-nitro toluene and nitro glycerene are common explosives
- Smelling salt is ammonium carbonate
- Potassium nitrate or Nitre or Indian salt petre is used as Gun powder.
- The paste applied to the side of a match box is a mixture of Phosphorous Trisulphide, glass powder and sand to cause frictions and glue. The match head contains a readily combustible substance like atimony trisulphide, potassium chlorate which maintain the combustion and a binding material like glue.
- Marble is calcium carbonate
- Methylated spirit is a mixture of methyl alcohol and ethyl alcohol
- Urea is the first organic compound prepared in the laboratory
- Carbonic acid is soda water

- Mercaptans leakage in L.P.G. cylinders is easily detected.
- Hydrazine is used to propel rockets
- Coke is obtained by healthy wood out of contact with air
- Terylene and nylon are synthetic fibres produced by a process of polymerization. Terylene is a polyester and Nylon a polymide.
- Pyrene is carbon tetrachloride specially used to extinguish electrical fires.
- Tincture iodine is a solution of iodine in alcohol.
- Nickel is used in conversion of oil into solid fat.
- Coal gas is the product of destructive distillation of coal i.e. heating coal out of contact of air
- Rust is hydrated ferric oxide
- The chief component of pearl is ferric component

# ═══ IMPORTANT GLOSSARY ═══

*Aerosol:* A colloid in which solid particles or liquid droplets are suspended in a gas. Smoke is a solid aerosol; fog is a liquid aerosol.

*Abrasive:* A very hard, brittle, heat-resistant substance that is used to grind the edges or rough surfaces of an object. boron carbide, diamond, and corundum are abrasives.

*Activated charcoal:* A porous form of carbon that acts as a powerful adsorbent , used to decolorize liquids, recover solvents, and remove toxins from water and air.

*Alkaloid:* A class of bitter-tasting, basic organic compounds with nitrogen-containing rings. Alkaloids often have powerful effects on living things. Examples are cocaine, nicotine, strychnine, caffeine, and morphine

*Allotrope:* Some elements occur in several distinct forms called allotropes. Allotropes have different chemical and physical properties. For example, graphite and diamond are allotropes of carbon.

*Antioxidant:* Antioxidants are compounds that slow oxidation processes that degrade foods, fuels, rubber, plastic, and other materials.

*Avogadro number:* The number of particles in one mole, equal to $6.02214199 \times 10^{23}$ $mol^{-1}$.

**Colloid:** A colloid is a heterogeneous mixture composed of tiny particles suspended in another material. Milk is an example of a colloid.

*Caffeine:* A substance found in tea, coffee, and cola that acts as a stimulant.

*Buffer:* A solution that can maintain its pH value with little change when acids or bases are added to it.

*Diamond:* A crystalline form of carbon, made of a network of covalent, tetrahedrally bound carbon atoms.

*Dry cell:* A electrolytic cell that uses a moist paste rather than a liquid as an electrolyte. Flashlight batteries are dry cells with a zinc cup for an anode, a carbon rod for a cathode, and a paste made of powdered carbon, $NH_4Cl$, $ZnCl_2$, and $MnO_2$ for an electrolyte.

*Distillation:* Distillation is a technique for separating components of a mixture on the basis of differing boiling points.

***Ethanol or ethyl alcohol or grain alcohol:*** A colorless, flammable liquid produced by fermentation of sugars.

***Emulsion:*** A colloid formed from tiny liquid droplets suspended in another, immiscible liquid. Milk is an example of an emulsion

***Ketone:*** An organic compound that contains a carbonyl group. For example, methyl ethyl ketone is $CH_3COCH_2CH_3$ is used in some adhesives.

***Efflorescent:*** Efflorescent substances lose water of crystallization to the air. The loss of water changes the crystal structure, often producing a powdery crust.

***Ester:*** An ester is a compound formed from an acid and an alcohol.

***Gel:*** A gell is a sol in which the solid particles fuse or entangle to produce a rigid or semirigid mixture. Fruit jellies are gels.

***Foam:*** A colloid in which bubbles of gas are suspended in a solid or liquid. eg. Aerogel (solid smoke) and Styrafoam.

***Reverse osmosis:*** Solvent molecules flow spontaneously from a dilute solution through a semipermeable membrane to a more concentrated solution (osmosis). Reverse osmosis is used to produce fresh water from sea water.

***Isomers:*** Isomers have identical molecular formulas but different structural formulas

***Hydrazine:*** A colorless, fuming, corrosive liquid that is a powerful reducing agent. It is used in jet and rocket fuels.

***Endothermic:*** A process that absorbs heat. eg. Cooking food, Melting of ice.

***Exothermic:*** A process that releases heat. eg. freezing of water.

***Sol:*** A colloid with solid particles suspended in a liquid. Examples are protoplasm, starch in water, and gels.

***Tyndall effect:*** Light passing through a colloid is scattered by suspended particles. The light beam becomes clearly visible; this phenomenon is called the Tyndall effect.

# MULTIPLE CHOICE QUESTIONS

1. Which of the following is an antibiotic?
   (a) Aspirin      (b) Paracetamol
   (c) Penicillin      (d) Sulphadizine

2. A thermostat is used to:
   (a) purify air
   (b) regulate humidity
   (c) regulate temperature
   (d) regulate air pressure

3. Heat from the sun reaches the earth by:
   (a) reflection      (b) conduction
   (c) convection      (d) radiations

4. An aeroplane is able to fly because;
   (a) it is lighter than air
   (b) it is heavier than air
   (c) it is made of very light materials
   (d) moving air can lift objects

5. The most abundant gas in the air is:
   (a) oxygen
   (b) carbon dioxide
   (c) nitrogen
   (d) hydrogen

6. Which is the element common to brass and bronze?
   (a) Copper      (b) Iron
   (c) Zinc      (d) Aluminium

7. The densest element known so far is:
   (a) iron      (b) mercury
   (c) osmium      (d) tungsten

8. The most ductile element is:
   (a) gold      (b) silver
   (c) iron      (d) aluminium

9. The metal having highest melting point is;
   (a) chromium      (b) tungsten
   (c) diamond      (d) silver

10. The gas which constitutes most of Venus's atmosphere is:
    (a) oxygen      (b) nitrogen
    (c) hydrogen      (d) carbon dioxide

11. The most common acid found in the nature is:
    (*a*) acetic acid
    (*b*) citric acid
    (*c*) lactic acid
    (*d*) hydrochloric acid

12. The bomb that cannot destroy the property but can damage the life only is:
    (*a*) atom bomb
    (*b*) hydrogen bomb
    (*c*) fission bomb
    (*d*) neutron bomb

13. Which of the following is the best conductor of electric current?
    (*a*) Aluminium  (*b*) Copper
    (*c*) Silver  (*d*) Gold

14. Tungsten is mainly used for making filament of electric bulbs because of its:
    (*a*) low cost
    (*b*) high melting point
    (*c*) high electrical conductivity
    (*d*) low thermal conductivity

15. The element common to bone and cement is:
    (*a*) silicon  (*b*) calcium
    (*c*) nitrogen  (*d*) phosphorus

16. The raw material common to cement and glass is:
    (*a*) soda  (*b*) rock
    (*c*) gypsum  (*d*) sand

17. Which of the following gases does not pollute air?
    (*a*) Carbon dioxide
    (*b*) Carbon monoxide
    (*c*) Nitrogen dioxide
    (*d*) Sulphur dioxide

18. Which form of gold is the softest?
    (*a*) 16 Carat  (*b*) 18 Carat
    (*c*) 20 Carat  (*d*) 22 Carat

19. Barometer measures:
    (*a*) wind velocity
    (*b*) atmospheric pressure
    (*c*) amount of rainfall
    (*d*) atmospheric moisture

20. Anemometer measures:
    (*a*) amount of rainfall
    (*b*) atmospheric pressure
    (*c*) wind velocity
    (*d*) amperage of an electrical current

21. Sphygmomanometer measures:
    (*a*) specific heat, latent heat, heat of chemical combination and other thermal properties
    (*b*) intensity of light
    (*c*) distance covered, or steps taken, by a person walking
    (*d*) blood pressure

22. Vegetables can be cooked quickly in a pressure cooker because:
    (*a*) steam can boil vegetables faster than water
    (*b*) boiling point increases with the increase in pressure
    (*c*) high pressure lowers the boiling point
    (*d*) All the above

23. Which of the following is common in all acids?
    (*a*) Hydrogen
    (*b*) Oxygen
    (*c*) Nitrogen
    (*d*) None of the above

24. One of the main constituents of Gobar gas is:
    (*a*) thyamine
    (*c*) methane
    (*c*) phosphate
    (*d*) carbon monoxide

25. Quartz is softer than:
    (*a*) Diamond  (*b*) Corundum
    (*c*) Topaz  (*d*) All the above

26. Emerald and diamond are made of:
    (*a*) Beryllium and Carbon
    (*b*) Carbon
    (*c*) Silica
    (*d*) Silica and Beryllium

27. Arrange the three forms of iron in descending order of carbon contents and other impurities in them:

I. wrought iron    II. cast iron
III. pig iron
(*a*) III, II, I      (*b*) III, I, II
(*c*) I, II, III      (*d*) II, I, III

**28.** Which one of the following has maximum nitrogen content?
(*a*) Sodium nitrate
(*b*) Urea
(*c*) Ammoniam sulphate
(*d*) None of the above has enough nitrogen

**29.** Radio carbon dating is used for determining the age of:
(*a*) fossils      (*b*) buildings
(*c*) babies      (*d*) rocks

**30.** Pasteurization of milk means:
(*a*) heating of milk upto 100°C
(*b*) heating of milk at 65°C
(*c*) cooling of milk at 100°C
(*d*) cooling of milk upto 0°C

**31.** A diamond is a:
(*a*) form of fossilised mammal of ancient times
(*b*) crystalline form of pure carbon
(*c*) hard rolled under sea stone made into a diamond by the saliva of huge sea monsters and thereafter dug out from the mines
(*d*) natural crystallized glass

**32.** The filament of electric bulb is made of:
(*a*) iron      (*b*) tungsten
(*c*) nichrome      (*d*) silver

**33.** The lightning rod used for protecting building from lightning is made of:
(*a*) glass      (*b*) cement
(*c*) copper      (*d*) plastic

**34.** Iron is heavier than water, still the ship floats on the sea because:
(*a*) weight of the ship is less than the weight of water in the sea
(*b*) weight of the ship is more than sea water
(*c*) weight of the ship is less than the weight of water that the ship displaces
(*d*) weight of ship is equal to the weight of water that ship displaces

**35.** What do fertilisers contain?
(*a*) Calcium      (*b*) Sodium
(*c*) Phosphorus      (*d*) Nitrogen

**36.** In which the purest form of carbon is found?
(*a*) Coke      (*b*) Diamond
(*c*) Graphite      (*d*) Coal

**37.** What is Tritium?
(*a*) Compound of hydrogen
(*b*) Isobar of hydrogen
(*c*) Isotope of hydrogen
(*d*) Oxide of hydrogen

**38.** Which of the properties of elements have a whole number?
(*a*) Atomic number
(*b*) Atomic weight
(*c*) Molecular weight
(*d*) Equivalent weight

**39.** What does the process in which a heavy nucleus breaks to give two or more small nuclei and large amount of energy is called:
(*a*) electrolysis      (*b*) fission
(*c*) fusion      (*d*) ionization

**40.** What is the process in which two or more small nuclei join to form a large nucleus with evolution of energy is called:
(*a*) electrolysis      (*b*) fission
(*c*) fusion      (*d*) diffusion

**41.** Which one is wrongly matched?
(*a*) Phosphorus -Match
(*b*) Potassium Sulphate -Fertilizer
(*c*) Methyl Isocynate -Tyre
(*d*) Silicon-Glass

**42.** The gas which helps in burning is:
(*a*) Carbon Monoxide
(*b*) Hydrogen
(*c*) Oxygen
(*d*) Nitrogen

**43.** The instrument used to measure radio activity is called:
(*a*) Gyroscope
(*b*) Nephoscope
(*c*) Machmeter
(*d*) Geiger Counter

**44.** Hygrometer is used to measure:
  (*a*) humidity of the atmosphere
  (*b*) density of milk
  (*c*) speed of sound in water
  (*d*) None of the above

**45.** The process of making an object white, by destroying its colour is known as:
  (*a*) corrosion  (*b*) bleaching
  (*c*) dehydration  (*d*) pyrolysis

**46.** Primary gold has a purity of ....... carats
  (*a*) 14  (*b*) 22
  (*c*) 23  (*d*) 24

**47.** What colour does copper turn a flame?
  (*a*) Red  (*b*) Green
  (*c*) Yellow  (*d*) Mauve

**48.** Vanadium is:
  (*a*) an element used in nuclear fission
  (*b*) a metal used as a substitute of gold
  (*c*) a metal used to make steel strong
  (*d*) a metal found without any alloy

**49.** What are the tapes in tape- recorders coated with?
  (*a*) Magnesium oxide
  (*b*) Silver bromide
  (*c*) Iron oxide
  (*d*) Zinc oxide

**50.** The Isotope of Uranium which is very much radioactive is:
  (*a*) U 235  (*b*) U 238
  (*c*) U 233  (*d*) All the above

**51.** A cut diamond sparkles because of its:
  (*a*) hardness
  (*b*) emission of light
  (*c*) high polish
  (*d*) high refractive index

**52.** The best known and most commonly used artificial fibre is:
  (*a*) Rayon
  (*b*) Terryfibre
  (*c*) Cellulose
  (*d*) Protein based fibres

**53.** Brass is an:
  (*a*) alloy of copper and tin
  (*b*) alloy of copper and zinc
  (*c*) alloy of zinc and tin
  (*d*) amalgam of zinc and tin

**54.** Main constituent of pearl is:
  (*a*) calcium carbonate and magnesium carbonate
  (*b*) calcium carbonate
  (*c*) calcium sulphate and calcium carbonate
  (*d*) calcium oxide and ammonium chloride

**55.** Which of the following metals has the lowest melting point?
  (*a*) Silver  (*b*) Zinc
  (*c*) Gold  (*d*) Tin

**56.** An important metal used with iron to produce stainless steel is:
  (*a*) aluminium  (*b*) tin
  (*c*) chromium  (*d*) carbon

**57.** Lode stone is:
  (*a*) a very hard stone
  (*b*) a blue variety of stone
  (*c*) a natural magnet
  (*d*) an artificial magnet

**58.** Which do you not find in the nucleus of an atom?
  (*a*) A proton  (*b*) A neutron
  (*c*) An electron  (*d*) None of these

**59.** What element has the lightest atom of all?
  (*a*) Oxygen  (*b*) Copper
  (*c*) Carbon  (*d*) Hydrogen

**60.** How would you make dry ice from carbon-dioxide?
  (*a*) By heating it  (*b*) By baking it
  (*c*) By freezing it  (*d*) By drying it

**61.** The "fizz" in soda water is caused by:
  (*a*) oxygen  (*b*) hydrogen
  (*c*) carbon dioxide (*d*) nitrogen

**62.** The terminals of the torch cells are made with:
  (*a*) zinc-copper
  (*b*) carbon-silver
  (*c*) carbon-copper
  (*d*) zinc-silver

**63.** The process of coating iron with zinc is known as :
(*a*) galvanization
(*b*) synthetic coating
(*c*) electroplating
(*d*) None of the above

**64.** 'Electrum' is a/an:
(*a*) alloy of gold and silver
(*b*) sub-atomic particle
(*c*) unit of measuring size of small particles
(*d*) a homoeopathic me:cticinc

**65.** The hardness of water is due to:
(*a*) oxygen
(*b*) dissolved substances
(*c*) hydrogen
(*d*) too much salt

**66.** Urea is prepared by the chemical reaction of:
(*a*) ammonia and carbon dioxide
(*b*) ammonia and sulphuric acid
(*c*) acetamide and ethyl alcohol
(*d*) calcium phosphate and sulphuric acid

**67.** German Silver is an alloy of:
(*a*) iron and tin
(*b*) brass and bronze
(*c*) copper, zinc and nickel
(*d*) copper and silver

**68.** The density of water is maximum at:
(*a*) 40°C        (*b*) 0°C
(*c*) 4°C         (*d*) 42°C

**69.** Copper is not used for long distance lighting wires because:
(*a*) copper is not a very good conductor of heat and electricity
(*b*) copper melts at high in temperature
(*c*) copper wires would cost very high
(*c*) copper wires would cost very high

**70.** The refrigerant liquid inside a refrigerator is:
(*a*) carbon dioxide
(*b*) ammonia
(*c*) nitrogen
(*d*) methane

**71.** Dry ice is prepared with:
(*a*) carbon dioxide

(*b*) nitrogen
(*c*) oxygen
(*d*) None of the above

**72.** What metals are used for manufacturing stainless steel?
(*a*) Copper and Steel
(*b*) Chromium and Steel
(*c*) Zinc and Aluminium
(*d*) Manganese and Mercury

**73.** Which one of the following cannot help remove the permanent hardness of water?
(*a*) Boiling
(*b*) Application of Caustic Soda
(*c*) Distillation
(*d*) Adding of Soda

**74.** Dacron is
(*a*) polyester
(*b*) ester
(*c*) polyamide
(*d*) halogen derivative

**75.** With a limited amount of HI, glycerol gives
(*a*) 1, 2, 3 triodo propane
(*b*) $\alpha$, $\beta$ glycerol tricodo hydron
(*c*) allyl iodide
(*d*) glycol

**76.** Which of the following when heated with glycerol will give acrylic aldehyde?
(*a*) $P_2O_5$       (*b*) $KHSO_4$
(*c*) $H_2SO_4$     (*d*) All of these

**77.** Oxalic acid is present in the plants of
(*a*) solanace family
(*b*) malvaceae family
(*c*) Numex family
(*d*) None of these

**78.** Cellulose is
(*a*) $C_2H_5OCH_2CH_2OCH_2CH_2OH$
(*b*) $CH_2OHCHOHCOOH$
(*c*) $2CH_2OH\ CH_2OH$
(*d*) $CH_3CH_2O.CH_2CH_2OH$

**79.** Sweet water is
(*a*) glycerol (aq)

(*b*)  oxalic acid (aq)
(*c*)  glycol (aq)
(*d*)  NaCl (aq)

**80.**  Fenton's reagent is
(*a*)  $FeSO_4$ and anhyd. $ZnCl_2$
(*b*)  $FeSO_4$ and $H_2O_2$
(*c*)  $FeSO_4$ and NaOBr
(*d*)  $FeSO_4$ and NaOH

**81.**  Which of the following is a dibasic acid?
(*a*)  Glycolic acid
(*b*)  Acetic acid
(*c*)  Oxalic acid
(*d*)  Lactic acid

**82.**  Dynamite was discovered by
(*a*)  Alfred Nobel  (*b*)  Gay Lussac
(*c*)  Wholer        (*d*)  Rutherford

**83.**  Glycerine is
(*a*)  $CHOCHOHCH_2OH$
(*b*)  $CH_2OHCHOHCH_2OH$
(*c*)  $CH_2OH. CH_2OHCHOH$
(*d*)  $CHOCHOHCHO$

**84.**  Which of the following vitamins contain cobalt?
(*a*)  Vitamin $B_1$    (*b*)  Vitamin $B_{12}$
(*c*)  Vitamin $B_9$   (*d*)  None of these

**85.**  Insulin regulates the metabolism of
(*a*)  carbohydrates  (*b*)  mineral salts
(*c*)  glucose         (*d*)  fructose

**86.**  Greater the of unsaturation in the lipid
(*a*)  lower is the solubility in water
(*b*)  lower is the melting point
(*c*)  greater is the solubility in water
(*d*)  higher is the melting point

**87.**  Which of the following vitamins can be synthesised in our body?
(*a*)  D          (*b*)  E
(*c*)  K          (*d*)  C

**88.**  Which of the following is known as anti- haemorrhagic vitamin?
(*a*)  E          (*b*)  K
(*c*)  D          (*d*)  C

**89.**  The chemical messages are
(*a*)  hormones     (*b*)  pulses
(*c*)  lipids       (*d*)  vitamins

**90.**  The coiled form of a fibrous protein is known as
(*a*)  β form
(*b*)  α form
(*c*)  globular
(*d*)  All of the above

**91.**  Unsaturated fatty acids in the duct can
(*a*)  prevent the deposition of cholesterol
(*b*)  prevent the hardening of arteries
(*c*)  strengthen the arteries
(*d*)  harden the arteries

**92.**  Deficiency of which of the following vitamins will cause xerophthalmia?
(*a*)  A          (*b*)  D
(*c*)  E          (*d*)  K

**93.**  Vitamin $D_2$ is
(*a*)  cephalin     (*b*)  thiamine
(*c*)  tocopherol   (*d*)  calciferol

**94.**  Oxalic acid is prepared in the laboratory by
(*a*)  heating glycerol
(*b*)  heating potassiuum oxalate
(*c*)  heating sodium formate
(*d*)  oxidation of cane sugar with $V_2O_5$

**95.**  Oxidation of oxalic acid is done with
(*a*)  bromine water
(*b*)  acetic acid
(*c*)  acidified $KMnO_4$ solution
(*d*)  None of these

**96.**  Which out of the following does not represent the proper application of glycerol?
(*a*)  In medicines for throat pains
(*b*)  As a reagent in volumetric analysis
(*c*)  As an antifreeze 41 automobile radiators
(*d*)  For preparing nitro-glycerine

**97.** Upon reduction with zinc and acid, oxalic acid gives
(*a*) ethane     (*b*) oxalic acid
(*c*) glycolic acid   (*d*) acetic acid

**98.** Which out of the following is optically active?
(*a*) Acetic acid
(*b*) Tartaric acid
(*c*) Oxalic acid
(*d*) All of the above

**99.** Sodium formate upon heating
(*a*) remains unaffected
(*b*) gives oxalic acid and $H_2$
(*c*) gives sodium oxalate and $H_2$
(*d*) gives $CO_2$ and NaOH

**100.** Electro metallurgical process (electrolysis of fused salt) is employed to extract
(*a*) iron     (*b*) lead
(*c*) sodium     (*d*) silver

**101.** Acetamide is treated separately with the following reagents. Which one of these would give methyl amine?
(*a*) sodalime
(*b*) hot conc. HCl
(*c*) $PCl_5$
(*d*) NaOH + $Br_2$

**102.** The compound that will not give iodoform on treatment with alkali and iodine is
(*a*) diethyl ketone
(*b*) isopropyl alcohol
(*c*) ethanol
(*d*) acetone

**103.** Heavy water is
(*a*) water obtained by repeated distillation
(*b*) water at 20°C
(*c*) $D_2O$
(*d*) $H_2O$

**104.** A gas that can be collected over water is
(*a*) $N_2$     (*b*) $O_2$
(*c*) $PH_3$     (*d*) All of these

**105.** Red lead is
(*a*) $PbO$     (*b*) $PbO_2$
(*c*) $Pb_3O_4$     (*d*) $Pb_2O_3$

**106.** The low boiling point of molecular solid is most closely associated with
(*a*) van der Waals attraction
(*b*) hydrogen bonds
(*c*) covalent forces
(*d*) ionic attraction

**107.** Which of the following statement is correct regarding hydride of VA group elements (Nitrogen family)?
(*a*) Reducing character of the hydrides increases down the group
(*b*) Thermal stability of the hydrides decreases down the group
(*c*) Basic strength of the hydrides decreases down the group
(*d*) All of the above

**108.** Which of the following contain phosphorus?
(*a*) Fluorapatite
(*b*) Chloropatite
(*c*) Rock phosphate
(*d*) All of the above

**109.** When a solution of KBr treated with each of the following, which one would liberate bromine?
(*a*) HCl     (*b*) $I_2$
(*c*) $H_2S$     (*d*) $Cl_2$

**110.** Which of the following statements is not correct regarding nitrogen?
(*a*) It has *d*-orbitals available for bonding
(*b*) Its electronegativity is very low
(*c*) It is a typical non-metal
(*d*) It has a small size

**111.** Which of the following will give nitrogen on heating?
(*a*) $NH_4NO_3$
(*b*) $NH_4Cl$
(*c*) $NaNO_3$
(*d*) $(NH_4)_2 Cr_2O_7$

**112.** Nitrogen is produced by heating
   (*a*) $NH_4Cl$
   (*b*) $NaNO_3$
   (*c*) $NH_4Cl + NaNO_2$
   (*d*) $NH_4Cl + NaNO_3$

**113.** In which of the following acid of phosphorus, the oxidation number of phosphorus is different from the other?
   (*a*) $HPO_3$     (*b*) $H_3PO_3$
   (*c*) $H_3PO_4$     (*d*) $H_4P_2O_7$

**114.** Nitrogen fails to form $NCl_5$ because its
   (*a*) atom does not have vacant *d*-orbitals
   (*b*) ionization energy is very small
   (*c*) electronegativity is very low
   (*d*) size is very small

**115.** When $Cl_2$ is passed through hot and conc. solution of NaOH, it produces sodium chloride and
   (*a*) sodium hypochlorate
   (*b*) sodium perchlorate
   (*c*) sodium hypochlorite
   (*d*) sodium chlorate

**116.** Nitrogen is inert because
   (*a*) it has stable electronic configuration
   (*b*) its dissociation energy is high
   (*c*) it is a typical non-metal
   (*d*) it has a small size

**117.** Bromine vapours turn starch iodide paper
   (*a*) black     (*b*) brown
   (*c*) blue     (*d*) red

**118.** The percentage of nitrogen in air remains almost constant due to the
   (*a*) effect of lighting and bacteria
   (*b*) activity of symbiotic bacteria
   (*c*) nitrogen cycle in Nature
   (*d*) fixation of nitrogen

**119.** An hydride of nitrogen, which is acidic in nature
   (*a*) $NH_3$     (*b*) $N_3H$
   (*c*) $NH_4$     (*d*) None of these

**120.** Which of the following properties of white phosphorus are shared by red phosphorus?
   (*a*) It dissolves in carbon disulphide
   (*b*) It burns when heated in air
   (*c*) It reacts with hot aqueous NaOH to give phosphine
   (*d*) It phosphoresces in air

**121.** Which one has the highest percentage of nitrogen?
   (*a*) $KMnO_4$     (*b*) $NH_4NO_3$
   (*c*) Urea     (*d*) $CaCN_2$

**122.** Phosphorus is kept in
   (*a*) ammonia     (*b*) alcohol
   (*c*) hot water     (*d*) cold water

**123.** Phosphorus combines with metal to form
   (*a*) phosphate
   (*b*) phosphite
   (*c*) phosphide
   (*d*) metaphosphite

**124.** Atomicity of phosphorus is
   (*a*) two     (*b*) four
   (*c*) five     (*d*) seven

**125.** Oxygen is evolved when water reacts with
   (*a*) sodium peroxide
   (*b*) sodium dichromate
   (*c*) dioxide of metals
   (*d*) oxide of alkali metal

**126.** Which of the following will give nitrogen on heating with paste of sodium hypobromite?
   (*a*) Nitric acid     (*b*) Nitrous acid
   (*c*) Ammonia     (*d*) Amide

**127.** Sodium nitrate on heating with zinc dust and caustic soda solution yields
   (*a*) $NH_3$     (*b*) $N_2H_5$
   (*c*) $NaNO_2$     (*d*) NO

**128.** When white phosphorus is boiled with concentrated solution of potassium hydroxide, .......... is produced.
   (*a*) potassium phosphate
   (*b*) potassium phosphide

(*c*) white phosphorus
(*d*) phosphine

**129.** Calcium carbide reacts with......at 1000°C to form calcium cyanide.
  (*a*) white phosphorus
  (*b*) red phosphorus
  (*c*) oxygen
  (*d*) nitrogen

**130.** Which one of the following does not form oxygen on heating?
  (*a*) $KMnO_4$        (*b*) $K_2Cr_2O_7$
  (*c*) $(NH_4)_2 Cr_2O$ (*d*) $KClO_3$

**131.** In the preparation $Cl_2$ from HCl, $MnO_2$ acts as
  (*a*) dehydrating agent
  (*b*) reducing agent
  (*c*) oxidising agent
  (*d*) dehydrogenating agent

**132.** Of the different allotropes of phosphorus the one which is most reactive is
  (*a*) black phosphorus
  (*b*) scarlet phosphorus
  (*c*) white phosphorus
  (*d*) red phosphorus

**133.** Phosphorus reduces copper sulphate to
  (*a*) copper sulphide
  (*b*) cuprous sulphate
  (*d*) copper phosphide
  (*d*) copper

**134.** Which of the following on heating yields pure sample of nitrogen?
  (*a*) $Ba(N_3)_2$
  (*b*) $NH_2ONH_2 + HNO_2$
  (*c*) $NH_3 + NaOCl$
  (*d*) $NH_3 + CuO$

**135.** The most acidic oxide of the following compounds is
  (*a*) $Ni_2O_3$        (*b*) $As_2O_3$
  (*c*) $N_2O_3$        (*d*) $P_2O_3$

**136.** Among the hydrides of oxygen family elements, water shows anomalous properties due to

  (*a*) ionic bonding
  (*b*) covalent bonding
  (*c*) hydrogen bonding
  (*d*) co-ordinate bonding

**137.** Which of the following can be used to dry chlorine?
  (*a*) Concentrated sulphuric acid
  (*b*) Caustic potash
  (*c*) Quicklime
  (*d*) Conc. $HNO_3$

**138.** Which of the following is most volatile?
  (*a*) HCl        (*b*) HF
  (*c*) HI        (*d*) HBr

**139.** Select the one which is strongest oxidising agent in the following :
  (*a*) $F_2$        (*b*) $N_2$
  (*c*) $Cl_2$        (*d*) $O_2$

**140.** Oxygen and sulphur are alike in that they both
  (*a*) exist in atomic state
  (*b*) have atoms of same size
  (*c*) can form covalent hydrides
  (*d*) can form covalent compound with metals

**141.** An example of superoxide is
  (*a*) $Mn_2O_7$        (*b*) $KO_2$
  (*c*) $BaO_2$        (*d*) $H_2O_2$

**142.** Which of the following elements is extracted commercially by electrolysis of an aqueous solution of one of its compounds?
  (*a*) Aluminium    (*b*) Chlorine
  (*c*) Bromine        (*d*) Iodine

**143.** The strength of $HClO_3$, $HBrO_3$ and $HIO_3$ is in the order
  (*a*) $HIO_3 > HClO_3 > HBrO_3$
  (*b*) $HIO_3 > HBrO_3 > HClO_3$
  (*c*) $HBrO_3 > HClO_2 > HIO_3$
  (*d*) $HClO_3 > HBrO_3 > HIO_3$

**144.** $Cl_2 + H_2S \rightarrow 2HCl + S$, in this equation the oxidation number of sulphur changes from

(*a*) 0 to 2      (*b*) 2 to 0
(*c*) 2 to 0      (*d*) same

**145.** Which of the following will result in the oxidation of halide ion?
(*a*) Iodine is added to hydrobromic acid
(*b*) Bromine is added to aqueous sodium bromide
(*c*) Bromine is added to aqueous sodium chloride
(*d*) Chlorine is added to aqueous hydrogen iodide

**146.** Which of the following oxide of nitrogen is isoelectronic with carbon dioxide?
(*a*) NO      (*b*) $NO_2$
(*c*) $N_2O_5$      (*d*) $N_2O$

**147.** Which of the following gives of oxygen on moderate heating?
(*a*) Mercuric oxide
(*b*) Zinc oxide
(*d*) Cupric oxide
(*d*) Barium oxide

**148.** A solution of chlorine in water contains
(*a*) only HCl
(*b*) only HOCl
(*c*) Both (*a*) and (*b*)
(*d*) HCl, HOCl and chlorine

**149.** Vinegar contains
(*a*) 50% acetic acid
(*b*) 6-10% acetic acid
(*c*) 10-20% acetic acid
(*d*) 25% acetic acid

**150.** A product of distructive distillation of wood is
(*a*) acetic acid
(*b*) ethyl alcohol
(*c*) petrol
(*d*) glycerol

## ANSWERS

| 1 | 2 | 3 | 4 | 5 | 6 | 7 | 8 | 9 | 10 |
|---|---|---|---|---|---|---|---|---|---|
| (*c*) | (*c*) | (*d*) | (*d*) | (*c*) | (*a*) | (*c*) | (*a*) | (*b*) | (*d*) |
| **11** | **12** | **13** | **14** | **15** | **16** | **17** | **18** | **19** | **20** |
| (*a*) | (*d*) | (*c*) | (*b*) | (*b*) | (*c*) | (*a*) | (*d*) | (*b*) | (*c*) |
| **21** | **22** | **23** | **24** | **25** | **26** | **27** | **28** | **29** | **30** |
| (*d*) | (*b*) | (*a*) | (*c*) | (*d*) | (*a*) | (*a*) | (*b*) | (*a*) | (*b*) |
| **31** | **32** | **33** | **34** | **35** | **36** | **37** | **38** | **39** | **40** |
| (*b*) | (*b*) | (*c*) | (*c*) | (*d*) | (*b*) | (*c*) | (*a*) | (*b*) | (*c*) |
| **41** | **42** | **43** | **44** | **45** | **46** | **47** | **48** | **49** | **50** |
| (*c*) | (*c*) | (*d*) | (*b*) | (*b*) | (*d*) | (*b*) | (*c*) | (*c*) | (*b*) |
| **51** | **52** | **53** | **54** | **55** | **56** | **57** | **58** | **59** | **60** |
| (*d*) | (*a*) | (*b*) | (*b*) | (*d*) | (*c*) | (*c*) | (*c*) | (*d*) | (*c*) |
| **61** | **62** | **63** | **64** | **65** | **66** | **67** | **68** | **69** | **70** |
| (*c*) | (*a*) | (*a*) | (*a*) | (*b*) | (*a*) | (*c*) | (*c*) | (*c*) | (*b*) |
| **71** | **72** | **73** | **74** | **75** | **76** | **77** | **78** | **79** | **80** |
| (*a*) | (*b*) | (*b*) | (*c*) | (*c*) | (*d*) | (*c*) | (*d*) | (*a*) | (*b*) |

| 81 | 82 | 83 | 84 | 85 | 86 | 87 | 88 | 89 | 90 |
|----|----|----|----|----|----|----|----|----|----|
| (c) | (a) | (b) | (b) | (c) | (b) | (a) | (b) | (a) | (b) |
| 91 | 92 | 93 | 94 | 95 | 96 | 97 | 98 | 99 | 100 |
| (b) | (a) | (d) | (d) | (c) | (b) | (c) | (b) | (c) | (d) |
| 101 | 102 | 103 | 104 | 105 | 106 | 107 | 108 | 109 | 110 |
| (d) | (a) | (c) | (d) | (c) | (a) | (d) | (d) | (d) | (a) |
| 111 | 112 | 113 | 114 | 115 | 116 | 117 | 118 | 119 | 120 |
| (d) | (c) | (c) | (a) | (d) | (b) | (c) | (c) | (b) | (b) |
| 121 | 122 | 123 | 124 | 125 | 126 | 127 | 128 | 129 | 130 |
| (c) | (d) | (c) | (b) | (a) | (c) | (a) | (d) | (d) | (c) |
| 131 | 132 | 133 | 134 | 135 | 136 | 137 | 138 | 139 | 140 |
| (c) | (c) | (d) | (a) | (d) | (c) | (a) | (a) | (a) | (c) |
| 141 | 142 | 143 | 144 | 145 | 146 | 147 | 148 | 149 | 150 |
| (b) | (b) | (d) | (c) | (d) | (d) | (a) | (a) | (b) | (a) |

★ ★ ★ ★ ★

# BIOLOGY

The term *biology* derived from the Greek work, bios, "life" and the suffix-*logia*, "study of." **Biology** is a natural science concerned with the study of life and living organisms.

═══ BRANCHES OF BIOLOGY ═══

| | |
|---|---|
| **Apiculture** | Culture of Bee |
| **Cytology** | Study of Cells |
| **Dermatology** | Study of Skin |
| **Entomology** | Study of Insects |
| **Evolution** | Study of Origin of new from old |
| **Floriculture** | Study of Flower Yielding Plants |
| **Genetics** | Study of heredity and Variations |
| **Gynaecology** | Study of Female Reproductive Organ |
| **Horticulture** | Study of Garden Cultivation |
| **Haematology** | Study of Blood |
| **Mycology** | Study of Fungi |
| **Nephrology** | Study of Kidneys |
| **Neurology** | Study of Nervous System |
| **Obstetrics** | Branch of Medicine Dealing with Pregnancy |
| **Ophthalmology** | Study of Eyes |
| **Ornithology** | Study of Birds |
| **Osteology** | Study of Bones |
| **Palaeontology** | Study of Fossils |
| **Phycology** | Study of Algae |
| **Pisciculture** | Study of Fish |
| **Pomology** | Study of Fruits |
| **Sericulture** | Culture of Silk Moth and Pupa |
| **Serpentology** | Study of Snakes |
| **Virology** | Study of Virus |

═══ CELL ═══

1. **Cell Membrane:** Cells are enclosed by a thin film like membrane called plasma membrane, cytoplasmic membrane or plasma lemma.
   *Endocytosis:* Taking substance inside the cell by the plasma membrane. It is of two types: *Phagocytosis:* Cell Eating. *Pinocytosis:* Cell drinking. *Exocytosis:* Reverse of Endocytosis.
2. **Cytoplasm:** It is a part of protoplasm lying between plasma membrane and nucleus.
3. **Cell Wall:** Cells of most fungi, prokaryotes (bacteria and blue - green algae) and plants (except gametes) are surrounded by the cell wall. It is absent in animals.

4. **Nucleus:** Discovered by Robert Brown. Nucleus controls the metabolic activities of the cell by controlling the synthesis of enzymes.
   - Contains nucleoplasm (nuclear sap) which contains chromatin.
   - Chromatin organizes itself into thread like structures called Chromosomes.
   - The function of chromosomes is to carry genetic information from one cell generation to another.
   - Nucleolus is also present which helps in the production of ribosomes.
5. **Chromosomes:** Waldeyer coined the term chromosome. Each chromosome is made up of DNA.
   - Chromosome number is constant for a particular species. Diploid number (2n) of chromosomes are present in somatic cells and haploid number (n) of chromosomes are there in gametes.
   - In humans, the diploid number is 46.
6. **Mitochondria :** Powerhouse of the cell and energy is stored as ATP
   - They are semi-autonomous organelles. They contain DNA.
   - Mitochondria is enclosed by a double-membraned envelope.
7. **Endoplasmic Reticulum :** Provides an increased surface area for various metabolic activities within the cell. Types: Rough ER and smooth ER.
8. **Golgi Complex :** Main function is secretion. Secretions are in the form of granules in cytoplasm.
9. **Lysosomes :** Also called Suicidal bags. Contain enzymes acid hydrolases which digest worn - out or unnecessary parts of the cell, or even whole cells by process called 'Autophagy'.
10. **Ribosomes :** Made of RNA and proteins in equal amounts. Sites of protein synthesis.
11. **Vacuoles :** Large vacuole found in plant cells. Membrane surrounding the vacuole is tonoplast. Regulation of water, in osmoregulation, in storage and in digestion.
12. **Plastids :** Found only in plant cells.
    - *Chloroplast :* Green contains the pigment chlorophyll.
    - *Leucoplasts :* Colorless, occur in large no in cells of fruits, seeds, etc. They store nutrients (e.g., amyloplasts of potato store starch).
    - *Chromoplasts :* Colored, containing fat soluble yellow, orange and red pigments. Found in flowers and fruits.
13. **Centrosome :** Found in animal cells and cells of lower plants (e.g., Algae) only. The first indication that the cell is about to divide is generally given by the centrosome.

# BALANCED DIET

A Balanced Diet comprising of healthy and diverse foods is key to promoting good health. The components of food are:

1. **Carbohydrates:** Constitutes 3 elements : Carbon, Hydrogen and Oxygen. 1 gm gives 17 kJ of energy (or 4.1 kcal of energy). Carbohydrates form a better fuel than proteins and fats because their molecules have relatively more oxygen.
   - Cellulose is present in the cell - wall of plants.
   - D - fructose is the sweetest of sugars. It is found in Fruit Juices, Honey, etc.
   - Excess Sugar is stored as Glycogen in liver.

- *Sources of Carbohydrates are :* Cereals (Wheat, Rice and Maize), Sugarcane, Milk (contains Lactose - a type of Sugar), Fruits, Honey, Beet, etc.
- *Types of Carbohydrates:* **(i) Monosaccharides :** They are the simplest carbohydrates consist of one unit (eg: glucose, fructose, galactose). **(ii) Disaccharides :** Consist of 2 units of monosaccharides (eg : sucrose, lactose and 1 maltose). **(iii) Polysaccharides :** Consist of more than three monosaccharide units (eg: starch in plants and glycogen in animals).

2. **Fats:** Provides twice the energy of carbohydrates (1 gm provides 37 kJ or 9 kcal of energy). Acts as the reserve food material, excess fat is stored in the liver and adipose tissue.
   - *Types of fatty acids :* Saturated and Unsaturated. **(i) Saturated Fatty Acids :** Solids at room temperature. **(ii) Unsaturated Fatty Acids :** Liquids at room temperature.
   - Excess of saturated fats increases the blood - cholesterol level and may cause arteriosclerosis (hardening of arteries). This may lead to heart attack.
   - Essential Fatty Acids include Linoleic, Linolenic and Arachidonic Acids are present in Groundnut Oil, Sunflower Oil.
   - *Hydrogenation :* Process by which unsaturated fatty acids are converted into saturated fatty acids by the addition of Hydrogen.

3. **Proteins :** Made up of Carbon, Hydrogen, Oxygen, Nitrogen and Sulphur. Important for growth and repair of the body (75% of our body is proteins only).
   - *Types of Amino acids are:* **(i) Essential Amino Acids :** They cannot be synthesised in the body. eg. isoleucine, leucine, lysine, methionine, phenylalanine, threonine, tryptophan and valine. **(ii) Non - Essential Amino Acids :** They are synthesized in the body. eg. Alanine, Arginine, Asparagine, Aspartic Acid, Cysteine, Glutamine, Glutamic Acid, Glycine, Histidine, Proline, Serine and Tyrosine.
   - *Some important Proteins are: Enzymes:* eg. Pepsin, Trypsin. **Hormone:** eg. Insulin, Glucogon, **Carrier:** eg. Haemoglobin - Transports O2 in blood, Myoglobin - Stores O2 in muscles. **Contractile Proteins:** eg. Actin and Myosin. **Structural Proteins:** eg. Collagen – Component of Bones, Tendons, Cartilage. Keratin - Component of Skin, Feathers, Nails, Hair, Horn. **Protective Proteins:** eg. Gamma globulins. **Visual Proteins :** Rhodopsin and Iodopsin of rods and cones. (present in Retina of the eye).
   - *Protein Energy Malnutrition :i. Kwashiorkar :* Due to deficiency of protein. Abdomen and feet swells, Skin becomes Dark and Scaly, Enlarged Liver, Anaemia. **ii. Marasmus :** Deficiency of Proteins. Losing of body weight, wasting of muscles, ribs look prominent. (Oedema and skin pigmentation absent).

4. **Minerals:** Minerals maintain water balance and nutrition in the body
   - *Types of mineral nutritution :* **(i)** Macroelements (required in amount more than 1 gm). **(ii)** Microelements (required in trace amounts less than 1 gm)

# ═══ MINERALS REQUIRED IN HUMAN BEINGS ═══

| Minerals | Sources | Functions | Deficiency |
|---|---|---|---|
| **Macro Elements** | | | |
| Calcium | Milk, Cheese | Formation of Teeth and Bones | Weak Teeth and Bones |
| Phosphorus | Milk, Meat, | Component of ATP, DNA, RNA | Weak Teeth & Bones; Retarded Growth |
| Sulphur | Proteins of Food | Component of Amino Acids | Disturbed Protein Metabolism. |
| Potassium | Meat, Milk, Cereals, Fruits | Water Regulation. | Weak Muscles; Risk of Paralysis |
| Chlorine | Table salt | Acid-Base Balance | Loss of Appetite; Muscle Cramps. |
| Sodium | Table salt | Acid - Base and Water Balances | Low Blood Pressure, Loss of Appetite; |
| Magnesium | Cereals, Green Vegetables | Cofactor of Enzymes | Affects Nervous Functions. |
| Iron | Meat, Eggs, Cereals | Component of haemoglobin | Anaemia, Weakness |
| Iodine | Sea Food, Iodized Salt | Component of Thyroxine | Goitre, Cretinism |
| **Micro Elements** | | | |
| Flourine | Drinking Water, Tea, Sea Food | Maintenance of Bones and Teeth | Weak Teeth, |
| Manganese | Dry Fruits, Cereals, | Cofactor of some Enzymes | Irregular Growth of Bones, Cartilages |

# ═══ VITAMINS REQUIRED IN HUMAN BEINGS ═══

*Vitamins :* Discovered by Funk. It do not provide energy but help in different physiological processes.

| Vitamin | Sources | Effect of Deficiency |
|---|---|---|
| **Water - Soluble Vitamins** | | |
| $B_1$ (Thiamine) | Rice Bran, Whole Wheat Flour | Beri - beri |
| $B_2$ (Riboflavin) | Cheese, Eggs, Yeast, | Cheilosis Keratitis of Cornea |
| $B_3$ (Nicotinic Acid) | Fresh Meat, Liver, Fish, | Pellagra, Muscle Atrophy, |
| $B_6$ (Pyridoxine) | Milk, Cereals, Fish, Meat Liver, | Dermatitis, Convulsions, Nausea, Mental Disorders |
| $B_5$ (Pantothenic Acid) | Yeast, Liver, Kidneys, Eggs, Meat, | Dermatitis, Anaemia, Fatigue, Nausea. |
| H (Biotin) | Yeast, Vegetables, Fruits, Eggs, | Skin Lesions, Loss of Appetite, Hair Fall. |
| Folic Acid Group | Green Vegetables, Soyabean, | Retarded Growth. |
| $B_{12}$ (Cyanocobabmine) | Meat, Fish, Liver, Eggs, | Pernicious Anaemia |
| C (Ascorbic acid) | Lemon, Orange, and | Scurvy |
| **Fat - Soluble Vitamins** | | |
| A (Retinol) | Milk, Butter, Egg Yolk, Liver, | Xerophthalmia |
| D (Cholecalciferol) | Synthesized in skin cells | Rickets, Osteomalacia. |
| E (Tocopherol) | Green Vegetables | Causes sterility, Muscular dystrophy, |
| K (Phylloauinone) | Carrots, Lettuce, | Haemorrhages, delayed blood clotting, |

# ═══ DIGESTIVE SYSTEM OF HUMANS ═══

The process of converting food into energy giving substances is carried out by this system.

1. **Buccal Cavity :** In the mouth salivary glands secrete saliva which contains the enzyme Ptyalin
   - *Teeth :* They are produced in two sets - Temporary and Permanent. The teeth are of four types : Incisors, Canines, Premolars and Molars.
   - *Structure of a Tooth :* A tooth consists of 3 Regions : Crown, Neck and Root. Enamel is the hardest substance in the human body.
   - *Dental Formula :* 2123 / 2123, means that there are 2 incisors, 1 canine, 2 Premolars and 3 molars in half of the upper jaw and exactly the same arrangement in half of the lower jaw.
   - In elephants, incisors of the upper jaw grow into huge tusks.
   - Canines are very large in predators such as cat, dog and lion.
   - Rabbit and squirrel lack canines. In walrus, the upper canines are enlarged into projecting tusks.
   - The last molars are called the wisdom teeth.
2. **Pharynx :** Links Buccal Cavity to Oesophagus. Food is carried by peristaltic movement. Trachea opens into Pharynx through an aperture called Glottis.
3. **Oesophagus :** 25 cm Long Tube. Longitudinal folds keep its cavity almost closed, except during swallowing of food.
4. **Stomach :** Oesophagus opens into it. In stomach, the food is called chyme. Has 3 Parts : Fundus, Cardiac and Pyloric. Gastric juices produced in the stomach help in digestion of food. Also contains HCI which provides acidic medium. Besides it activates pepsinogen to pepsin and prorennin to rennin.
   - Ruminents (Cattle, Buffaloes, Goats, Sheep, Deer, Camel) have their stomach consisting of 4 Chambers : Rumen, Reticulum, Omasum and Abomasum.
5. **Small Intestine :** Here the food from the stomach is mixed with bile and pancreatic juice.
   - Duodenum receives the bile - pancreatic duct formed by the union of bile duct and pancreatic duct.
   - Both jejunum and ileum have numerous figure like projections called the villi. The villi contain blood vessels to absorbe digested food.
6. **Large Intestine:** It receives undigested material from the small intestine and absorbs water.
   - Caecum is the diverted part of intestine. Cellulose digestion takes place in it. It is very large in herbivores.
   - Vermiform appendix is a part of caecum. Both caecum and appendix are vestigial in humans.

# ═══ BLOOD IN HUMAN BODY ═══

Blood is a fluid connective tissue. It is 6.8 litres in man and 500 ml less in woman. 6 - 8% of body weight (pH 7.4)

1. **Red Blood Corpuscles:** Also called Erythrocytes, disc - shaped (for increased Surface Area), no nucleus contains a pigment called Haemoglobin, which gives blood its Red Color.
   - *Amount of Haemoglobin* is 14 - 15.6 gm / 100 cc of blood (11 - 14 in woman).
   - Life of RBC is 120 days after which they are broken down in spleen or liver.
   - Product of breakdown of haemoglobin is a pigment (yellow colour), called bilirubin. Retention of bilirubin leads to jaundice.
2. **White Blood Corpuscles:** Also called Leucocytes, rounded, with a nucleus, far less numerous than RBCs, life 3 - 4 days.
   - *Types* : Granulocytes (Basophils, Eosinophils, Neutrophils) and Agranulo-cytes (Monocytes, Lymphocytes)
   - *Basophils :* Take up basic stains. Have an S-shaped nucleus. Secrete an anti - coagulant Heparin, which prevents clots within the blood vessels.
   - *Eosinophils or Acidophils :* Take up acidic stains. Assists in defence mechanism.
   - *Neutrophils :* Most numerous of the WBCs (65 - 70%). Defence.
   - *Monocytes :* Largest of all. Very motile. Defence.
   - *Lymphocytes :* 25% of the WBC. Takes part in antigen and antibody formation.
3. **Platelets :** Also called Thrombocytes, formed in bone marrow, life 3 - 7 days, sets off blood clotting.

   **Plasma (65%) :** Watery part of blood, clear, yellow fluid. Contains about 90% water, proteins and organic salts.
   - *Lymph :* Lymph = Blood - RBC, i.e., Plasma + WBC. All interchanges of nutrients and waste products between blood and tissue takes place through lymph only.
   - Spleen produces lymph. At the same time it also acts as the graveyard of lymph.

   **Blood Groupings**
   - *Father of Blood Grouping:* Karl Landsteiner. He discovered A, B and O blood groups in 1900.
   - Decastello and Sturle in 1902 discovered AB blood group.
   - ABO system of blood groups is based on antigens and antibodies.
   - AB: Universal recipient
   - O: Universal donor

*RH Factor:* It is based on Rh antigen. Discovered in 1940 by Landsteiner and A.S. Veiner. It discovered in Rhesus monkey. A person can be Rh+ or Rh-.
   - In world population Rh+ are 85% and Rh- are 15% only.
   - Blood transfusion technique was first developed by James Blundell in 1825.

# EXCRETORY SYSTEM OF HUMANS

Waste materials excreted in animals are of many kinds : Nitrogenous Substances, Carbon - Dioxide, Pigments, Excess Water, etc.

The Nitrogenous Waste can be excreted in the following forms :

- **Ammonia :** Highly Toxic. In aquatic animals (called Ammoniotelic).
- **Urea :** Far less toxic than ammonia In Mammals, Alligators, Turtles (called Ureotelic).
- **Uric Acid :** In animals where conservation of water is needed. In Birds, Insects, Land Reptiles (called Uricotelic).

## Excretory System of Mammals

1. **Kidneys :** A kidney is composed of 1.2 million microscopic structural and functional units called nephrons or uriniferous tubules.
2. **Ureters :** Open into Urinary Bladder
3. **Urinary Bladder :** Size depends upon the amount of mine in it (up to 700 - 800 ml).
   The lower part is guarded by 2 Sphinctors : inner involuntary and outer voluntary.
4. **Urethra :** Leads to the exterior. In females, it carries only urine. In males it carries urine as well as spermatic fluid.
   **Nephron :** Functional unit of kidney. It is a long tube differentiated into 4 regions.
1. **Bowman's Capsule :** Contains a globular bunch of capillaries, the glomerulus. In glomerular filtrate: water (99%), inorganic salts, amino acids, fatty acids, glucose, urea, uric acid, hormones, vitamins are present.
2. **Proximal Convoluted Tubule :** Starts from the neck of Bowman's capsule and is highly twisted. Almost whole of the glucose and vitamins, amino acids, Na and K, Ca and Mg and water is absorbed.
3. **Loop of Henle:** U-shaped. Consist of 2 straight limbs: descending and ascending. No water is absorbed in ascending limb.
4. **Distal Convoluted Tubule :** Greatly twisted. Reabsorbs some Na and Cl. Leads to Collecting Tubules which lead to ureters.
   - The yellow colour of urine is caused by the pigment urochrome, which is a breakdown product of haemoglobin from worn out RBCs.
   - The urine gives a pungent smell due to conversion of urea into ammonia by bacteria.
   - Kidney stones: Calcium Oxalate

# RESPIRATORY SYSTEM OF HUMANS

I. **Anaerobic Respiration :** When nutrients are oxidized without using $O_2$ (also called fermentation). eg. Ascaris, Fasciola, Taenia also respire anaerobically. It is a low energy yielding process.

II. **Aerobic Respiration :** Cells utilize $O_2$ for oxidizing nutrients. It is found in most plants and animals. It involves:
   1. **External Respiration:** Gaseous exchange of $O_2$ and $CO_2$ between blood and air (or water).
   2. **Internal Respiration:** Gaseous exchange between blood and tissues.
   3. **Cellular Respiration:** Oxidation of nutrients in the cells and liberation of energy.

# ENDOCRINE SYSTEM OF HUMANS

Formed by endocrine glands (or Ductless Glands). They secrete hormones directly into the blood stream.

**Hypothalamus :** Forms a part of fore - brain, secretes neurohormones, which effect the release of hormones from pituitary.

**Pituitary Gland:** Also called Master Gland. It is the smallest endocrine gland. It secretes:

1. *Somatotrophic Hormone :* Controls the general growth of the body. Hypersecretion leads to acromegaly and gigantism and hyposecretion leads to dwarfness.
2. *Gonadotrophic Hormone :* Stimulates the primary sex hormones, i.e. ovaries and testes.
3. *Lactogenic Hormone :* Initiates milk production in the pregnant females.
4. *Thyrotrophic Hormone :* Aids in the regulation of thyroid secretion.
5. *Adrenocorticotrophic Hormone :* Influences the secretion from the cortex of adrenal glands.
6. *Oxytocin or Pitocin :* Stimulates smooth muscle contractions during child birth. Also helps in the secretion of milk in females.
8. *Vasopressin (Anti - Diuretic Hormone) :* Regulates reabsorption of water from the kidney tubules, causing increase in Blood Pressure.

**Thyroid Gland :** It is the largest endocrine gland located in the neck between the trachea and larynx.

1. *Thyroxine :* Regulates physical, mental and sexual development.
   * Poor in iodine is insufficient for the synthesis of thyroxin, leads to simple goitre.
2. *Thyrocalcitonin :* It controls the amount of calcium in the body.
   * *Hashimoto Disease :* Due to age factor or injury in thyroid gland secretion of thyroid reduces.

**Parathyroid Gland :** Secretes Parathormone. It influences calcium and phosphorus metabolism.

**Thymus Gland :** Situated near the heart. Produces Thymine. Preventing development of gonads.

**Pancreas :** It is an exocrine as well as an endocrine gland. Its endocrine part is known as Islets of Langerhans. Beta cells secrete Insulin which controls the amount of sugar in the blood.

**Adrenal Glands :** Consists of 2 Distinct Parts : Outer cortex and inner medulla.

1. Adrenal Medulla secretes Adrenaline or epinephrine which effects liberation of glucose from glycogen stored in liver.
2. Adrenal Cortex secretes two types of Hormones :
   (a) *Mineralo Corticoids :* Maintain electrolyte balance. Its hyposecretion results in Addison's disease
   (b) *Gluco Corticoids :* It influences carbohydrate metabolism. Its hypersecretion leads to Cushing Disease.

# REPRODUCTIVE SYSTEM OF HUMANS

It is the process by which an individual multiplies in number by producing more individuals of its own type.

I. **Asexual Reproduction :** Asexual Reproduction is the process of multiplication of individuals without the formation or fusion of gametes.

   **Binary Fission :** It involves the division of the nucleus followed by that of the cytoplasm, breaking the body into two young ones. e.g., Amoeba, Euglena, Paramecium, etc.

II. **Sexual Reproduction :** The process of sexual reproduction involves the formation and fusion of gametes (Syngamy) and results in the formation of a new organism genetically different from parent.

   **Mammalian Reproductive System :** The reproductive system of sexually reproducing animals consists of:

| Sex | Primary Sex Organs | Secondary Sex Organs |
|---|---|---|
| Male | Testes | Epididymis, Vas deferens, Ejaculatory duct, Urethra Seminal vesicle Prostate Gland Cowper's gland Penis |
| Female | Ovary | Fallopian tubes, Uterus, Vagina External Genitalia / Vulva Bartholian's Gland Mammary glands |

# SENSORY ORGANS OF HUMANS

**Eye :** Eye is made up of 3 Layers : Upper Sclerotic, Middle Choroids, Inner Retina

1. *Sclerotic Layer :* The Transparent bulging, circular part of sclerotic layer which lies in the front is called cornea. Cornea is covered by the thin Conjunctiva.
2. *Choroid Layer :* Choroid layer starts from iris which is next to cornea. The circular aperture of iris is called pupil.
   - Lens is a proteinous. It is biconvex in nature.
3. *Retina :* Image of the object is formed on retina. Retina is composed of 2 types of Cells :
   - *Rod Cells :* Sensitive to dim light and contain the pigment Rhodopsin (in nocturnal animals more)
   - *Cone Cells :* Color sensitive for 3 primary colors (Red, Blue and Green). They are found more in diurnal animals.

**Yellow Spot (Macula Lutea) :** On retina, finest image is formed here. Favea centralis is the depression in the middle of yellow spot.

**Blind Spot :** No image formation takes place here as the optic nerves innervate the eyeball here.
   - Cornea is donated in Eye Donation.
   - Eyes glow in animals due to tapetum.

**Defects of Eye**

1. *Myopia:* Cannot see distant objects, image formed before retina, concave lens is used.

2. *Hypermetropia* : Cannot see near objects, image formed behind retina, convex lens is used.
3. *Astigmatism* : Curvature of cornea becomes irregular and image is not clear cylindrical lens is used.
4. *Cataract* : Due to defective protein metabolism the lens becomes opaque Operation is needed.
5. *Gloucoma* : Due to defect in aqueous humour.
6. *Presbiopia* : In this, power of accommodation of lens decreases due to age factor and defected metabolism. Can be removed by bifocal lens.
   **Ear** : Divided into 3 Parts :
1. *External Ear* : Pinna + External Auditary Meatus
   * Has wax glands which produce cerumen to trap dust particles.
2. *Middle Ear* : It encloses 3 Ear Ossicles : Malleus (Hammer - Shaped), Incus (Anvil - Shaped), Stapes (Stirrup - Shaped)

**Fanastra Ovalis** : Connects middle ear to internal ear. Middle ear is connected to the pharynx by Eustachian tube.

3. *Internal Ear (Membranous Labyrinth)* : Most delicate part. Enclosed by parotic bone. It perform two functions : Maintenance of balance and hearing.
   * In the internal ear are 3 semi - circular canals and utriculus which are filled with a fluid, endolymph.

# DISEASES IN HUMAN

| Human Viral Diseases | Human Bacterial Diseases |
|---|---|
| Chickenpox | Cholera |
| Measles | Diphtheria |
| Polio | Tuberculosis |
| Rabies | Leprosy |
| Mumps | Tetanus |
| Influenza | Typhoid |
| Hepatitis | Plague |
| Herpes | Whooping Cough |
| AIDS | Sore Throat |
| Trachoma (of Cornea) | Pneumonia |
| **Human Protozoans Diseases** | Gonorrhoea |
| Amoebiasis | Syphilis |
| Malaria | Botulism |
| Sleeping Sickness | **Human Fungal Diseases** |
| Kalazar | Ringworm |
| Diarrhoea | Athlete's foot |
| Piarrhoea | Dhobie itch |

# ═══ SOME IMPORTANT FACTS OF HUMAN BODY ═══

| | |
|---|---|
| Length of Alimentary Canal | Approximately 8 metres |
| Number of Cells in Body | 75 trillion |
| Longest Bone | Femur (Thigh bone) |
| Smallest Bone | Ear ossicle, stapes |
| Weight of Brain | 1400 gms |
| Blood Volume | 6.8 litres (in 70 kg body) |
| Normal B.P | 120/80 mm Hg |
| Number of R.B.C | (*a*) In Male : 4.5 - 5.0 million/cubic mm. |
| | (*b*) In Female : 4.0 - 4.5 million/cubic mm |
| Life Span of R.B.C | 120 days |
| Normal W.B.C Count | 5000 - 1000/cubic mm |
| Life Span of W.B.C | 3 - 4 days |
| D.L.C. (Differential Leucocyte Count) | (*a*) Basophils : 0.5 - 1% |
| | (*b*) Eosinophils : 1 - 3% |
| | (*c*) Monocytes : 3 - 8% |
| | (*d*) Neutrophils : 40 - 70% |
| | (*e*) Lymphocytes : 2 - 25% |
| Blood Platelets Count | 2,00,000 - 4,00,000/cubic mm |
| Haemoglobin | (*a*) In Male : 14 - 15.6 gm/100 c.c. of blood |
| | (*b*) In Female : 11 - 14 gm/100 c.c. of blood |
| Hb Content in Body | 500 - 700 gm |
| Universal Blood Donor | O Rh-ve |
| Universal Blood Recipient | AB |
| Blood Clotting Time | 2 - 5 minutes |
| Average Body Weight | 70 kg |
| Normal Body Temperature | 98.4° F or 37°C |
| Breathing Rate | 16 - 20/minute |
| Dental Formula | Adult : 2123 / 2123 = 32; |
| | Child : 2120 / 2120 = 22 Milk Teeth |
| Number of Cranial Nerves | 12 pairs |
| Number of Spinal Nerves | 31 pairs |
| Largest Endocrine Gland | Thyroid |
| Gestation Period | 9 months (253 - 266 days) |
| Normal Heart Beat | 72 - 75/minute |
| Largest Gland | Liver |
| Largest Muscle in the Body | Gluteus maximus (Buttock Muscle) |
| Smallest Muscle in the Body | Stapedius |
| Largest Artery | Abdominal Aorta |
| Largest Vein | Inferior Venacava |
| Greatest Regeneration Power | In liver |
| Longest Nerve | Sciatic |
| Longest Cell | Neuron (Nerve Cell) |
| Minimum Regeneration Power | In Brain Cells |
| pH of Gastric Juice | 1.4 |
| pH of Urine | 6.0 |
| pH of Blood | 7.35 - 7.45 |
| Total Number of Muscles in the Body | 639 |
| Total Number of Bones in the Body | 206 |

# ═══ MEDICAL INVENTIONS AND DISCOVERIES ═══

| Name | Medical Inventions |
| --- | --- |
| Ronald Rose | Malaria Parasite |
| Salk, Jonas E. | Anti-Polio Vaccine |
| Simpson and Harrison | Chloroform |
| Waksman | Streptomycin |
| Banting | Insulin |
| Barnard, Christian | Replacing the human heart |
| Brahmachari, U.N. | Cure of Kala-azar fever |
| Eijkman | Cause of Beri-Beri |
| Fleming, Alexander | Penicillin (in 1929) |
| Harvey | Circulation of Blood |
| Hahnemann | Homoeopathy (Founder) |
| Hopkins, Frederick | Vitamin D |
| Jenner | Smallpox Vaccination |
| Koch | Tubercle Bacillus |
| Lainnec | Stethoscope |
| Lister, Lord | Antiseptic Treatment |
| Pasteur, Louis | Treatment of Rabies; Cure of Hydrophobia |

# ═══ MULTIPLE CHOICE QUESTIONS ═══

1. Digestion of food starts in:
   (*a*) mouth     (*b*) liver
   (*c*) stomach     (*d*) intestines

2. By taking the pulse rate of the human body, a doctor determines:
   (*a*) heartbeat
   (*b*) functioning of heart valves
   (*c*) the amount of blood in body
   (*d*) the condition of liver

3. The souring of milk is caused by the action of;
   (*a*) a protozoa
   (*b*) bacteria
   (*c*) viruses
   (*d*) None of these

4. The smallest living thing that can cause disease in the human body is:
   (*a*) flea     (*b*) bacteria
   (*c*) a protozoa     (*d*) viruses

5. What is essentially required to digest the food in stomach?
   (*a*) Air     (*b*) Water
   (*c*) Enzymes     (*d*) Minerals

6. Polio is a disease caused due to:
   (*a*) bacterial infection
   (*b*) virus infection
   (*c*) protozoal infection
   (*d*) food poisoning

7. Filtration of wastes from the blood in human body is done by:
   (*a*) heart     (*b*) lungs
   (*c*) kidney     (*d*) intestines

8. Oil, water and gas can be present in a well in the ascending order of:
   (*a*) water, oil, gas
   (*b*) gas, water, oil
   (*c*) water, gas, oil
   (*d*) oil, water, gas

9. A person suffering from which of the following cannot see with clarity the horizontal and vertical lines simultaneously?
   (*a*) Myopia
   (*b*) Hypermitropia
   (*c*) Astigmatism
   (*d*) Squint

**10.** Excessive intake of alcohol damages a person's:
(*a*) kidneys
(*b*) liver
(*c*) stomach
(*d*) All the above to a certain degree

**11.** After boiling, rice grains grow in volume and weight because:
(*a*) starch swells in water and heat
(*b*) heat enlarges solid
(*c*) rice is a fatty grain
(*d*) All the above

**12.** Plants are grown along river banks in order to check:
(*a*) siltage and floods
(*b*) pollution
(*c*) rainfall
(*d*) All the above

**13.** In a village where fuel is not available and people are poor, which of the following measures is the most suitable to prevent disease through contaminated water from the wells?
(*a*) Using chemicals to purify water
(*b*) Boiling the water
(*c*) Use of micro-organisms to purify water
(*d*) None of the above

**14.** Human brain receives and sends signals as:
(*a*) chemical impulses
(*b*) physical impulses
(*c*) electrical impulses
(*d*) mechanical impulses

**15.** The ductless glands secreting hormones directly into human blood are known as:
(*a*) exocrine glands
(*b*) endocrine glands
(*c*) metabolic glands
(*d*) ductlands

**16.** Foot and mouth diseases attack:
(*a*) cattle, sheep and pigs
(*b*) cattle only
(*c*) cattle and pigs only
(*d*) cattle and sheep only

**17.** Ranikhet disease affects:
(*a*) dogs
(*b*) cows
(*c*) poultry
(*d*) sheep

**18.** Wisdom teeth appear in a human being between:
(*a*) 17 and 20 years of age
(*b*) 30 and 40 years of age
(*c*) 10 and 17 years of age
(*d*) 4 and 8 years of age

**19.** Decomposition of matter takes place due to the effect of:
(*a*) bacteria
(*b*) virus
(*c*) fungi
(*d*) algae

**20.** Bile is secreted by:
(*a*) pancreas
(*b*) small intestine
(*c*) stomach
(*d*) liver

**21.** Polio myelitis which causes polio is spread by:
(*a*) mosquito
(*b*) virus
(*c*) water
(*d*) adulterated food

**22.** Which of the following is a genetically transmitted disease?
(*a*) Myopia
(*b*) Long sightedness
(*c*) Colour blindness
(*d*) Night blindness

**23.** Which of the following is a metal?
(*a*) Arsenic
(*b*) Sulphur
(*c*) Potassium
(*d*) Carbon

**24.** How does weedicide remove weeds?
(*a*) It removes the water required for growth
(*b*) It destroys the roots of the weeds
(*c*) It destroys the nutrients required for the growth of weeds
(*d*) All of the above

**25.** High heel and/or pointed shoes are harmful because:
(*a*) they injure the feet
(*b*) they weaken the eyesight
(*c*) they cause polio
(*d*) they cause backache and sleeplessness

26. Respiration is:
    (*a*) to change the food into energy
    (*b*) the process during which food is oxidized and its chemical energy is transformed into useful form
    (*c*) a sort of exercise
    (*d*) interconversion of food and energy
27. Dialysis is:
    (*a*) the same process as osmosis
    (*b*) the diffusion of sugar molecules through water
    (*c*) the process involved in the diffusion of toxic substance through a membrane
    (*d*) the evaporation of surplus sugar
28. Mycology is the study of:
    (*a*) Mica
    (*b*) Ants
    (*c*) Changes of environment
    (*d*) Fungi
29. In human body, quantity of water is about:
    (*a*) 10%        (*b*) 20%
    (*c*) 65%        (*d*) 80%
30. What does the urine of a man contain mainly?
    (*a*) Urea
    (*b*) Sugar
    (*c*) Salt
    (*d*) None of the above
31. Deficiency of insulin causes:
    (*a*) Beri-Beri        (*b*) Fever
    (*c*) Diabetes         (*d*) Anaemia
32. Photosynthesis results in:
    1. release of oxygen
    2. release of carbon dioxide
    3. formation of carbohydrates
    4. intake of carbon dioxide
    (*a*) 1, 2, 3 are correct
    (*b*) 1,3,4 are correct
    (*c*) 2,3,4 are correct
    (*d*) only 1 is correct
33. Which one of the following definitions is wrong?

    (*a*) *Amino Acids:* Large chemical substances containing carbon and oxygen
    (*b*) *Proteins:* Giant molecules of carbon, nitrogen and oxygen which are broken into small molecules during digestion
    (*c*) *Carbohydrates:* Big molecules used for getting energy
    (*d*) *Lipids:* A group of organic compounds found in living cells
34. Which one of the following is a contagious disease?
    (*a*) Malaria        (*b*) Small pox
    (*c*) Cholera        (*d*) Tuberculosis
35. DNA is concentrated in the:
    (*a*) Microsome      (*b*) Nucleus
    (*c*) Chromatin      (*d*) Cell wall
36. Vinegar is obtained by the fermentation process; what does it contain?
    (*a*) Acetic acid     (*b*) Formic acid
    (*c*) Nitric acid     (*d*) Oxalic acid
37. When the leaves of a plant show chlorosis, the possible cause can be:
    (*a*) increase in nitrate content in the soil
    (*b*) increase in chloride content in the soil
    (*c*) decrease in phosphorus content in the soil
    (*d*) deficiency of trace elements in the soil
38. The main endocrine gland present in the human body is:
    (*a*) Adrenal gland
    (*b*) Pituitary gland
    (*c*) Thyroid gland
    (*d*) Pancreas gland
39. Which one of the following pairs is incorrect?
    (*a*) Malaria        – Mosquitoes
    (*b*) Small Pox      – Virus
    (*c*) Typhoid        – Fungi
    (*d*) Cholera        – Water

40. Which one group of the following belongs to 'lichens'?
    (*a*) Algae and bacteria
    (*b*) Virus and bacteria
    (*c*) Algae and fungi
    (*d*) All the above

41. Arrange the following elements, present in human body, in the descending order of their percentage:
    1. Oxygen
    2. Nitrogen
    3. Carbon
    (*a*) 1 and 2 only (*b*) 1 and 3 only
    (*c*) 1, 3, 2     (*d*) 2 and 3 only

42. Which one of the following is given to a typhoid patient?
    (*a*) Chloroquin    (*b*) Vitamin A
    (*c*) Chloromycetin(*d*) Sulphur

43. Which one of the following is called a growth gland?
    (*a*) Adrenal
    (*b*) Thyroid
    (*c*) Pituitary
    (*d*) None of the above

44. Which one of the following is a rich source of vitamin A?
    (*a*) Potato tuber   (*b*) Carrot root
    (*c*) Onion bulb    (*d*) Maize grains

45. Which one is the most popular fodder for poultry?
    (*a*) Barley       (*b*) Maize
    (*c*) Wheat      (*d*) Bajra

46. Pencillin is given to a patient in order to:
    (*a*) cure hereditary diseases
    (*b*) cure all diseases
    (*c*) prevent any rise in bodily temperature
    (*d*) prevent the growth of several types of disease-causing bacteria

47. For getting instant energy an athlete should take:
    (*a*) Carbohydrate
    (*b*) Protein
    (*c*) Vitamin
    (*d*) Chewing Gum

48. The amoeba type organisms in the human body, causing malaria and amoebic dysentery are known as:
    (*a*) bacteria      (*b*) virus
    (*c*) fungi        (*d*) protozoa

49. Seeds are best preserved in:
    (*a*) hot and dry condition
    (*b*) cool but dry condition
    (*c*) dry condition
    (*d*) wet and cool condition

50. Which originates from a plant?
    (*a*) Chloromycetin
    (*b*) Quinine
    (*c*) Insulin
    (*d*) Aspirin

51. Shortage of Vitamin A results in:
    (*a*) Beri Beri
    (*b*) Rickets
    (*c*) Scurvy
    (*d*) Night blindness

52. The process by which plants make food is called:
    (*a*) Phototropism
    (*b*) Photosynthesis
    (*c*) Transpiration
    (*d*) Hydrotropism

53. Which of the following is a gas?
    (*a*) Carbon dioxide(*b*) Alcohol
    (*c*) Mercury     (*d*) Latex

54. Which animal fights snakes?
    (*a*) Monkey     (*b*) Mongoose
    (*c*) Tiger       (*d*) Jackal

55. In a human body, the basic building block is:
    (*a*) Muscle      (*b*) Cell
    (*c*) Bones       (*d*) Nerves

56. Which disease does virus cause?
    (*a*) Typhoid fever
    (*b*) Conjunctivitis
    (*c*) Malarial fever
    (*d*) Cholera

57. What causes decomposition of animal remains?
    (*a*) Bacteria     (*b*) Hormones
    (*c*) Enzymes    (*d*) Insects

**58.** The drug most widely used to relieve pain is:
(*a*) opium     (*b*) aspirin
(*c*) morphine     (*d*) baralgan

**59.** A vitamin that has vital influence on organs of reproduction and is found in germinating wheat is:
(*a*) A     (*b*) B
(*c*) E     (*d*) D

**60.** Diptheria and influenza are caused by:
(*a*) bacteria and virus respectively
(*b*) bacteria
(*c*) virus and bacteria respectively
(*d*) None of the above

**61.** Vitamin K deficiency causes:
(*a*) sexual disorders
(*b*) Haemorrhages
(*c*) night blindness
(*d*) weakness

**62.** Which of the following should be avoided by a heart patient?
(*a*) Bread     (*b*) Cream
(*b*) Apple     (*d*) Rice

**63.** Which of the following is indispensable for the growth of teenagers?
(*a*) Carbohydrate
(*b*) Protein
(*c*) Vitamin
(*d*) Fat

**64.** Which of the following is available in the sea in plenty and is given to patients suffering from a deficiency disease?
(*a*) Planktons
(*b*) Iodine
(*c*) Vitamin A
(*d*) None of the above

**65.** Which one of the following blood groups is universal recipient?
(*a*) AB     (*b*) A
(*c*) O     (*d*) B

**66.** Identify which one of the following is not a parasite?
(*a*) Housefly     (*b*) Louse
(*c*) Mosquito     (*d*) Tick

**67.** Which one of the following determines the sex of a child?
(*a*) Rh factor of the parents
(*b*) Chromosomes of the father
(*c*) Blood group of the mother
(*d*) Chromosomes of the mother

**68.** Triple Antigen prevents:
(*a*) whooping cough, tetanus, diphtheria
(*b*) polio tetanus, small pox
(*c*) small pox, typhoid, malaria
(*d*) tetanus, diptheria, malaria

**69.** What is the normal range of the adult human heart-beat per minute?
(*a*) 50 to 59     (*b*) 60 to 80
(*c*) 81 to 90     (*d*) 91 to 110

**70.** What would be the effect of breathing air without oxygen?
(*a*) One would collapse within 30 seconds and be dead within 5 minutes
(*b*) One would become uncon- scious but be living for few days
(*c*) One would start vomiting and be dead in 2 hours
(*d*) One would be alive for few days

**71.** A person in normal health requires per day:
(*a*) 1 ,000 — 1,800 calories
(*b*) 4,000 — 5,000 calories
(*c*) 2,500 — 3,000 calories
(*d*) 3,000 — 4,000 calories

**72.** 'ELISA' test is done for detection of:
(*a*) AIDS     (*b*) Kalazar
(*c*) Cancer     (*d*) Diabetes

**73.** Which one of the following is credited for developing blood grouping method?
(*a*) Karl Landsteiner
(*b*) Robert Koch
(*c*) William Harvey
(*d*) Louis Pasteur

**74.** Plants take nitrogen in the form of:
(*a*) nitrate    (*b*) element N
(*c*) nitrite    (*d*) ammonia

**75.** Red blood corpuscles are produced in:
(*a*) spleen
(*b*) liver
(*c*) bone marrow
(*d*) kidneys

**76.** Bile is stored in:
(*a*) lungs    (*b*) kidney
(*c*) heart    (*d*) lever

**77.** Insulin is used in the treatment of:
(*a*) diabetes    (*b*) cancer
(*c*) small pox    (*d*) plague

**78.** Radium is used to cure which disease?
(*a*) Cancer
(*b*) Bright's disease
(*c*) Haemophilia
(*d*) Typhoid fever

**79.** Which of the following helps to drive out harmful germs from the body?
(*a*) RBC    (*b*) WBC
(*c*) Kidney    (*d*) Liver

**80.** In which among the following iron is found in plenty?
(*a*) Oranges
(*b*) Eggs
(*c*) Green vegetables
(*d*) Milk

**81.** Which one of the following is wrong about Vitamins?
(*a*) Useful for digestion
(*b*) Useful for growth
(*c*) Useful for metabolic action
(*d*) For creating energy

**82.** Hydroponics refers to:
(*a*) an instrument
(*b*) soil free cultivation of plants
(*c*) a kind of soil preservation technique
(*d*) None of the above

**83.** Find the odd man out:
(*a*) Diabetes
(*b*) Scurvy
(*c*) Rickets
(*d*) Xerophthalmia

**84.** Malaria and yellow fever germs are carried by:
(*a*) birds    (*b*) flies
(*c*) mosquitoes    (*d*) gnats

**85.** 'Beri-Beri' is caused by the deficiency of Vitamin:
(*a*) A    (*b*) B
(*c*) C    (*d*) D

**86.** 'Scurvy' is caused by the deficiency of Vitamin:
(*a*) A    (*b*) B
(*c*) C    (*d*) D

**87.** Fatty things contain Vitamin:
(*a*) A    (*b*) B
(*c*) C    (*d*) D

**88.** In oranges and lemons we fmd mostly Vitamin:
(*a*) A    (*b*) B
(*c*) C    (*d*) D

**89.** The Genetic Code of DNA is carried from the nucleus to the ribosomes by:
(*a*) s—DNA    (*b*) ATP
(*c*) m—RNA    (*d*) r—DNA

**90.** Meningitis is the infection of the:
(*a*) Eyes    (*b*) Skin
(*c*) Brain    (*d*) Throat

**91.** Transpiration rate reaches its maximum with:
(*a*) low temperature
(*b*) high temperature and low humidity
(*c*) high humidity
(*d*) None of the above

**92.** For the treatment of which organ dialysis is resorted to?
(*a*) Lung    (*b*) Liver
(*c*) Kidney    (*d*) Brain

**93.** Vitamin C is also known as:
(*a*) ascorbic acid  (*b*) acetic acid
(*c*) lactic acid    (*d*) None of the above

**94.** During processing, the maximum amount of food substance lost is:
(*a*) protein    (*b*) vitamins
(*c*) fat    (*d*) carbohydrate

**95.** Liver helps to:
- (*a*) promote digestion of food
- (*b*) store glucose as glycogen
- (*c*) promote respiration
- (*d*) All the above

**96.** Pests attack stored grains because of:
- (*a*) moisture of grains
- (*b*) temperature of grains
- (*c*) smell of grains
- (*d*) All the above

**97.** Deficiency of chlorine in human body cause
- (*a*) week teeth
- (*b*) loss of appetite
- (*c*) osteophorosis
- (*d*) All of above

**98.** Sleeping under a tree at night is dangerous since:
- (*a*) there is poor oxygen release from tree
- (*b*) trees release carbon dioxide
- (*c*) larger amount of oxygen release from trees might bring about sudden death of a person
- (*d*) animals and insects may bite a man

**99.** The chief ingredient of the mosquito repellent cream is derived from :
- (*a*) tulsi         (*b*) neem
- (*c*) lemon       (*d*) rice bran

**100.** Dialysis is resorted to when a patient suffers from:
- (*a*) liver trouble
- (*b*) kidney trouble
- (*c*) lung trouble
- (*d*) heart trouble

**101.** One of the reasons why people in India suffer from Anaemia is that they have deficiency of:
- (*a*) iron          (*b*) iodine
- (*c*) calcium     (*d*) potassium

**102.** Which one of the following three grows fast?
- (*a*) eucalyptus
- (*b*) coconut
- (*c*) banyan
- (*d*) shorea robusta

**103.** Reserpine is used to:
- (*a*) alleviate high blood pressure
- (*b*) alleviate low blood pressure
- (*c*) cure heart ailments
- (*d*) None of the above

**104.** Cancer is :
- (*a*) reduced cell division
- (*b*) excess cell division
- (*c*) cell division plus pus formation
- (*d*) excess and uncontrolled cell division

**105.** The sickle cell anaemia results in :
- (*a*) leukaemia    (*b*) polycythemia
- (*c*) polycemia    (*d*) polio

**106.** The groups of micro-organisms requiring living cells for growth and multiplication are :
- (*a*) viruses and fungi
- (*b*) fungi and bacteria
- (*c*) bacteria and rickettsiae
- (*d*) viruses and rickettsiae

**107.** Treatment with alloxan destroys :
- (*a*) STH cells
- (*b*) Cells of Sertoli
- (*c*) Cells of Leydig
- (*d*) Beta cells of Islets of Langerhans of Pancreas

**108.** Which of the following is not a viral disease?
- (*a*) Measles
- (*b*) Mumps
- (*c*) Chicken pox and small pox
- (*d*) Plague

**109.** AIDS abbreviation stands for :
- (*a*) All India Disease Scheme
- (*b*) All India Diphtheria Society
- (*c*) Acquired Immune Deficiency Syndrome
- (*d*) Acquired Immune Deficiency Society

**110.** A severe form of Jaundice is caused by :
(*a*) Hepatitis-C    (*b*) HIV
(*c*) Hepatitis-A    (*d*) Hepatitis-B

**111.** Very fast dehydration of the body is caused by :
(*a*) an attack by *Mycobacterium tuberculosis*
(*b*) an attack by *Salmonella typhi*
(*c*) an attack by *Vibrio coma*
(*d*) an attack by *Corynebacterium diphtheria*

**112.** Lysozyme is an important antimicrobial secretion present in :
(*a*) tears    (*b*) saliva
(*c*) nasal mucus    (*d*) all of these

**113.** Swelling of salivary glands is the symptom of :
(*a*) diphtheria    (*b*) mumps
(*c*) tetany    (*d*) rubella

**114.** In fever too much of sugar may increase the elimination in urine of :
(*a*) sodium chloride (*b*) glucose
(*c*) uric acid    (*d*) phosphates

**115.** *Chenopodium* oil is used in :
(*a*) tuberculosis    (*b*) typhoid
(*c*) ascariasis    (*d*) small pox

**116.** A chemical which prevents blood clotting is useful in the treatment of :
(*a*) leukaemia
(*b*) anaemia
(*c*) haemophilia
(*d*) coronary thrombosis

**117.** It is said that wherever there are more houseflies there is greater incidence of Amoebic dysentry. It is because :
(*a*) house flies infect human food and water with cysts of *Entamoeba histolytica*
(*b*) part of the life cycle of *Entamoeba histolytica* passes in the blood of houseflies
(*c*) houseflies and *Entamoeba histolytica* have a common host
(*d*) both houseflies and *Entamoeba histolytica* thrive separately in similar conditions

**118.** Which of the following are psychotropic drugs?
(*a*) Barbiturates and LSD
(*b*) Morphine and cocaine
(*c*) Cocaine and LSD
(*d*) Barbiturates, LSD, cocaine and morphine

**119.** A fatal disease of anaemia of the mediterranean region is :
(*a*) Haemoophilia
(*b*) Brachydactyly
(*c*) Thallassemia
(*d*) Tay Sachs disease

**120.** Haemophilia disease is caused due to lack of :
(*a*) ADH    (*b*) STH
(*c*) AHF    (*d*) ACTH

**121.** Filariasis does not stimulate excessive growth of
(*a*) arms    (*b*) legs
(*c*) scrotal sacs    (*d*) neck region

**122.** What is the study of senescence and senility called?
(*a*) Dendrology    (*b*) Gerontology
(*c*) Paleontology    (*d*) Craniology

**123.** To which types of reproduction does Schizogony belong?
(*a*) Budding
(*b*) Fragmentation
(*c*) Binary fission
(*d*) Multiple fission

**124.** The eggs of reptiles and birds are :
(*a*) alecithal    (*b*) isolecithal
(*c*) telolecithal    (*d*) homolecithal

**125.** Leathery eggs are found in :
(*a*) amphibians    (*b*) mammals
(*c*) birds    (*d*) reptiles

**126.** Colour blindness is caused due to :
  (*a*) deficiency of vitamin C
  (*b*) sex-linked abnormality
  (*c*) absence of rods in retina
  (*d*) absence of visual purple in retina

**127.** The science dealing with study of inheritance and variation is :
  (*a*) Genetics      (*b*) Evolution
  (*c*) Morphology    (*d*) Cytology

**128.** One of these is an important source of evolution of new species :
  (*a*) Cloning
  (*b*) Mutation
  (*c*) Asexual reproduction
  (*d*) Autogamy

**129.** In the four blood groups A, B, AB and O the letters stand for :
  (*a*) antigens carried by RBC
  (*b*) antigens carried by WBC
  (*c*) antibodies carried by RBC
  (*d*) antibodies carried by WBC

**130.** A person of blood group.....cannot donate blood to people belonging to other groups.
  (*a*) Only AB      (*b*) A
  (*c*) B           (*d*) O

**131.** In the blood group of AB :
  (*a*) A antigens and b antibodies are present
  (*b*) Both A and B antigens are present
  (*c*) Both a and b antibodies are present
  (*d*) B antigens and b antibodies are present

**132.** The science of improving hereditary characters in human being is :
  (*a*) Epigenesis      (*b*) Genetics
  (*c*) Eugenics      (*d*) Metagenesis

**133.** Haemophilia is :
  (*a*) albinism
  (*b*) diabetes mellitus
  (*c*) bleeders' disease
  (*d*) None of these

**134.** Blood agglutination means :
  (*a*) blood transfusion
  (*b*) blood typing
  (*c*) clumping of blood due to antigen and antibody reaction
  (*d*) None of these

**135.** A polysome is a :
  (*a*) ribosome plus tRNA
  (*b*) ribosome plus mRNA
  (*c*) ribosome plus tRNA and mRNA
  (*d*) many ribosomes attached to mRNA at a time

**136.** Cell membranes are composed mainly of :
  (*a*) sugar and proteins
  (*b*) lipids and proteins
  (*c*) starch and lipids
  (*d*) sugar and lipids

**137.** Hydrolytic enzymes are abundant in :
  (*a*) peroxisomes    (*b*) microsomes
  (*c*) lysosome      (*d*) lomasome

**138.** Ribosomes are the centre of :
  (*a*) respiration
  (*b*) photosynthesis
  (*c*) protein synthesis
  (*d*) fat synthesis

**139.** In plant cell vacuole contains :
  (*a*) water
  (*b*) cytoplasm
  (*c*) air
  (*d*) water and dissolved substance

**140.** The cellwall was discovered by :
  (*a*) Robert Hooke
  (*b*) Robert Brown
  (*c*) Antony Van Leeuwenhoek
  (*d*) Carolus Linnaeus

**141.** Semi-Genetic autonomy is seen in :
  (*a*) ribosomes      (*b*) dictyosomes
  (*c*) lysosomes      (*d*) chloroplast

**142.** Bile helps in :
  (*a*) producing enzymes

(*b*)  esterification
(*c*)  both (*a*) and (*b*)
(*d*)  emulsification of fats
143.  Water-soluble vitamins are :
    (*a*)  A, B and C    (*b*)  C and D
    (*c*)  B and C    (*d*)  None of these
144.  Vitamin containing a cobalt cyanide linkage is :
    (*a*)  A    (*b*)  B
    (*c*)  $B_6$    (*d*)  $B_{12}$
145.  Scurvy is caused due to dificiency of :
    (*a*)  Vitamin-C    (*b*)  Vitamin-D
    (*c*)  Vitamin-K    (*d*)  Vitamin-A
146.  Pellagra is caused by the deficiency of :
    (*a*)  thiamine
    (*b*)  ascorbic acid
    (*c*)  nicotinic acid (Niacin)
    (*d*)  calciferol
147.  Beri-beri is caused due to deficiency of :
    (*a*)  Vitamin-$B_1$    (*b*)  Proteins
    (*c*)  Enzymes    (*d*)  Vitamin-$B_2$
148.  The enzymes are chemically speaking :
    (*a*)  proteins    (*b*)  lipids
    (*c*)  vitamins    (*d*)  none of these
149.  The essential mineral for the formation of body protein is :
    (*a*)  calcium    (*b*)  sodium
    (*c*)  magnesium    (*d*)  potassium
150.  Anaemia is caused due to deficiency of :
    (*a*)  biotin    (*b*)  folic acid
    (*c*)  niacin    (*d*)  ascorbic acid

## ANSWERS

| 1 | 2 | 3 | 4 | 5 | 6 | 7 | 8 | 9 | 10 |
|---|---|---|---|---|---|---|---|---|---|
| (*a*) | (*a*) | (*b*) | (*d*) | (*c*) | (*b*) | (*c*) | (*a*) | (*c*) | (*d*) |
| **11** | **12** | **13** | **14** | **15** | **16** | **17** | **18** | **19** | **20** |
| (*a*) | (*a*) | (*a*) | (*a*) | (*b*) | (*a*) | (*c*) | (*a*) | (*a*) | (*d*) |
| **21** | **22** | **23** | **24** | **25** | **26** | **27** | **28** | **29** | **30** |
| (*b*) | (*c*) | (*c*) | (*d*) | (*d*) | (*b*) | (*b*) | (*d*) | (*c*) | (*a*) |
| **31** | **32** | **33** | **34** | **35** | **36** | **37** | **38** | **39** | **40** |
| (*c*) | (*b*) | (*a*) | (*b*) | (*c*) | (*a*) | (*d*) | (*b*) | (*c*) | (*c*) |
| **41** | **42** | **43** | **44** | **45** | **46** | **47** | **48** | **49** | **50** |
| (*c*) | (*c*) | (*b*) | (*b*) | (*b*) | (*d*) | (*a*) | (*d*) | (*b*) | (*b*) |
| **51** | **52** | **53** | **54** | **55** | **56** | **57** | **58** | **59** | **60** |
| (*d*) | (*b*) | (*a*) | (*b*) | (*b*) | (*b*) | (*a*) | (*b*) | (*c*) | (*a*) |
| **61** | **62** | **63** | **64** | **65** | **66** | **67** | **68** | **69** | **70** |
| (*b*) | (*b*) | (*b*) | (*b*) | (*a*) | (*a*) | (*b*) | (*a*) | (*b*) | (*a*) |
| **71** | **72** | **73** | **74** | **75** | **76** | **77** | **78** | **79** | **80** |
| (*c*) | (*a*) | (*a*) | (*a*) | (*c*) | (*d*) | (*a*) | (*a*) | (*b*) | (*c*) |
| **81** | **82** | **83** | **84** | **85** | **86** | **87** | **88** | **89** | **90** |
| (*d*) | (*b*) | (*a*) | (*c*) | (*b*) | (*c*) | (*d*) | (*c*) | (*d*) | (*c*) |

| 91 | 92 | 93 | 94 | 95 | 96 | 97 | 98 | 99 | 100 |
|----|----|----|----|----|----|----|----|----|-----|
| (b) | (c) | (a) | (b) | (b) | (a) | (b) | (b) | (b) | (b) |
| 101 | 102 | 103 | 104 | 105 | 106 | 107 | 108 | 109 | 110 |
| (a) | (a) | (a) | (d) | (a) | (d) | (d) | (c) | (a) | (d) |
| 111 | 112 | 113 | 114 | 115 | 116 | 117 | 118 | 119 | 120 |
| (c) | (a) | (b) | (b) | (c) | (d) | (a) | (d) | (c) | (c) |
| 121 | 122 | 123 | 124 | 125 | 126 | 127 | 128 | 129 | 130 |
| (d) | (b) | (d) | (c) | (b) | (b) | (a) | (b) | (a) | (a) |
| 131 | 132 | 133 | 134 | 135 | 136 | 137 | 138 | 139 | 140 |
| (b) | (c) | (b) | (c) | (d) | (b) | (c) | (c) | (d) | (a) |
| 141 | 142 | 143 | 144 | 145 | 146 | 147 | 148 | 149 | 150 |
| (d) | (d) | (c) | (d) | (a) | (c) | (a) | (a) | (c) | (b) |

1805

★ ★ ★ ★ ★

# GENERAL KNOWLEDGE

# INDIA

## Facts About India

(1) **Area** = 32, 87,263 sq. km.

(2) **Land Frontier** = 15, 200 km

(3) **Total Coast line** = 7516.6 km

(4) **Population (2011 census)** = 1,21,08,54,977 (62,32,70,258 males and 58,75,84,719 females)

(5) **Average Density of Population:** 382 per sq. km.

(6) **Total Literacy** = 73.0%
   - *(i)* Male literacy = 80.9%
   - *(ii)* Female literacy = 64.6%

(7) **India is -**
   - *(i)* 7th largest country in the world in area.
   - *(ii)* 2nd largest populous country in the world.
   - *(iii)* home of more than 16 per cent of world population (2011 census) and accounts for 2.42 per cent of the total world area.

(8) **India's neighbour's**
   - *(i)* in the north — China, Nepal and Bhutan
   - *(ii)* in the east — Myanmar (Burma)
   - *(iii)* Bangladesh lies wedged between India's north-eastern States and West Bengal
   - *(iv)* in the west and north-west — Pakistan
   - *(v)* in the south — Sri Lanka

(9) India's States and Union Territories
   - *(i)* India has 29 States and 7 Union Territories.

**STATES OF INDIA**

| State | Capital | Principal Language(s) | Area in (sq. km) | Population 2011 |
|---|---|---|---|---|
| 1 | 2 | 3 | 4 | 5 |
| 1. Andhra Pradesh | Hyderabad | Telugu, Urdu | 1,60,205 | 4,93,86799 |
| 2. Arunachal Pradesh[#] | Itanagar | Monpa, Miji, etc. | 83,743 | 1383727 |
| 3. Assam | Dispur[1] | Assamese, Bengali | 78,438 | 31205576 |
| 4. Bihar | Patna | Hindi | 94,163 | 104099452 |
| 5. Chhattisgarh | Raipur | Hindi | 1,35,192 | 25545198 |
| 6. Goa | Panaji | Konkani, Marathi | 3,702 | 1458545 |
| 7. Gujarat | Gandhi Nagar | Gujarati | 1,96,024 | 60439692 |
| 8. Haryana | Chandigarh | Hindi | 44,212 | 25351462 |
| 9. Himachal Pradesh | Simla | Hindi, Pahari | 55,673 | 6864602 |
| 10. Jammu & Kashmir | Srinagar[2] | 3 | 2,22,236[4-5] | 12541302 |
| 11. Jharkhand | Ranchi | Hindi | 79,714 | 32988134 |
| 12. Karnataka | Bengaluru | Kannada | 1,91,791 | 61095297 |
| 13. Kerala | Thiruvananthapuram | Malayalam | 38,863 | 33406061 |
| 14. Madhya Pradesh | Bhopal | Hindi | 3,08,000 | 72626809 |
| 15. Maharashtra | Mumbai | Marathi | 3,07,713 | 112374333 |
| 16. Manipur | Imphal | Manipuri | 22,327 | 2855794 |
| 17. Meghalaya | Shillong | Khasi, Garo, English | 22,429 | 2966889 |
| 18. Mizoram | Aizawl | Mizo, English | 21,081 | 1097206 |
| 19. Nagaland | Kohima | 6 | 16,579 | 1978502 |
| 20. Odisha | Bhubaneswar | Odiya | 1,55,707 | 41974218 |
| 21. Punjab | Chandigarh | Punjabi | 50,362 | 27743308 |
| 22. Rajasthan | Jaipur | Hindi, Rajasthani | 3,42,239 | 68548437 |
| 23. Sikkim | Gangtok | 7 | 7,096 | 610577 |

4

| No. | State/UT | Capital | Language | Area (sq km) | Population |
|---|---|---|---|---|---|
| 24. | Tamil Nadu | Chennai | Tamil | 1,30,058 | 72147030 |
| 25. | Tripura | Agartala | 8 | 10,491 | 3673917 |
| 26. | Uttarakhand | Dehradun (Provisional) | Hindi | 53,483 | 10086292 |
| 27. | Uttar Pradesh | Lucknow | Hindi, Urdu | 2,40,928 | 199812341 |
| 28. | West Bengal | Kolkata | Bengali | 88,752 | 91276115 |
| 29. | Telangana | Hyderabad | Telugu, Urdu | 1,14,840 | 3,51,93,978 |

## UNION TERRITORIES

| No. | Union Territory | Capital | Language | Area (sq km) | Population |
|---|---|---|---|---|---|
| 1. | Andaman & Nicobar Islands | Port Blair | 9 | 8,249 | 380581 |
| 2. | Chandigarh | Chandigarh | Hindi, Punjabi, English | 114 | 1055450 |
| 3. | Dadar & Nagar Haveli | Silvassa | Gujarati and Hindi | 491 | 343709 |
| 4. | Daman & Diu | Daman | Gujarati | 112 | 243247 |
| 5. | Delhi | Delhi | Hindi, Urdu, Punjabi | 1,483 | 16787941 |
| 6. | Lakshadweep | Kavaratti | Malayalam | 32 | 64473 |
| 7. | Puducherry | Pudducherry | Tamil, French, Telugu English and Malayalam | 490 | 1247953 |

1. Pragjyotishpur will be the new capital of Assam; 2. In winter the capital shifts to Jammu; 3. Kashmiri, Dogri, Gujri, Urdu, Balti, Dadri, Pahari, Ladakhi, Punjabi; 4. Includes 78,114 sq km under illegal occupation of Pakistan, 5,180 sq. km illegaly handed over by Pakistan to China and 37,555 sq km under illegal occupation of China; 5. The population figure excludes population of area under unlawful occupation of Pakistan and China. 6. Angami, Ao, Chang, Konyak, Lotha, Sangtam, Sema and Chakhesang; 7. Bhutia, Nepali, Lepcha and Limbu; 8. Bengali, Kakborak and Manipuri, 9. Hindi, Nicobarese, Bengali, Malayalam, Tamil & Telugu. # This State enjoys special status on traditional and customary laws.

**Note:** The figures are based on Final Census of India 2011.

**States:**

| | | |
|---|---|---|
| *(i)* | Largest in population | : Uttar Pradesh (about 19.9 crore) |
| *(ii)* | Smallest in population | : Sikkim (about 6 lakh) |
| *(iii)* | Largest in area | : Rajasthan (about 3.4 Lakh sq. km) |
| *(iv)* | Smallest in area | : Goa (3702 sq. km) |
| *(v)* | Highest density of population | : Bihar (1106) |
| *(vi)* | Lowest density of population | : Arunachal Pradesh (17) |
| *(vii)* | First to achieve 100% rural electrification | : Haryana |
| *(viii)* | First to achieve total Literacy | : Kerala |
| *(ix)* | Lowest percentage of literacy | : Bihar (61.8%) |
| *(x)* | With high number of females than males | : Kerala (1084 females for 1000 males) |

**Union Territories**

| | | |
|---|---|---|
| *(i)* | Largest in population | : Delhi (over 1.6 crore) |
| *(ii)* | Smallest in population | : Lakshadweep (over 64 thousand) |
| *(iii)* | Largest in area | : Andaman & Nicobar Islands (8249 sq. km) |
| *(iv)* | Smallest in area | : Lakshadweep (32 sq. km) |
| *(v)* | Highest density of population | : Delhi (11,320) |
| *(vi)* | Lowest density of population | : Andman & Nicobar Islands (46) |
| *(vii)* | Highest percentage of Literacy | : Lakshadweep (91.8%) |
| *(viii)* | Lowest percentage of Literacy | : Dadra & Nagar Haveli (76.2%) |

**National Flag:**

(1) It is horizontal tricolour.

(2) Three equal horizontal strips : *(a)* Deep saffron at the top
: *(b)* White in the middle
: *(c)* Dark Green at the bottom.

(3) Ratio of width to length : 2:3.

(4) In the centre of the white stripe : a wheel in navy blue.

(5) Number of spokes in the wheel : 24.

(6) The wheel is a replica of the wheel on the capital of the Ashoka Pillar at Sarnath.

(7) The National Flag was adopted *(i)* by the Constituent Assembly of India, *(ii)* on July 22, 1947.

(8) Its use and display are regulated by a code.

**National Emblem:**

(1) National Emblem is an adaptation from the Sarnath Lion Capitol of Ashoka.
(2) It depicts three lions.
(3) A wheel appears in relief in the centre of the abacus with a bull on the right and a horse on the left.
(4) Below the abacus appear *Satyameva Jayate* in the devanagari script.
(5) *Satyameva Jayate* has been taken from Mundaka Upanishad.
(6) *Satyameva Jayate* means "Truth Alone Triumphs."
(7) The National Emblem was adopted by the Government of India on January 26, 1950.

**National Anthem:**

(1) *Jana-gana-mana* composed by Rabindranath Tagore is our national anthem.
(2) The Constituent Assembly of India adopted it as the national anthem on January 24, 1950.
(3) It was first sung on December 27, 1911 at the Calcutta Session of the Indian National Congress.
(4) It was first published under caption 'Bharat Vidhata' in January 1912 in the magazine named *'Tatva Bodhini'*.
(5) Playing time of the full version of the national anthem is approximately 52 seconds.
(6) *Vande Mataram*, composed by Bankim Chandra Chatterjee has an equal status with *Jana-gana-mana*.
(7) It was first sung at the 1896 session of the Indian National Congress.
(8) This song occurs in the novel *Anand Math*, written by Bankim Chandra Chatterjee.

**National Calendar**

(1) India's National Calendar is based on *Saka* Era.
(2) It was adopted and introduced on March 22, 1957.
(3) It has a normal year of 365 days.
(4) *Chaitra* is the first month and *Phalguna* is the last month of the year.
(5) 1 *Chaitra* falls on March 22 in a normal year and on March 21 in a leap year.

**National Animal and National Bird**

(1) Tiger is the national animal of India.
(2) Peacock is the national bird of India.

## History of India – Some Facts

1. The discovery of the Indus Valley Civilisation was made in 1921.
2. The main centres of the Indus Valley Civilisation were – Harappa, Mohenjodaro, Kali Bangan, Luthal, etc.

3. The Aryans came into India from Central Asia and settled first in *Sapta Sindhu.*

4. The Indus Valley Civilisation was urban whereas the Aryan Civilisation was rural.

5. The Vedas are four: *(i)* Rig Ved, *(ii)* Yajur Ved, *(iii)* Sam Ved, and *(iv)* Atharva Ved.

6. Of the four Vedas, Rig Ved is the oldest.

7. Jainism and Buddhism were founded during the 6th century B. C.

8. Jainism was founded by Lord Mahavir whereas Buddhism was founded by Lord Buddha.

9. Buddha was born at Lumbini.

10. Buddhism got maximum state patronage from Ashoka.

11. Buddha delivered his first sermon at Sarnath (near Varanasi)

12. Megasthenese was the Greek ambassador to the Court of Chandragupta Maurya.

13. The capital of the Mauryan Empire was Pataliputra.

14. Kanishka was the most important Kushana ruler who ruled from Purushpur (Peshawar).

15. Gupta Period is known as the Golden Age of ancient India.

16. Ashoka vowed never to wage a war (after his victory in Kalinga War) and converted himself to Buddhism.

17. Chinese Buddhist monk Hiuen Tsang visited India during the reign of Harshavardhana.

18. Sind (in India) was the first victim of Arab invasion.

19. Mahmud Ghaznavi plundered Somnath temple in 1026.

20. Mohammad Ghori defeated Prithviraj Chauhan in the second battle of Tarain.

21. Qutb-ud-din Aibak was the first Muslim ruler of India.

22. Razia Begum was the first woman who sat on the throne of Delhi Sultanate.

23. The founder of the Mughal Empire in India was Babar.

24. First battle of Panipat (1526) laid the foundation of Mughal rule in India.

25. Akbar was the greatest of the conquerors, administrators and empire builders amongst the Mughal rulers.

26. *Din-e-Ilahi* was a religious sect founded by Akbar.

27. Akbar founded Fatehpur Sikri and constructed beautiful buildings there.

28. Shahjehan died as a prisoner in the jail.

29. Aurangzeb had to face a great challenge from the Marathas.

30. The English established their first factory at Surat in 1615.

31. Portuguese were the first European traders to come to India.

32. Robert Clive was the real founder of British power in India.

33. It was Robert Clive who set up double government in Bengal.

34. Lord Wellesley followed the policy of Subsidiary Alliance to make Indian rulers as subordinate allies of the British power in India.

35. Lord William Bentinck abolished the *Sati* system.

36. During the tenure of William Bentinck English was made medium of instruction in India.

37. The last Governor General of British India was Lord Canning.

38. Lord Dalhousie sowed the seeds of 1857 Sepoy Mutiny.

39. Doctrine of Lapse was used against the Indian rulers by Lord Dalhousie.

40. Warren Hastings introduced the Permanent Settlement of land revenue in Bengal.

41. Lord Curzon partitioned Bengal in 1905.

42. The Sepoy Mutiny of 1857 started from Meerut on May 10, 1857.

43. The glorious leaders of the Revolt of 1857 were — Nana Saheb, Rani Lakshmi Bai of Jhansi, Mughal Emperor Bahadur Shah II Zafar, Kunwar Singh and Tantia Tope.

44. Indian National Congress was founded by A.O. Hume in 1885.

45. Netaji Subhash Chandra Bose founded the Indian National Army (INA) at Singapore.

46. Jallianwala Bagh massacre took place at Amritsar in 1919.

47. Indian National Congress put forth the demand of Complete Independence in 1929.

48. Swadeshi movement became very popular during mass agitation against Partition of Bengal (1905).

49. Gandhiji's Dandi March is associated with the salt law.

50. 'Quit India' slogan was given by the Indian National Congress in 1942.

51. Indian Muslim League was founded in 1906.

52. India achieved Independence in 1947 during the tenure of Lord Mountbatten.

53. With the Partition of India the British Rule ended; two ''Independent States'' India and Pakistan were created; Mountbatten became the first Governor-General of Free India in 1947.

54. Assassination of Mahatma Gandhi (January 30, 1948) by Nathu Ram Godse; Kashmir acceded to India; C. Rajgopalachari took over as the first Indian Governor-General (1948).

55. Integration of the Princely States into the Indian Union (1948-50).

56. Indian Constitution was signed and adopted on November 26, 1949.

57. India became Sovereign Republic (January 26, 1950). Sardar Patel died (December 15, 1950); Dr. Rajendra Prasad became the first President of India (1950).

## India's Armed Forces

1. President of India is the Supreme Commander of the Armed Forces of India.

2. Union Cabinet is responsible for national defence.

3. Operational control of the armed forces is exercised by the Ministry of Defence.

4. The armed forces consist of three services namely: *(i)* Army, *(ii)* Navy and *(iii)* Air Force.

5. The three services function under their respective Chiefs of Staff namely: *(i)* Chief of the Army Staff, *(ii)* Chief of the Naval Staff and *(iii)* Chief of the Air Staff.

### Army

1. Army Headquarters is in New Delhi.

2. Army is organised into Six operational Commands, *viz.* *(i)* Southern, *(ii)* Eastern, *(iii)* Western, *(iv)* Central, *(v)* Northern and *(vi)* South Western.

3. Army has also a training Command in Shimla (Himachal Pradesh).

4. Each Command is under a General Officer Commanding-in-Chief.

5. Army consists of a number of arms and services such as *(i)* Armoured Corps, *(ii)* Regiment of Artillery, *(iii)* Corps of Air Defence, *(iv)* Army Aviation Corps, *(v)* Corps of Engineers/Signals, *(vi)* Infantry, *(vii)* Army Medical/ Nursing Corps, *(viii)* Army Education Corps, *(ix)* Corps of Military Police etc.

### Navy

1. Navy Headquarters is in New Delhi.

2. The Navy has 3 commands — *(i)* Western, *(ii)* Eastern, and *(iii)* Southern.

3. Each Command is headed by a Flag Officer Commanding-in-Chief.

4. The Western and the Eastern Commands are operational commands with their fleets while the Southern Command is responsible for all training activities of Indian Navy.

5. Fleets of Indian Navy comprise warships, submarines, aircraft carriers, etc.
6. There are two major naval bases at Mumbai and Vishakhapatnam.
7. Coast Guard was constituted in 1978 with its headquarters at New Delhi. It is responsible for defence and security of India's marine interests and assets.

## Air Force

1. Air Force Headquarters is in New Delhi.
2. Air Force is organised into 5 operational Commands — *(i)* Western Air Command, *(ii)* South-Western Air Command, *(iii)* Central Air Command, *(iv)* Eastern Air Command, and *(v)* Southern Air Command.
3. There are two functional commands — *(i)* Maintenance Command, and *(ii)* Training Command.
4. Air Force fleet consists of fighter bombers, fighters, Transport, Interceptors and logistic aircrafts and helicopters. Strike aircrafts are MIG-21, MIG-23, MIG-25, MIG-27 and Jaguar, Air Defence Aircrafts are MIG 29, Mirage-2000. Transport fleet consists of AN-32, Boeing - 737, HS-748. Helicopters are — MI-8, MI-17, Chetak/Cheetah.
5. Chetak/Cheetah helicopters are manufactured by HAL.

## Commissioned Ranks in Defence Services

| *Army* | *Navy* | *Air Force* |
|---|---|---|
| General | Admiral | Air Chief Marshal |
| Lieutenant-General | Vice-Admiral | Air Marshal |
| Major-General | Rear-Admiral | Air Vice-Marshal |
| Brigadier | Commodore | Air Commodore |
| Colonel | Captain | Group Captain |
| Lieutenant-Colonel | Commander | Wing Commander |
| Major | Lt. Commander | Squadron Leader |
| Captain | Lieutenant | Flight Lieutenant |
| Lieutenant | Sub-Lieutenant | Flying Officer |

## Non-Commissioned and Junior Commissioned Ranks in Defence Services

| *Army* | *Navy* | *Air Force* |
|---|---|---|
| Subedar Major | Master Chief Petty Officer I | Master Warrant Officer |
| Subedar | Master Chief Petty Officer II | Warrant Officer |
| Naik Subedar | Chief Petty Officer | Junior Warrant Officer |
| Havildar | Petty Officer | Sergeant |
| Naik | Leading Sailor I | Corporal |
| Lance Naik | Leading Sailor II | Leading Aircraftsman |
| Jawan | Sailor | Aircraftsman |

**Training Institutions:**

- *(i)* ***Training Institutions for Army:*** National Defence Academy, Khadakwasla; The National Defence College, New Delhi; The Indian Military Academy, Dehra Dun; Defence Service Staff College, Wellington; Armed Forces Medical College, Pune; The Officers Training School, Chennai; Army Ordnance Corps School, Jabalpur; Army Defence College, Pune; College of Defence Management, Secunderabad; The School of Artillery, Deolali; Military College of Telecommunication Engineering, Mhow and The College of Military Engineering, Kirkee.

- *(ii)* ***Training Institutions for Navy:*** INS Shivaji, Lonavala; INS Valsura, Jamnagar; INS Vendruthy, Kochi; INS Chilka, Odisha; INS Satavahan, Vishakhapatnam; INS Garuda, Kochi; INS Mandovi, Goa; INS Dronacharya, Kochi and INS Hamla, Malad (Mumbai).

- *(iii)* ***Training Institutions for Air Force:*** Air Force Academy, Hyderabad; Fighter Training Wing, Hakim; Elementary Flying School, Bidar; Air Force Technical College, Jalahalli; College of Air Warfare, Secunderabad; Air Force Administrative College, Coimbatore and Institute of Aviation Medicine, Bengaluru.

***Defence Production Undertakings:*** There are eight public sector enterprises under the Department of Defence Production:- 1. Hindustan Aeronautics Ltd. (HAL); 2. Bharat Electronics Ltd. (BEL); 3. Bharat Earth Movers Ltd. (BEML); 4. Mazagon Dock Ltd. (MDL); 5. Garden Reach Shipbuilders & Engineers Ltd. (GRSE); 6. Goa Shipyard Ltd. (GSL); 7. Bharat Dynamics Ltd. (BDL); 8. Mishra Dhatu Nigam Ltd. (MIDHANI).

**Second Line of Defence:**

- (a) **Territorial Army:** Organised in 1949.
- (b) **Border Security Force:** Set up in 1965.
- (c) **Home Guards :** Organised in 1962.
- (d) **N.C.C. (National Cadet Corps)**

N.C.C., the premier youth organisation of the country was established in 1948 (15th July). Its motto is "Unity and Discipline" and its aims are:

1. To develop qualities of character, courage, comradeship, discipline, leadership, secular outlook, spirit of adventure, sportsmanship.
2. NCC is headed by a Director General NCC, located at New Delhi.
3. NCC consist of 3 divisions—(i) Senior division for college student, (ii) Junior division for secondary school boys and girls, and (iii) Girls division.
4. The senior and junior divisions are composed of three wings: Army, Navy and Air Force.

**Miscellaneous Facts**

**Indian Missiles:**
- *(i)* Prithvi — Surface to surface
- *(ii)* Nag — Anti-Tank
- *(iii)* Trishul — Surface to air
- *(iv)* Akash — Surface to air
- *(v)* Agni — Air to air
- *(vi)* Brahmos — Supersonic Cruise Missile (It is a product of India-Russia Cooperation)

**Main Battle Tank:** Arjun

**First Indigenous Tank:** Vijayanta

**Multi-barrel Rocket System:** Pinaka

# Indian Transport System

## 1. Railways

*(i)* Indian Railway System is our country's biggest national undertaking.

*(ii)* It is largest in Asia and the second largest in the world.

*(iii)* As on March 31, 2016, the total route length was 67,312 km.

*(iv)* Indian Railway is organised into 17 zones.

*(v)* Gatiman Express is the fastest train in India with a permissible speed of 160 km per hour.

*(vi)* The first Shatabdi Express was introduced on July 10, 1988 between New Delhi and Jhansi.

*(vii)* *Locker on Wheels* is a service introduced in Feb. 1995 for passengers of Shatabdi Express trains with 100% guaranteed delivery on the same day.

*(viii)* There are six main production units under the Indian Railways: (1) Chittaranjan Locomotive Works (West Bengal), (2) Diesel Locomotive Works (Varanasi, Uttar Pradesh), (3) Diesel Component Works (Patiala, Punjab), (4) Integral Coach Factory (Perambur, Tamil Nadu), (5) Rail Coach Factory (Kapurthala, Punjab), (6) Wheel & Axles Plant, Yelahanka (Bangalore, Karnataka).

### *Miscellaneous Facts*

1. The first train in India was introduced between Mumbai and Thana, a stretch of 34 km on April 16, 1853.
2. The first electric train was opened in February 1925 on Mumbai sub-urban railway on Mumbai VT-Kurla branch line.
3. As on 31-3-2016 the electrified route was about 43 per cent of the route km.
4. The largest rail platform in India is at Gorakhpur (1355.4 mt.), Uttar Pradesh.

5. The longest railway tunnel is Banihal–Qazigund tunnel (J&K, 11 km).
6. At present Indian Railways have 17 zones.
7. The largest marshalling yard is at Mughalsarai.
8. The third class in the Indian Railways was abolished in 1974.
9. The Railways have more than 1.32 million employees.
10. The steam engines are being phased out and diesel and electric locomotives are being introduced.
11. India's first Metro Railway was opened in Calcutta (now Kolkata) on Oct. 24, 1984.
12. *Palace on Wheels* is Rajasthan's prestigious tourist train.
13. Computer reservation is 95%.

## 2. Shipping

1. Shipping Corporation of India came into being in 1961.
2. Four major shipyards in the public sector are: *(i)* Garden Reach Shipbuilders & Engineers Ltd, Kolkata, *(ii)* Mazagon Dock Ltd, Mumbai, *(iii)* Hindustan Shipyard Ltd, Vishakhapatnam, *(iv)* Cochin Shipyard, Cochin.
3. The major ports on Western Coast are: Kandla, Mumbai, Mormugao, New Mangalore, Cochin and Nhava Sheva (Jawaharlal Nehru Port).
4. The major ports on Eastern Coast are: Tuticorin, Chennai, Vishakhapatnam, Paradip and Kolkata-Haldia.
5. In respect of shipping tonnage, India ranks second in Asia and fifteenth in the world.
6. The first passenger ship built in India is Harshavardhana.

## 3. Civil Aviation:

1. All air routes and air companies in India were nationalised in 1953.
2. Air India Corporation and Indian Airlines Corporation were established in 1953.
3. In 1994, these Corporations were converted into public limited companies and private sector was allowed in the field.
4. Jet Airways, Jetlite Airlines, Go Airlines, Kingfisher Airlines, Spicejet Ltd, Paramount Airways and IndiGo are private carriers.
5. In India main International Airports are:

   *(i)* Mumbai, *(ii)* Kolkata, *(iii)* Delhi, *(iv)* Chennai, *(v)* Thiruvananthapuram, *(vi)* Ahmedabad.
6. Vayudoot was set up in January 1981.
7. Helicopter Corporation of India (*Pavan Hans*) was inaugurated on October 15, 1985.

# Communications

## 1. Akashvani and Doordarshan

1. All India Radio was named *Akashvani* in 1957.
2. Akashvani covers 91.37% area and 99.13% of the population of India.
3. *Vividh Bharati* service was started in 1957.
4. Sponsored Programmes were introduced in May 1970.
5. Television in India was started in Delhi on September 15, 1959.
6. Doordarshan was separated from Akashvani in 1976.
7. Doordarshan turned commercial from January 1, 1976.
8. Satellite technology came into operation in 1975.
9. Doordarshan National Programme was introduced on August 15, 1984.
10. International Channel of Doordarshan was started on March 14, 1995.

## 2. Post-Telecommunications

(i) Postal Department was set up in 1854.
(ii) Money Order service was introduced in 1880.
(iii) Air Mail Service started in 1911.
(iv) PIN Code system started in 1972.
(v) Speed Post was introduced in 1986.
(vi) Satellite Money Order service started in December 1994.

# Scientific Research

(i) Atomic Energy Commission was set up in 1948.
(ii) Atomic Power Stations are located at : *(a)* Tarapore (Maharashtra), *(b)* Rawathbhata (Rajasthan), *(c)* Kalpakkam (Tamil Nadu), *(d)* Narora (UP), *(e)* Kakrapara (Gujarat), *(f)* Kaiga (Karnataka) and *(g)* Kudankulam (Tamil Nadu).
(iii) The first heavy water plant was set up in 1961 in Nangal.
(iv) India coducted her first underground atomic explosion at Pokhran (Rajasthan) on May 18, 1974.
(v) Space Commission was set up in 1972.
(vi) Squadran Leader Rakesh Sharma became the first Indian to go into Space on April 3, 1984.
(vii) Department of Ocean Development was set up in July 1981.
(viii) *Dakshin Gangotri and Maitri* are the two stations set up by India in Antarctica.

# Planning

(1) Planning Commission was constituted in March 1950. 'NITI Aayog' replaced it from January 1, 2015.

(2) Prime Minister is the Chairman of the NITI Aayog.

(3) The Five-Year Plans are finally approved by the National Development Council.

(4) The 12th Five-Year Plan started in 2012.

(5) The First Five-Year Plan started in 1951.

# Finance

(1) Finance Commission is appointed by the President of India.

(2) Finance Commission is appointed every 5 years.

(3) All currency notes are issued by the Reserve Bank of India.

(4) One rupee notes are issued by the Ministry of Finance.

(5) Decimal system of coins was introduced in India from April 1, 1957.

(6) 14 major banks were nationalised in July 1969.

(7) Reserve Bank of India is the Central Bank of India.

(8) The largest commercial bank in public sector is State Bank of India.

(9) Life Insurance Corporation of India was set up in September 1956.

(10) Unit Trust of India (UTI) was set up in 1964.

# Wildlife Sanctuaries and National Parks

| Wildlife Sanctuaries & National Parks | State |
| --- | --- |
| Kanha National Park | Madhya Pradesh |
| Shivpuri National Park | Madhya Pradesh |
| Kaziranga Sanctuary | Assam |
| Manas Sanctuary | Assam |
| Hazaribagh National Park | Jharkhand |
| Ghana Bird Sanctuary | Rajasthan |
| Sariska Game Sanctuary | Rajasthan |
| Corbett National Park | Uttarakhand |
| Chandraprabha Sanctuary | Uttar Pradesh |
| Rangathittoo Bird Sanctuary | Karnataka |
| Bandipur Sanctuary | Karnataka |
| Vendanthangal Bird Sanctuary | Tamil Nadu |
| Mudumalai Sanctuary | Tamil Nadu |
| Periyar Sanctuary | Kerala |

| | |
|---|---|
| Eravikulam Rajmallay National Park | Kerala |
| Sultanpur Bird Sanctuary | Haryana |
| Todoba National Park | Maharashtra |
| Semlipal National Park | Odisha |
| Nal Sarovar Bird Sanctuary | Gujarat |
| Rohia National Park | Himachal Pradesh |
| Jaldapara Sanctuary | West Bengal |

# Agriculture, Industries and Minerals

## I. Agriculture

| *Crop* | *Chief Producers* |
|---|---|
| Wheat | Punjab, Haryana and UP |
| Rice | West Bengal |
| Rubber | Kerala |
| Tea | Asom and West Bengal |
| Cotton | Maharashtra |
| Sugar | UP |
| Tobacco | Andhra Pradesh |
| Cashew nut | Kerala |
| Pulses | UP, Bihar and Madhya Pradesh |

## II. Industries

| *Places* | *Associated with Industries* |
|---|---|
| Khetri | Copper |
| Raniganj & Jheria | Coal |
| Durgapur | Steel |
| Ahmedabad | Cotton Textiles |
| Barauni | Oil Refinery |
| Nepanagar | Newsprint |
| Sindri | Fertilisers |
| Anand | Dairy |
| Avadi | Heavy Vehicle Factory |
| Dalmia Nagar | Cement |
| Digboi | Oil wells |
| Katni | Cement |
| Koyali | Petro-Chemicals |
| Narora | Atomic Power Station |
| Nangal | Fertilisers |

| | |
|---|---|
| Nasik | Currency Note Press |
| Obra | Thermal Power Station |
| Pimpri | Antibiotic Drugs |
| Renukoot | Aluminium plant |
| Sivakasi | Match Box and Fire works |
| Hoshangabad | Security Paper Mills |

**III. Minerals**

| *Minerals* | *States* |
|---|---|
| Coal | Jharkhand |
| Iron | Jharkhand |
| Mica | Jharkhand |
| Gold | Karnataka (Kolar) |
| Uranium | Jharkhand |
| Diamond | Madhya Pradesh (Panna) |

# Constitution of India

(1) Constitution of India came into force on January 26, 1950.

(2) President of India is elected for a term of five years.

(3) Sessions of Parliament are summoned by President.

(4) Vice-President of India is the ex-offico Chairman of Rajya Sabha.

(5) Lok Sabha is elected for a term of five years.

(6) Speaker, Lok Sabha is elected by the members of Lok Sabha.

(7) Council of Ministers is appointed by the President on the recommendation of the Prime Minister.

(8) The Union Council of Ministers is responsible to Lok Sabha.

(9) Rajya Sabha is a permanent body and cannot be dissolved.

(10) Members of Rajya Sabha have a term of 6 years.

(11) Judges of Supreme Court are appointed by the President.

(12) State Governors are appointed by the President.

# President

The President is the Constitutional head of the Republic of India. He is more or less the titular head of the executive. Really speaking, he is the constitutional head but not the real executive.The real power is vested in the hands of the Council of Ministers.

**Qualifications:** (*i*) Indian citizen, (*ii*) age not less than 35 years, (*iii*) should have qualification for election to Lok Sabha, (*iv*) should not hold any office of profit, (*v*) should not be a Member of Parliament or State Legislature.

**Powers:** He makes appointments to all the constitutional posts. He can address either House of Parliament and dissolve Lok Sabha. All Bills passed by Parliament must receive his assent to become an Act. He issues ordinances when Parliament is not in session. No Money Bill can be introduced in Lok Sabha without his recommendation. He can grant pardon, reprieve or remit punishment and he can commute death sentences, can declare national emergency, state emergency and financial emergency.

**Term and Emolument:** The President holds the office for a period of five years. He is eligible for re-election. He draws a fixed salary. He is also entitled to rent free official residence called Rashtrapati Bhawan.

## Vice-President

The Vice-President acts as the ex-officio Chairman of the Council of States (Rajya Sabha). He is elected by an electoral college consisting of the members of both Houses of Parliament in accordance with the system of proportional representation by means of the single transferable vote. He must be a citizen of India, not less than 35 years of age, and should be eligible for election as a member of the Council of States. Disputes in connection with election of a president or a vice-president are to be a dealt with in accordance with Article-71. Such disputes shall be decided by the Supreme Court.

## Prime Minister

The constitution lays down that there shall be a Council of Ministers headed by the Prime Minister to aid and advise the President in the exercise of his functions. The Prime Minister is the head of the Cabinet. Other Ministers are appointed by the President on his advice. He is the leader of the majority party in the Lok Sabha.

## First in India

| | |
|---|---|
| First Person to get Nobel Prize | Rabindranath Tagore (1913) |
| First President of Indian Republic | Dr. Rajendra Prasad |
| First Prime Minister | Pt. Jawaharlal Nehru |

20

| | |
|---|---|
| First Woman Prime Minister | Smt. Indira Gandhi |
| First Woman President | Pratibha Patil |
| First President of the Indian National Congress | W.C. Banerjee |
| First Woman Governor of a State | Smt. Sarojini Naidu |
| First Woman Chief Minister of a State | Smt. Sucheta Kripalani |
| First Indian President of the International Court of Justice | Dr. Nagendra Singh |
| First Indian in the British Parliament | Dadabhai Naoroji |
| First Field Marshal | S.H.F.J. Manekshaw |
| First Indian to conquer Mt. Everest | Tenzing Norgay |
| First Indian Cosmonaut | Rakesh Sharma |
| First Indian to address UN General Assembly in Hindi | Atal Bihari Vajpayee |
| First Indian to get Special Oscar Award | Satyajit Ray |
| First Indian Satellite | Aryabhatta |
| First person to get Bharat Ratna | C. Rajagopalachari |
| First Woman to get Bharat Ratna | Smt. Indira Gandhi |
| First Governor-General of Free India | C. Rajagopalachari |

## Largest, Highest, Biggest & Longest in India

| | |
|---|---|
| Highest Gate way | Buland Darwaja (Fatehpur Sikri, Agra) |
| Highest Dam | Tehri Dam on Bhagirathi river in Uttarakhand (855 f.) |
| Highest Tower (minar) | Qutub Minar (Delhi) |
| Highest Waterfall | Gersopa Waterfall (Karnataka) |
| Highest Peak | K-2* |
| Highest Civilian Award | Bharat Ratna |
| Highest Rainfall | Mowsyrnam near Cherapunji (Meghalaya) |
| Highest Literacy | Kerala |
| Largest lake | Wular lake (Kashmir) |
| Largest Dome | Gol Gumbaj (Bijapur) |
| Biggest Cattle Fair | Sonepur Fair (Bihar) |
| Biggest Mosque | Jama Masjid (Delhi) |
| Longest Platform | Gorakhpur (Uttar Pradesh) |
| Longest River Bridge | Bhupen Hazarika Bridge (Assam) |
| Oldest Mountain Range | Aravali Range |

## Important Architectures, Monuments and Places of Interest

| | |
|---|---|
| Meenakshi Temple | Madurai (Tamil Nadu) |
| Khajuraho Temple | Madhya Pradesh |

* Highest peak in the world is Mount Everest, which is in Nepal, K-2 is the second highest peak in the world.

21

| | |
|---|---|
| Lingaraja Temple | Bhubaneswar (Odisha) |
| Jagannath Temple | Puri (Odisha) |
| Gateway of India | Mumbai (Maharashtra) |
| Buland Darwaja | Fatehpur Sikri (UP) |
| Victory Tower | Chittorgarh (Rajasthan) |
| Gol Gumbaj | Bijapur (Karnataka) |
| Golden Temple | Amritsar (Punjab) |
| Dilwara Temples | Mt. Abu (Rajasthan) |
| Sarnath Temple | Varanasi (UP) |
| Rameshwaram | Tamil Nadu |
| Amarnath Temple | Jammu & Kashmir |
| Sambhar Lake | Rajasthan |
| Dal Lake | Srinagar (Jammu & Kashmir) |
| Thumba (Rocket Launching Station) | Kerala |
| Sriharikota (Satellite Launching Station) | Andhra Pradesh |
| Ajanta and Ellora Caves | Aurangabad (Maharashtra) |
| Taj Mahal | Agra (UP) |
| Char Minar | Hyderabad (Telangana) |
| Sabarmati | Ahmedabad (Gujarat) |
| Sanchi (Stupa) | Madhya Pradesh |
| Vivekanand Rock | Tamil Nadu (near Kanyakumari) |

## Samadhis

| Name | Associated with |
|---|---|
| Rajghat | Mahatma Gandhi |
| Shantivan | Jawahar Lal Nehru |
| Samta Sthal | Jagjivan Ram |
| Vijayghat | Lal Bahadur Shastri |
| Shakti Sthal | Indira Gandhi |
| Vir Bhumi | Rajiv Gandhi |

## Important Towns on River Banks

| Town | River | Town | River |
|---|---|---|---|
| Agra | Yamuna | Ahmedabad | Sabarmati |
| Allahabad | Confluence of Ganga & Yamuna | Kolkata | Hooghli |
| | | Cuttack | Mahanadi |
| Ayodhya | Saryu | Kanpur | Ganga |

| Town | River | Town | River |
| --- | --- | --- | --- |
| Kota | Chambal | Delhi | Yamuna |
| Serivrangapatnam | Cauveri | Hardwar | Ganga |
| Ujjain | Chhipra | Jabalpur | Narmada |
| Vijayawada | Krishna | Dibrugarh | Brahamputra |
| Sambalpur | Mahanadi | Srinagar | Jhelum |
| Nasik | Godavari | Surat | Tapti |
| Mathura | Yamuna | Varanasi | Ganga |
| Lucknow | Gomati | Guwahati | Brahamputra |
| Patna | Ganga | Vijaywada | Krishna |

# Nicknames of Rivers and Cities

| | |
| --- | --- |
| Bengal's Sorrow | Damodar River |
| City of Palaces | Kolkata |
| Gateway of India | Mumbai |
| Land of Five Rivers | Punjab |
| Pink City | Jaipur |
| Blue Mountains | Nilgiri Hills |

# Important Days

| | |
| --- | --- |
| National Youth Day | January 12 |
| Army Day | January 15 |
| Republic Day | January 26 |
| Martyr's Day | January 30 |
| National Science Day | February 28 |
| Independence Day | August 15 |
| Teacher's Day | September 5 |
| Mahatma Gandhi's Birthday | October 2 |
| Air Force Day | October 8 |
| Energy Conservation Day | October 14 |
| National Intergration Day | October 31 |
| Children's Day | November 14 |
| Navy Day | December 4 |
| Flag Day | December 7 |

# Books and Authors

| | |
| --- | --- |
| Ain-e-Akbari | Abul Fazl |
| Anand Math | Bankim Chandra Chatterjee |

| | |
|---|---|
| Arthasastra | Kautilya |
| Chidambara | Sumitranandan Pant |
| Devdas | Sarat Chandra Chatterjee |
| Discovery of India | Jawaharlal Nehru |
| Geet Govind | Jaya Dev |
| Geetanjali | Rabindranath Tagore |
| Godan | Munshi Prem Chand |
| Idols | Sunil Gavaskar |
| India Divided | Dr. Rajendra Prasad |
| India Wins Freedom | Abul Kalam Azad |
| Kamayani | Jaishankar Prasad |
| Mahabharat | Ved Vyas |
| My Experiments with Truth | Mahatma Gandhi |
| Ramayan | Valmiki |
| Ram Charit Manas | Tulsidas |
| Saket | Maithili Sharan Gupta |
| Pancha Tantra | Vishnu Sharma |

## Important Slogans & Quotations

**Slogans**

| | |
|---|---|
| *Dilli Chalo* | Netaji Subhash Chandra Bose |
| *Jai Jawan Jai Kisan* | Lal Bahadur Shastri |
| *Garibi Hatao* | Indira Gandhi |
| *Quit India* | Mahatma Gandhi |

**Quotations**

| | |
|---|---|
| Swarajya is my birth right and I shall have it. | *Bal Gangadhar Tilak* |
| Give me blood, I shall give you freedom. | *Subhas Chandra Bose* |

## Popular Names

| *Popular Name* | *Real Name* |
|---|---|
| Iron Man | Sardar Vallabhbhai Patel |
| Bapu, Father of Nation | Mahatma Gandhi |
| Chachaji | Jawaharlal Nehru |
| Gurudev | Rabindranath Tagore |
| Lokmanya | Bal Gangadhar Tilak |
| Netaji | Subhas Chandra Bose |
| Punjab Kesari | Lala Lajpat Rai |

| Popular Name | Real Name |
|---|---|
| Mahamana | Madan Mohan Malviya |
| Baba Saheb | Dr. B.R. Ambedkar |
| Grand Old Man of India | Dada Bhai Naoroji |
| Lok Nayak | Jay Prakash Narain |
| Nightingale of India | Sarojini Naidu |
| Bal, Pal, Lal | Bal Gangadhar Tilak, Bipin Chandra Pal, Lala Lajpat Rai |

## Festivals (Regional)

| Festival | State |
|---|---|
| Teej | Rajasthan |
| Vaisakhi | Punjab and Haryana |
| Ganesh Chaturthi Puja | Maharashtra |
| Durga Puja | West Bengal |
| Onam | Kerala |
| Pongal | Tamil Nadu and Andhra Predesh |
| Lohri | Punjab & Haryana |
| Bhageli Bihu | Assam |
| Ugadi | Karnataka |

## Popular Dances

| | |
|---|---|
| Bharat Natyam | Tamil Nadu |
| Kathakali | Kerala |
| Kathak | North India |
| Manipuri | Manipur |
| Odissi | Orissa |
| Kuchipudi | Andhra Pradesh |
| Bhangra | Punjab |
| Bihu | Assam |
| Garba | Gujarat |
| Ghoomar | Rajasthan |

## National Honours & Awards

**I. Civilian Awards**

1. **Bharat Ratna:** This is India's highest civilian award. It is given for exceptional work in art, literature, science, sport and recognition of public service

of the highest order. Government servants are not eligible for it.

2. **Padma Vibhushan:** This award is given for exceptional and distinguished service in any field, including service rendered by Government servants.

3. **Padma Bhushan:** This award is given for distinguished service of a high order in any field, including service rendered by Government servants.

4. **Padma Shri:** This award is given for distinguished service in any field, including service rendered by Government servants.

## II. Gallantry Awards

1. **Param Vir Chakra:** The highest award for bravery or some daring and pre-eminent act of valour of self-sacrifice in the presence of the enemy, whether on land, at sea or in the air.

2. **Mahavir Chakra:** It is the second highest decoration and is awarded for acts of conspicuous gallantry in the presence of the enemy, whether on land, at sea or in the air.

3. **Vir Chakra:** It is the third in order of awards given for acts of gallantry in presence of enemy, whether on land, at sea or in the air.

4. **Ashok Chakra:** This medal is awarded for the most conspicuous bravery or some daring or pre-eminent act of valour or self-sacrifice on land, at sea or in the air but not in the presence of enemy.

5. **Vishistha Sewa Medal:** It is awarded to personnel of all the three Services in class I, II and III in recognition of distinguished service of the "most exceptional" and "exceptional" and a "high" order respectively. Prefixes *Parma* and *Ati* added before first two categories of medals respectively.

6. **Jeewan Raksha Padak:** Awarded for meritorious acts or a series of acts of human nature displayed in saving life from drowning, fire and rescue operations in mines etc.

## III. Other awards

| *Awards* | *Related to* |
|---|---|
| Jnanpith Award | Outstanding contribution to Indian Literature. |
| Dada Saheb Phalke Award | Outstanding contribution to Indian cinema (films). |
| Arjuna Awards | Given to sportspersons who distinguish themselves in different sports disciplines. |
| Dronacharya Awards | Given to outstanding Indian Sports Coaches. |
| Bhatnagar Awards | Given for important contribution to any field of science. |
| Krishi Pandit Award | It is given to agriculturist showing maximum per acre production. |

# Sports

## Cups and Trophies

**Cricket:** Ranji Trophy—National Championship, C.K. Naidu Trophy, Asia Cup, Ashes (Australia-England), Baria Trophy (Inter University), Benson & Hedges, Sharjah Cup, Nehru Gold Cup.

**Hockey:** Rangaswamy Trophy—National Championship, Agha Khan Cup, Indira Gold Cup, Jawaharlal Nehru Gold Cup, Obaidullah Gold Cup, Sultan Ajlan Shah Cup, Beighton Cup, Champions Trophy, Lady Ratan Tata Trophy (Women), Sindhya Gold Cup, Asia Cup.

**Football:** Santosh Trophy—National Championship, Durand Cup, DCM Trophy, IFA Shield, Rovers Cup, Subroto Mukherji Cup (Inter School), Scissors Cup, Federation Cup, Kalinga Cup, Airlines Gold Cup, Merdeka, Asia Cup, Jules Rimet Trophy—World Cup.

**Badminton:** Rahimtoola Cup, Chadha Cup, Thomas Cup—World Championship Men, Uber Cup—World Championship Women.

**Table Tennis:** Corbillion Cup (Women), Asia Cup, Swaythling Cup (Men).

**Lawn Tennis:** Davis Cup, Wimbledon Trophy.

**Golf:** Walker Cup.

**Billiards:** Arthur Walker Trophy.

## Sport Terms

**Badminton:** Mixed doubles; Deuce; Drop; Smash; Let; Foot work; Setting.

**Base Ball:** Pitcher; Put out; Strike; Home; Bunt.

**Billiards:** Cue; Jigger; Pot; Break; In Baulk; In Off; Corom; Cannons.

**Boxing:** Upper cut; Round; Punch; Bout; Knock down; Hitting below the belt; Ring.

**Bridge:** Finesse; Dummy; Revoke; Grand Slam; Little Slam; No Trump; Rubber.

**Chess:** Bishop, Gambit; Checkmate; Stalemate.

**Cricket:** L.B.W. *(leg before wicket)*; Creases, Popping-creases; Stumped; Bye; Leg-Bye; Googly; Hat-trick; Maiden over; Drive; Bowling; Duck; Follow on; No ball; Leg Break; Gulley; Silly point; Cover point; Hit-wicket; Late-cut; Slip; Off-spinner; Leg-spinner; In-swing; Night watchman.

**Football:** Off side; Block; Drop-kick; Penalty-kick (or *goal kick*); Corner-kick; Free-kick; Dribble; Thrown-in; Foul.

**Golf:** Boggy; Foursome; Stymic; Tee; Put; Hole; Niblic; Caddie; Links; The green; Bunker.

**Hockey:** Carried; Short Corner; Bully; Sticks; Off side; Roll in; Striking Circle; Under-cutting; Dribble.
**Horse racing:** Jockey; Punter.
**Polo:** Bunker; Chukker; Mallet.
**Tennis:** Back hand drive; Volley; Smash; Half-volley; Deuce; Service; Let; Grand Slam.

# WORLD

## Facts About UNO

- UNO officially came into existence on October 24, 1945.
- UNO headquaters are located at New York.
- UN Charter was signed on June 26, 1945 by 50 countries at San Francisco.
- Objectives of the UN are:-
  (1) Security, (2) Welfare, (3) Protection of Human Rights
- UN Flag is light blue in colour and emblazoned in white in its centre is the UN symbol — a polar map of the world embraced by twin olive branches open at the top.
- UN is financed by the contibution from member countries.
- UN membership is open to all peace-loving countries. New members are admitted by the General Assembly on the recommendation of the Security Council.
- The six major organs of the UNO are:
  (1)  General Assembly
  (2)  Security Council
  (3)  Economic and Social Council
  (4)  Trusteeship Council
  (5)  International Court of Justice
  (6)  Secretariat
- The General Assembly meets once a year.
- The General Assembly elects its President for a year.
- The General Assembly passes the entire budget of the UN.
- The Security Council has 15 members — 5 permanent members and 10 non-permanent members.
- The permanent members of the Security Council are — USA, UK, Russia, France and China.
- The non-permanent members of the Security Council are elected by the General Assembly for a term of 2 years.

- The right to veto is available to only 5 permanent members of the Security Council.
- Presidency of the Security Council is held for one month in rotation by member states in the English alphabetical order of their names.
- The Secretary General of the UNO is appointed on the recommendation of the Security Council.
- The International Court of the Justice has 15 Judges elected by the General Assembly and the Security Council sitting independently.
- The term of office of the Judges of the International Court of Justice is 9 years.
- The seat of the International Court of Justice is the Hague (Netherlands).
- The official languages of the UN are — English, French, Chinese, Russian, Arabic and Spanish. However, the languages mostly used are English and French.
- The International Labour Organisation (ILO) was established in 1919. Its headquarters are located at Geneva (Switzerland).
- The Food and Agriculture Organisation (FAO) has its headquarters at Rome (Italy).
- The United Nations Educational, Scientific and Cultural Organisation (UNESCO) with its headquarters at Paris (France) seeks to promote peace through international collaboration in education for all.
- Taiwan is not member of the UNO.
- At present 193 countries are members of the UNO.

## Years Observed by the UNO

*1972:* International Book Year; *1973:* Copernicus Year; *1974:* World Population Year; *1975:* International Women's Year; *1979:* International Year of the Child; *1981:* International Year of Disabled; *1983:* World Communication Year; *1985:* International Youth Year; *1986:* International Year of Peace; *1987:* International Year of Shelter for the Homeless; *1990:* International Literacy Year; *1992:* International Space Year; *1993:* International Year for World's Indigenous People; *1994:* International Year of Family; *1995:* International Year of Tolerance; *1999:* International Year of Older Persons; *2000:* International Year of the Culture of Peace; *2001:* Internation Year of Volunteer; *2002:* International Year of Ecotourism; *2003:* International year of Fresh Water; *2004:* International year of Rice; *2005:* International year of Sport and Physical Education; *2006:* International year of deserts and desertification; *2008:* International Year of Potato; *2009:* International Year of Astronomy; *2010:* International Year of Bio-Diversity; *2011:* International Year of Forest; *2012:* International Year of Cooperatives; *2013:* International Year of Water Cooperation; *2014:* International Year of Family Farming; *2015:* International Year of Soils; *2016:* International Year of Pulses; *2017:* International Year of Sustainable Torism for Development; *2019:* International Year of Indigenous Languages.

## National Games of Some Countries

| | |
|---|---|
| USA | Baseball |
| Australia | Cricket |
| Canada | Ice Hockey |
| Spain | Bull Fighting |

| Britain | Cricket |
|---------|---------|
| India | Hockey |
| Japan | Jujitsu |

– Olympic Games are held every four years.
– Asian Games are held every four years.

## Capitals & Currencies of Countries

| Country | Capital | Currency |
|---------|---------|----------|
| Afghanistan | Kabul | Afghani |
| Algeria | Algiers | Dinar |
| Angola | Luanda | New Kwanza |
| Argentina | Buenos Aires | Peso |
| Austria | Vienna | Euro |
| Azerbaijan | Baku | Ruble |
| Bangladesh | Dhaka | Taka |
| Belgium | Brussels | Euro |
| Bhutan | Thimpu | Ngultrum |
| Bosnia | Sarajevo | Dinar |
| Brazil | Brasillia | Cruzeiro |
| Bulgaria | Sofia | Lev |
| Byelorussia | Minsk | Ruble, Zaichik |
| Cambodia | Phnom-Penh | Riel |
| Canada | Ottawa | Dollar |
| Chile | Santiago | Peso |
| China | Beijing | Yuan |
| Colombia | Bogota | Peso |
| Congo | Brazzaville | Franc |
| Croatia | Zegerb | Dinar |
| Cuba | Havana | Peso |
| Cyprus | Nicosia | Pound |
| Czech | Prague | Crown |
| Denmark | Copenhagen | Krone |
| Egypt | Cairo | Pound |
| Ethiopia | Addia Ababa | Birr |
| Finland | Helsinki | Euro |
| France | Paris | Euro |

| Country | Capital | Currency |
|---|---|---|
| Germany | Berlin | Euro |
| Ghana | Accra | Cedi |
| Greece | Athens | Euro |
| Hong Kong | Victoria | Dollar |
| Hungary | Budapest | Forints |
| India | New Delhi | Rupee |
| Indonesia | Jakarta | Rupiah |
| Iran | Tehran | Rials |
| Iraq | Baghdad | Dinar |
| Ireland | Dublin | Euro |
| Israel | Jerusalem | Shekel |
| Italy | Rome | Euro |
| Jamaica | Kingston | Dollar |
| Japan | Tokyo | Yen |
| Jordan | Amman | Dinar |
| Kazakhstan | Alma Ata | Ruble |
| Kenya | Nairobi | Shilling |
| Korea (S) | Seoul | Won |
| Korea (N) | Pyongyang | Won |
| Kuwait | Kuwait City | Dinar |
| Laos | Vientiane | Kip |
| Lebanon | Beirut | Pound |
| Libya | Tripoli | Dinar |
| Malaysia | Kuala Lumpur | Ringgit |
| Maldives | Male | Rufiyya |
| Mauritius | Port Louis | Rupee |
| Mexico | Mexico City | Peso |
| Morocco | Rabat | Dirham |
| Mozambique | Maputo | Metical |
| Myanmar (Burma) | Yangon (Rangoon) | Kyat |
| Nepal | Kathmandu | Rupee |
| Netherlands | Amsterdam | Euro |
| New Zealand | Wellington | Dollar |
| Nigeria | Abuja | Naira |
| Norway | Oslo | Kroner |
| Oman | Muscat | Rial |

| Country | Capital | Currency |
|---|---|---|
| Pakistan | Islamabad | Rupee |
| Phillippines | Manila | Peso |
| Poland | Warsaw | Zloty |
| Portugal | Lisbon | Euro |
| Romania | Bucharest | Leu |
| Russia | Moscow | Ruble |
| Saudi Arabia | Riyadh | Rial |
| South Africa | Capetown (Legislative) Pretoria (Administrative) | Rand |
| Spain | Madrid | Euro |
| Sri Lanka | Colombo | Rupee |
| Sweden | Stockholm | Krona |
| Switzerland | Berne | Swiss Francs |
| Syria | Damascus | Pound |
| Taiwan | Taipei | Dollar |
| Tanzania | Dodoma | Shilling |
| Thailand | Bangkok | Baht |
| Turkey | Ankara | Lira |
| United Arab Emirates | Abu Dhabi | Dirham |
| U.K. | London | Pound Sterling |
| U.S.A. | Washington | Dollar |
| Uzbekistan | Tashkent | Ruble |
| Vietnam | Hanoi | Dong |
| Zimbabwe | Harare | Dollar |
| Zaire | Kinshasa | Zaire |
| Zambia | Lusaka | Kwacha |

# Nicknames of Countries, Lakes and Cities

| China's Sorrow | Hwang-Ho |
|---|---|
| Cockpit of Europe | Belgium |
| Dark Continent | Africa |
| Empire City | New York |
| Eternal City/City of Seven Hills | Rome |
| Forbidden City | Lhasa (Tibet) |
| Gift of the Nile | Egypt |
| Hermit Kingdom | Korea |

| | |
|---|---|
| Holy Land | Jerusalem (Palestine) |
| Island of Cloves | Zanzibar |
| Key to the Mediterranean | Gibraltar |
| Land of Maple Leaf/Lillies | Canada |
| Land of the Rising Sun | Japan |
| Land of the Thousand Lakes | Finland |
| Land of Golden Fleece | Australia |
| Land of Kangaroo | Australia |
| Land of Midnight Sun | Norway |
| Land of the White Elephants | Thailand |
| Manchester of the Orient | Osaka (Japan) |
| Playground of Europe | Switzerland |
| Queen of the Adriatic | Venice (Italy) |
| Roof of the world | Pamirs |
| Sickman of Europe | Turkey |
| Sugar Bowl of the World | Cuba |
| Venice of the North | Stockholm (Sweden) |

## Important Days

| | |
|---|---|
| Women's Day, International | March 8 |
| Consumers' Rights Day, World | March 15 |
| Disabled Day, World | March 15 |
| Health Day, World | April 7 |
| May Day, World | May 1 |
| Red Cross Day, World | May 8 |
| Commonwealth Day | May 24 |
| No Tobacco Day, World | May 31 |
| Environment Day, World | June 5 |
| International Yoga Day | June 21 |
| International Day against Drug abuse and illicit Trafficking | June 26 |
| Population Day, World | July 11 |
| Hiroshima Day | August 6 |
| Literacy Day, World | September 8 |
| Ozone Day, World | September 16 |
| Tourism Day, World | September 27 |
| Habitat Day, World | October 3 |
| Standards Day, World | October 14 |

| | | | |
|---|---|---|---|
| Food Day, World | | | October 16 |
| U.N. Day, World | | | October 24 |
| Human Rights Day, World | | | December 10 |

## Important Towns on River Banks

| Town | River | Town | River |
|---|---|---|---|
| Alexandria | Nile | Lisbon | Tagus |
| Bangkok | Chao Phraya | London | Thames |
| Baghdad | Tigris | Madrid | Menzanares |
| Belgrade | Danube | Moscow | Moskwa |
| Berlin | Spree | New York | Hudson |
| Bonn | Rhine | Paris | Seine |
| Budapest | Danube | Prague | Vltava |
| Buenos Aires | La Plata | Quebec | St. Lawrence |
| Cairo | Nile | Rome | Tiber |
| Dublin | Liffey | St. Louis | Mississippi |
| Karachi | Indus | Sydney | Darling |
| Khartoum | Nile | Vienna | Danube |
| Lahore | Ravi | Warsaw | Vistula |
| Leh | Indus | Washington | Potomac |

## Major Producers of Crops, Minerals and Industrial Goods

| Items of Production | Country |
|---|---|
| Aluminium | China |
| Coal | China |
| Coffee | Brazil |
| Copper | Chili |
| Cotton | China |
| Gold | China |
| Grapes | Italy |
| Iron ore | Australia |
| Jute | India, Bangladesh |
| Manganese | South Africa |
| Diamond | Russia |
| Rice | China |

| *Items of Production* | *Country* |
| --- | --- |
| Rubber | Thailand |
| Silver | Mexico, Peru |
| Steel | China |
| Sugar | Brazil |
| Tea | China, India |
| Tin | China |
| Wheat | China, India |
| Wool | Australia |
| Mica | China |

## First in the World

| | |
| --- | --- |
| First Chinese visitor to India | Fahien |
| First foreign invader of India | Alexander, the Great (Greek) |
| First person to climb Mt. Everest | Tenzing Norgay (Indian) |
| First atom bomb dropped at | Hiroshima (Japan) |
| First man in the space | Yuri Gagarin (former USSR) |
| First woman in the space | Valentina Tereshkova (former USSR) |
| First person to land on the moon | Neil Armstrong (USA) |
| First person to climb Mt. Everest twice | Nawang Gombu |
| First President of the USA | George Washington |
| First woman Prime Minister | Sirimavo Bandaranaike (Sri Lanka) |
| First person to swim across English Channel | Mathew Webb |
| First woman to swim across English Channel | Gertrude Caroline Ederle |
| First woman to climb Mt. Everest | Junko Tabei (Japan) |
| First test-tube Baby | Louise Brown (UK; 1978) |
| First person to reach South Pole | R. Amundsen (Norway) |
| First person to reach North Pole | Robert Peary (USA) |

## Famous Books and Authors

| | |
| --- | --- |
| Aesop's Fables | Aesop |
| Comedy of Errors, Julius Caesar, Merchant of Venis, Hamlet, As you Like it | William Shakespeare |
| Apple Cart, Doctor's Dilemma | G.B. Shaw |
| A Tale of Two Cities | Charles Dickens |

| | |
|---|---|
| Das Kapital | Karl Marx |
| Good Earth | Pearl S. Buck |
| Indica | Megasthenese |
| Light of Asia | A. Arnold |
| Lajja | Taslima Nasreen |
| Long Walk to Freedom | Nelson Mandela |
| Man Eaters of Kumayun | Jim Corbett |
| Mein Kampf | Adolf Hitler |
| Mother | Maxim Gorky |
| Paradise Lost | John Milton |
| The Satanic Verses | Salman Rushdie |
| The Moor's Last Sigh | Salman Rushdie |
| Shahnama | Firdausi |
| Rubaiyat | Omar Khayyam |
| Unto the Last | John Ruskin |
| War and Peace | Leo Tolstoy |
| Wealth of Nations | Adam Smith |

## Some Famous Quotations

| | |
|---|---|
| Abraham Lincoln | Government of the People, by the people and for the people. |
| Neil Armstrong | A single step for a man, a giant leap for the mankind. |
| John Milton | Better to reign in Hell than to serve in the Heaven. |
| William Shakespeare | Cowards die many times before their death; The valiant never taste of death but once. |
| Napoleon Bonaparte | Give us good mothers and I shall give you good nation. |
| Goldsmith | Where wealth accumulates, men decay. |
| John F. Kennedy | We do not fear to negotiate, but we do not negotiate out of fear. |

## Important Official Residences

| | |
|---|---|
| Buckingham Palace (London) | King/Queen of Britain |
| 10, Downing Street (London) | Prime Minister, Britain |
| Elysee Palace (Paris) | President, France |
| Rashtrapati Bhawan (New Delhi) | President, India |
| White House (Washington) | President, USA |
| Vatican (Rome) | Pope |
| 7, Race Course (New Delhi) | Prime Minister, India |

# Wonders of the World

**Seven Wonders of the Ancient World :** *(1)* the Pyramids of Egypt, built in approximately 2700 BC; *(2)* the Hanging Gardens at Babylon; *(3)* the temple of Artemis at Emphesus; *(4)* the statue of Zeus at Olympia; *(5)* the tomb of Mausolus at Halicarnassus, built in nearly 350 BC; *(6)* the Colossus of Rhodes, built in nearly 280 BC; *(7)* the Pharos Lighthouse at Alexandria.

**Seven Wonders of the Medieval World :** *(1)* the Colosseum of Rome; *(2)* the Great Wall of China; *(3)* the Porcelain Tower of Nanking; *(4)* the Mosque at St. Sophia (Constantinople); *(5)* Stonehenge; *(6)* the Catacombs of Rome; *(7)* the Leaning Tower of Pisa.

**Seven New Wonders of the World :** *(1)* Taj Mahal of Agra (India); *(2)* Pyramid at Chichen Itza (Mexico); *(3)* Machu Picchu (Peru); *(4)* Statue of Christ The Redeemer (Brazil); *(5)* Great Wall of China; *(6)* Roman Colosseum, Italy; *(7)* Ruins of Petra, Jordan.

# Symbols and Signs

| | |
|---|---|
| Red Triangle | Family Planning |
| Red Cross | Hospital (or medical aid) |
| Lotus | Culture and Civilization |
| Olive Branch | Peace |
| Red Light | Danger; Traffic signal for 'stop' |
| Green Light | Traffic signal for 'go' |
| Black arm-band | Sign of mourning or protest |
| Dove | Peace |
| Two bones crossing each other diagonally with a skull in the upper quadrant | Danger |
| Flag upside down | Distress |
| Flag flown at half mast | National mourning |
| Red Flag | Revolution |
| White Flag | Truce |
| Wheel | Progress |
| Two hands protecting a lamp | Life Insurance Corporation of India |
| V (letter) | Victory |

# Names of Parliaments of Some Countries

| *Country* | *Name of the Parliament* |
|---|---|
| Afghanistan | Shora |
| Canada | Parliament: Senate (Upper House); House of Commons (Lower House) |
| China | National People's Congress |
| Denmark | Folketing |

| Country | Name of the Parliament |
| --- | --- |
| Germany | Bundestag (Lower House); Bandesrat (Upper House) |
| Iceland | Althing |
| India | Sansad : Lok Sabha (Lower House); Rajya Sabha (Upper House) |
| Iran | Majlis |
| Israel | Knesset |
| Japan | Diet |
| Korea (North) | Supreme People's Assembly |
| Mongolia | Great People's Khural |
| Nepal | National Panchayat |
| Netherlands | The States General |
| Norway | Storting |
| Poland | Sejm |
| Russia | Federation Council (Upper House); Duma (Lower House) |
| Spain | Cortes |
| Sweden | Riksdag |
| UAR | Darul Avam |
| U.K. | Parliament: House of Commons (Lower); House of Lords (Upper) |
| USA | Congress: Senate (Upper House); House of Representatives (Lower House) |

# Highest, Biggest, Largest, Longest, etc. in the World

| | |
| --- | --- |
| Animal, *tallest* | Giraffe |
| Bird, *largest* | Ostrich |
| Canal, *longest* | Suez canal |
| Church, *largest* | St. Peter's Church (Rome) |
| City, *largest in population* | Tokyo (Japan) |
| Continent, *largest* | Eurasian Landmass (Europe and Asia) |
| *smallest* | Australia |
| Country, *largest* | |
| *(i)* in population | China |
| *(ii)* in area | Russia |
| *Smallest* | Vatican |

| | |
|---|---|
| Desert, *largest* | Sahara (N. Africa) |
| Gulf, *largest* | Gulf of Mexico |
| Island, *biggest* | Greenland |
| Lake, *largest* | Caspian Sea |
| *largest* (fresh water) | Superior Lake (USA—Canada border) |
| Mountain, *highest peak* | Mt. Everest |
| Ocean, *largest and deepest* | The Pacific Ocean |
| Place, *rainiest* | Mowsyrnam near Cherapunji (Meghalaya) |
| Planet, *biggest* | Jupiter |
| *brightest* | Venus |
| *nearest to the sun* | Mercury |
| Railway Line, *longest* | Trans-Siberian Railway |
| River, *longest* | *(i)* Nile (6670 km) |
| | *(ii)* Amazon (6570 km) |
| Building, *tallest* | Burj Khalifa, Dubai (2010), 818 m |
| Tower, *tallest*★ | Guangzhou TV Tower, China (2010), 2001 ft. |
| Waterfall, *highest* | Salto-Angel (Venezuela) |

★ C.N. Tower, Toronto, Canada (1815 ft) is now second in the world

# INVENTIONS AND DISCOVERIES

## IMPORTANT INVENTIONS

| Name of Invention | Inventor | Nationality | Year |
|---|---|---|---|
| Aeroplane | Orville & Wilbur Wright | U.S.A | 1903 |
| Ball-Point Pen | John J. Loud | U.S.A. | 1888 |
| Barometer | Evangelista Torrcelli | Italy | 1644 |
| Bicycle | Kirkpatrick Machmillan | Britain | 1839-40 |
| Bifocal Lens | Benjamin Franklin | U.S.A. | 1780 |
| Car (Petrol) | Karl Benz | Germany | 1888 |
| Celluloid | Alexander Parkes | Britain | 1861 |
| Cinema | Nicolas and Jean Lumiere | France | 1895 |
| Clock (mechanical) | I-Hsing & Liang Ling-Tsan | China | 725 |
| Diesel Engine | Rudolf Diesel | Germany | 1895 |
| Dynamo | Hypolite Pixii | France | 1832 |
| Electric Lamp | Thomas Alva Edison | U.S.A. | 1879 |
| Electric Motor (DC) | Zenobe Gramme | Belgium | 1873 |
| Electric Motor (AC) | Nikola Tesla | U.S.A. | 1888 |
| Electromagnet | William Sturgeon | Britain | 1824 |
| Electronic Computer | Dr. Alan M Turing | Britain | 1943 |
| Film (moving outlines) | Louis Prince | France | 1885 |
| Film (musical sound) | Dr. Le de Forest | U.S.A. | 1923 |
| Fountain Pen | Lewis E. Waterman | U.S.A. | 1884 |

| Name of Invention | Inventor | Nationality | Year |
|---|---|---|---|
| Gramophone | Thomas Alva Edison | U.S.A. | 1878 |
| Helicopter | Etienne Oehnichen | France | 1924 |
| Jet Engine | Sir Frank Whittle | Britain | 1937 |
| Laser | Charles H. Townes | U.S.A. | 1960 |
| Lift (Mechanical) | Elisha G. Otis | U.S.A. | 1852 |
| Locomotive | Richard Trevithick | Britain | 1804 |
| Machine Gun | James Puckle | Britain | 1718 |
| Microphone | Alexander Graham Bell | U.S.A. | 1876 |
| Microscope | Z. Janssen | Netherlands | 1590 |
| Motor Cycle | G. Daimler | Germany | 1885 |
| Photography (on film) | John Carbutt | U.S.A. | 1888 |
| Printing Press | Johann Gutenberg | Germany | 1455 |
| Razor (safety) | King C. Gillette | U.S.A. | 1895 |
| Refrigerator | James Harrison & Alexander Catlin | U.S.A. | 1850 |
| Safety Pin | Walter Hunt | U.S.A. | 1849 |
| Sewing machine | Barthelemy Thimmonnier | France | 1829 |
| Ship (steam) | J.C. Perier | France | 1775 |
| Ship (turbine) | Hon. Sir C. Parsons | Britain | 1894 |
| Skyscraper | W. Le Baron Jenny | U.S.A. | 1882 |
| Slide Rule | William Oughtred | Britain | 1621 |
| Steam Engine(condenser) | James Watt | Britain | 1765 |
| Steel Production | Henry Bessemer | Britain | 1855 |
| Steel (stainless) | Harry Brearley | Britain | 1913 |
| Submarine | David Bushnell | U.S.A. | 1776 |
| Tank | Sir Ernest Swinton | Britain | 1914 |
| Telegraph | M. Lammond | France | 1787 |
| Telegraph Code | Samuel F.B. Morse | U.S.A. | 1837 |
| Telephone (perfected) | Alexander Graham Bell | U.S.A. | 1876 |
| Television (mechanical) | John Logie Baird | Britain | 1926 |
| Television (electronic) | P.T. Farnsworth | U.S.A. | 1927 |
| Thermometer | Galileo Galilei | Italy | 1593 |
| Transformer | Michael Faraday | Britain | 1831 |
| Transistor | Bardeen, Shockley & Brattain | U.S.A. | 1948 |
| Washing Machine (elect.) | Hurley Machine Co. | U.S.A. | 1907 |
| Zip-Fastener | W.L. Judson | U.S.A. | 1891 |

## GEOGRAPHICAL EXPLORATIONS/DISCOVERIES

| Place | Explorer/Discoverers | Nationality | Year |
|---|---|---|---|
| America | Christopher Columbus | Italy | 1492 |
| Hawaii Islands (Sandwich Islands) | Captain James Cook | England | 1778 |
| Newfoundland | John Cabot | England | 1497 |

| Place | Explorer/Discoverers | Nationality | Year |
|---|---|---|---|
| New Zealand | Abel Janszoon Tasman | Holland | 1642 |
| North Pole | Robert Peary | U.S.A. | 1909 |
| Sea Route to India (via Cape of Good Hope) | Vasco da Gama | Portugal | 1498 |
| South Pole | Ronald Amundsen | Norway | 1911 |

## IMPORTANT DISCOVERIES

| Discovery | Discoverer | Nationality | Year |
|---|---|---|---|
| Aluminium | Hans Christian Oerstedt | Denmark | 1827 |
| Atomic number | Henry Moseley | England | 1913 |
| Atomic structure of matter | John Dalton | England | 1803 |
| Chlorine | C.W. Scheele | Sweden | 1774 |
| Electromagnetic induction | Michael Faraday | England | 1831 |
| Electromagnetic waves | Heinrich Hertz | Germany | 1886 |
| Electromagnetism | Hans Christian Oersted | Denmark | 1920 |
| Electron | Sir Joseph Thomson | England | 1897 |
| General theory of relativity | Albert Einstein | Switzerland | 1915 |
| Hydrogen | Henry Cavendish | England | 1766 |
| Law of electric conduction | Georg Ohm | Germany | 1827 |
| Law of electromagnetism | Andre Ampere | France | 1826 |
| Law of falling bodies | Galileo | Italy | 1590 |
| Laws of gravitation & motion | Isaac Newton | England | 1687 |
| Laws of planetary motion | Johannes Kepler | Germany | 1609-19 |
| Magnesium | Sir Humphry Davy | England | 1808 |
| Neptune (Planet) | Johann Galle | Germany | 1846 |
| Neutron | James Chadwick | England | 1932 |
| Nickel | Axel Cronstedt | Sweden | 1751 |
| Nitrogen | Daniel Rutherford | England | 1772 |
| Oxygen | Joseph Priestly | England | 1772 |
|  | C.W. Scheele | Sweden |  |
| Ozone | Christian Schonbein | Germany | 1839 |
| Pluto (Planet) | Clyde Tombaugh | U.S.A. | 1930 |
| Plutonium | G.T. Seaborg | U.S.A. | 1940 |
| Proton | Ernest Rutherford | England | 1919 |
| Quantum Theory | Max Planck | Germany | 1900 |
| Radioactivity | Antoine Henery Bacquerel | France | 1896 |
| Radium | Pierre and Marie Curie | France | 1898 |
| Silicon | Jons Berzelius | Sweden | 1824 |
| Special theory of relativity | Albert Einstein | Switzerland | 1905 |
| Sun as centre of solar system | Copernicus | Poland | 1543 |
| Uranium | Martin Klaproth | Germany | 1789 |
| Uranus (Planet) | William Herschel | England | 1781 |
| X-rays | Willhelm Roentgen | Germany | 1895 |

# ABBREVIATIONS

**A.D.:** Anno Domini (in the year of our Lord)
**A.H.Q.:** Air Head Quarters: Army Head Quarters
**A.I.:** Air India, Artificial Intelligence
**A.I.D.S.:** Acquired Immune Deficiency Syndrome
**A.I.I.M.S.:** All India Institute of Medical Sciences
**A.M.:** Ante Meridiem (before noon), Amplitude Modulation
**A.S.L.V.:** Augmentated Satellite Launch Vehicle
**B.C.:** Before Christ, Backward Class
**B.S.F.:** Border Security Force
**C.B.I.:** Central Bureau of Investigation
**C.D.S.:** Combined Defence Services
**C-in-C.:** Commander-in-Chief
**CTBT:** Comprehensive Test Ban Treaty
**DoT:** Department of Telecommunication
**E. & O.E.:** Errors and Omission Excepted
**FAX:** Fascimile Exchange
**FDI:** Foreign Direct Investment
**F.I.R.:** First Information Report
**G.A.T.T.:** General Agreement on Tariffs and Trade
**G.M.T.:** Greenwich Mean Time
**H.R.D.:** Human Resource Development
**I.C.A.R.:** Indian Council of Agricultural Research
**I.L.O.:** International Labour Organisation
**I.M.F.:** International Monetary Fund
**I.S.R.O.:** Indian Space Research Organisation
**LASER:** Light Amplification by Stimulated Emission of Radiation
**L.I.C.:** Life Insurance Corporation (of India)
**N.A.S.A.:** National Aeronautics and Space Administration (of U.S.A.)
**N.C.C.:** National Cadet Corps
**N.C.E.R.T.:** National Council of Educational Research and Training
**N.D.A.:** National Defence Academy
**N.H.R.C.:** National Human Rights Commission
**P.I.N.:** Postal Index Number
**P.M.:** Post Meridiem (afternoon); Prime Minister
**P.S.U.:** Public Sector Undertaking
**P.T.I.:** Press Trust of India
**P.W.D.:** Public Works Department
**R.B.C.:** Red Blood Corpuscles
**R.B.I.:** Reserve Bank of India
**S.O.S.:** Save our Souls
**S.S.B.:** Service Selection Board
**U.N.O.:** United Nations Organisation
**U.N.E.S.C.O.:** United Nations Educational, Scientific and Cultural Organisation
**V.I.P.:** Very Important Person
**W.H.O.:** World Health Organisation

# COMMON TERMS

**Adult Franchise:** It is a voting right conferred on every adult, without distinction, to elect any candidate he or she may choose.

**By-election:** It is the special election to a seat tendered vacant during the running term of an elected person (by death, resignation, disqualification).

**Coalition:** It is a temporary union of political parties for special purpose. It is formed either deal with some crisis situation or when no party is able to secure absolute majority in a legislature.

**Coup d' Etat:** It is a sudden change of government by force, brought about by those who already hold some governmental or military power.

**Federation:** It is a political unit on which a number of smaller political units devolve certain power over themselves and their citizens and to which they usually entrust the conduct of their foreign affairs.

**Fili buster:** It is a parliamentary device of long winded speeches, not necessarily relevant to obstruct, delay or bargain over a measure under consideration for voting.

**Impeachment:** It is a prosecution of a very high public officials by the legislature for alleged offences otherwise beyond the normal reach of law.

**Lame-ducks:** These are the members of the Parliament who failed to get re-elected.

**Martial Law:** It is an administration of a certain area passing into the hands of military authorities superseding all civil law.

**Mid-term election:** It is an election to the legislature before completion of its full term usually, because of dissolution.

**Ombudsman:** A vigilance officer who hears citizens complaints against the government.

**Plebiscite:** Direct vote of electors on a political issue of importance.

**Proportional Representation:** An electrical system under which a legislature reflects the strength of the various political parties among the electorate at large, it has several form.

**Question Hour:** Session of legislature usually beings with question hour in which members can ask questions on any aspect of administration. Each member is allowed a quota of five questions per day.

**Ratification:** The formal adoption by a state of a treaty signed by its representatives. It is effected by an exchange of documents, embodying their formal adoption of the treaty between the states concerned.

**Referendum:** A reference of a particular political question to the electorate for a direct decision by popular vote.

**Republic:** This is a form of government by people and for people.

**Secession:** Formal withdrawal from an organisation such as party, church or state. A session from a state is often preceded by a revolt.

**Separation:** A belief that a particular group or area should be separated from the larger organisation of which it forms a part applied to political movements that advocate independence.

**Snap Vote:** A vote taken unexpectedly without voters having been briefed in advance.

**Supplementary question:** Question asked in parliament based on answer to the main question.

**Veto:** The right to reject.

**Zero Hour:** Time allotted in the House every day for miscellaneous business, *i.e.,* call attention notice, question on official statements and adjournment motion.

**Solid Smoke:** Aerogels are known as solid smoke. They are composite materials- the-lightest solid known. They are made of silica, alumina and carbon. It can weigh lesser than the same volume of air. A lump of this frozen smoke the size of a man would weigh less than half-a-kilogram, but could bear the weight of a car.

**Super acids:** Acids are substances capable of giving hydrogen ions for chemical reaction. An acid is called a super acid if it is stronger than 100% sulphuric acid, the strongest classical acid which is also considered to be a super acid. Super acids are a trillion times stronger than the dilute sulphuric acid used to kill bacteria in swimming pool which spreads just a few ions through a large volume of water and yet the solution is weakly acid.

**Neutrons:** Uncharged sub atomic particle, mass approximately equal to that of the proton, which enters into the structure of atomic nuclei.

**Superliquid:** Helium may well be the strongest element in the universe. For poorly understood reasons, at very low temperatures it becomes a superfluid, a substance that flows without friction.

**Cypher:** Cypher is a prototype car-size flying machine with a global positioning satellite receiver and radar tied into a remote laptop computer. All an operator has to do is to indicate on a computer map where he wants his machine to go and immediately it plots a route, takes off and navigates itself.

**Galaxies:** Galaxies are huge congregations of stars held together by force of gravity. They are so big that they have some times been called islands universes. They are so big that they have some times been called islands universes. It seems to be scattered in space. It tend to be grouped together into clusters, and some clusters appear to be grouped into superclusters.

**The Milky Way:** The Milky Way is our home galaxy. A peculiar feature of this galaxy is a bright band of light that runs almost in a perfect circle through it. Milky way belongs to a cluster of some 24 galaxies called the local group.

**Black Hole:** Strange things happen to a star at the end of its life of its mass is more than three times the mass of the sun. It will collapse, becoming more and more compact. The collapse continues until the star becomes so dense that nothing, not even light, can escape from its gravity. Hence, the object is dark and can't be viewed directly.

**Asteroids:** They are rocky debris upto 1000 km in diameter, although most are much smaller. They are remains from the nebulac, out of which the Solar System formed. Most of them orbit the sun in the asteroid belt, which lies between the orbit of Mars and Jupiter.

**Comets:** Comets may originate in a huge cloud called the Oort cloud that is supposed to surround Solar System. When first viewed through a telescope the bright head of a comet, called coma, looks like a hazy dot. Comets have very low density. It can move into new orbits.

**Meteors:** As the earth travels in its orbit around the Sun, it continually encounters meteoroides head on. On a clear, dark night one may see more than 10 meteors/hours. Sometimes an unusually large number of small meteors can be seen in rapid succession perhaps more than 50/hour. Such a display is called a meteorids.

**Lithosphere:** The lithosphere is the top crust of the Earth on which our continents and ocean basins rest. It is the thickest in the continental regions where it has an average thickness of 40 km and thinest in the oceans where it may have a maximum thickness of 10 to 12 km. It constitutes about 1% of the Earth's volume and 0.4% of its mass.

**Mountains:** Mountains are conventionally divided into four type, according to their male of origin: fold mountains, Block mountains, Volcanic mountains and Residual mountains.

**Richter Scale:** The Richter is a logarithmic scale, devised in 1935 by geophysicist Charles Richter, for representing the energy released by earthquake. A figure of 2 is barely perceptible, which an earthquake measuring over 5 may be destructive.

**Earthquakes:** The earthquake is a shaking of the ground. Caused by the sudden breaking and shifting of large sections of the Earth's rocky outer shell. A severe earthquake may release energy 10,000 times as great as that of the first atomic bomb. Earthquake can trigger landslides that causes great damage and loss of life.

**Volcanos:** Volcano is an opening in the Earth's surface through which lava, hot gases, and rock fragments erupt. Such an opening forms when melted rock form deep within the earth blasts through the surface.

**Desert:** Desert is a part of Earth's surface that is too dry to support plant or animal life and is usually sparsely inhabited or uninhabited by man.

**Hydrosphere:** It is estimated that the hydrosphere contains about 1,460,000 cubic km of water of this 97.3% is in the oceans and inland seas. The rest 2.7% is formed as glaciers and ice caps, fresh water lakes, rivers and underground water.

# RELIGIONS FOUNDERS AND FOLLOWERS

| Religion | Founder | Followers |
|---|---|---|
| Christianity | Jesus Christ | Christians |
| Islam | Prophet Mohammed | Muslims |
| Hinduism | Aryans | Hindus |
| Buddhism | Gautama Buddha | Buddhists |
| Judaism | Prophet Moses | Jews |
| Zoroastrianism | Zaratushtra | Parsis |
| Sikhism | Guru Nanak | Sikhs |
| Jainism | Mahavira | Jains |

# GEOGRAPHY

## Soils

**Types of Soils**

**Sandy Soil:** It contains sand in large quantity.

**Clay Soil:** It contains a good quantity of clay.

**Black Soil:** It is formed by disintegration of basalt rocks.

**Yellow Soil:** It is deposited by winds from deserts.

## Rocks

**Types of Rocks**

(a) **Igneous Rocks :** These are formed by cooling of hot masses of the earth. *e.g.*, granite and basalt rocks.

(b) **Aqueous Rocks :** These are formed by the action of water and have layers of clay, chalk or sandstone.

(c) **Sedimentary Rocks :** These are formed by layers of sediments which are brought by rivers.

(d) **Organic Rocks :** These are formed by remains of plants and animals.

## Mountains

**Types of Mountains**

**Fold Mountains :** These mountains are mainly made up of folded strata of sedimentary rocks. These rocks are folded when they are compressed. These are the highest mountains of the world. The Alps, the Himalayas and Rockies are fold mountains.

**Block Mountains :** These are parts of the earth's crust which have been uplifted due to the earth's movement along the line of weakness called faults.

**Residual Mountains :** These are formed by the differences in the rates of erosion.

**Volcanic Mountains :** These mountains are formed by accumulation of material erupted from the interior of the earth.

## MOUNTAIN PEAKS

| Name | Country | Range | Height (m) | Dt. of first ascent |
|---|---|---|---|---|
| Mt. Everest | Nepal-Tibet | Himalayas | 8,848 | May 29, 1953 |
| K-2 (Godwin Austin) | India | Karakoram | 8,611 | July 31, 1954 |
| Kanchenjunga | Nepal-India | Himalayas | 8,598 | May 25, 1955 |
| Lhotse | Nepal-China | Himalayas | 8,511 | May 18, 1956 |
| Makaly | Tibet-Nepal | Himalayas | 8,481 | May 15, 1955 |
| Dhaulagiri-I | Nepal | Himalayas | 8,172 | May 13, 1960 |
| Nanga Parbat | India | Himalayas | 8,124 | July 03, 1953 |
| Nanda Devi | India | Himalayas | 7,817 | Aug. 29, 1960 |

## MAJOR PORTS

There are 13 major ports and about 200 non-major ports along the coast line of (about 7,516.6 km.) India. The major ports on the west coast of India are Mumbai, Kandla, Mormugao, New Mangaluru, Kochin and Jawaharlal Nehru port at Nhava Sheva. On the east coast, the major ports are Tuticorin, Chennai, Visakhapatnam, Paradip and Kolkata (Haldia).

# INDIAN LANGUAGES

There are 22 national languages recognized by the Indian Constitution and these are spoken in over 1600 dialects. India's official language is Hindi in the Devanagri script. However, English continues to be the official working language. The country has a wide variety of local languages and in many cases the State boundaries have been drawn on linguistic lines. Besides Hindi and English, the other languages recognised in the Indian Constitution are Assamese, Bengali, Gujarati, Kannada, Nepali, Kashmiri, Konkani, Sanskrit, Sindhi, Tamil, Malayalam, Marathi, Punjabi, Odiya, Telugu, Urdu, Bodo, Maithili, Santhali and Dogri.

Some Indian languages have evolved from the Indo-European group of languages and these were the languages of the Aryans who invaded India. This set is known as the Indic group of languages. The other set of languages are Dravidian and are native to South India, though a distinct influence of Sanskrit and Hindi is evident in these languages.

# BATTLES AND WARS IN INDIA

| War | Year | Result |
|---|---|---|
| *Battle of Kalinga* | (261 B.C.) | Ashoka defeated the king of Kalinga |
| *Second battle of Tarain* | (1192 A.D.) | Muhammad Gori defeated Prithviraj Chauhan |
| *First battle of Panipat* | (1526 A.D.) | Babar defeated Ibrahim Lodi |
| *Battle of Khandawa* | (1527 A.D.) | Babar defeated Rana Sanga |
| *Battle of Chausa* | (1539 A.D.) | Shershah Suri defeated Humayun and became ruler of Delhi |
| *Second Battle of Panipat* | (1556 A.D.) | Akbar defeated Hemu |

| War | Year | Result |
|---|---|---|
| *Battle of Talikota* | (1565 A.D.) | Allied forces of Bijapur, Bidar, Golkunda and Ahamadnagar defeated the King of Vijay Nagar |
| *Battle of Haldighati* | (1576 A.D.) | Rana Pratap was defeated by Akabar |
| *Battle of Palasey* | (1757 A.D.) | British forces defeated Nawab of Bengal Sirajudoulla |
| *Battle of Wandiwash* | (1760 A.D.) | British forces defeated the French |
| *Third battle of Panipat* | (1761 A.D.) | Maratha were defeated by Ahmad Shah Abadali |
| *Battle of Buxar* | (1764 A.D.) | British forces defeated the combined forces of Mir Quasim. Shah Alam Mughal empire and Awadh's Nawab |
| *Third Anglo-Maratha War* | (1792 A.D.) | Maratha were conclusively defeated |
| *Fourth Anglo-Mysore War* | (1799 A.D.) | Tipu Sultan died fighting the British forces |
| *Second Anglo-Sikh War* | (1848 A.D.) | British forces annexed Punjab from Sikh rulers |
| *Indo-China War* | (1962 A.D.) | China attacked India unilaterally and annexed some area |
| *Indo-Pak War* | (1965 A.D.) | Pakistan attacked India but had to suffer severe setbacks |
| *Indo-Pak War* | (1971 A.D.) | Pak declear war against India. |

## Short Biography of Historical Personalities

**Aurobindo Ghosh (1872-1950):** He began his life as ICS officer but became a revolutionary. He played an important role during partition of Bengal. He was among the first Indian leaders to demand independence. He was tried for waging war against the state but the British could not prove their allegations. Later, he became a philosopher and thinker. He went to Pondicherry and lived rest of his life in Aurobindo Ashram.

**Chandra Shekhar Azad (1906-1931):** He was one of the leading revolutionary of Indian freedom struggle who showed exemplary courage at very young age. Once when he was arrested, he said his name was Azad, father's name was Swatantrata and his residence was jail. He was a member of Azad Hindustan Socialist Republic Party which carried out several acts like Kakori dacoity, bomb blast in assembly, Saunders's murder etc. He was killed in an encounter.

**Sardar Bhagat Singh (1907-1931):** He was another great revolutionary. He spread the spirit of nationalism throughout the country. He was involved in killing of English officer Saunders. He, along with Battukeshwar Dutt, decided to throw a bomb in the Central Assembly to draw attention of Lawmakers towards their demand. After throwing bomb, they did not run away and made patriotic slogans. Later, Rajguru and Sukhdev were also arrested on the doubt of being involved in the case. Bhagat Singh, Rajguru and Sukhdev were hanged in Lahore Jail on March 23, 1931.

**Lokmanya Bal Gangadhar Tilak (1856-1920):** He was a great Indian freedom fighter who revived the festival in memory of Shivaji and Ganesh festival to make people interested in nationalistic activities. He started "Kesri" and "Maratha" newspapers to spread the message. He belonged to the extremist wing and did not believe in the politics of petitions and passing resolutions. He coined the slogan that "Swaraj is our birthright".

**Subhash Chandra Bose (1897-1945):** He started his life as an ICS officer but quit it, joined the national movement. He joined the Congress and took strong stand against the British rule. He was elected President of the Congress in 1938 and 1939 but due to differences with Gandhiji, he resigned from the post. He launched Forward Bloc. After the start of Second World War, the Congress initially was not in favour of taking strong position against the British but he announced a non-cooperation movement. He was put under house arrest but he escaped from there to Germany. He tried to form an armed force against the British. He came to Singapore and with the help of Indians living in South-East Asia, he launched Azad Hind Fauj (INA). It marched towards India, with the slogan "Delhi Chalo". It liberated Andaman and Nicobar Islands. It reached upto Kohima but setbacks to Japan and Germany in World War forced INA to slow down the march. Subhash Chandra Bose is known as Netaji. His death has been shrouded with mystery.

**Acharya Vinoba Bhave (1895-1982):** His full name was Vinayak Narhari Bhave. He was a self-taught multilinguist and was proficient in Hindi scriptural books Gandhiji had great faith in him and chose him for managing the Wardha Ashram, and participating in the famous 'Dandi March'. He started the Bhoodan movement to bring about fundamental social and economic changes in society by peaceful means.

**Baba Kharak Singh:** He was the Grand Old Man of Punjab during the freedom struggle. He urged the Sikhs to throw in their lot with the Congress against imperialism. He took active part in the Gurudwara liberation movement. The British Government, afraid of indomitable will and spirit of sacrifice, put him in jail for a long time but he continued his efforts for the freedom of the  country.

**Sardar Patel (1875-1950):** He is known in history as the "Iron Man of India". His real name was Vallabhbhai Patel. He began his political career in Kheda district of Gujarat by launching "no tax" campaign. He led the peasants agitation against an increase in land revenue at Bardoli and won a signal victory. Gandhiji described him as the "Sardar". He was a very able negotiator and played a vital role in discussions with the British Government. He was a trusted lieutenant of Gandhiji. He joined interim government as a minister Incharge of Home Affairs and Information and Broadcasting and played important role in uniting the country and maintaining order. In independent India, he became the Deputy Prime Minister and accomplished the tough task of integrating various States in India.

**Raja Rammohan Roy (1772-1833):** He was the pioneer of social and religious reforms in the country. He was a scholar in English, Sanskrit and Persian. He was close to the Englishmen. He opposed the Sati system in the country and worked for its abolition. He established Brahamo Samaj. He wrote several books. He asked the British to introduce reforms in India.

# Objective General Knowledge

## History

1. 'Abhinav Bharat' was organized by
   A. Bhai Parmanand
   B. Khudiram Bose
   C. Vir Savarkar
   D. None of these

2. The ancient name of Bengal was
   A. Kamrupa   B. Vasta
   C. Gauda     D. Vallabhi

3. Ashoka belonged to:
   A. Maurya dynasty
   B. Gupta dynasty
   C. Kushan dynasty
   D. Saka dynasty

4. Morish traveller, Ibn Batutah, came to India during the time of
   A. Ala-ud-din Khilji
   B. Firoz Shah Tughluq
   C. Balban
   D. Muhammad-bin-Tughluq

5. The relics of Indus Valley Civilisation indicates that the main occupation of the people was
   A. Agriculture
   B. Cattle rearing
   C. Commerce
   D. Hunting

6. The Mahabalipuram temples were built by the king of .......... dynasty
   A. Gupta
   B. Chola
   C. Pallava
   D. Kushana

7. The first telegraph line between Calcutta (Kolkata) and Agra was opened in
   A. 1852     B. 1853
   C. 1854     D. 1855

8. The first discourse of Buddha in Sarnath is called
   A. Mahabhiniskraman
   B. Mahaparinirvana
   C. Mahamastakabhisheka
   D. Dharmachakrapravartan

9. The political and cultural centre of the Pandyas was
   A. Vengi
   B. Madurai
   C. Kanchipuram
   D. Mahabalipuram

10. What is the correct chronological order of the dynasties in which they invaded India?
    1. Huns      2. Kushanas
    3. Aryans    4. Greeks
    A. 4, 3, 2, 1   B. 3, 4, 2, 1
    C. 4, 2, 3, 1   D. 3, 4, 1, 2

11. Who wrote Mitakshara, a book of Hindu law?
    A. Nayachandra
    B. Amoghvarsa
    C. Vijnaneswara
    D. Kumban

12. Gupta empire declined in the fifth century A.D. as a consequence of
    A. Chalukya raids
    B. Greek invasion
    C. Hun invasion
    D. Pallava raids

**13.** Who founded the Hindu Shahi dynasty of Punjab?
A. Vasumitra
B. Kallar
C. Jayapala
D. Mahipala

**14.** The main external threat to the Sultanate of Delhi was posed by the
A. Mughals
B. Afghans
C. Iranians
D. None of these

**15.** Who among the following was a leading exponent of Gandhian thoughts?
A. J.L. Nehru
B. M.N. Roy
C. Vinoba Bhave
D. Jayaprakash Narayan

**16.** Who were the immediate successors of the Imperial Mauryas in Magadha?
A. Kushanas
B. Pandyas
C. Satvahanas
D. Sungas

**17.** Both Mahavira and Buddha preached during the reign of
A. Ajatashatru
B. Bimbisara
C. Nandivardhan
D. Uday

**18.** Jahangiri Mahal is located in
A. Delhi
B. Fatehpur Sikri
C. Agra Fort
D. Sikandara

**19.** The main contribution of the Chola dynasty is in the field of
A. Systematic provincial administration
B. A well planned revenue system
C. A well organised central government
D. An organised local self government

**20.** Who founded the philosophy of Pustimarga?
A. Chaitanya
B. Nanak
C. Surdas
D. Ballabhacharya

**21.** Which of the following battles changed the destiny of a Mughal ruler of India?
A. Haldighati
B. Panipat II
C. Khanwah
D. Chausa

**22.** "The Vedas contain all the truth" was interpreted by
A. Swami Vivekanand
B. Swami Dayanand
C. Swami Shraddhanand
D. S. Radhakrishnan

**23.** Match the colums

| **Column I** | | **Column II** | |
|---|---|---|---|
| (a) | Second Battle of Panipat | 1. | Decline of Vijayanagar empire |
| (b) | Second Battle of Tarain | 2. | British rule in India |
| (c) | Battle of Talikota | 3. | Turkish rule in India |
| (d) | Battle of Plassey | 4. | Mughal rule in India |
| | | 5. | Slave dynasty in India |

**Codes:**

|  | (a) | (b) | (c) | (d) |
|---|---|---|---|---|
| A. | 2 | 3 | 4 | 1 |
| B. | 3 | 1 | 2 | 4 |
| C. | 5 | 3 | 2 | 1 |
| D. | 4 | 3 | 1 | 2 |

24. Babur entered India for the first time from the west through
    A. Kashmir  B. Sind
    C. Punjab  D. Rajasthan
25. Which was the first among the following?
    A. Doctrine of Lapse
    B. Subsidiary Alliance
    C. Permanent Settlement
    D. Double Government
26. The name of Lord Cornwallis is associated with the
    A. Dual government
    B. Maratha wars
    C. System of subsidiary
    D. Permanent settlement
27. Sir Charles Wood's Despatch of 1854 dealt with
    A. Administrative reforms
    B. Social reforms
    C. Economic reforms
    D. Educational reforms
28. Which of the following pairs is correct?
    A. Ashvaghosa — Vikramaditya
    B. Banabhatta — Harshvardhan
    C. Harisena — Kanishka
    D. Kalidasa — Samudragupta
29. 4th July, 1776 is important in world history because
    A. battle fo Plassey started
    B. Sea route to India was discovered
    C. English King Charles II was executed
    D. American Congress adopted the Declaration of Independence
30. Rawlatt Act was passed in the year
    A. 1917  B. 1919
    C. 1921  D. 1923
31. The court language of Delhi Sultanate was
    A. Urdu  B. Persian
    C. Hindi  D. Arabic
32. Where did Buddha attain Mahaparinirvana?
    A. Kushinagar
    B. Kapilvastu
    C. Pava
    D. Kundagramma
33. In Afghanistan, two towering Buddha statues were destroyed at
    A. Kandahar B. Yakaolong
    C. Bamiyan D. Mazar-i-Sharif
34. Kalibangan, the Indus Valley site is in
    A. Rajasthan
    B. Gujarat
    C. Madhya Pradesh
    D. Uttar Pradesh
35. Which of the following materials was mainly used in the manufacture of harappan seals?
    A. Terracota B. Bronze
    C. Copper  D. Iron
36. The Grand Trunk Road in India was got constructed by
    A. Ashoka  B. Shershah Suri
    C. Akbar  D. Humayun
37. 'Tripitaka' is the religious book of the
    A. Jains  B. Buddhists
    C. Sikhs  D. Hindus

38. Which among the following states was forced to merge itself with the Union of India after 1947?
A. Hyderabad
B. Kashmir
C. Patiala
D. Mysore

39. Alexander the Great died in 323 B.C. in
A. Persia
B. Babylon
C. Macedonia
D. Taxila

40. Who gave the slogan—"Jai Hind"?
A. Subhash Chandra Bose
B. Jawaharlal Nehru
C. Moti Lal Nehru
D. Mahatma Gandhi

41. The most glorious king of the Chola dynasty who conquered Ceylon was
A. Rajaraja I
B. Rajaraja II
C. Rajendra Chola
D. Gangai Konda Chola

42. Name the Chera King known as the "Red Chera", who built a temple for Kannagi?
A. Elara
B. Karikala
C. Senguttuvan
D. Nedenjerai Alan

43. The first Indian ruler to accept Subsidiary Alliance offered by Lord Wellesley in 1798 was
A. Nawab of Oudh
B. Nizam of Hyderabad
C. Nawab of Carnatic
D. King of Mysore

44. The first Viceroy of India was
A. Lord Hastings
B. Lord Canning
C. Lord Minto
D. Lord Curzon

45. The Satavahanas formerly worked as local officials under the
A. Nandas    B. Mauryas
C. Cholas    D. Cheras

46. Who was the first woman President of the Indian National Congress?
A. Sarojini Naidu
B. Bhikaji Cama
C. Annie Besant
D. Vijaya Lakshmi Pandit

47. During the Indian Freedom Struggle, who of the following founded the Parathana Samaj?
A. Atmaram Pandurang
B. Gopal Hari Deshmukh
C. Ishwar Chandra Vidyasagar
D. Keshav Chandra Sen

48. Which one of the following periodicals was published by Mahatma Gandhi during his stay in South Africa?
A. Afrikanes
B. Indian Opinion
C. India Gazette
D. Navjivan

49. During the Civil Disobedience Movement, who led the 'Red Shirts' of North-Western India?
A. Abul Kalam Azad
B. Khan Abdul Ghaffar Khan
C. Mohammad Ali Jinnah
D. Shaukat Ali

50. Match List-I with List-Il and select the correct answer using the codes given below the lists—

**List-I**

**(Name of the Author)**

(a) Abul Fazal

(b) Nizamuddin Ahmed

(c) Krishnadeva Raya

(d) Kalhana

**List-II**

**(Name of the Book)**

1. Tabqat-i-Akbari

2. Akbarnama

3. Rajatarangini

4. Amuktamalyada

**Codes:**

|   | (a) | (b) | (c) | (d) |
|---|-----|-----|-----|-----|
| A. | 2 | 4 | 1 | 3 |
| B. | 3 | 1 | 4 | 2 |
| C. | 2 | 1 | 4 | 3 |
| D. | 3 | 4 | 1 | 2 |

51. Which one of the following pairs is not correctly matched?

A. Sheikh Shihab-ud-din Suharawardi — Sufi Saint

B. Chaitanya Maha Prabhu — Bhakti Saint

C. Minhaj-us Siraj — Founder of Sufi order

D. Lalleshwari — Bhakti Saint

52. Who of the following kings was an ardent follower of Jainism?

A. Bimbisara

B. Mahapadma Nanda

C. Kharavela

D. Pulakesin II

53. To which dynasty did Ashoka belong?

A. Vardhana B. Maurya

C. Kushan   D. Gupta

54. Which one of the following battles was fought between Babar and the Rajputs in 1527?

A. The First Battle of Panipat

B. The Battle of Khanwah

C. The Battle of Ghagra

D. The Battle of Chanderi

55. Aryabhat,ta and Varahamihira belong to which age?

A. Guptas   B. Cholas

C. Mauryas D. Mughals

56. Consider the· following statements about Amir Khusro:

1. He was a disciple of Nizamuddin Auliya.

2. He was the founder of both Hindustani classical music and Qawwali.

Which of the statements given above is/are correct?

A. 1 only

B. 2 only

C. Both 1 and 2

D. Neither 1 nor 2

57. Panini, the first Grammarian of Sanskrit language in India, lived during the

A. 2nd Century B.C.

B. 6th-5th Century B.C.

C. 2nd Century A.D.

D. 5th-6th Century A.D.

58. Who among the following was associated with the foundation of Ghadar party?

A. Lala Lajpat Rai

B. Lala Hardayal

C. C.R. Das

D. Bipin Chandra Pal

**59.** The Treaty of Bassein (1802) was signed between
A. Madhav Rao and the British
B. Baji Rao II and the British
C. Mahadji Scindia and the British
D. Holkar and the British

**60.** The words 'Satyameva Jayate' in the State Emblem of India, have been adopted from which one of the following?
A. Brahma Upanishad
B. Mudgala Upanishad
C. Maitreyi Upanishad
D. Mundaka Upanishad

**61.** Match List-I with List-II and select the correct answer using the codes given below the lists—
**List-I**
**(Symbol)**
(*a*) Elephant
(*b*) Tree
(*c*) Empty Throne
(*d*) Horse
**List-II**
**(Important event of life of Buddha)**
1. Renouncement of worldly pleasures
2. Birth of Buddha
3. Enlightenment
4. Representation of royalty
**Codes:**

|   | (*a*) | (*b*) | (*c*) | (*d*) |
|---|---|---|---|---|
| A. | 2 | 4 | 3 | 1 |
| B. | 3 | 1 | 4 | 2 |
| C. | 3 | 4 | 1 | 2 |
| D. | 2 | 3 | 4 | 1 |

**62.** When was Mahatma Gandhi, the father of the nation, born?
A. 1889　　B. 1859
C. 1869　　D. 1879

**63.** Chinese pilgrim Hiuen-Tsang came to and lived in India under whose rule?
A. Harshavardhan
B. Chandragupta Maurya
C. Ashok
D. Samudragupta

**64.** Who had founded the Slave dynasty in India?
A. Qutb-ud-din Aibak
B. Iltutmish
C. Mohammed Gauri
D. Balban

**65.** Which British Governor-General had started the *Doctrine of Lapse* policy in India?
A. Lord William Bentinck
B. Lord Dalhousie
C. Lord Canning
D. Lord Hardinge

**66.** "Liberty is our birth right, we shall seize it." Who said it?
A. Bhagat Singh
B. Ramprasad Bismil
C. Bal Gangadhar Tilak
D. Mahatma Gandhi

**67.** The most important Sufi shrine in India is located at
A. Pandua
B. Bidar
C. Ajmer
D. Shahjahanabad

**68.** The 'Ajivikas' were a
A. Sect contemporary to the Buddha
B. Breakaway branch of the Buddhists
C. Sect founded by Charvaka
D. Sect founded by Shankaracharya

**69.** The Indian Universities were first founded during the time of
A. Macaulay
B. Warren Hastings
C. Lord Canning
D. Lord William Bentinck

**70.** One of the following was **not** involved in the Chittagong Armoury Raid, 1934. Who was he?
A. Kalpana Dutt
B. Surya Sen
C. Pritilata Woddedar
D. Dinesh Gupta

**71.** Which of the following is associated with Sufi saints?
A. Tripitaka B. Dakhma
C. Khanqah D. Synagogue

**72.** Which Indian statesman used these, magic words, "Long years ago we made a tryst with destiny, and now the time comes when we shall redeem our pledge ... "?
A. Mohandas Karamchand Gandhi
B. Sardar Vallabhbhai Patel
C. Netaji Subhas Chandra Bose
D. Jawaharlal Nehru

**73.** In which century did French Revolution begin?
A. 16th century
B. 17th century
C. 18th century
D. 19th century

**74.** Under whose patronage was the Khandariya Mahadeo Temple at Khajuraho built?
A. Solankis
B. Rashtrakutas
C. Tomaras
D. Chandellas

**75.** During the period of which of the following was 'Panchtantra' written?
A. Nandas   B. Mauryas
C. Guptas   D. Sungas

**76.** Who wrote the book called Kitab-i-Nauras?
A. Amir Khusro
B. Badauni
C. Ibrahim Adil Shah II
D. Ala-ud-din Bahmani

**77.** Who among the following, Mughal rulers granted the English Company *Dewani* over Bengal, Bihar and Orissa, by Treaty of Allahabad?
A. Ahmad Shah
B. Alamgir II
C. Shah Alam II
D. Akbar Shah II

**78.** During the Indian freedom struggle, what accusation was made against Master Amir Chand, Awadh Bihari, Bal Mukund and Basant Kumar Biswas?
A. Assassination of the Commissioner of Poona
B. Throwing a bomb on Viceroy's procession in Delhi
C. Attempt to shoot the Governor of Punjab
D. Looting an armoury in Bengal

**79.** Which of the following pairs is/ are correctly matched?
1. Regulating Act : Hastings
2 Widow Remarriage Act : Bentinck
3. Vernacular Press Act : Lytton

Select the correct answer using the codes given below:
A. 1 only     B. 2 and 3
C. 1 and 3   D. 1, 2 and 3

80. Which among the following is referred to as the Montague-Chelmsford Reforms?
A. Indian Council Act, 1909
B. Government of India Act, 1919
C. Rowlatt Act
D. Government of India Act, 1935

81. Consider the following statements:
1. Lord Cornwallis introduced the Permanent Land Settlement in Bengal.
2. Lord Wellesley introduced the Subsidiary Alliance system.
Which of the statements given above is/are correct?
A. 1 only
B. 2 only
C. Both 1 and 2
D. Neither 1 nor 2

82. Who was the Governor-General when the Revolt of 1857 started?
A. Lord Canning
B. Lord Cornwallis
C. Lord Dalhousie
D. Lord Ellenborough

83. Which of the following pairs is correctly matched?
A. Mahatma : Home Rule
   Gandhi
B. Annie : Non-Coopera-
   Besant         tion Movement
C. Jawaharlal : Khilafat
   Nehru          Movement
D. Lala : Hindustan
   Hardayal     Ghadar Party

84. For which of the following movements did Mahatma Gandhi give the slogan "Do or Die"?
A. Kheda Satyagraha
B. Non-Cooperation Movement
C. Civil Disobedience Movement
D. Quit India Movement

85. Who among the following was the founder of the Servants of India Society?
A. Bal Gangadhar Tilak
B. Dadabhai Naoroji
C. Gopal Krishna Gokhale
D. Lala Lajpat Rai

86. Which of the following pairs is *not* correctly mathced?
A. Lord Wellesley : Subsidiary
                         Alliance
B. Lord Dalhousie : Doctrine of
                          Lapse
C. Lord Ripon : Vernacular
                       Press Act
D. Lord Curzon : Partition of
                       Bengal

87. Which of the following territories was outside the boundaries of the Mughal Empire during the reign of Akbar?
A. Khandesh B. Kabul
C. Bijapur   D. Kashmir

88. Which Sultan of Delhi enforced a strict market control system during his time?
A. Ala-ud-din Khilji
B. Mohammad-bin-Tughlaq
C. Firoz Shah Tughlaq
D. Bahlol Lodi

**89.** Which of the following pairs is *not* correctly matched?
  A. Kautilya    : Arthashastra
  B. Hala        : Gathasaptasati
  C. Banabhatta : Buddha Charita
  D. Kalidasa    : Abhijnana Shakuntalam

**90.** With which of the following countries is the famous 'October Revolution' associated?
  A. China       B. Cuba
  C. France      D. Russia

**91.** Who is the author of "Das Kapital"?
  A. Karl Marx
  B. Friedrich Engels
  C. Joseph Stalin
  D. Vladimir Lenin

**92.** Who was the Commander of the American forces during the American War of Independence?
  A. Alexander Hamilton
  B. Thomas Jefferson
  C. George Washington
  D. Major Samuel Shaw

**93.** Who fought the Battle of Buxar?
  A. Humayun and Sher Shah Suri
  B. Ahmad Shah Abdali and Marathas
  C. English and Mir Kasim
  D. English and Marathas

**94.** Who of the following started the newspaper 'Samvad Kaumudi' in the early 19th century?
  A. Ishwar Chandra Vidyasagar
  B. Keshav Chandra Sen
  C. Raja Rammohan Roy
  D. Satyendranath Tagore

**95.** Match List-I (Movements) with List-II (Leaders) and select the correct answer using the codes given below the lists:

| List-I (Movements) | List-II (Leaders) |
| --- | --- |
| A. Home Rule movement | 1. Maulana Abul Kalam Azad |
| B. Bhudan movement | 2. Bal Gangadhar Tilak |
| C. Aligarh movement | 3. Sayyid Ahmad Khan |
| D. Khilafat movement | 4. Vinoba Bhave |

**Codes:**

|   | (a) | (b) | (c) | (d) |
| --- | --- | --- | --- | --- |
| A. | 1 | 4 | 3 | 2 |
| B. | 2 | 4 | 3 | 1 |
| C. | 2 | 3 | 4 | 1 |
| D. | 1 | 3 | 4 | 2 |

**96.** When the Moroccan traveller Ibn Batutah visited India, who was the Delhi Sultan?
  A. Jalaluddin Khilji
  B. Ala-ud-din Khilji
  C. Giasuddin Tughlaq
  D. Muhammad-bin Tughlaq

**97.** The Lingaraja Temple built during the medieval period is at
  A. Bhubaneswar
  B. Khajuraho
  C. Madurai
  D. Mount Abu

**98.** Which of the following is Considered as an encyclopaedia of Indian medicine?
  A. Charakasamhita
  B. Lokayata

C. Brihatsamhita

D. Suryasiddhanta

**99.** Which of the following is not included in the 'eight-fold path' of Buddhism?
  A. Right Speech
  B. Right Contemplation
  C. Right Desire
  D. Right Conduct

**100.** During India's freedom struggle, the 'Sepoy Mutiny' started from which of the following places?
  A. Agra      B. Gwalior
  C. Jhansi    D. Meerut

## Geography

**101.** Match List-I (Historical Site) with List-II (State) and select the correct answer using the codes given below the lists:

| List-I (Historical Site) | List-II (State) |
|---|---|
| (a) Shore temple | 1. Karnataka |
| (b) Bhimbetka | 2. Tamil Nadu |
| (c) Kesava temple (Hoysala (Monuments) | 3. Kerala |
| (d) Hampi | 4. Madhya Pradesh |
| | 5. Rajasthan |

Codes :

|   | (a) | (b) | (c) | (d) |
|---|---|---|---|---|
| A. | 3 | 5 | 2 | 1 |
| B. | 2 | 4 | 1 | 1 |
| C. | 3 | 4 | 2 | 2 |
| D. | 2 | 5 | 1 | 4 |

**102.** Where are the maximum numbers of major ports located in India?
  A. Maharashtra
  B. Kerala
  C. Goa
  D. Tamil Nadu

**103.** Match List-I (Beach Resort) with List-II (State) and select the correct answer using the codes given below the lists:

| List-I (Beach Resort) | List-II (State) |
|---|---|
| (a) Digha | 1. Kerala |
| (b) Covelong | 2. West Bengal |
| (c) Cherai | 3. Maharashtra |
| (d) Murud-Janjira | 4. Tamil Nadu |

Codes :

|   | (a) | (b) | (c) | (d) |
|---|---|---|---|---|
| A. | 2 | 4 | 1 | 3 |
| B. | 3 | 1 | 4 | 2 |
| C. | 2 | 1 | 4 | 3 |
| D. | 3 | 4 | 1 | 2 |

**104.** Match List-I (Produce) with List-II (Major Producer State) and select the correct answer using the codes given below the lists:

| List-I (Produce) | List-II (Major Producer State) |
|---|---|
| (a) Rubber | 1. Andhra Pradesh |
| (b) Soyabean | 2. Tamil Nadu |
| (c) Groundnut | 3. Madhya Pradesh |
| (d) Wheat | 4. Kerala |
| | 5. Uttar Pradesh |

**Codes :**

|   | (a) | (b) | (c) | (d) |
|---|-----|-----|-----|-----|
| A. | 4 | 1 | 2 | 5 |
| B. | 5 | 3 | 1 | 4 |
| C. | 4 | 3 | 1 | 5 |
| D. | 5 | 1 | 2 | 4 |

**105.** Match List-I (Railway Zone) with List-II (Headquarters) and select the correct answer using the codes given below the lists:

| **List-I** | **List-II** |
|---|---|
| **(Railway Zone)** | **(Headquarters)** |
| (a) East-Central Railway | 1. Hubli |
| (b) North-Western Railway | 2. Allahabad |
| (c) North-Central Railway | 3. Hajipur |
| (d) South-Western Railway | 4. Jabalpur |
|  | 5. Jaipur |

**Codes :**

|   | (a) | (b) | (c) | (d) |
|---|-----|-----|-----|-----|
| A. | 3 | 5 | 2 | 1 |
| B. | 2 | 1 | 4 | 5 |
| C. | 3 | 1 | 2 | 5 |
| D. | 2 | 5 | 4 | 1 |

**106.** Match List-I (Wildlife Sanctuary) with List-II (State) and select the correct answer using the codes given below the lists:

| **List-I** | **List-II** |
|---|---|
| **(Wildlife Sanctuary)** | **(State)** |
| (a) Bhitar Kanika | 1. Andhra Pradesh |
| (b) Pachmarhi | 2. Karnataka |
| (c) Pocharam | 3. Madhya Pradesh |
| (d) Sharavathi | 4. Orissa |
|  | 5. Uttar Pradesh |

**Codes :**

|   | (a) | (b) | (c) | (d) |
|---|-----|-----|-----|-----|
| A. | 4 | 2 | 1 | 3 |
| B. | 1 | 3 | 5 | 2 |
| C. | 4 | 3 | 1 | 2 |
| D. | 1 | 2 | 5 | 3 |

**107.** Which one of the following is *not* a tributary of the river Godavari?

A. Koyna    B. Manjra
C. Pranhita   D. Wardha

**108.** Which one of the following is the correct statement?

A. Spring tides occur on the full moon day only
B. Neap tides occur on the new moon day only
C. The West coast of India experiences tides four times a day
D. Tides do not occur in the gulfs

**109.** Which one of the following pairs is *not* correctly matched?

| City | River |
|---|---|
| A. Ahmedabad: | Sabarmati |
| B. Hyderabad : | Musi |
| C. Lucknow : | Gomti |
| D. Surat : | Narmada |

**110.** Match List-I (Famous Place) with List-II (Country) and select the correct answer using the codes given below the lists:

|  | List-I<br>(Famous Place) | List-II<br>(Country) |
|---|---|---|
| (a) | Alexandria | 1. Turkey |
| (b) | Blackpool Pleasure Beach | 2. Great Britain |
| (c) | Constantinople | 3. Italy |
| (d) | Florence | 4. Greece |
|  |  | 5. Egypt |

**Codes :**

|  | (a) | (b) | (c) | (d) |
|---|---|---|---|---|
| A. | 1 | 3 | 4 | 2 |
| B. | 5 | 2 | 1 | 3 |
| C. | 1 | 2 | 4 | 3 |
| D. | 5 | 3 | 1 | 2 |

111. Match List-I (Institute) with List-II (City) and select the correct answer using the codes given below the lists:

|  | List-I<br>(Institute) | List-II<br>(City) |
|---|---|---|
| (a) | Rashtriya Sanskrit Vidyapeeth | 1. Hyderabad |
| (b) | Maharishi Sandipani Rashtriya Veda Vidhya Pratishthan | 2. Varanasi |
| (c) | Central Institute of Indian Languages | 3. Mysore |
| (d) | Central Institute of English and Foreign Languages | 4. Tirupati |
|  |  | 5. Ujjain |

**Codes :**

|  | (a) | (b) | (c) | (d) |
|---|---|---|---|---|
| A. | 2 | 3 | 1 | 5 |
| B. | 4 | 5 | 3 | 1 |
| C. | 2 | 5 | 3 | 1 |
| D. | 4 | 3 | 1 | 5 |

112. Consider the following statements:
   1. Kaziranga National park is a World Heritage Site recognised by the UNESCO
   2. Kaziranga National Park is a home to sloth bear and hoolock gibbon.

   Which of the statements given above is/are correct?
   A. 1 only
   B. 2 only
   C. Both 1 and 2
   D. Neither 1 nor 2

113. Which country among the following is the biggest producer of cotton?
   A. China
   B. India
   C. Indonesia
   D. USA

114. Where is the Holy Shrine of Imam Ali in Najaf located?
   A. Saudi Arabia
   B. Iraq
   C. Iran
   D. Kuwait

115. Match List-I (Institute) with List-II (Location) and select the correct answer using the codes given below the lists:

|  | List-I<br>(Institute) | List-II<br>(Location) |
|---|---|---|
| (a) | Indian Institute of Public Administration | 1. Faridabad |

(b) V.V. Giri National Labour Institute    2. Bangalore

(c) National Institute of Financial Management    3. NOIDA

(d) National Law School of India University    4. Mumbai

     5. Delhi

**Codes :**

|   | (a) | (b) | (c) | (d) |
|---|-----|-----|-----|-----|
| A. | 1 | 2 | 4 | 3 |
| B. | 5 | 3 | 1 | 2 |
| C. | 1 | 3 | 4 | 2 |
| D. | 5 | 2 | 1 | 3 |

**116.** Which river feeds "Tehri dam"?
A. Alaknanda
B. Bhagirathi
C. Gandak
D. Ghaghara

**117.** Which of the following winds are known as "Anti-trade winds"?
A. Chinook
B. Cyclones
C. Typhoons
D. Westerlies

**118.** Geostationary orbit is at a height of
A. 6 km
B. 1000 km
C. 3600 km
D. 36000 km

**119.** The orbits of planets around the Sun can be
A. Elliptic and parabolic
B. Parabolic and hyperbolic
C. Circular and hyperbolic
D. Circular and elliptic

**120.** What is Super Nova?
A. A black hole
B. A dying star
C. An asteroid
D. A comet

**121.** Which State is irrigated by the Gang Canal?
A. Uttar Pradesh
B. Bihar
C. West Bengal
D. Rajasthan

**122.** Among the following Indian cities, which one is located most southward?
A. Hyderabad
B. Visakhapatnam
C. Panaji
D. Belgaum

**123.** Match List I (National Highway) with List II (Connected Cities) and select the correct answer using the codes given below the Lists:

| List-I (National Highway) | List-II (Connected Cities) |
|---|---|
| A. NH 3 | 1. Delhi-Lucknow |
| B. NH 4 | 2. Agra-Bikaner |
| C. NH 11 | 3. Agra-Mumbai |
| D. NH 24 | 4. Chennai-Thane (Mumbai) |

**Codes :**

|   | (a) | (b) | (c) | (d) |
|---|-----|-----|-----|-----|
| A. | 3 | 1 | 2 | 4 |
| B. | 2 | 4 | 3 | 1 |
| C. | 3 | 4 | 2 | 1 |
| D. | 2 | 1 | 3 | 4 |

**124.** Match List-I (Defence Institute) with List-II (City) and select the correct answer using the codes given below the Lists:

| List-I (Defence Institute) | List-II (City) |
|---|---|
| (a) College of Defence Management | 1. Panchmarhi |
| (b) Army Air Defence College | 2. Bengaluru |
| (c) Army Supply Corps (ASC) Centre and College | 3. Secunderabad |
| (d) Army Education Corps (AEC) Training College and Centre | 4. Gopalpur |

**Codes :**

|   | (a) | (b) | (c) | (d) |
|---|---|---|---|---|
| A. | 3 | 4 | 2 | 1 |
| B. | 1 | 2 | 4 | 3 |
| C. | 3 | 2 | 4 | 1 |
| D. | 1 | 4 | 2 | 3 |

**125.** Which of the following are Defence Public Sector Undertakings?
1. Goa Shipyard Limited
2. The Bharat Dynamics Limited
3. Mishra Dhatu Nigam Limited

Select the correct answer using the codes given below:
A. 1 and 2   B. 2 and 3
C. 1 and 3   D. 1, 2 and 3

**126.** Which one of the following pairs is *not* correctly matched?
A. Gol Gumbaz : Hyderabad
B. Tomb of Itmad-ud-daula : Agra
C. Tomb of Sher Shah : Sasaram
D. Tomb of Rani Rupmati : Ahmedabad

**127.** Where is the Baglihar Hydro-electric Project located?
A. Firozepur District of Punjab
B. Doda District of Jammu and Kashmir
C. Faridkot District of Punjab
D. Baramulla District of Jammu and Kashmir

**128.** Match List-I (Temple/Cathedral) with List-II (Place) and select the correct answer using the code given below the Lists:

**List-I (Temple/Cathedral)**
(a) Brihadeswara Temple
(b) Vishwanatha Temple
(c) Kamakhya Temple
(d) Santhom Cathedral

**List-II (Place)**
1. Guwahati
2. Chennai
3. Thanjavur
4. Khajuraho

**Codes :**

|   | (a) | (b) | (c) | (d) |
|---|---|---|---|---|
| A. | 3 | 2 | 1 | 4 |
| B. | 1 | 4 | 3 | 2 |
| C. | 3 | 4 | 1 | 2 |
| D. | 1 | 2 | 3 | 4 |

**129.** Match List-I (World Heritage Site) with List-II (State) and select the correct answer using the code given below the Lists:

**List-I (World Heritage Site)**
(*a*) Manas Wildlife Sanctuary
(*b*) Mahabodhi Temple Complex
(*c*) Group of Monuments, Pattadakal
(*d*) Nandadevi National Park

**List-II (State)**
1. Bihar
2. Uttarakhand
3. Asom
4. Karnataka

**Codes :**

|  | (*a*) | (*b*) | (*c*) | (*d*) |
|---|---|---|---|---|
| A. | 2 | 4 | 1 | 3 |
| B. | 3 | 1 | 4 | 2 |
| C. | 2 | 1 | 4 | 3 |
| D. | 3 | 4 | 1 | 2 |

**130.** Consider the following statements:
1. Black soils occur mainly in Maharashtra, Western Madhya Pradesh and Gujarat.
2. Alluvial soils are confined mainly to the northern plains.

Which of the statements given above is/are correct?
A. 1 only
B. 2 only
C. Both 1 and 2
D. Neither 1 nor 2

**131.** What is the new name of the old colony of Northern Rhodesia?
A. Zambia  B. Zimbabwe
C. Uganda  D. Tanzania

**132.** Which is the smallest (in area) of the following Union Territories?
A. Chandigarh
B. Dadra and Nagar Haveli
C. Daman and Diu
D. Lakshadweep

**133.** The Sundarbans or the 'Mangrove' forests are found in
A. Kutch Peninsula
B. Western Ghats
C. Konkan Coast
D. Deltaic West Bengal

**134.** On which river has the Hirakud dam been built?
A. Mahanadi
B. Godavari
C. Cauvery
D. Periyar

**135.** Where is "Ground Zero"?
A. Greenwich
B. New York
C. Indira Point
D. Sriharikota

**136.** The maximum concentration of scheduled caste population is in the
A. Indo-Gangetic Plains
B. North-East India
C. Western Coast
D. Eastern Coast

**137.** When was the first passenger train run in India?
A. January 1848
B. April 1853
C. May 1857
D. April 1852

**138.** Which is the major area where 'Garba' dance form is common?
A. Maharashtra  B. Gujarat
C. Rajasthan  D. Punjab

**139.** Where is India's most prized tea grown?
A. Jorhat    B. Darjeeling
C. Nilgiris   D. Mannar

**140.** Which is the largest cotton growing State in India?
A. Maharashtra
B. Madhya Pradesh
C. Andhra Pradesh
D. Gujarat

**141.** Which one of the following is the first shipyard of India?
A. Cochin
B. Visakhapatnam
C. Mazagaon
D. Paradeep

**142.** Which of the following Indian States is the largest producer of Cardamom?
A. Kerala
B. Tamil Nadu
C. Karnataka
D. Jammu & Kashmir

**143.** Vikram Sarabhai Space Centre is located in
A. Peenya
B. Ahmedabad
C. Thiruvananthapuram
D. Dehradun

**144.** The Sardar Sarovar Dam is associated with
A. Tapti river valley project
B. Mahanadi river valley project
C. Narmada project
D. Bhakra-Nangal project

**145.** In which of the following states in India is the bird, Great Indian Bustard found?
A. Rajasthan
B. Bihar

C. Karnataka
D. Andhra Pradesh

**146.** The Indian state with smallest population is
A. Sikkim
B. Arunachal Pradesh
C. Goa
D. Mizoram

**147.** On which of the following rivers Nasik is situated?
A. Ganges
B. Krishna
C. Godavari
D. Cauvery

**148.** Atacama Desert is in
A. South America
B. North America
C. South Africa
D. Russia

**149.** Which place in India is a reference for determining Indian Standard Time?
A. Delhi    B. Allahabad
C. Kolkata   D. Mumbai

**150.** Which of the following does not share a boarder with India?
A. Pakistan
B. Bangladesh
C. Burma
D. Afghanistan

**151.** The Dachigam Wildlife Sanctuary is in
A. Himachal Pradesh
B. Asom
C. Jammu & Kashmir
D. Karnataka

**152.** How many days does the moon take to complete 1 revolution around the earth?

A. $26\frac{1}{3}$ days

B. $27\frac{1}{3}$ days

C. $24\frac{1}{3}$ days

D. $28\frac{1}{2}$ days

**153.** A high growth rate of population is characterised by
A. High birth and high death rates
B. High birth and low death rates
C. Low birth and low death rates
D. Low birth and high death rates

**154.** The Indian Sub-continent was originally a part of
A. Jurassic-land
B. Angara-land
C. Aryavarta
D. Gondwana-land

**155.** The tropical grassland is called
A. Pampas　B. Llanas
C. Savanah　D. Veld

**156.** The atmosphere is heated mainly by
A. Insolation
B. Conduction
C. Radiation
D. Convection

**157.** Which one of the following countries is the largest producer of uranium in the world?
A. Canada　B. South Africa
C. Namibia　D. USA

**158.** Which of the following methods does not help in conserving soil fertility and moisture?
A. Contour ploughing
B. Dry farming
C. Strip cropping
D. Shifting agriculture

**159.** Mudumalai Wildlife Sanctuary is located in the State of
A. Kerala
B. Karnataka
C. Tamil Nadu
D. Andhra Pradesh

**160.** The narrow stretch of water connecting two seas is called
A. Bay　　B. Peninsula
C. Isthmus　D. Strait

**161.** The topography of plateau is ideal for
A. Cultivation
B. Forestry
C. Mining
D. Generation of hydel power

**162.** Naga Khasi and Garo hills are located in
A. Purvanchal Ranges
B. Karakoram Ranges
C. Zaskar Ranges
D. Himalayas Ranges

**163.** In which of the following States, Jawahar Tunnel is located?
A. Himachal Pradesh
B. Jammu & Kashmir
C. Uttarakhand
D. Goa

**164.** Where was India's first submarine museum established?
A. Kochi
B. Panjim
C. Visakhapatnam
D. Mumbai

**165.** Which two countries are connected by an under-water tunnel?
A. England and Spain
B. Malaysia and Singapore
C. England and Belgium
D. France and England

**166.** Which of the following is correctly matched with regard to thermal power projects?
A. Korba — Uttar Pradesh
B. Ramagundam — Tamil Nadu
C. Talcher — Andhra Pradesh
D. Kawas — Gujarat

**167.** Sundarbans of Eastern India is an example of
A. Forest Ecosystem
B. Mangrove Ecosystem
C. Grassland Ecosystem
D. Marine Ecosystem

**168.** The deepest trench of the world—'The Mariana Trench' is located in the
A. Indian Ocean
B. Atlantic Ocean
C. Arctic Ocean
D. Pacific Ocean

**169.** Which of the following is a landlocked sea?
A. Timor Sea
B. Arafura Sea
C. Greenland Sea
D. Aral Sea

**170.** Match the dams and the states in which they are situated:

| | Dam | State |
|---|---|---|
| (a) | Hirakud | 1. Chhattisgarh |
| (b) | Mettur | 2. Orissa |
| (c) | Mahanadi | 3. Karnataka |
| (d) | Almatti | 4. Tamil Nadu |

**Codes :**

| | (a) | (b) | (c) | (d) |
|---|---|---|---|---|
| A. | 3 | 2 | 4 | 1 |
| B. | 2 | 4 | 1 | 3 |
| C. | 1 | 3 | 2 | 4 |
| D. | 4 | 1 | 3 | 2 |

**171.** Which of the following territories does not have a border with Arunachal Pradesh?
A. Asom
B. Nagaland
C. Bhutan
D. Manipur

**172.** Which of the following 'rivers does *not* originate in the Indian territory?
A. Mahanadi
B. Brahamaputra
C. Ravi
D. Chenab

**173.** Land and sea-breezes occur due to
A. Conduction
B. Convection
C. Radiation
D. Tides

**174.** Which of the following is *not* correctly matched with regard to Project Tiger Reserves?
A. Sariska — Alwar
B. Valmiki — Hazaribagh
C. Pench — Garhwal
D. Nagarjunasagar — Sri Sailam

**175.** Trade winds blow from the
- A. Equatorial low pressure
- B. Polar high pressure
- C. Subtropical high pressure
- D. Subpolar low pressure

**176.** Most of the Indians belong to which of the following racial stocks?
- A. Caucasoid
- B. Negroid
- C. Australoid
- D. Mongoloid

**177.** Which of the following signifies the American Indians living in the US?
- A. Bushmen
- B. Alpine
- C. Amerindus
- D. Mestizoes

**178.** Which region is most famous for citrus fruits?
- A. Deserts
- B. Monsoon regions
- C. Temperate grasslands
- D. Mediterranean regions

**179.** The leading sulphur producing country in the world is
- A. USA
- B. Russia
- C. Japan
- D. Mexico

**180.** The largest producer of mercury is
- A. USA
- B. Canada
- C. China
- D. Spain

**181.** The largest amount of saffron comes from
- A. Uttar Pradesh
- B. Tamil Nadu
- C. Jammu and Kashmir
- D. Kerala

**182.** The boundary between Germany and Poland is called the
- A. Hindenberg Line
- B. Maginot Line
- C. Durand Line
- D. 17th Parallel

**183.** The boundary between North and South Korea is marked by the
- A. Radcliffe Line
- B. 38th Parallel
- C. 49th Parallel
- D. 17th Parallel

**184.** Which countries are separated by the 49th Parallel?
- A. France and Germany
- B. USA and Mexico
- C. USA and Canada
- D. Russia and China

**185.** Echo-sounding is the technique applied to
- A. Measure the depth of the sea
- B. Measure the amplitude of sound waves
- C. Record earthquake waves
- D. Record the density of air in the atmosphere

**186.** On which of the rivers is the famous Kariba Dam situated?
- A. Nile
- B. Niger
- C. Zambezi
- D. Amazon

**187.** The northernmost limit of India is
- A. $36°4'$ N latitude
- B. $37°8'$ N latitude
- C. $37°6'$ N latitude
- D. $36°12'$ N latitude

188. The length of India's coastline is about
    A. 4,500 km
    B. 5,900 km
    C. 7,000 km
    D. 7,516 km

189. The total area of India is about
    A. 31 lakh sq km
    B. 33 lakh sq km
    C. 320 lakh sq km
    D. 35 lakh sq km

190. Where is the Gulf of Mannar located?
    A. West of Gujarat
    B. East of Tamil Nadu
    C. West of Kerala
    D. South of Kanyakumari

191. The Sivaliks stretch between
    A. Indus and Sutlej
    B. Potwar Basin and Teesta
    C. Sutlej and Kali
    D. Sutlej and Teesta

192. The territorial waters of India extend up to
    A. 12 nautical miles
    B. 6 nautical miles
    C. 15 nautical miles
    D. 10 nautical miles

193. The deepest lake in the world is
    A. Pushkar Lake
    B. Lake Superior
    C. Victoria Lake
    D. Baikal Lake

194. Simlipal Tiger Reserve is located at
    A. Assam
    B. Gujarat
    C. Orissa
    D. Bihar

195. Which of the following rivers flow through a rift valley?
    A. Ganga
    B. Narmada
    C. Brahmaputra
    D. Krishna

196. What is the most important characteristic of the islands (Indian) located in the Arabian Sea?
    A. They are all very small in size
    B. They are all of coral origin
    C. They have a very dry climate
    D. They are extended parts of the mainland

197. The Thar Desert is believed to be expanding. The most suitable way to check it would be by
    A. Afforestation
    B. Artificial rain
    C. Canal irrigation
    D. Using the area for cattle rearing

198. Which one is a land-locked State?
    A. Gujarat
    B. Andhra Pradesh
    C. West Bengal
    D. Bihar

199. Which area in India gets the summer monsoon?
    A. The Himalayas
    B. The Eastern Ghats
    C. The Western Ghats
    D. The Indo-Gangetic plains

200. In which of the following areas is maximum precipitation received from the summer monsoon?
    A. The Coromandel coast

B. The North-Eastern hilly region
C. The Central Indian hills
D. The Western Himalayas

## Indian Polity and Constitution

**201.** Which Schedule of the Constitution lists the languages recognised by it?
A. Eighth Schedule
B. Sixth Schedule
C. Seventh Schedule
D. Ninth Schedule

**202.** Which of the following Union Territories has a Chief Minister?
A. Andaman and Nicobar Islands
B. Puducherry
C. Chandigarh
D. Dadra and Nagar Haveli

**203.** Who among the following administers the Oath of Office to the President of India?
A. The Vice-President of India
B. The Chief Justice of India
C. The Chairman of Rajya Sabha
D. The Prime Minister

**204.** Parliament of India consists of
A. Directly elected members only
B. Directly elected and nominated members
C. Directly elected and indirectly elected members
D. Directly elected, indirectly elected and nominated members

**205.** In a Unitary Government
A. All powers are vested in the Centre
B. Powers are divided between the Centre and the States under a Constitution
C. Powers are divided by mutual consent of the Centre and the States through Parliamentary statute
D. The Judiciary must be independent

**206.** Article 360 of the Constitution of India relates to
A. National Emergency
B. Emergency in a State
C. To conduct Parliament Elections
D. Financial Emergency

**207.** Panchayati Raj was recommended by
A. Sarkaria Commission
B. Fazlali Commission
C. Balwantrai Mehta Committee
D. Rajamannar Committee

**208.** Name the first woman Governor of an Indian State
A. Padmaja Naidu
B. Lakshmi N. Menon
C. Sarojini Naidu
D. Sucheta Kriplani

**209.** Gangtok is the capital of
A. Nagaland
B. Meghalaya
C. Sikkim
D. Arunachal Pradesh

**210.** Who appoints the Chief Justice of a High Court in India?

A. The President of India
B. The Governor of the State concerned
C. The Chief Justice of the Supreme Court
D. An Appointment Committee in the Union Ministry of Law

**211.** In India, how did the Planning Commission come into existence?
A. By an Act of Parliament
B. By an executive order
C. Under the provisions of the Constitution
D. As an attached office of the Union Ministry of Finance

**212.** Which is the first executive tier of the Panchayati Raj system from below?
A. Gram Sabha
B. Gram Panchayat
C. Mandal Parishad
D. Panchayat Samiti

**213.** After the Constitution of India, came into force, when did the Parliament enact the Untouchability (Offences) Act?
A. 1953     B. 1954
C. 1955     D. 1956

**214.** Which of the following pairs is *not* correctly matched?

| State/U.T. | High Court |
| --- | --- |
| A. Goa | — Bombay |
| B. Andaman and Nicobar Islands | — Calcutta |
| C. Sikkim | — Guwahati |
| D. Puducherry | — Madras |

**215.** The procedure for the Amendment of the Constitution of India is given under
A. Article 315
B. Article 358
C. Article 360
D. Article 368

**216.** Which of the following Articles of the Constitution of India has provision for the President to proclaim emergency?
A. Article 352
B. Article 355
C. Article 356
D. Article 360

**217.** Which of the following offices is held during the pleasure of the President of India?
A. Vice-President
B. Chief Justice of India
C. Governor of a State
D. Chairman of the Union Public Service Commission

**218.** Article 370 of the constitution is applicable to the state of
A. Nagaland
B. Mizoram
C. Manipur
D. Jammu & Kashmir

**219.** In the parliamentary practices when did the "Zero-hour" interventions emerge in India?
A. 1952     B. 1962
C. 1972     D. 1982

**220.** "Vote on Account" means legislative vote
A. On the Appropriation Bill
B. On the Finance Bill

C. On the accounts and audit report submitted by the CAG

D. Authorising expenditure in respect of the demands for grants pending the passing of the Appropriation Bill

**221.** Which of these words is not in the preamble of the constitution of India?

A. Socialist

B. Sovereign

C. Secular

D. Public Welfare

**222.** Which of the following has **not** been mentioned in the Indian Constitution as a Right?

A. Political and Social Rights

B. Educational Rights

C. Economic Rights

D. Religious Rights

**223.** Which one of the following is **not** stated in the Preamble of the Indian Constitution?

A. Justice

B. Fraternity

C. Adult franchise

D. Equality of status

**224.** In framing the Constitution of India, from which country did we borrow the scheme of the federal set up?

A. U.S.A.     B. U.K.

C. Canada    D. Switzerland

**225.** Who among the following was **not** a member of the Constituent Assembly set up in July 1946?

A. Dr. Rajendra Prasad

B. K.M. Munshi

C. Mahatma Gandhi

D. Abul Kalam Azad

**226.** Which article of the Indian Constitution provides for the institution of Panchayati Raj?

A. Art. 36   B. Art. 39

C. Art. 40   D. Art. 48

**227.** Which of the following is a bulwark of personal freedom?

A. Mandamus

B. Habeas Corpus

C. Quo Warranto

D. Certiorari

**228.** Who is the highest civil servant of the Union Government?

A. Attorney-General

B. Cabinet Secretary

C. Home Secretary

D. Principal Secretary to the Prime Minister

**229.** Article 1 of the Constitution declares India as

A. Federal State

B. Quasi-Federal State

C. Unitary State

D. Union of States

**230.** Which functionary can be invited to give his opinion in the Parliament?

A. Attorney-General of India

B. Chief Justice of India

C. Chief Election Commissioner of India

D. Comptroller and Auditor-General of India

**231.** Which of the following countries has an Unwritten Constitution?

A. USA      B. UK

C. Pakistan  D. India

232. The Drafting Committee of the Constitution, including the chairman, comprised of
A. Seven members
B. Five members
C. Nine members
D. Three members

233. Which one of the following exercised the most profound influence on the Indian Constitution?
A. The Government of India Act 1935
B. The US Constitution
C. British Constitution
D. The UN Charter

234. Which one of the following features was borrowed by the Indian Constitution from the British Constiution?
A. Parliamentary system of government
B. Rule of Law
C. Law-making procedure
D. All the above

235. India borrowed the idea of a federal system with a strong centre from
A. USA        B. Canada
C. Australia  D. New Zealand

236. The emergency provisions of the constitution of India were greatly influenced by
A. The Government of India Act 1935
B. The Weimar Constitution of Germany
C. The Constitution of United States

D. The Constitution of Canada

237. India borrowed the idea of Directive Principles of State Policy from the Constitutions of
A. The Weimar Republic of Germany
B. The Republic of Ireland
C. The South Africa
D. None of the above

238. If the President wishes to tender his resignation before the expiry of his normal term, he has to address the same to
A. The Vice-President of India
B. The Speaker of Lok Sabha
C. The Chief Justice of India
D. The Election Commission

239. Who among the following got the Bharat Ratna Award before becoming the President of India?
A. Dr. Zakir Hussain
B. Dr. Rajendra Prasad
C. V.V. Giri
D. Dr. S. Radhakrishnan

240. The Council of Ministers is collectively responsible to
A. The President of India
B. The Parliament
C. The Prime Minister
D. The Rajya Sabha

241. The office of the Prime Minister of India
A. Has been created by the Constitution
B. Is extra-constitutional growth
C. Has been created by a Parliamentary Statute
D. Is the combination of all the above

**242.** The minimum age at which a person can be appointed Prime Minister of India?
A. 21 years  B. 25 years
C. 30 years  D. 35 years

**243.** The first Amendment of the constitution was made in the year:
A. 1950        B. 1949
C. 1954        D. 1958

**244.** Which of the following is the maximum time limit of 'Zero Hour' during the Parliament session in India?
A. 30 minutes
B. One hour
C. Two hours
D. None of the above

**245.** Who among the following summons the joint session of Lok Sabha and Rajya Sabha?
A. Speaker
B. Chairman of Rajya Sabha
C. President
D. Minister of Parliamentary Affairs

**246.** Which of the following is India's Contribution to parliamentary system of democracy?
A. Zero Hour
B. Cut Motion Resolution
C. Adjournment Motion
D. Guillotine

**247.** The total number of members in the Legislative Council of a State cannot exceed
A. one-fourth of the total number of members in the Legislative Assembly

B. one-third of the total number of members of the legislative Assembly
C. one-sixth of the total number of members of the Legislative Assembly
D. No such limit has been fixed

**248.** Sikkim was made an integral part of India under the
A. 42nd Amendment
B. 40th Amendment
C. 39th Amendment
D. 36th Amendment

**249.** The number of Anglo-Indians who can be nominated by the President to the Lok Sabha is
A. 2          B. 3
C. 4          D. 5

**250.** Money Bills can be introduced in the State Legislature with the prior consent of
A. the Speaker
B. the Chief Minister
C. the Governor
D. the President

## Economy

**251.** The apex bank for industrial credit in India is
A. RBI        B. NABARD
C. ICICI      D. IDBI

**252.** The prominent function of the Central Statistical Organisation is
A. To determine the money supply
B. To collect national income estimates
C. To collect employment details
D. To determine prices

**253.** Planning and control are related in such a way that
- A. Planning precedes control
- B. Control precedes planning
- C. Both are concurrent
- D. Both go hand in hand with each other in a cyclical manner

**254.** 'Gresham's Law' states that
- A. Good money drives away bad money out of circulation
- B. Bad money drives away good money out of circulation
- C. Good money promotes bad money in the system
- D. Bad money promotes good money in the system

**255.** National income refers to
- A. Money value of goods and services produced in a country during a year
- B. Money value of stocks and shares of a country during a year
- C. Money value of capital goods produced by a country during a year
- D. Money value of consumer goods produced by a country during a year

**256.** Which of the following taxes is/are lived by the Union and collected and appropriated by the States?
- A. Service tax
- B. Stamp duties
- C. Estate duty
- D. Passenger and goods tax

**257.** Which of the following is *not* shared by the Centre and the States?
- A. Income tax
- B. Excise duty
- C. Corporation duty
- D. Sales tax

**258.** Expenditure on which of the following is *not* considered as an investment in the theory of income determination?
- A. Factory construction
- B. A computer
- C. Increase in stocks of unsold goods
- D. Stocks or shares in a joint stock company

**259.** With what aspect of commerce are "Bull" and "Bear" associated?
- A. Banking
- B. E-Commerce
- C. International trade
- D. Stock market

**260.** FDI means—
- A. Foreign Direct Investment
- B. Full Dog Cost
- C. Full Direct Cost
- D. Finance Institute

**261.** If the tax rate increases with the higher level of income, it shall be called
- A. Proportional tax
- B. Progressive tax
- C. Lump sum tax
- D. Regressive tax

**262.** In India, one-rupee coins and notes and subsidiary coins are issued by
A. The Reserve Bank of India
B. The Central Government
C. The State Bank of India
D. The Unit Trust of India

**263.** Which is the highest body that approves Five-Year Plans in the country?
A. NITI Aayog
B. Union Cabinet
C. National Development Council
D. Parliament

**264.** Prime cost is equal to
A. Variable cost plus administrative cost
B. Variable cost plus fixed cost
C. Variable cost only
D. Fixed cost only

**265.** New capital issue is placed in
A. Secondary market
B. Grey market
C. Primary market
D. Black market

**266.** Bank deposits that can be withdrawn without notice are called
A. Account payee deposits
B. Fixed deposits
C. Variable deposits
D. Demand deposits

**267.** An expenditure that has been made and cannot be recovered is called
A. Variable cost
B. Opportunity cost
C. Sink cost
D. Operational cost

**268.** The practice of selling goods in a foreign country at a price below their domestic selling price is called
A. 'Diplomacy'
B. 'Discrimination'
C. 'Dumping'
D. 'Double pricing'

**269.** Who propounded the 'market law'?
A. Adam Smith
B. J.B. Say
C. T.R. Malthus
D. Dravid Ricardo

**270.** National income is based on the
A. total revenue of the state
B. production of goods and services
C. net profit earned and expenditure made by the state
D. the sum of all factors of incomes

**271.** 'Utility' in economics means the capacity to
A. provide comforts
B. earn an income
C. satisfy human wants
D. satisfy human motives

**272.** Labour welfare does not include
A. education facilities
B. health facilities
C. housing facilities
D. quick promotion in job

**273.** 'Sellersmarket' denotes a situation where
A. Commodities are available at competitive rates
B. Demand exceeds supply

C. Supply exceeds demand

D. Supply and demand are evenly balanced

**274.** "Legal Tender Money" refers to
A. Cheques
B. Drafts
C. Bills of exchange
D. Currency notes

**275.** The sum total of incomes received for the services of labour, land or capital in a country is called
A. Gross domestic product
B. National income
C. Gross domestic income
D. Gross national income

**276.** The measurement of poverty line is based on the criteria of
A. Their dwelling houses
B. The nature of employment
C. Coloric consumption
D. Level of education

**277.** Capital is that wealth
A. Which is used for the production of wealth
B. Which is kept in boxes and lockers
C. Which is buried in the land
D. Which is stored for consumption

**278.** The poverty line has been defined in the
A. Seventh Five–Year Plan
B. Sixth Five–Year Plan
C. Eight Five–Year Plan
D. Fifth Five–Year Plan

**279.** Perfect market means there are
A. Many sellers and many buyers
B. A few sellers and a few buyers
C. A few sellers and many buyers
D. A few buyers and many sellers

**280.** A hard currency is the one
A. Whose external value is increasing
B. Which can be acquired only with official permission
C. Which can be obtained only against sale of gold
D. Which is really accepted in international transactions

**281.** Which of the following is not a Central Government Tax?
A. Income Tax
B. Customs
C. Land Revenue
D. Corporation Tax

**282.** Who is called the father of White Revolution?
A. Dr. Kurien Verghese
B. Nanjunda Swamy
C. M.S. Swaminathan
D. U.R. Rao

**283.** The major source of revenue in India is through
A. Direct Taxes
B. Indirect Taxes
C. Internal Borrowings
D. External Borrowings

**284.** The Reserve Bank of India was established in
A. 1927     B. 1935
C. 1947     D. 1949

**285.** Finance Commission is appointed by
A. Prime Minister
B. President of India
C. Ministry of Finance
D. None of these

**286.** Which of the following groups suffer the most from inflation?
A. Debtors
B. Creditors
C. Business class
D. Holders of real assets

**287.** Which one of the following is not an example of indirect tax?
A. Sales tax
B. Excise duty
C. Customs duty
D. Expenditure tax

**288.** The major aim of devaluation is to
A. Encourage imports
B. Encourage exports
C. Encourage both exports and imports
D. Discourage both exports and imports

**289.** Which of the following is a cash crop?
A. Wheat
B. Rice
C. Sugarcane
D. Maize

**290.** NAFED is connected with
A. Animal husbandry
B. Conservation of fuels
C. Agricultural marketing
D. Agricultural implements

**291.** Which Commission replaced Planning Commission in 2015?
A. NIYAM Aayog
B. NAGRIK Aayog
C. NITI Aayog
D. None of these

**292.** The one-rupee notes bear the signatures of the
A. Governor, Reserve Bank of India
B. Secretary, Ministry of Finance
C. Deputy Governor, Reserve Bank of India
D. Joint Secretary, Ministry of Finance

**293.** Whose approval is necessary before the Five-Year Plan can start?
A. The Finance Minister
B. National Development Council
C. The Prime Minister
D. Parliament

**294.** NABARD stands for
A. National Bank of Agriculture and Regional Development
B. National Bank for Agriculture and Rural Development
C. National Bureau of Aeronautical Research and Development
D. None of these

**295.** 'Bottle neck inflation' means
A. No rise in prices despite increase in aggregate demand
B. Rise in prices without increase in the aggregate demand

C. Decline in prices due to increase in aggregate demand
D. None of these

**296.** The main cause of International Trade is
A. Equal cost difference
B. Absolute cost difference
C. Comparative cost difference
D. Equal and comparative cost difference

**297.** Which one of the following taxes is not shared by the Central Government with the States?
A. Union excise duties
B. Customs duty
C. Income tax
D. Estate duty

**298.** A dualistic economy is one in which
A. both rich and poor people co-exist side by side
B. it has both foreign trade and internal trade
C. industry and agriculture exist side by side
D. modern sector and traditional sector exist side by side

**299.** Whose signatures are found on the 10 rupee note in India?
A. Prime Minister of India
B. President of India
C. Finance Minister of India
D. Governor, Reserve Bank of India

**300.** "Green Revolution" began in India during the year
A. 1967-68  B. 1966-67
C. 1968-69  D. 1969-70

## General Science

**301.** Deep blue colour is imparted to glass by the presence of
A. Cobalt Oxide
B. Cupric Oxide
C. Ferrous Oxide
D. Nickel Oxide

**302.** Which of the following fibres is least prone to fire?
A. Nylon     B. Cotton
C. Rayon     D. Terry Cott

**303.** Which of the following is used as a filler in rubber tyres?
A. Carbon black
B. Coal
C. Coke
D. Graphite

**304.** Which of the following alloys is used for making magnets?
A. Duralumin
B. Stainless Steel
C. Alnico
D. Magnalium

**305.** Which of the following elements is obtained from sea weeds?
A. Argon
B. Sulphur
C. Vanadium
D. Iodine

**306.** Where are Mesons found?
A. Cosmic rays
B. X-rays
C. $\gamma$-rays
D. Laser beams

**307.** Milk tastes sour when kept in the open for sometime due to the formation of
A. Lactic acid
B. Citric acid
C. Acetic acid
D. Carbonic acid

**308.** Polythene is industrially prepared by the polymerisation of
A. Methane
B. Styrene
C. Acetylene
D. Ethylene

**309.** Which of the following chemicals responsible for the depletion of ozone layer in the atmosphere?
A. Nitrous oxide
B. Carbon dioxide
C. Chlorofluorocarbons
D. Sulphur dioxide

**310.** Plants die in winter by frost because
A. There is no transpiration
B. No photosynthesis takes place at such low temperatures
C. Respiration ceases at such low temperatures
D. Of desiccation and mechanical damage to tissues

**311.** Which of the following is *not* a constituent of chlorophyll?
A. Hydrogen
B. Magnesium
C. Carbon
D. Calcium

**312.** Which is the chief nitrogenous waste in humans?
A. Ammonia
B. Urea
C. Uric acid
D. Ammonium nitrate

**313.** Which is the largest living bird?
A. Peacock   B. Ostrich
C. Dodo      D. Turkey

**314.** Hormones are normally absent in
A. Rat       B. Monkey
C. Bacteria  D. Cat

**315.** Dengue fever is caused by
A. Fungi     B. Bacteria
C. Protozoa  D. Virus

**316.** Which of the following is considered to be good cholesterol?
A. VLDL      B. LDL
C. HDL       D. Triglycerides

**317.** "Thalassaemia" is a hereditary disease affecting
A. Blood     B. Kidney
C. Lungs     D. Heart

**318.** Which of the following is a proper food chain showing a producer, a herbivore and the carnivore?
A. Grass-Insect-Elephant
B. Plants-Rabbit-Tiger
C. Fish-Insect-Whale
D. Tiger-Rabbit-Owl

**319.** Aspirin is
A. Methoxy Benzoic acid
B. Methyl Salicylate
C. Acetyl Salicylic acid
D. Phenyl Salicylate

**320.** The medical instrument sphygmomanometer is used to examine
A. hormonal activity
B. brain tumor
C. the functions of intestine
D. blood pressure

**321.** Onion is a modified form of
A. stem      B. root
C. leaves    D. fruit

**322.** Weight of the body
- A. remains the same everywhere on the earth's surface
- B. is maximum at the poles
- C. is maximum at the equator
- D. is more on mountains than plains

**323.** Most of the nutrients are absorbed into blood through
- A. large intestine
- B. mouth
- C. small intestine
- D. abdomen

**324.** The path of Halley's comet in its orbit around the Sun is
- A. circular
- B. elliptical
- C. parabolic
- D. hyperbolic

**325.** Atoms of the same element having the same atomic number but different atomic weights are called
- A. Isotopes
- B. Polymers
- C. Isomers
- D. Isobars

**326.** The chief constituent of gobar gas is
- A. Nitrogen
- B. Ethane
- C. Hydrogen
- D. Methane

**327.** Law of heredity was put forward by
- A. Mendel
- B. Mendeleev
- C. Pavlov
- D. Koch

**328.** A device used for converting a.c. into d.c. is called
- A. Transformer
- B. Rectifier
- C. Induction oil
- D. Dynamo

**329.** An antibiotic is
- A. A chemical synthesised by a human cell against a micro-organism
- B. A chemical synthesised by a micro-organism against another micro-organism
- C. A substance produced by blood cells against bacteria
- D. A substance produced by blood cells against infection

**330.** Which one of the following can be synthesized by Liver?
- A. Vitamin-A
- B. Vitamin-E
- C. Vitamin-D
- D. Vitamin-K

**331.** Fluid part of blood devoid of corpuscles is called
- A. Tissue fluid
- B. Plasma
- C. Serum
- D. Lymph

**332.** Heart murmur indicates a
- A. Defective valve
- B. Poor oxygenation
- C. Dislocation of the heart
- D. Improper development of muscles

**333.** The language used in writing the scientific name of animals is
- A. French
- B. Latin
- C. German
- D. Dutch

**334.** Energy of Ultra-violet rays is greater than
- A. Infra-red rays

B. Gamma rays
C. X-rays
D. Cosmic rays

**335.** By-product obtained by soap-industry is
A. Caustic soda
B. Glycerol
C. Naphthalene
D. Caustic potash

**336.** Ripe grapes contain
A. Fructose
B. Sucrose
C. Galactose
D. Glucose

**337.** Polythene is polymer of
A. Ethylene
B. Propylene
C. Acetylene
D. Aniline

**338.** Which one of the following is pure water?
A. Rain water
B. Filter water
C. Tubewell water
D. Distilled water

**339.** Which silver salt is used for making film for photography?
A. Silver bromide
B. Silver chloride
C. Silver sulphate
D. Silver nitrate

**340.** To an astronaut sky appears
A. White
B. Rich blue
C. Light blue
D. Dark

**341.** The instrument used to measure the speed of the wind is
A. Altimeter

B. Anemometer
C. Chronometer
D. Dosimeter

**342.** Who defined the law of gravitation?
A. Newton    B. Archimedes
C. Galileo    D. Faraday

**343.** The metal used to make lightning conductors is
A. Iron        B. Aluminium
C. Copper    D. Zinc

**344.** 'IC' in computers stands for
A. Integrated Charge
B. Integrated Current
C. Integrated Circuits
D. Internal Circuits

**345.** A hydrogen balloon floats up because of
A. Air pressure decreases with decrease in height
B. Air pressure decreases with decrease in weight
C. Weight of the balloon is less than the weight of air displaced by it
D. The pressure inside the balloon is more than the pressure outside it

**346.** In a rechargeable cell what kind of energy is stored within the cell?
A. Electrical energy
B. Potential energy
C. Chemical energy
D. Kinetic energy

**347.** M.R.I. stands for
A. Metered Resonance imaging
B. Magnetic Resonance Imaging

C. Magnetic Reaction Imaging
D. Metered Reaction Imaging

**348.** The American space shuttle which exploded in space killing astronaut Kalpana Chawla, was known as
A. Challenger
B. Columbia
C. Discovery
D. Columbus

**349.** For determination of the age of which among the following is carbon dating method used?
A. Fossils
B. Rocks
C. Trees
D. A and B

**350.** Which is the hottest planet in the Solar System?
A. Jupiter      B. Saturn
C. Venus      D. Uranus

## State

**351.** Telangana became India's 29th State in
A. 2014      B. 2013
C. 2012      D. 2011

**352.** In which State would you find Jim Corbett National Park?
A. Assam
B. Uttar Pradesh
C. Maharashtra
D. Uttarakhand

**353.** Jharia mines are situated in which of the following States?
A. Jharkhand
B. West Bengal
C. Bihar
D. Odisha

**354.** 'Sardar Sarovar' project is in which of the following States?
A. Rajasthan
B. Madhya Pradesh
C. Uttar Pradesh
D. Gujarat

**355.** The new name of Rajasthan canal is
A. Gandhi canal
B. Indira Gandhi canal
C. Jawahar canal
D. Subhash canal

**356.** Which of the following lakes in Rajasthan is saline?
A. Ana Sagar
B. Pichola
C. Sambhar
D. Jaisamand

**357.** In which state is the district of Udham Singh Nagar situated?
A. Punjab
B. Uttarakhand
C. Uttar Pradesh
D. Rajasthan

**358.** Which amongst the following States has the highest population density as per census 2011?
A. Kerala
B. Madhya Pradesh
C. Uttar Pradesh
D. Bihar

**359.** Which one among the following states is smallest in area?
A. Andhra Pradesh
B. Gujarat
C. Karnataka
D. Tamil Nadu

**360.** In which State is Nalsarovar Bird Sanctuary located?

A. Maharashtra
B. Odisha
C. Gujarat
D. Rajasthan

**361.** Which of the following is the 28th State of India?
A. Jharkhand
B. Uttarakhand
C. Chhattisgarh
D. Gorkhaland

**362.** In which State is Ghana Bird Sanctuary located?
A. U.P.
B. M.P.
C. Assam
D. Rajasthan

**363.** Which of the following States does not have border with China?
A. Uttarakhand
B. U.P.
C. H.P.
D. Sikkim

**364.** What is the capital of the State of Chhattisgarh?
A. Raipur
B. Patna
C. Jamshedpur
D. Bokaro

**365.** With which State would you associate the festival of Dev Devali?
A. Bihar
B. West Bengal
C. Uttar Pradesh
D. Maharashtra

**366.** Areawise, which is the smallest State in India?
A. Goa  B. Sikkm
C. Manipur  D. Tripura

**367.** The capital of Lakshadweep is
A. Aizwal  B. Port Blair
C. Kavaratti  D. Agartala

**368.** The famous Kanha Wildlife Sanctuary is located in the State of:
A. Assam
B. Bihar
C. Madhya Pradesh
D. Karnataka

**369.** Which one of the following State is most populous?
A. Odisha
B. Uttar pradesh
C. Maharashtra
D. Bihar

**370.** Bhangra is a folk dance of
A. Punjab
B. Madhya Pradesh
C. Odisha
D. Assam

**371.** Kaziranga Animals Sanctuary is situated in the State of
A. Assam
B. Uttar Pradesh
C. Madhya Pradesh
D. Rajasthan

**372.** Konark temple is situated in the State of
A. Odisha
B. Kerala
C. Madhya Pradesh
D. Andhra Pradesh

**373.** The State which produces maximum Uranium in India is
A. Rajasthan
B. Kerala
C. Jharkhand
D. West Bengal

**374.** Lumbini, the birth place of Gautam Buddha is in
A. Bihar    B. Sikkim
C. Nepal    D. Uttar Pradesh

**375.** Which of the following is the least densely populated State?
A. Sikkim
B. Meghalaya
C. Mizoram
D. Arunachal Pradesh

**376.** "Dudhawa National Park" is situated in
A. Madhya Pradesh
B. Bihar
C. Uttar Pradesh
D. Karnataka

**377.** Sandal wood is found in
A. Tamil Nadu
B. Himachal Pradesh
C. Karnataka
D. Maharashtra

**378.** The chief producer of 'Jute' in India is
A. West Bengal
B. Karnataka
C. Tamil Nadu
D. Asom

**379.** The Ghat and Bhor Ghat are the important passes in
A. Kerala
B. Maharashtra
C. Gujarat
D. Rajasthan

**380.** The famous monolithic statue of Jain Saint Bahubali is situated in the state of
A. Andhra Pradesh
B. Bihar
C. Karnataka
D. Tamil Nadu

**381.** Which state of India is the largest exporter of marine products?
A. Andhra Pradesh
B. Gujarat
C. Kerala
D. Maharashtra

**382.** After Uttar Pradesh, which State leads in the production of sugarcane?
A. Bihar
B. Andhra Pradesh
C. Maharashtra
D. Tamil Nadu

**383.** Goa was liberated from the Portuguese in
A. 1964    B. 1961
C. 1963    D. 1962

**384.** The State which accounts for more than 90 per cent of total rubber production in India is
A. Karnataka
B. Kerala
C. Tamil Nadu
D. Andhra Pradesh

**385.** Which one of the following States has no common border with UP?
A. Punjab
B. Haryana
C. Madhya Pradesh
D. Uttarakhand

**386.** Name the State in which the Hirakud Dam is located?
A. Orissa    B. Karnataka
C. U.P.    D. Gujarat

**387.** Panna in Madhya Pradesh is associated with
A. Manganese
B. Mica
C. Copper
D. Diamond

**388.** The holy city Hardwar is in which of the State?
- A. Uttar Pradesh
- B. Haryana
- C. Bihar
- D. Uttarakhand

**389.** According to the census of 2011 the only State in India that shows excess of females over males is
- A. Uttar Pradesh
- B. Kerala
- C. Maharashtra
- D. Jammu and Kashmir

**390.** Which States share the Tungabhadra multipurpose project?
- A. Karnataka and Madhya Pradesh
- B. Orissa and Madhya Pradesh
- C. Andhra Pradesh and Karnataka
- D. Tamil Nadu and Andhra Pradesh

## Organisations

**391.** The headquarter of World Trade Organisation (WTO) is located at
- A. Rome
- B. New York
- C. Geneva
- D. Washington DC

**392.** Which of the following countries is not a member of SAARC?
- A. Nepal
- B. China
- C. Pakistan
- D. India

**393.** Where is SAARC secretariat situated?
- A. Islamabad
- B. Colombo
- C. New Delhi
- D. Kathmandu

**394.** What is the activity of the INTERPOL?
- A. Central record keeping agency of the international crimes
- B. Investigative agency of the UN
- C. An organisation to coordinate the police activities of the participating nations
- D. A terrorist outfit

**395.** The six official languages of the UN are Russian, Chinese, English, French, Spanish and
- A. Hindi     B. Urdu
- C. Arabic     D. Japanese

**396.** What does SAPTA stands for?
- A. South Asian Preferential Trade Agreement
- B. South Asian Post Trade Agreement
- C. SAARC Preferential Trade Agreement
- D. SAARC Prevention Trade Agreement

**397.** The Association of South East Asian Nations (ASEAN) has its headquarters at
- A. Manila
- B. Jakarta
- C. Kuala Lumpur
- D. Bangkok

**398.** The normal term of office of UN Secretary General is
- A. 3 years
- B. 4 years
- C. 5 years
- D. 6 years

**399.** Which of the following countries is not a member of the G-7 Group?
- A. France
- B. Italy
- C. Spain
- D. Germany

**400.** Which of the following is NOT a permanent member of the UN Security Council?
- A. Germany
- B. France
- C. Great Britain
- D. China

**401.** The first Secretary General of the United Nations was:
- A. Mrs. Vijay Lakshmi Pandit
- B. Trygve Lie
- C. Dag Hammarskjoeld
- D. U. Thant

**402.** Who was the first Indian to be the President of U.N. General Assembly?
- A. Natwar Singh
- B. V.K. Krishna Menon
- C. Smt. Vijay Lakshmi Pandit
- D. Romesh Bhandari

**403.** Where is the headquarters of the International Court of Justice?
- A. The Hague (Netherlands)
- B. Paris (France)
- C. Rome (Italy)
- D. Washington (U.S.A)

**404.** How many Judges are there in the International Court of Justice?
- A. 9
- B. 10
- C. 11
- D. 15

**405.** When was the United Nations Organisation founded?
- A. 20th October, 1945
- B. 11th, November, 1944
- C. 24th October, 1945
- D. 26th June, 1945

**406.** The headquarters of the Organisation of Petroleum Exporting Countries is at
- A. Teheran
- B. Vienna
- C. Abu Dhabi
- D. Doha

**407.** How many members does the Security Council of UN have?
- A. Ten
- B. Fifteen
- C. Sixteen
- D. Twenty

**408.** Which country is not a member of ASEAN?
- A. Indonesia
- B. Cambodia
- C. Singapore
- D. Philippines

**409.** Where is the Head Quarter of Asian Development Bank?
- A. Washington
- B. Manila
- C. Paris
- D. Canberra

**410.** The headquarters of the U.N.O. is located in
- A. Washington
- B. New York
- C. Philadelphia
- D. Chicago

## Awards

**411.** 'Pulitzer' prizes are awarded to Americans for excellence in
A. Films
B. Social work
C. Journalism
D. Medicine

**412.** When was the Nobel Prize started?
A. 1901     B. 1905
C. 1934     D. 1900

**413.** 'Bharat Ratna' Award was given for the first time in
A. 1956     B. 1957
C. 1952     D. 1954

**414.** Saraswati Samman is awarded by
A. K.K. Birla Foundation
B. Government of India
C. Bharatiya Jnanpith
D. Sahitya Academy

**415.** Who was the first Asian to win a Nobel Prize?
A. Hideki Yuka
B. Har Gobind Khurana
C. C.V. Raman
D. Rabindranath Tagore

**416.** The highest Gallantry Award given in India is
A. Ashok Chakra
B. Mahavir Chakra
C. Param Vir Chakra
D. None of these

**417.** On which day every year National Awards for Teachers are announced?
A. September 5
B. November 14
C. November 19
D. August 15

**418.** Dronacharya Awards are given
A. to outstanding athletes
B. to outstanding coaches
C. for best performance in archery
D. for invention in science

**419.** Dr. C.V. Raman was awarded Nobel Prize in
A. Chemistry
B. Literature
C. Physics
D. Medicine

**420.** The first recipient of Rajiv Gandhi Khel Ratna Award is
A. Leander Paes
B. Viswanathan Anand
C. Kapil Dev
D. Limba Ram

**421.** The highest civilian award of India is
A. Bharat Ratna
B. Padam Vibhushan
C. Padam Bhushan
D. Padma Shri

**422.** Which of the following Indians awarded 'Legion D Award', the highest civilian award of France?
A. Satyajit Ray
B. Pandit Ravi Shankar
C. Lok Nayak Jayaprakash
D. J.L. Nehru

**423.** Dhanvantari Awards are given for the best performance in the field of
A. Medical Sciences
B. Nuclear Sciences
C. Economics
D. Space Research

**424.** Nobel Prizes are not given for which of the following fields?
A. Music    B. Chemistry
C. Peace    D. Physics

**425.** Dadasaheb Phalke Award is given for:
A. drama    B. social welfare
C. films    D. literature

**426.** In which year Nehru Award for International Understanding was instituted?
A. 1969    B. 1984
C. 1964    D. 1966

**427.** Who among the following has not been awarded the Bharat Ratna?
A. Indira Gandhi
B. Mahatma Gandhi
C. Sardar Patel
D. Radhakrishnan

**428.** Which one of the following is the second highest Civilian award in India?
A. Padma Shri
B. Bharat Ratna
C. Padma Bhushan
D. Padma Vibhushan

**429.** 'Victory Medal' is awarded in:
A. the USA
B. the UK
C. Russia
D. France

**430.** National film Awards were instituted in the year
A. 1954    B. 1950
C. 1961    D. 1969

**431.** In which year was the Nobel Prize for Economics announced for the first time?
A. 1969    B. 1901
C. 1919    D. 1970

**432.** Borlaug Award was instituted for recognising outstanding contribution in the field of
A. agriculture
B. ecology
C. journalism
D. medicine

**433.** Jesse Owens Global Award is given in the field of
A. Literature
B. Journalism
C. Science
D. Sports

**434.** Noble Alfred Bernhard after whom Nobel Prizes are given was
A. Engineer
B. Chemist
C. Both (A) and (B)
D. Doctor

**435.** Who was the first winner of Nehru Award for International Understanding?
A. Martin Luther King
B. Mother Teresa
C. U. Thant
D. Dr. Jonas Salk

## Sports

**436.** In which International Championship, 'Thomas Cup' is given
A. Football
B. Cricket
C. Badminton
D. Tennis

**437.** 'Gambit' is related to which among the followings sports?
A. Carrom   B. Bridge
C. Chess   D. Billiards

**438.** The term 'Grandmaster' is used in which of these games?
A. Chess   B. Judo
C. Bridge   D. Karate

**439.** In the game of Volleyball, the number of players on each side is
A. Eight   B. Five
C. Seven   D. Six

**440.** The term ''Cue'' is associated with which game?
A. Hockey   B. Football
C. Billiards D. Cricket

**441.** With which game is Geet Sethi Associated?
A. Basketball
B. Snooker
C. Chess
D. Tennis

**442.** How many players are there in each side in the game of Netball?
A. 7   B. 6
C. 9   D. 11

**443.** 'Uber Cup' is associated with which of the following?
A. Tennis   B. Badminton
C. Chess   D. Cricket

**444.** Where is the annual Australian Open Tennis tournament held?
A. Sydney   B. Melbourne
C. Canberra D. Brisbane

**445.** The Olympic Motto is
A. Health is wealth
B. Promote Universal brotherhood
C. Faster, higher, stronger
D. Excellence is the goal

**446.** The term 'Tee' is associated with which of the following sports?
A. Polo   B. Table Tennis
C. Golf   D. Judo

**447.** Which Indian sportsman is known as Hockey Wizard throughout the world?
A. A.B. Subbiah
B. Jude Felix
C. Dhyan Chand
D. Ajitpal Singh

**448.** When did India become World Cricket champion?
A. 1980   B. 1982
C. 1983   D. 1986

**449.** ''Googly'' is associated with:
A. Cricket   B. Table-Tennis
C. Hockey   D. Billiards

**450.** With which game are the terms bull's eye, muzzle and plug associated?
A. Shooting B. Solitaire
C. Billiards D. Rowing

**451.** Who is the first Indian to take a hat trick in an international test?
A. Kapil Dev
B. Jasu Patel
C. Harbhajan Singh
D. B.S. Chandrashekhar

**452.** Who was declared by wisden as '' The Best Indian Bowler of the Century'' (20th Century)?
A. Kapil Dev
B. B.S. Chandrashekhar

C. B.S. Bedi
D. Subhash V. Gupte

**453.** '' Jab'' and ''Parry'' are terms used in which sport?
A. Wrestling
B. Boxing
C. Billiards
D. Weightlifting

**454.** India's national game is
A. Football   B. Cricket
C. Tennis   D. Hockey

**455.** Davis Cup is associated with the sport of
A. Tennis   B. Football
C. Cricket   D. Hockey

**456.** The term 'breast stroke' is associated with:
A. Skating
B. Croquet
C. Swimming
D. Rifle Shooting

**457.** What is the National Game of the USA?
A. Cricket   B. Baseball
C. Soccer   D. Billiards

**458.** Roger Federer is associated with
A. Hockey   B. Lawn Tennis
C. Golf   D. Badminton

**459.** 'Merdeka Cup' is associated with
A. Golf   B. Football
C. Squash   D. Hockey

**460.** Who among the following has become the first woman in the world to swim across seven seas?
A. Shikha Tandon
B. Bula Chowdhury
C. Amanda Beard
D. Arti Saha

---

| **Books** |

**461.** The famous book 'Geet Govind' is written by
A. Banabhatt
B. Jaydev
C. Mirabai
D. Kalidas

**462.** 'Ain-e-Akbari' was written by
A. Farista   B. Ibn Batuta
C. Abul Fazal   D. Birbal

**463.** Who wrote '' Vande Mataram''?
A. Rabindra Nath Tagore
B. Sumitra Nandan Pant
C. Bankim Chandra Chatterji
D. Vivekanand

**464.** Who among the following is the author of 'Das Kapital'?
A. Lenin
B. J.M. Keynes
C. Robert Owen
D. Karl Marx

**465.** 'Panchatantra' was written by
A. Jai Dev
B. Ved Vyas
C. Bhavbhuti
D. Vishnu Sharma

**466.** Patanjali is well known for the compilation of
A. Yoga Sutra
B. Panchatantra
C. Brahma Sutra
D. Ayurveda

**467.** Who among the following has written the book, 'The Wings of Fire: An Autobiography'?
A. K.R. Narayan
B. Sobha De

C. A.B. Vajpayee
D. A.P.J. Abdul Kalam

**468.** Who compiled the 'Adi Granth'?
A. Guru Nanak
B. Guru Ramdas
C. Guru Arjun
D. Guru Gobind Singh

**469.** The famous book 'Anandmath' was authored by
A. Rabindranath Tagore
B. Bankim Chandra Chattopadhyaya
C. Sarojini Naidu
D. Sri Aurobindo

**470.** Which one of the following pairs is *not* correctly matched?
A. Mudrarakshasa : Visakhadatta
B. Rajtarangini : Kalhana
C. Kadambari : Bana Bhatta
D. Ratnavali : Bilhana

**471.** 'Harry Potter and the Deathly Hallows' is written by
A. Robert Ludlum
B. J.K. Rowling
C. Sidney Sheldon
D. Spencer Johnson

**472.** 'Arthashastra' was written by
A. Kalidas
B. Kautilya
C. R.K. Narayan
D. Bana Bhatta

**473.** Name the author of book ''The Post Office (Dak Ghar)''?
A. R.K. Narayan
B. Rabindra Nath Tagore
C. Prem Chand
D. Krishan Chandra

**474.** Who wrote the nursery rhyme, ''Twinkle, twinkle, little star''?
A. Lovelace
B. Ann Taylor
C. William Ross Wallace
D. William Shakespeare

**475.** Ashtadhyayi is a book written by
A. Panini
B. Patanjali
C. Vishnu Sharma
D. None of these

**476.** 'Prithviraj Raso' was written by:
A. Kalhan
B. Chand Bardai
C. Bhavbhuti
D. Bhule Shah

**477.** The book 'Prison Diary' was written by
A. Mahatma Gandhi
B. V.D. Savarkar
C. Jai Prakash Narayan
D. Morarji Desai

**478.** ''Runs and Ruins'' is written by
A. Nawab Pataudi
B. Vivian Richards
C. Clive Lloyd
D. Sunil Gavaskar

**479.** Who is the author of the book, 'The God of small Things'?
A. Ali Sardar Jafri
B. Vikram Chandra
C. Padma Seth
D. Arundhati Roy

**480.** India-2020 is a book written by
A. Montek Singh Ahluwalia
B. A.P.J. Abdul Kalam
C. G. Ganeshan
D. Indra Kumar Gujral

## Computer

**481.** Which one of the following has earned the title "Father of Modern Computer"?
A. Blaise Pascal
B. Charles Babbage
C. Herman Hollerith
D. Jack Kilby

**482.** Which one of the following is the first generation computer?
A. UNIVAC-1
B. EDVAG
C. IBM 1201
D. IBM 1104

**483.** Which one of the following is a hardware?
A. Integrated circuit
B. Compiler
C. DOS
D. FORTRAN

**484.** What is the measuring unit of memory?
A. Watt
B. Words
C. Bit
D. None of these

**485.** How many bits are there in one byte?
A. 1
B. 2
C. 8
D. 1024

**486.** Digital computers deal with
A. discrete quantities
B. physical quantities
C. both discrete and physical quantities
D. neither discrete nor physical quantities

**487.** What is nibble?
A. A group of 2 bits
B. A group of 4 bits
C. A group of 8 bits
D. A group of 12 bits

**488.** Which one of the following is not a package?
A. BASIC
B. dBase
C. Pagemaker
D. Wordstar

**489.** Who invented the punched card?
A. Jack Kilby
B. John Napier
C. Gottfried Leibnitz
D. None of these

**490.** Which of the following does not represent an I/O device?
A. Speaker which beeps
B. Plotter
C. Joystick
D. ALU

**491.** A set of instructions is called a
A. compiler
B. program
C. assembler
D. information

**492.** Data is a collection of
A. raw material
B. number of alphabets
C. facts and entities relevant to user
D. input material for a computer

**493.** Which one of the following is part of the CPU?
A. Memory
B. Compiler
C. Control unit
D. Joystick

**494.** Which one of the following is not a system software?
A. Operating system
B. Compiler

C. Assembler
D. Software for railway reservation

**495.** What are the main limitations of computers?
A. Lack of decision-making power
B. Zero IQ
C. Lack in innovations
D. All the above

**496.** What do you understand by IPO cycle?
A. Information and Programming Operations cycle
B. Innovating and Programming Operations cycle
C. Input-Program-Output cycle
D. None of these

**497.** Calculations are made in computer with the help of its
A. Memory
B. ALU
C. CU
D. Input device

**498.** Results are obtained from computer through its
A. input unit
B. output unit
C. CPU
D. memory

**499.** Who, among the following invented the method of logarithm?
A. John Napier
B. Blaise Pascal
C. Joseph Jacquard
D. Charles Babbage

**500.** The modern age of data processing began with the completion of the computer

A. Analytical Engine
B. Napier's 'Logs' and 'Bones'
C. ENIAC
D. Leibnitz's Calculator

## Miscellaneous

**501.** Who is called the First Citizen of India?
A. President of India
B. Prime Minister of India
C. Mahatma Gandhi
D. Dr. B.R. Ambedkar

**502.** Panini was a famous scholar of
A. Language and grammar
B. Ayurveda
C. Astronomy
D. Biology

**503.** Which of the following is not a mineral?
A. Slate
B. Limestone
C. Coal
D. Calcite

**504.** The state of rising prices due to an enhancement in the quantity of money in circulation, is termed as
A. Inflation
B. Deflation
C. Demonetisation
D. Devaluation

**505.** Name the minerals that are essential for bone and teeth formation in human
A. Calcium and Phosphorus
B. Magnesium and Potassium
C. Sodium and Iron
D. Iodine and Sulphur

**506.** Ripe mangoes contain
A. Vitamin A
B. Vitamin B
C. Vitamin C
D. Vitamin E

**507.** In which one of the following places, the boiling point of water is the highest?
A. Dead Sea
B. Mt. Everest
C. Nile Delta
D. Sunderbans Delta

**508.** The primary colours used in a colour TV are
A. Green, Yellow, Violet
B. Violet, Red, Orange
C. Blue, Green, Red
D. Blue, Geen, Violet

**509.** Which one of the following is not a Fundamental Right guaranteed by the Indian Constitution?
A. Freedom to manage religious affairs
B. Free and compulsory education up to primary stage
C. Prohibition of employment of children in factories
D. Freedom to propagate religion

**510.** The chief merit of a federal government is that it
A. Ensures a strong government at the centre
B. Integrates national unity with regional autonomy
C. Keeps a check on the multiparty system
D. Is very less expensive

**511.** The first Assamese to become the President of India was
A. Saiyeda Anowara Taimur
B. Gopinath Bordoloi
C. Fakhruddin Ali Ahmed
D. Syed Abdul Malik

**512.** Match List I with List II and select the correct answer using the codes given below the lists:

| | List-I | List-II |
|---|---|---|
| (a) | Amjad Ali Khan | 1. Flute |
| (b) | Bismillah Khan | 2. Sarod |
| (c) | Hari Prasad Chaurasia | 3. Tabla |
| (d) | Alla Rakha | 4. Shehnai |

**Codes:**

| | (a) | (b) | (c) | (d) |
|---|---|---|---|---|
| A. | 2 | 1 | 3 | 4 |
| B. | 4 | 2 | 1 | 3 |
| C. | 2 | 4 | 1 | 3 |
| D. | 1 | 2 | 3 | 4 |

**513.** A dentist's mirror is a
A. Cylindrical mirror
B. Plane mirror
C. Convex mirror
D. Concave mirror

**514.** Which of the following is the largest producer of raw silk?
A. Asom
B. Karnataka
C. Andhra Pradesh
D. Jammu and Kashmir

**515.** The Gandhara School of Sculpture was a blend of
A. Indian and Greek styles
B. Indian and Persian styles
C. Purely Indian in origin
D. Indian and South East Asian style

516. Which one of the following languages is used in Tripura?
A. Hindi    B. Mizo
C. Khasi    D. Bengali

517. How many schedules are there in the Constitution of India?
A. Eight    B. Ten
C. Twelve   D. Fourteen

518. The term 'cloning' is related with
A. Environment
B. Genetics
C. Space technology
D. Trade

519. The planet nearest to the Earth is
A. Jupiter    B. Venus
C. Mercury    D. Mars

520. Hard water can be used in
A. Boilers
B. Textile industry
C. Paper industry
D. Drinking

521. Ras Leela, Yaosang, Lai Haraoba are the festivals of
A. Assemese people
B. Karbi people
C. Manipuri people
D. Bodo people

522. The Tigris river flows mainly through
A. Turkey    B. Syria
C. Iraq      D. Iran

523. "India is a secular State". It means that the Indian State
A. Favours irreligious citizens
B. Favours the religions of the majority community
C. Favours the religions of the minority community
D. Favours no particular religion

524. The second largest linguistic unit in India is
A. Tamil    B. Hindi
C. English  D. Telugu

525. The oldest inhabitants of India are considered to be
A. Mongoloids
B. Negritos
C. Indo-Aryan
D. Mediterranean

526. The International Date Line passes through
A. Malacca Strait
B. Gibraltar Strait
C. Bering Strait
D. Florida Strait

527. The last three digits of a PIN code represent
A. Zone
B. Subzone
C. Sorting District
D. Mailing route

528. Which state has the largest number of sugar mills?
A. Punjab
B. Haryana
C. Tamil Nadu
D. Uttar Pradesh

529. The first oil well in India was dug at
A. Bombay High
B. Moran
C. Digboi
D. Naharkatiya

**530.** Which of the following is *not* a rabi crop?
A. Wheat  B. Maize
C. Mustard  D. Gram

**531.** The state with the largest area under waste land is
A. Gujarat
B. Madhya Pradesh
C. Jammu and Kashmir
D. Rajasthan

**532.** Mixed farming involves
A. Growing more than one crop on a farm
B. Growing specialised crops
C. Growing crops and keeping livestock
D. Intensive and extensive agriculture

**533.** The country with the highest population density is
A. China  B. Bangladesh
C. India  D. France

**534.** When the first metal came into being, it was used for
A. Pot making
B. House-building
C. Clearing jungles
D. Making wheels

**535.** To whom does Vasudeva-Krishna address all his teachings in the Bhagvad Gita?
A. Arjuna
B. Duryodhana
C. Yudhishthira
D. The common people

**536.** Who raised the simple slogan 'Do or Die' for the Quit India Movement?
A. Mahatma Gandhi
B. Subhash Chandra Bose
C. Jawahar Lal Nehru
D. J.B. Kripalani

**537.** The salary and perquisities of the Prime Minister of India are decided by the
A. Constitution
B. Cabinet
C. Parliament
D. President

**538.** At what age can one exercise the right to vote in the general elections?
A. 18 years  B. 21 years
C. 25 years  D. 19 years

**539.** The Supreme Court was set up
A. By an act of Parliament
B. By the Constitution
C. Under the Government of India Act, 1935
D. By the Presidential order

**540.** A party to be recognised as a National Party must be in at least_____states.
A. Three  B. Four
C. Five  D. Six

**541.** Which of the following places is well known for the embroidery form of ''Chikankari''?
A. Hyderabad
B. Jaipur
C. Bhopal
D. Lucknow

**542.** Match the following

| Folk form | States where popular |
|---|---|
| (a) Heer song | 1. Bengal |
| (b) Bhatiali song | 2. Punjab |

(*c*) Garba dance    3. U.P.
(*d*) Raas dance    4. Gujarat

|     | (*a*) | (*b*) | (*c*) | (*d*) |
| --- | --- | --- | --- | --- |
| A. | 1 | 2 | 3 | 4 |
| B. | 1 | 3 | 2 | 4 |
| C. | 2 | 1 | 4 | 3 |
| D. | 2 | 3 | 4 | 1 |

**543.** Which is the most ancient musical instrument of India?
A. Flute    B. Tabla
C. Veena    D. Sitar

**544.** Who was the pioneer of the Bengal School of Art?
A. Nandlal Bose
B. B.C. Sanyal
C. Jamini Roy
D. Abanindranath Tagore

**545.** The proposed sea-route "Sethu Samudram" is a canal through which of the following sea-lanes?
A. Gulf of Mannar
B. Malacca Strait
C. Gulf of Kutch
D. Andaman and Nicobar Islands

**546.** The English established their first factory in India at
A. Bombay (Mumbai)
B. Surat
C. Sutanati
D. Madras (Chennai)

**547.** Which one of the following is a political right?
A. Right to freedom
B. Right to contest elections
C. Right to equality before law
D. Right to life

**548.** The main function of the judiciary is
A. Law formulation
B. Law execution
C. Law adjudication
D. Law application

**549.** 'Sakshat' is
A. A missile
B. An artificial satellite
C. A railway project
D. A website

**550.** Who started the first English newspaper in India?
A. Bal Gangadhar Tilak
B. Raja Rammohan Roy
C. J.A. Hickey
D. Lord William Bentinck

**551.** Mahatma Gandhi's autobiography—'My Experiments with Truth' was originally written in—
A. English    B. Hindi
C. Marathi    D. Gujarati

**552.** Who commanded the army of Bahadur Shah Zafar in 1857 revolt in Delhi ?
A. Azimulla
B. General Bakht Khan
C. Haqim Ahsanulla
D. Khan Bahadur

**553.** People greet one another in French language with—
A. GutenTag
B. Bonjour
C. Ahlan Wasahlan
D) None of these

**554.** Which among the following is *not* a correct match—
A. Thomas Cup—Badminton
B. Rovers Cup—Hockey
C. Deodhar Trophy—Cricket
D. Durand Cup—Football

**555.** What is Gene ?
- A. A segment of RNA, DNA and Histone
- B. A segment of DNA and RNA
- C. A segment of DNA
- D. A segment of DNA and Histone

**556.** Water pollution is mainly caused by-
- A. Pesticides
- B. $NH_3$
- C. Industrial waste
- D. Detergent

**557.** In the constitution of India, India has been described as—
- A. A federation
- B. A secular of federation
- C. A quasi-federal organization
- D. A union of states

**558.** Damodar Valley Project is sponsored by West Bengal and—
- A. Orissa
- B. Jharkhand
- C. U.P.
- D. All the above

**559.** Which among the following is a riverine port ?
- A. Cochin
- B. Kolkata
- C. Kanca
- D. Mormugao

**560.** Budapest is the capital of—
- A. Haiti
- B. Honduras
- C. Hungary
- D. Czech Republic

**561.** Among the following, which state capital is not situated near the bank of a river ?
- A. Lucknow
- B. Patna
- C. Bombay
- D. Kolkata

**562.** Which is the storehouse of salt in human body ?
- A. Liver
- B. Skin
- C. Kidneys
- D. Neck

**563.** Pyorrhoea affects which part of the body ?
- A. The gums
- B. The teeth
- C. Salivary glands
- D. Lips

**564.** Who was the author of 'Geet Govind' ?
- A. Vidyapati
- B. Jayadeva
- C. Magha
- D. Sriharsha

**565.** Thermocole is made from—
- A. Polystyrene
- B. Perspex
- C. Polythene
- D. Teflon

**566.** Printing for the blind was invented by—
- A. Berliner
- B. N.R.Finsen
- C. Louis Braile
- D. J. L. Baird

**567.** Which is the heaviest flying bird?
- A. Bustard
- B. Penguin
- C. Ostrich
- D. Vulture

**568.** Economic development of a country is directly based on—
- A. Natural resources
- B. Capital formation
- C. Availability of market
- D. None of these

**569.** The term Ikebana is associated with which country ?
- A. Thailand
- B. Japan
- C. England
- D. Australia

570. The largest irrigation canal in India is called the—
    A. Yamuna canal
    B. Sirhind canal
    C. Lower Baridoab canal
    D. Indira Gandhi canal

571. Horns of most mammals are made of—
    A. Bones    B. Cartilage
    C. Keratin    D. Chitin

572. Rigveda is divided into how many Mandals ?
    A. 10 mandals
    B. 7 mandals
    C. 15 mandals
    D. 20 mandals

573. The constitution of UNO is known as—
    A. Peace agreement
    B. Magna Carta
    C. Declaration
    D. Charter

574. December 10 is observed as—
    A. World Mental Health Day
    B. World Sight Day
    C. World Red Cross Day
    D. Human Rights Day

575. The Durand Line is the international border between—
    A. Afghanistan and Pakistan
    B. Iran and Syria
    C. India and Bangladesh
    D. India and Nepal

576. Washington is situated at the bank of—
    A. Vistula    B. Moskava
    C. Potomac    D. Tagus

577. The term 'Rook' is linked with—
    A. Golf    B. Archery
    C. Chess    D. Badminton

578. 'Fan', a widely spoken language of the world belongs to—
    A. Laos    B. Kenya
    C. Tibet    D. Myanmar

579. Which among the following is matched incorrectly ?
    A. Mahatma Gandhi  — Bapu
    B. Lajpat Rai — Punjab Kesari
    C. C.F. Andrews—
                         Deshabandhu
    D. Subhash Chandra Bose —
                         Netaji

580. Supreme Court in India was established in Calcutta in :
    A. 1771    B. 1774
    C. 1775    D. 1776

581. The first radio-programme in India was broadcast by Radio Club of Bombay in:
    A. 1924    B. 1923
    C. 1926    D. 1927

582. In India, the first state to institute a Human Rights Commission is :
    A. A.P.    B. Kerala
    C. W. Bengal    D. Rajasthan

583. The 'Vikram Sarabhai Space Centre is located at :
    A. Bangalore
    B. Hyderabad
    C. Chennai
    D. Thiruvananthapuram

584. The first film actor to be nominated to Rajya Sabha was :
    A. Ashok Kumar
    B. Dilip Kumar
    C. Jeevan
    D. Prithviraj Kapoor

**585.** The first Indian Institute of Technology was set up in India in 1950 at :
   A. Kolhapur    B. Kanpur
   C. Kharagpur    D. Bangalore

**586.** Which state has the maximum forest cover amongst all Indian States and Union Territories?
   A. T.N.    B. A.P.
   C. M.P.    D. U.P.

**587.** Manas Wildlife Sanctuary housing tigers is in:
   A. Sikkim
   B. Asom
   C. Karnataka
   D. Arunachal Pradesh

**588.** Who wrote 'Long Walk To Freedom' ?
   A. Nelson Mandela
   B. Aung San Su Kyi
   C. Abraham Lincoln
   D. Moti Lal Nehru

**589.** The currency of Bhutan is :
   A. Lote    B. Rupiah
   C. Ngultrum    D. Shekel

**590.** Who discovered X-rays in 1895 ?
   A. Mackintos
   B. B. Certois
   C. Belard
   D. Prof. Roentgen

**591.** The melting point of iron is :
   A. 1600°C    B. 1535°C
   C. 1765°C    D. 1650°C

**592.** The headquarters of European Union is :
   A. Rome    B. Paris
   C. Brussels    D. Dublin

**593.** Commonwealth Day is observed by Member Countries on :
   A. 26 August
   B. 24 May
   C. 27 December
   D. 29 January

**594.** IMF (International Monetary Fund) was established in :
   A. 1950    B. 1965
   C. 1945    D. 1980

**595.** The distance covered by wheeled vehicle is measured by :
   A. Sextant
   B. Odometer
   C. Speedometer
   D. Stroboscope

**596.** Diphtheria, a disease, attacks :
   A. Lungs    B. Eyes
   C. Gums    D. Throat

**597.** Phrenology is the study of :
   A. Language
   B. Teeth
   C. Skull and brain
   D. Nerves

**598.** If the President of India wants to submit his resignation, to whom, would he submit his resignation?
   A. Speaker of the Lok Sabha
   B. Chief Justice of Supreme Court
   C. Vice President
   D. Prime Minister

**599.** Rose is the national emblem of :
   A. Italy    B. Iran
   C. Israel    D. Iraq

**600.** 'Akash' is India's—
   A. Air to air missile
   B. Anti-tank guided missile
   C. Surface to surface missile
   D. Surface to air missile

**601.** Tapti river originates from :
A. Amarkantak
B. Panchmarhi
C. Trimbakeshwar
D. Satpura range

**602.** The first municipal corporation in India was established in Madras in :
A. 1687      B. 1699
C. 1685      D. 1690

**603.** RAW (Research and Analysis Wing) works under:
A. Ministry of Home
B. Ministry of Personnel
C. PMO
D. Cabinet Secretariat

**604.** The first spacecraft sent by Europe to the moon is :
A. Atlantis      B. Discovery
C. Odyssey      D. SMART-I

**605.** Siyam is the old name of :
A. Vietnam      B. Thailand
C. Myanmar      D. Laos

**606.** The number of states which do not touch international boundary and are completely landlocked is :
A. 3      B. 5
C. 4      D. 6

**607.** Which state of India touches the boundary of most other states?
A. A.P.      B. M.P.
C. Asom      D. U.P.

**608.** Which of the Mughal rulers promoted painting most?
A. Babar      B. Akbar
C. Jahangir      D. Shahjahan

**609.** The subject matter of the fourth schedule of the Constitution of India is :
A. Administration of tribal areas
B. Forms of oath or Affirmation
C. Languages
D. Allocation of seats of the Rajya Sabha to states

**610.** Vice-President is the part of :
A. Legislature
B. Executive
C. Rajya Sabha
D. None of these

## ANSWERS

| 1 | 2 | 3 | 4 | 5 | 6 | 7 | 8 | 9 | 10 |
|---|---|---|---|---|---|---|---|---|---|
| C | C | A | D | C | C | B | D | B | B |
| **11** | **12** | **13** | **14** | **15** | **16** | **17** | **18** | **19** | **20** |
| C | C | C | D | C | D | B | C | D | D |
| **21** | **22** | **23** | **24** | **25** | **26** | **27** | **28** | **29** | **30** |
| B | B | D | B | D | D | D | B | D | B |
| **31** | **32** | **33** | **34** | **35** | **36** | **37** | **38** | **39** | **40** |
| B | A | C | A | A | B | B | B | A | A |
| **41** | **42** | **43** | **44** | **45** | **46** | **47** | **48** | **49** | **50** |
| C | C | B | B | B | C | A | B | B | C |
| **51** | **52** | **53** | **54** | **55** | **56** | **57** | **58** | **59** | **60** |
| C | C | B | B | A | C | B | B | B | D |

| 61 | 62 | 63 | 64 | 65 | 66 | 67 | 68 | 69 | 70 |
|---|---|---|---|---|---|---|---|---|---|
| D | C | A | A | B | C | C | A | C | D |
| 71 | 72 | 73 | 74 | 75 | 76 | 77 | 78 | 79 | 80 |
| C | D | C | D | C | C | C | B | C | B |
| 81 | 82 | 83 | 84 | 85 | 86 | 87 | 88 | 89 | 90 |
| C | A | D | D | D | C | C | A | C | D |
| 91 | 92 | 93 | 94 | 95 | 96 | 97 | 98 | 99 | 100 |
| A | C | C | C | B | D | A | A | C | D |
| 101 | 102 | 103 | 104 | 105 | 106 | 107 | 108 | 109 | 110 |
| B | D | A | C | A | C | A | A | D | B |
| 111 | 112 | 113 | 114 | 115 | 116 | 117 | 118 | 119 | 120 |
| B | C | A | B | B | B | D | D | D | B |
| 121 | 122 | 123 | 124 | 125 | 126 | 127 | 128 | 129 | 130 |
| D | C | C | A | D | A | D | C | B | C |
| 131 | 132 | 133 | 134 | 135 | 136 | 137 | 138 | 139 | 140 |
| B | D | D | A | B | A | B | B | B | D |
| 141 | 142 | 143 | 144 | 145 | 146 | 147 | 148 | 149 | 150 |
| B | A | C | C | A | A | C | A | B | D |
| 151 | 152 | 153 | 154 | 155 | 156 | 157 | 158 | 159 | 160 |
| C | B | B | C | C | D | A | D | C | D |
| 161 | 162 | 163 | 164 | 165 | 166 | 167 | 168 | 169 | 170 |
| B | D | B | C | D | D | B | D | D | B |
| 171 | 172 | 173 | 174 | 175 | 176 | 177 | 178 | 179 | 180 |
| D | B | B | C | C | C | A | D | A | C |
| 181 | 182 | 183 | 184 | 185 | 186 | 187 | 188 | 189 | 190 |
| C | A | B | C | B | C | C | D | B | D |
| 191 | 192 | 193 | 194 | 195 | 196 | 197 | 198 | 199 | 200 |
| D | A | D | C | B | B | A | D | D | C |
| 201 | 202 | 203 | 204 | 205 | 206 | 207 | 208 | 209 | 210 |
| A | B | B | D | A | D | C | C | C | A |
| 211 | 212 | 213 | 214 | 215 | 216 | 217 | 218 | 219 | 220 |
| B | B | C | C | D | A | C | D | B | D |
| 221 | 222 | 223 | 224 | 225 | 226 | 227 | 228 | 229 | 230 |
| D | C | C | A | C | C | B | A | D | A |
| 231 | 232 | 233 | 234 | 235 | 236 | 237 | 238 | 239 | 240 |
| B | A | A | A | A | B | B | A | D | B |
| 241 | 242 | 243 | 244 | 245 | 246 | 247 | 248 | 249 | 250 |
| D | B | A | B | C | C | B | D | A | C |
| 251 | 252 | 253 | 254 | 255 | 256 | 257 | 258 | 259 | 260 |
| D | B | D | B | A | B | C | D | D | A |

| | | | | | | | | | |
|---|---|---|---|---|---|---|---|---|---|
| 261 | 262 | 263 | 264 | 265 | 266 | 267 | 268 | 269 | 270 |
| B | A | C | C | C | D | C | C | B | B |
| 271 | 272 | 273 | 274 | 275 | 276 | 277 | 278 | 279 | 280 |
| C | D | B | D | D | C | A | D | A | D |
| 281 | 282 | 283 | 284 | 285 | 286 | 287 | 288 | 289 | 290 |
| C | A | B | B | B | B | D | B | C | C |
| 291 | 292 | 293 | 294 | 295 | 296 | 297 | 298 | 299 | 300 |
| C | B | D | B | B | C | B | D | D | A |
| 301 | 302 | 303 | 304 | 305 | 306 | 307 | 308 | 309 | 310 |
| A | B | A | C | D | A | A | D | C | A |
| 311 | 312 | 313 | 314 | 315 | 316 | 317 | 318 | 319 | 320 |
| D | C | B | C | D | C | A | B | C | D |
| 321 | 322 | 323 | 324 | 325 | 326 | 327 | 328 | 329 | 330 |
| A | B | C | B | A | D | A | B | B | D |
| 331 | 332 | 333 | 334 | 335 | 336 | 337 | 338 | 339 | 340 |
| B | A | B | A | C | C | A | A | D | D |
| 341 | 342 | 343 | 344 | 345 | 346 | 347 | 348 | 349 | 350 |
| B | A | B, C | C | C | C | B | B | A | C |
| 351 | 352 | 353 | 354 | 355 | 356 | 357 | 358 | 359 | 360 |
| A | D | A | D | B | C | B | D | D | C |
| 361 | 362 | 363 | 364 | 365 | 366 | 367 | 368 | 369 | 370 |
| A | D | B | A | D | A | C | C | B | A |
| 371 | 372 | 373 | 374 | 375 | 376 | 377 | 378 | 379 | 380 |
| A | A | C | C | D | C | C | A | B | C |
| 381 | 382 | 383 | 384 | 385 | 386 | 387 | 388 | 389 | 390 |
| D | C | B | B | A | A | D | D | B | C |
| 391 | 392 | 393 | 394 | 395 | 396 | 397 | 398 | 399 | 400 |
| C | B | D | C | C | A | B | C | C | A |
| 401 | 402 | 403 | 404 | 405 | 406 | 407 | 408 | 409 | 410 |
| B | C | A | D | C | B | B | B | B | B |
| 411 | 412 | 413 | 414 | 415 | 416 | 417 | 418 | 419 | 420 |
| C | A | D | A | D | C | A | B | C | B |
| 421 | 422 | 423 | 424 | 425 | 426 | 427 | 428 | 429 | 430 |
| A | A | A | A | C | C | B | D | A | A |
| 431 | 432 | 433 | 434 | 435 | 436 | 437 | 438 | 439 | 440 |
| A | A | D | B | C | C | C | A | D | C |
| 441 | 442 | 443 | 444 | 445 | 446 | 447 | 448 | 449 | 450 |
| B | A | B | B | C | C | C | C | A | A |
| 451 | 452 | 453 | 454 | 455 | 456 | 457 | 458 | 459 | 460 |
| C | B | B | D | A | C | B | B | B | B |

| 461 | 462 | 463 | 464 | 465 | 466 | 467 | 468 | 469 | 470 |
|---|---|---|---|---|---|---|---|---|---|
| B | C | C | D | D | A | D | C | B | D |
| 471 | 472 | 473 | 474 | 475 | 476 | 477 | 478 | 479 | 480 |
| B | B | B | B | B | B | C | D | D | B |
| 481 | 482 | 483 | 484 | 485 | 486 | 487 | 488 | 489 | 490 |
| B | A | A | D | C | A | B | A | D | D |
| 491 | 492 | 493 | 494 | 495 | 496 | 497 | 498 | 499 | 500 |
| B | C | C | D | D | D | B | B | A | A |
| 501 | 502 | 503 | 504 | 505 | 506 | 507 | 508 | 509 | 510 |
| A | A | C | A | A | A | A | C | C | B |
| 511 | 512 | 513 | 514 | 515 | 516 | 517 | 518 | 519 | 520 |
| C | C | D | A | A | D | C | B | B | A |
| 521 | 522 | 523 | 524 | 525 | 526 | 527 | 528 | 529 | 530 |
| C | C | D | D | B | C | C | D | C | C |
| 531 | 532 | 533 | 534 | 535 | 536 | 537 | 538 | 539 | 540 |
| D | C | B | A | A | A | C | A | B | B |
| 541 | 542 | 543 | 544 | 545 | 546 | 547 | 548 | 549 | 550 |
| D | C | A | D | A | B | B | C | D | C |
| 551 | 552 | 553 | 554 | 555 | 556 | 557 | 558 | 559 | 560 |
| D | B | B | B | C | C | D | B | B | C |
| 561 | 562 | 563 | 564 | 565 | 566 | 567 | 568 | 569 | 570 |
| C | B | A | B | A | C | A | B | B | D |
| 571 | 572 | 573 | 574 | 575 | 576 | 577 | 578 | 579 | 580 |
| C | A | D | D | A | C | C | D | C | B |
| 581 | 582 | 583 | 584 | 585 | 586 | 587 | 588 | 589 | 590 |
| B | C | D | D | C | C | B | A | C | D |
| 591 | 592 | 593 | 594 | 595 | 596 | 597 | 598 | 599 | 600 |
| B | C | B | C | B | D | C | C | B | D |
| 601 | 602 | 603 | 604 | 605 | 606 | 607 | 608 | 609 | 610 |
| B | A | D | D | B | C | D | C | D | B |